——————— *A Journal Briefing* ———————

Whitewater
Volume VI

——————— *A Journal Briefing* ———————

Whitewater
Volume VI

*Impeachment Aftermath
and Election 2000*

From the Editorial Pages of
The Wall Street Journal.

Edited by Robert L. Bartley
with Micah Morrison & Melanie Kirkpatrick
and the Editorial Page staff

DOWJONES

Library of Congress Catalog Card Numbers:
94-79762

ISBN 1-881944-31-X

Printed in the United States of America

The Wall Street Journal.
Dow Jones & Company, Inc.
200 Liberty Street
New York, N.Y. 10281

Introduction

Conan's Clinton

Late-night talk show host Conan O'Brien has written an amusing essay for the Jan. 8 Time magazine on Bill Clinton. He writes: "Clinton was our first cartoon President. He ran off cliffs, was crushed by anvils and flattened by turn-of-the-century trains. Yet moments later, we always saw him, just like Wile E. Coyote or Daffy Duck, completely reassembled and eagerly pursuing his next crazy scheme." He concludes with this thought: "I'm going to miss Bill Clinton. And regardless of your politics, you will too." Just one question. How did Conan O'Brien ever get the impression that Bill Clinton was leaving? Beep, beep.

—The Wall Street Journal
January 12, 2001

As I write this, William Jefferson Clinton is gone from the White House, last seen ordering a sandwich at a deli in Chappaqua. His plea bargain with Independent Counsel Robert Ray has been signed and delivered, and he proved to Susan McDougal that he did feel her pain after all, granting her a Presidential pardon on his way out of the Oval Office. He pardoned some 140 others, most spectacularly fugitive arbitrageur Marc Rich, whose pardon plea was taken directly to the Oval Office by one of Mr. Clinton's former White House counsels and whose still-supportive former wife was a big Clinton contributor.

Hillary Clinton, of course, is just now being initiated into the World's Most Exclusive Club, the U.S. Senate. Senator Clinton and former President Clinton now dominate the New York Democratic Party, taking Harold Ickes as their political mastermind. Mr. Clinton has installed his peripatetic fund-raiser Terry McAuliffe as Democratic National Committee chairman. And any ex-president has powerful friends and connections that can be put to future use, as the Bush family has just demonstrated. Clearly a powerful political base remains. For those of us who've prematurely counted Mr. Clinton out before, the voice of experience warns, we may not yet have seen the Comeback Kid's last comeback.

At the moment, though, it seems that during the presidential transition Mr. Clinton's star dimmed decidedly. Any outgoing President will fade, indeed is expected to. But President Clinton's leave-taking seemed aptly to epitomize his eight years in office. It was self-centered, with three speeches on George W. Bush's inaugural day and several aspersions on the legitimacy of his victory. It tried to "spin away" criminal behavior, with spokesmen voicing caveats intended to cloud the written admissions to Mr. Ray and the Arkansas Bar. It was so Clintonian that hairs started to bristle on the necks of some who'd long given him the benefit of the doubt.

The self-serving pardons in particular stuck in the craw of some who'd opposed impeachment, for example Senate Democratic leader Tom Daschle. As it happens, I've long held doubts about the sweeping nature of the charges against Mr. Rich, since they arose from the Carter Administration's energy-policy conceit that it could make "old oil" sell for a much lower price than "new oil." But whatever your view of the charges, the procedures for the pardon, or rather the lack of them, suggest that the moving force was money-grubbing. Similarly, the closing days of the Clinton Presidency produced embarrassments about Mrs. Clinton's $8 million book deal, presents to decorate their new home and the expense of Bill's office overlooking Central Park.

On the pardon list, Mr. Rich merely headed a parade of Clinton allies and retainers. A President pardoning his own brother must certainly be a record. The pardon to Susan McDougal was clearly a reward for her willingness to serve jail time for contempt of court in refusing to answer questions about the Clintons' role in the Whitewater partnership. A host of even smaller fries from Whitewater and other Clinton Administration scandals received Presidential dispensations. President Clinton also commuted the sentences of four Hasidic men from the village of New Square in New York's Rockland County, where Hasidim had voted overwhelmingly for Mrs. Clinton's Senatorial campaign. Earlier, in the midst of Mrs. Clinton's campaign for the New York ethnic vote, he'd pardoned 16 jailed members of FLAN, a Puerto Rican terrorist group.

Many of the President's long-time defenders reacted with anger. Washington Post columnist Richard Cohen wrote that the Rich pardon was "a pie in the face of anyone who ever defended you. You may look bad, Bill, but we look just plain stupid."

This reaction, if I may indulge myself, is of some satisfaction to me and my staff on the editorial page of the Journal. We think we are the one media outlet that consistently stuck with the big story of the last eight years, to wit, Presidential character. Precisely how this story would play out was impossible to predict back when we asked "Who Is Bill Clinton?" during the 1992 campaign or "Who Is Webster Hubbell?" in the first weeks of the Clinton Presidency. But as it unwound through eight years and into the final weeks we—and our regular readers—were scarcely surprised.

We are now winding up this coverage by publishing a sixth volume of "A Journal Briefing—Whitewater." And, sensitive as we are to modern technology, we are also offering a searchable CD-ROM collection of all volumes, including an exhaustive chronology. No doubt we will find ourselves writing about former President Clinton and Senator Clinton in the future, but this final publication is intended to close out the Clinton Presidency. We hope, as the saying goes, to "move on."

This is a juncture for a few reflections; a truly comprehensive overview of these eight years will require the detachment of time. Some of the former Clintonites have been baring their souls, most particularly on ABC News. Mixed with the obvious need for absolution has been a lot of second-guessing. If only the President had settled the Paula Jones lawsuit, for example, there would have been no perjured testimony about Monica Lewinsky. If only Mrs. Clinton had cooperated with the Washington Post's request for documents on the original Whitewater land deals, the whole thing would have blown over.

There is a certain tactical craftiness in these speculations, but on another level the denouement seems somehow inevitable. To begin with, it is not in the nature of the Clintons to settle or cooperate with investigations; stonewalling has taken them so far both in Little Rock and Washington. But beyond that, there were reasons. As Monica said Mr. Clinton told her, there were "hundreds" of other women; doubtless many of them might have been tempted to sue if he had demonstrated a willingness to settle the Jones case. And no doubt Mrs. Clinton, unlike the aides seeking cooperation, was very much aware of the legal vulnerabilities surrounding Whitewater.

Before anyone knew Monica Lewinsky's name, after all, Kenneth Starr had won 14 convictions or pleas, including the Clintons' Whitewater partners Jim and Susan McDougal, Arkansas insider and former U.S. Associate Attorney General Webster Hubbell, and former Arkansas Governor Jim Guy Tucker. After years of stonewall delays and facing the prospect of jury nullification, Mr. Starr's successor decided not to prosecute Mrs. Clinton for Whitewater, the Castle Grande land flips, disappearing billing records or the Travel Office firings. Robert Ray's carefully parsed statements of prosecutorial discretion were spun by the Clintons as vindication. Meanwhile, Attorney General Janet Reno repeatedly refused to charter an independent investigation of the campaign finance-Chinese espionage issues, despite the recommendations of the FBI chief and her own task-force head.

But to ultimately succeed, this kind of behavior needs to fool all of the people all of the time. Somewhere along the way a slip was inevitable. It happened to be Monica, probably because sex was about the only thing the President could not delegate to a protective shield of aides and agents. So Mr. Clinton was the second president impeached, survived his trial and went on to further adventures detailed in Volume VI—the contempt of court finding in Arkansas, the strutting Mussolini-like speech at the Democratic National Convention, the exile from the Gore campaign, the Florida election count and on to the plea bargain and pardons in the final days. The election challenge was of a piece with the Clinton era; we now know that the Democrats hired a telemarketing firm, TeleQuest, to stir up doubts about the Florida outcome before the polls even closed, and that they deliberately launched a smear campaign against Secretary of State Katherine Harris.

Mr. Ray will now complete his final report not only on the plea bargain but on Whitewater and the other prosecutorial-discretion cases. I will be watching carefully for his comments on the Clinton's 1992 tax return; as detailed in these volumes, they did not report the gift from Jim McDougal when he assumed the Clinton share of Whitewater's debts, about $32,000. The return was prepared after Mr. Clinton was in office. Dodging a bit of tax to avoid the public relations bombshell of reporting gifts from Mr. McDougal is not exactly a "high crime or misdemeanor;" but the American taxpayers are entitled to take notice of their President hoodwinking his own IRS.

Especially so since it was the late Vincent Foster who prepared the return. The Clintons did report a capital gain of $1,000 in "selling" their Whitewater interest to Mr. McDougal, but Mr. Foster had to wrestle with the problem of the "basis" for this gain, in fact about $38,000 in the negative for the Clintons' share of accumulated debts. This was one of the many Clinton legal problems on Mr. Foster's mind in the months leading up to his suicide. These were detailed in a 114-page report by Independent Counsel Starr, "Report on the Death of Vincent W. Foster Jr." (Our own view was set out by Micah Morrison, "In Re: Vincent Foster," Nov. 25, 1997, included in Volume IV).

The Clinton spinmeisters tried to blame our editorials for driving Mr. Foster to suicide. There is in fact one thing I would like to go back and change: the last line of our editorial following his death. With more time for reflection, I would edit it to read that if a competent investigation concluded his death was clearly a suicide "perhaps his memory could do for depression what Betty Ford's problems did for alcoholism."

Yet the spin against us was the Clinton tactic, honed in Arkansas, of turning your own errors against your critics. In fact, Mr. Foster was bedeviled by his own legal maneuvers trying to protect the Clintons—involving the tax return, the secrecy of the First Lady's health care task force and the Travel Office firings, over which he was seeking independent legal counsel. He committed suicide on the day Louis Freeh was named head of the FBI.

To turn to a happier story, under Mr. Clinton the Republic shared his luck. There were no major foreign policy crises, though American troops intervened around the world. The economy prospered, and Mr. Clinton claims credit. In fact, the financial markets boomed when the Republicans captured the House of Representatives; the bond markets hit bottom that very day (see chart). President Clinton's most memorable legislative accomplishments—the North American Free Trade Agreement and welfare reform—were fundamentally Republican programs.

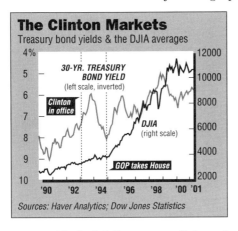

The Clinton Markets
Treasury bond yields & the DJIA averages

Sources: Haver Analytics; Dow Jones Statistics

While Mr. Clinton ran twice as a centrist Democrat, in his final years he had to reciprocate for support from his base during impeachment. This gave heady McGovernite liberalism a new breath of life. Over Mr. Clinton's two terms the Democratic Party declined. While the 2000 elections were essentially a tie, it is also true that for the first time in two generations the Republicans now control both the White House and the Congress. They will have the opportunity to address issues postponed in the Clinton years, in particular the looming Social Security problem. They also will have a chance to restore the rule of law shredded by his stonewalling and coverups.

While Bill Clinton caused some pretty good hiccups, in the end the system digested the problems created by his personal and political peccadilloes. As Adam Smith once put it, responding to a friend who declared that the loss of the American colonies would be the ruination of Britain: "Be assured, my young friend, that there is a great deal of ruin in a nation."

ROBERT L. BARTLEY
Editor
The Wall Street Journal
February 5, 2001

TABLE OF CONTENTS

	Introduction	*i*
	Impeachment Aftermath	*1*
Feb. 25, 1999	Good Counsel	3
March 12	The Starr Strategy	6
March 22	Whitewater: Back in Court	8
April 2	Does Character Matter Yet?	15
April 6	Clinton's Johnny	18
April 12	Zhu Knows	21
April 13	Mopping Up Whitewater	24
April 16	Does Clinton Have an 'Enemies List'?	28
	Clinton in Contempt	*31*
April 14	Someone Has to Do It	33
April 19	What's Wrong With Wright	36
May 14	Clinton's China Policy	40
May 26	The Banquo Report	44
June 16	Starr's Mandate	48
July 1	Watching the Watchdog	50
	The 2000 Campaign Begins	*55*
June 17	Gore's Chore	57
June 4	Victory Would Be Hillary's Best Revenge	59
July 9	The Icon Lady	62
July 8	The Natural	65
July 9	The Remaking of Hillary Rodham Clinton	69
July 13	Campaign Finance Statement	72
Aug. 4	The Counterattack Continues	73
Aug. 10	Bad Lawyer Joke?	76
Aug. 19	Something Happened	78
Aug. 30	Clinton's Other Perjury	82
Aug. 30	Perjury? Let the Courts Decide	85
Sept. 29	Vetting the Frontrunners: Albert Gore Jr. Occidental and Oriental Connections	87
	All About Scandals	*95*
Sept. 30	Obstruction of Justice Department?	97
Oct. 18	Mr. Ray's Decision	102
Oct. 19	Scandal Decisions: Indict Clinton? Free Archie?	105

Oct. 20	What We've Accomplished	108
Nov. 2	What Trie Got	112
Nov. 15	Swap Schemes: Campaign Finance On Trial	113
Nov. 18	Starry Eyed	116
Nov. 19	Where's Janet?	117
Nov. 22	Ms. White's Conviction	120

The Most Corrupt Administration Ever   *123*

Jan. 7, 2000	Will Mrs. Clinton Be Indicted?	125
Jan. 13	The Most Corrupt Administration Ever	129
Jan. 19	Pertinent Question: Will GOP Duck Clinton Character?	132
Feb. 4	Judicial Discretion	135
March 3	Mr. Gore's Scandal	137
March 13	Learned His Lesson?	140
March 20	Another Clinton Victim: The Integrity of the Federal Courts	145
March 30	The 'Crime-Fraud Exception'	149
April 20	Clinton Revisionism	152
May 1	Secrets Aren't Secure on Clinton's Watch	159
May 5	The Get-Lost Virus	162

Campaign Finance Scandals   *165*

May 11	Who Is Richard Trumka?	167
May 24	Truth and Consequences	170
June 14	How Reno Let the Big Fish Get Away	173
June 26	Reno Stonewall: Third Time a Charm?	178
June 29	Al Gore, Environmentalist and Zinc Miner	182
July 17	Malicious Discretion at Justice	189
July 18	The Big Stall	193
July 21	The Riady Connection	196
July 27	'Loose Enterprise'?	200

The Permanent Campaign   *203*

Aug. 3	Big Bill	205
Aug. 8	Gore's Clinton Fatigue	208

Aug. 11	How Different?	211
Aug. 14	Titan of the Media Age	214
Aug. 23	Abusing the INS	218
Aug. 25	Three-Ring Scandals	222
Sept. 19	The Wen Ho Lee Diversion	225
Sept. 21	The Coverup Worked	229

Election Day 2000 — *233*

Oct. 26	Who Is Harold Ickes?	234
Oct. 30	Ken Starr's Vindication	239
Nov. 6	What's It All About?	243
Nov. 6	Touring Cyberspace With DUI Story	246
Nov. 9	Moment for Leadership	250

Trying to Steal an Election — *253*

Nov. 13	Pandora's Politics	255
Nov. 13	Let the High Court Count	258
Nov. 13	Recount 'Em All, or None at All	262
Nov. 14	The Railroad	264
Nov. 15	The Gore Hurricane	267
Nov. 16	Florida's Political Swamp	270
Nov. 17	Al Gore's Class-Action	273
Nov. 17	The Donkey in the Living Room	277
Nov. 20	The Will of the Lawyers	282
Nov. 20	How Democrats Wage Political War	285
Nov. 24	President Dimples?	289
Nov. 24	Burgher Rebellion: GOP Turns Up Miami Heat	292
Nov. 27	Supremes to Al: Concede	295
Nov. 29	Some Road to the Presidency	298
Nov. 29	Gore Agonistes	301
Dec. 1	Dimples Wild?	306
Dec. 1	When the Going Gets Messy, There's Jesse	309
Dec. 4	Chad Buildup	313
Dec. 4	The Clinton Legacy: Rule or Ruin	316
Dec. 5	Controlling Legal Authority	320

Dec. 11	What's the Law For?	323
Dec. 13	7 to 2	326
Dec. 14	Supreme Irony	328

	End of an Era	*331*
Jan. 5, 2001	Yes, Indict Clinton	333
Jan. 5	Make Way for Hillary	338
Jan. 8	The Clinton Years	341
Jan. 8	A Photo-Op Presidency: The Finale	345
Jan. 11	Pending Justice: Labor v. Ashcroft	349
Jan. 15	Damaged Justice	352
Jan. 18	The Clinton Legacy: President Paradox	355
Jan. 19	Two Presidencies in One	359
Jan. 18	Who Is Bill Clinton?	363
Jan. 22	Bill Cops a Plea	367

A Whitewater Chronology	*370*
Acknowledgments	*411*
Index	*413*

Impeachment Aftermath

On February 12, 1999, the United States Senate acquitted President Clinton of two articles of impeachment, charging him with perjury and obstruction of justice. The President had "won," clinging to office behind the Constitutional requirement of a two-thirds Senate majority. But the House had officially impeached a President for the second time in U.S. history, and the public appeared broadly convinced that Mr. Clinton had committed perjury and obstruction.

The Senate vote turned out not to be the final curtain of the drama the Journal had followed closely for seven years. In the months after impeachment, other matters that had bedeviled the Clinton presidency moved to the fore, and new concerns emerged.

In March, Whitewater figure Susan McDougal went on trial in Little Rock on charges of criminal contempt and obstruction of justice related to the original inquiry into Bill and Hillary Clinton's Arkansas land dealings. Ms. McDougal already had served 22 months for Whitewater fraud and civil contempt. She faced a new trial for refusing to answer questions from a federal grand jury concerning allegations that Mr. Clinton, while serving as Governor of Arkansas, knew about illegal loans at the heart of the Whitewater inquiry.

Trial testimony disclosed that the independent counsel had drawn up a draft indictment of Mrs. Clinton in the Whitewater matter, and prosecutors presented strong evidence that the Clintons were the beneficiaries of illegal loan schemes. But in a highly charged political atmosphere, Ms. McDougal's trial ended with her acquittal on the obstruction charge and a hung jury on the criminal contempt charge. Whitewater was slowly drawing to a close. Yet its mark on the Clinton era would be profound. As the mother of all Clinton scandals, the charges of illegal benefit from a corrupt S&L owner, first sketched in a 1992 Resolution Trust Corp. inquiry, marked the first step on the long road to impeachment.

In Washington, attention slowly shifted toward Vice President Al Gore, Mr. Clinton's putative successor, as the 2000 presidential election began to loom over the political landscape. And new details continued to emerge about alleged Chinese government influence in the 1996 Clinton-Gore campaign.

REVIEW & OUTLOOK

Good Counsel

Twenty years after enactment of the Independent Counsel statute, we are said to have reached a "consensus" that the mechanism is not working. Senator Fred Thompson began hearings yesterday into whether the law should be revised, replaced or left to die.

The good news here is that Congress actually recognized one of its many laws went off the tracks. Most every other law Washington enacts provides lifetime work for Congress and the local bureaucracy. The Independent Counsel mostly provides jail time. Thus, it took them only 20 years to react.

This page warned back when the subject first came up that creating a prosecutorial function that operated outside the accountability of the established political system probably wouldn't work as planned. We feel some vindication 20 years later in seeing that our frequent liberal critics have come to agree; the past six years have proven the value of personal experience over mere theory.

Kenneth Starr

In any consideration of the Independent Counsel Act, the one word that must sit squarely before the Congress is "accountability." And, closely related is the cardinal principle in our political system called checks and balances. We doubt that the American system can function, much less survive, without both these principles actively serving as monitors on the behavior of elected and appointed political officials—people whom we invest with great power over all the rest of us, but who are after all merely men and women, like all the rest of us.

That said, we don't think the principle of accountability has been paid much honor the past six years, the years of the Clinton Presidency, by much of anyone who should know better—not Congress, not the Department of Justice, not the compliant and complicit members of the President's own party and not by those people in the media or politics who felt this President was the carrier of their political goals. Since 1993, political goals have trumped and smashed accountability.

In the face of this massive default by the Washington political community, it fell to one court-appointed officer, Independent Counsel Kenneth Starr, to carry their burden of accountability. Now, after the second Presidential impeachment in our history, this same court officer is the object of obliteration by the Justice Department and by Congress.

They will have to do better than this.

If the Independent Counsel law is not renewed, Justice and Congressional oversight are going to have to start to do their jobs. It would be reassuring if they did so before expiration, not after.

One of the great deficiencies of the Independent Counsel phenomenon is that the presence of these prosecutors effectively allowed all the other branches to walk away from their constitutionally assigned responsibilities. The consequences of that have been just awful.

With the Clintons passing over their generation's best and brightest to run Justice, the department degraded into a back room of cronies and cat's paws, culminating in Ms. Reno's shameless refusal to comply with the law and appoint a campaign-finance counsel. And while Justice fell apart, Congress slept, most notably the Senate Judiciary Committee's advise and consent function.

If we may say so, a relatively small number of the Washington journalistic community (relative, that is, to the hundreds employed to watch Washington) were tireless in their efforts to disclose to the public the details of the fund-raising abuses, Ron Brown's Commerce junkets, the bureaucracy's efforts to suppress Whitewater and the rest.

In defense of the Independent Counsel statute, its supporters argue with considerable persuasive force that the powers of people in politics and in high office to conceal their illicit behavior are simply too great, that only by investing an independent authority such as Ken Starr held can we even hope to overcome the political class's skills at diversion and escape.

In other words, someone needs subpoena power. The question now before the Thompson committee is, who gets it?

Ultimately, we think, it is not feasible to hold a wholly malign view of Washington's ability to police itself. As we all relearned only recently, the Founders placed the power of impeachment and trial in the hands of Congress, rather than judges, because they wanted the broadest possible judgment brought to bear on such malfeasance, and that includes political judgment. So too, with potential crimes by members of an administration or Congress. Both may hold subpoena power; the one should check and balance the other.

The Democratic legal community holds many men and women of integrity who could still restore Justice's honor, as Louis Freeh has done to the FBI. The small corps of men who made up the House Managers proved to our satisfaction that independent belief and principle still exist in a poll-obsessed Congress. Genuine accountability is by no means beyond the established system's abilities and powers.

If, however, in the coming weeks the only mantra that you hear from the Congress and from the pundits is that the job at hand is mainly to get rid of the "excesses" of the Independent Counsel assigned to this President, then you can be pretty sure we are not close to restoring responsibility, much less accountability, to the political culture in Washington. The burden now is theirs, not Ken Starr's.

REVIEW & OUTLOOK

The Starr Strategy

When last we surveyed White House attempts to demonize Independent Counsel Kenneth Starr, we reminded readers of some legal folk wisdom: If you can't win on the facts, argue the law; and if you can't win on the law or the facts, put the prosecutor on trial. Down in Little Rock this week, opening statements got under way in the criminal contempt and obstruction trial of Whitewater figure Susan McDougal, and it has been made explicit that the Clinton camp's efforts to delegitimize the prosecutor will be the focus of her defense.

So yesterday courtroom news of a Clinton connection to an illegal loan was matched by news of the resignation of Mr. Starr's press spokesman in a controversy over leaks. The campaign against this particular prosecutor has never stopped. In turn, media outlets deploy pollsters to test the public's reaction to this barrage, and a low job-approval rating echoes back, summarized as what "the American people" think about the prosecutor. Just this week the Attorney General announced that she reserves the right to investigate the investigator of her boss.

Ms. McDougal is charged with refusing to answer questions from a federal grand jury in Arkansas about whether Bill and Hillary Clinton were involved in fraud schemes related to the Whitewater Development Co. and Madison Guaranty Savings & Loan. Polls would no doubt echo back that people think Mr. Starr put Susan in prison for refusing these answers. No, a federal judge, Susan Webber

Wright, a former law student of Mr. Clinton's, ordered Ms. McDougal to answer, and it is she who sentenced Ms. McDougal to prison for contempt of her court.

Ms. McDougal's lawyer, Mark Geragos, said in Little Rock this week that he will put Mr. Starr on trial. During jury selection for the trial, perceptions of the Independent Counsel were highly negative. Mr. Geragos is the California attorney who won Ms. McDougal an acquittal in the Nancy Mehta embezzlement case. This week he flew in two of the Mehta jurors to Little Rock to complain about Mr. Starr to the assembled media. CNBC's Geraldo Rivera was standing by to air their complaints on his show, where he denounced Mr. Starr as a "terrorist."

Mr. Geragos paints Ms. McDougal in saintly hues, saying she was once willing to cooperate, but balked when Mr. Starr's office demanded she lie to the grand jury. Ms. McDougal "was not going to be used as a pawn by somebody else to get the President or First Lady," Mr. Geragos told the jury Wednesday.

Just how much Mr. Geragos will be allowed to get away with remains to be seen. The trial is presided over by U.S. District Judge George Howard Jr., a no-nonsense jurist who ran the McDougal-Tucker trial with a tight fist. In that 1996 trial, an Arkansas jury convicted the two McDougals and the state's sitting governor, Jim Guy Tucker, of felonies. Last week, Judge Howard ruled that Mr. Geragos could not raise issues of "prosecutorial vindictiveness," Ms. McDougal's prison conditions or her health. But he gave Mr. Geragos permission to make the case for admission of evidence of "outrageous government conduct" based on the allegation that the Office of Independent Counsel asked Ms. McDougal to lie.

She now sits before 12 Arkansans who will resolve her refusal of a judge's order to speak to a federal grand jury. As her lawyer strives to put Mr. Starr personally on trial before this jury, we will be reminded of Senator Robert Byrd's startling admonition to the Clinton media spinners before the impeachment trial: "Don't tamper with this jury." Senator Byrd offered an important insight into this White House. But it came a little late.

Editorial Feature

Whitewater: Back in Court

By Micah Morrison

LITTLE ROCK, Ark.—Whitewater figure Susan McDougal is on trial here for criminal contempt and obstruction of justice, but it was Hillary Rodham Clinton who sent wire service reporters running to the phones Thursday. The independent counsel's office, a witness revealed, had written up a draft indictment of the first lady.

The moment caught the essence of the trial. It is of little national importance whether the defendant goes back to jail, where she has already served 22 months for Whitewater fraud and civil contempt, or beats the rap, as she did at a recent California state trial on unrelated charges of embezzlement from Nancy Mehta, wife of the famed conductor. The larger meaning of the proceedings is what they tell us about the Clintons in general and the original Whitewater controversy in particular. To those of us who have followed Whitewater from the start, evidence revealed so far tells quite a lot about the Ozark land deal that, as the mother of all Clinton scandals, was the first step on the road to impeachment.

Ms. McDougal is on trial for twice refusing to answer questions from a federal grand jury concerning allegations that Bill Clinton was aware of illegal loans at the heart of the Whitewater inquiry. Since Ms. McDougal clearly did refuse to talk to the grand jury, and this clearly is contempt, her attorney, Mark Geragos, is putting the prosecutor on trial. His first witness was Deputy Independent Counsel Hickman Ewing Jr., who confirmed the longstanding rumor of deliberations over indicting Mrs. Clinton. Mr. Geragos did not ask the obvious follow-up question—just what were the draft charges?—and Mr. Ewing did not volunteer any information. The jury was rapt.

Presumably Mr. Geragos, the smooth Californian who won the acquittal in the Mehta case, raised the matter of Mrs. Clinton's possible indictment because he is trying to convince the jury that Ms. McDougal's contempt was justifiable due to fear of vindictive tactics by prosecutors under Independent Counsel Kenneth Starr. But Mr. Ewing was cool under questioning, and it's doubtful that revelation of the draft indictment was welcome news for Mrs. Clinton's putative Senate campaign in New York.

Similarly, new evidence offered by the prosecution in the opening phase of the trial could not have been welcome at 1600 Pennsylvania Avenue. It bolsters the case that the Clintons indeed were beneficiaries of illegal loans, as charged by Resolution Trust Corp. investigators as far back as 1992. And videotaped testimony by Mrs. Clinton includes an admission that revives a controversy about the 1992 joint tax return prepared in the White House by the late Vincent Foster.

Whitewater, of course, was a partnership among the Clintons, Ms. McDougal and her then husband, the late James McDougal; the McDougals owned Madison Guaranty Savings & Loan, which collapsed in 1989 at an estimated taxpayer loss of $60 million. During the 1992 presidential campaign, RTC investigator Jean Lewis drew up criminal referral No.C0004, naming the McDougals as suspects in an illegal check-kiting scheme involving Madison, Whitewater and other McDougal-controlled financial entities. Among the possible beneficiaries, the referral noted, were then-Gov. Clinton, Mrs. Clinton and Jim Guy Tucker, Mr. Clinton's gubernatorial successor. Nine other referrals followed, with more details on the Clintons and other members of the Arkansas political elite.

The Madison referrals were the burning fuse on a stick of political dynamite. The handling of a "heads up" on the confidential reports at the White House led to the resignation of several key administration officials. Ms. Lewis was taken off the case; later, congressional Democrats made charges, based on reconstruction of erased material from her computer, that the referrals were simply a partisan attack. Ultimately Mr. Starr convicted the McDougals and then-Gov. Tucker on multiple fraud counts arising from transactions first detailed in the referrals.

This month's proceedings here leave little doubt that, as Ms. Lewis concluded, the Clintons were indeed beneficiaries of illegal loan schemes. Prosecutors introduced two checks they say were uncovered following extensive debriefings of James McDougal, who became a cooperating government witness following his fraud convictions. One is a cashier's check from Madison Guaranty for $27,600 payable to "Bill Clinton." The other is a check drawn on a James McDougal trustee account for $5081.82, payable to Madison Guaranty; it is signed by Susan McDougal and bears the notation "payoff Clinton."

Prosecutors say the first check represents a loan to Mr. Clinton to retire the balance of a $30,000 loan to Whitewater from Madison Bank, a separate McDougal-controlled entity. The purpose of the transaction was to dress up Madison Bank's books and relieve pressure from federal regulators.

The "payoff Clinton" check represents the retirement of the $27,600 loan. At Ms. McDougal's trial this month, prosecutors alleged that Mr. McDougal handled this obligation through further kiting in the summer of 1983, by advancing a $25,000 nominee loan to a Madison associate, who immediately wrote a check to Madison S&L for the same amount. At the same time, Ms. McDougal wrote the $5081.82 "payoff Clinton" check to Madison Guaranty. The combined total of the two checks paid off the principal and interest on the $27,600 Clinton loan.

Prosecutors supported this scenario with other evidence—the minutes of a Madison Bank board meeting; a list of S&L borrowers noting one "B Clinton"; and a sheet of paper, apparently monthly interest calculations, with "$27,600" written at the top and "$5081.82" at the bottom.

Such fraudulent transactions benefited not only the McDougals but the Clintons as Whitewater partners. In the words of referral No.C0004, "The overdrafts and 'loan' transactions, or alleged check 'swapping' and kiting, between the combined companies' accounts ensured that loan payments and other corporate obligations were met, thus clearly benefiting the principals of each entity."

What remains at issue, and the reason Ms. McDougal is being tried for criminal contempt, is whether the Clintons knew of the kiting scheme and related matters, and thus were participants in an illegal conspiracy. The $27,600 check was not endorsed by Mr. Clinton before its deposit at Madison Bank. According to testimony at the current trial, Mr. McDougal told an FBI agent that Mr. Clinton had signed a loan document, which Mr. McDougal destroyed after the loan was paid off.

At the 1996 McDougal-Tucker trial, former Arkansas insider David Hale testified that he had met with Gov. Clinton and Mr. McDougal to discuss an illegal $300,000 loan for the "political family" from Mr. Hale's federally backed lending agency, Capital Management Service, to a front company set up in Susan McDougal's name. Mr. Hale, a cooperating witness for the government, himself earlier had pleaded guilty to several fraud schemes and was sentenced to 28 months in prison.

Another witness at the 1996 trial was FBI accounting expert Michael Patkus, who testified that he had traced nearly $50,000 springing from the $300,000 loan to two payments benefiting the Whitewater Co.—$24,455 to settle problems relating to a loan payment and $25,000 as a down payment on a land purchase from International Paper. Called as a defense witness in the 1996 trial and testifying via videotaped deposition, President Clinton said he was not aware of the $300,000 scheme and that he had never taken out a loan from Madison.

Ms. McDougal was convicted on four counts related to the $300,000 loan and sentenced to two years in prison. In September 1996 she was called before a federal grand jury and asked whether she had ever discussed the loan with Mr. Clinton, and whether to her knowledge he had testified truthfully at her trial. She refused to answer the questions and was jailed for civil contempt.

If Mr. Clinton was involved with Whitewater loans, he committed perjury at the 1996 trial; and of course perjury before a grand jury, pursuant to the Paula Jones/Monica Lewinsky matters, was one of the impeachment counts voted by the House of Representatives. The independent counsel says that the grand jury in Arkansas has a right to ask Ms. McDougal what she knows about suspect Whitewater transactions, including evidence developed after Ms. McDougal's first appearance. In April 1998, Mr. Starr brought Ms. McDougal back to the grand jury to ask about the new evidence. Again she refused to testify. Mr. Starr says Ms. McDougal's refusal to speak is an

assault on the rule of law—on the federal judge she disobeyed, on the federal grand jury she defied—and that she must be held accountable.

Mr. Geragos, Ms. McDougal's attorney, ridicules the prosecution's evidence as "nonsense" and asks what it has to with his client. Ms. McDougal is "not going to be used as a pawn by somebody else to get the president and first lady," he told the jury.

But Mr. Geragos doesn't appear to be doing the White House any favors. Last week, in addition to confirming reports of a draft indictment of Mrs. Clinton, he opened the door for the prosecution to play portions of a videotaped deposition Mrs. Clinton gave to the Little Rock grand jury in April 1998. It included her response to a question about the original Whitewater loan of $182,600. She said that loan "was never put into the corporation. I might be wrong about that, but certainly from my understanding we were always liable, personally liable."

This contradicts the Clintons' defense of their 1992 tax return, on issues raised by a 1995 report by House Banking Committee Chairman Jim Leach, and a 1996 analysis on these pages by John Hartigan, formerly general counsel of Philbro Inc. and Philbro-Salomon after the Philbro purchase of Salomon Brothers. They contend that since the Clintons had agreed to split any profits or expenses from Whitewater 50-50 with the McDougals, Mr. McDougal's 1992 agreement to assume the corporation's debt represented $58,000 in taxable income to the Clintons. Vincent Foster and Tyson Foods counsel Jim Blair extricated the Clintons from Whitewater by having Mr. McDougal buy their interest for $1,000 (provided by Mr. Blair). But at that point the McDougals had put $200,000 into Whitewater and the Clintons only $42,000. So under the 50-50 arrangement, they owed Mr. McDougal $58,000, and the IRS regards debt forgiveness as income.

Naturally, since the Clintons had said all along that they had not made money on Whitewater, it would be difficult to explain a $58,000 gift from James McDougal on their 1993 tax returns. They didn't mention it. A worried Foster, working on the return a few months before his suicide, reported the $1,000 payment from Mr. McDougal as a capital gain, but wrote notes pondering the tax basis of the gain. Rather than raise the true economic status of the Whitewater investment, which would show a loss covered by Mr. McDougal, he reported no basis. Whitewater was, he scrawled in a note to himself, a "can of worms you shouldn't open."

The Clinton defense of their tax position has been, in the words of attorney David Kendall's letter in response to the Hartigan article, that "the Clintons and McDougals transferred the Whitewater land, subject to the existing mortgage, into a newly formed corporation known as Whitewater Development Co. Inc." And that "once a corporation was formed, the Clintons became shareholders and their liability was accordingly limited." The White House has released a study by prestigious experts backing this view. But now Mrs. Clinton has testified that she does not believe the loan was brought into the corporation, and that their personal liability remained despite incorporation—the position long held by Mr. Hartigan and critics of the 1992 return. The Clintons have already gone back three times to pay additional taxes for improper Whitewater deductions and other errors, and the Senate Whitewater Committee raised further tax liability issues. Yesterday, House Banking Committee spokesman David Runkel told the Journal that the tax issue "has never been resolved and clearly shows that there were benefits flowing to the Clintons out of the Whitewater land deals."

Trial aficionados are savoring the battle here between two shrewd adversaries, which could produce further Whitewater revelations. Also, of course, Mr. Starr has indicted Clinton confidant Webster Hubbell on issues relating to Madison Guaranty and the thorny Castle Grande land deals; that indictment repeatedly alludes to Mrs. Clinton as the Rose Law Firm "billing partner," a sign that she and her billing records likely will figure prominently in Mr. Hubbell's trial. Meanwhile, Mr. Geragos promises that Ms. McDougal will take the stand, probably this week. Presumably she will provide answers that will implicate or defend Mr. Clinton. But maybe she should simply ask the Clintons for her money back.

Mr. Morrison is a Journal editorial page writer.

REVIEW & OUTLOOK

Does Character Matter Yet?

Less than a week into the bombing in Kosovo, the political establishment in Washington is beginning to criticize President Clinton severely for ignoring the advice of the military and CIA that ground troops would be necessary, that air power alone would not deter Milosevic and the Serbs. There is now talk of a military disaster. There are also reports that the White House resents this Monday-morning quarterbacking.

Bill Clinton

Ironically enough, we're inclined to agree, though not on the White House's terms. We would like to know where this establishment— the politicians, pundits and Beltway press—has been the past six years, when some of us were pressing the argument that Bill Clinton's handling of Whitewater, Gennifer Flowers, the draft, Filegate and all the rest were relevant to the character and conduct of his Presidency. We were told, long before Monica and even before the Lincoln Bedroom rentals, that it didn't matter.

And indeed it didn't matter in a political world willing to hold leaders to no higher standard than an ability to survive the Beltway Colosseum. Mr. Clinton's double-cross of the Breaux Medicare Commission just last month didn't cost him a political dime. Commentary after commentary told the President his skill at avoiding getting tagged with responsibility for anything was political genius.

Now some half-million refugees are streaming out of Kosovo, three beaten-up U.S. soldiers are in Serbian captivity and President Clinton was on primetime television Wednesday night telling his interviewer that he isn't sending ground troops into Kosovo and he doesn't think impeachment is a badge of shame. Some genius.

It now seems clear that the President went into this military commitment without having thought it through, and is getting himself, his troops, his nation and the NATO alliance into a deeper and deeper mess. It is well established by now that bombing an adversary's army while ruling out ground troops is a recipe for irresolution. Absent ground troops, the only option is bigger bombing, inevitably of civilians. The lesson of war is that if you are compelled to use force, use it overwhelmingly. This is also the responsible course; what saves lives is getting the war over quickly.

There is no reason to be surprised that the U.S. has arrived at this awful moment. Someone who behaves irresponsibly in much of his life is likely to behave irresponsibly in the rest of it. This is what we have meant by character.

Mr. Clinton's character problem is not, and never was, just about sex. From the first overseas engagement—in Haiti or Somalia—the criticism in this quarter of Bill Clinton's foreign policy has been that it's nothing more than managing the next news cycle in the interests of Presidential popularity. It has been a narcissistic foreign policy. Now we, and especially those three captured GIs, are paying the price.

There is danger here to broader U.S. interests. It is not merely a matter of Slobodan Milosevic; Saddam is taking the American President's measure. So obviously are the volatile North Koreans and those elements of the Chinese leadership that want to take Taiwan or who talked blithely awhile back of lobbing missiles at Los Angeles. Mr. Clinton has stumbled into this only six weeks after the impeachment vote that might have given us a new leadership; he has nearly two years left to go, and the price may mount.

Now a moment has arrived that offers Mr. Clinton a chance to prove us critics wrong. Having made this mess, the only thing that can redeem it is the removal from power of Milosevic. The crucial step is to declare removal as a goal. Currently we are slipping toward exactly the wrong way to try to compel this outcome, using escalating air power to attack civilian targets such as power grids.

After all, just over two years ago, these Serbian civilians took to Belgrade's streets to demonstrate against Milosevic. Before that, in 1991, some 200,000 of them demonstrated against Milosevic's war policies, which have been utterly devastating for the Serbs themselves. Indeed, once the goal of removal is in place, the U.S. could announce a pause in the bombing to see whether there are in fact dissidents in the Serbian military who might move against him.

Serbs who stood for election against Milosevic in the past, and did so bravely, could serve as the basis for a legitimate successor government. At the same time, NATO could assemble forces for an assault to change the Serbian government by overwhelming force if that proves necessary. Not so incidentally, this would also chill troublemakers around the world.

There is, in short, a way out of Mr. Clinton's current mess. However, it most certainly would require decisiveness, resolution and a willingness to spend political and personal capital. That is, precisely the traits of character Mr. Clinton has never before displayed.

REVIEW & OUTLOOK

Clinton's Johnny

Did Richard Nixon go to China so that his successor 25 years later could traffic in Chinese campaign contributions? Under Bill Clinton, the American political culture has traveled a long way down this road, which may be why it's hard to conceive of the current U.S. President accomplishing anything very grand during his time this week with Chinese Premier Zhu Rongji.

Johnny Chung

Mr. Zhu lands in Los Angeles just as a minor Los Angeles businessman named Johnny Chung has landed back in the news. Johnny Chung, recall, is the L.A. blast-fax magnate who somehow made 50 visits to the Clinton White House, who struck up a business partnership with a lieutenant-colonel in the Chinese army, and, who according to Sunday's Los Angeles Times, agreed to funnel $300,000 to the Clinton-Gore campaign at the behest of General Ji Shengde, the head of Chinese military intelligence.

Some of our friends have taken to asserting that the primary import of all these stories of Chinese missile espionage and campaign contributions is that China can't be trusted and should now be thought the modern analogue of the Soviet Union. China's 5,000-year history of spying is indeed an interesting subject, but we worry a lot more about seeing that the United States gets through the next one and a half years with a compromised U.S. President who still bears direct responsibility for formulating this country's foreign policy—whether in Belgrade or Beijing.

The Clinton legacy is especially troubling in this sphere because we are now seeing just how much collateral damage it has done to important American political institutions, not least the Democratic Party. GOP Senator Fred Thompson announced at the start of his July 1997 hearings into campaign fund raising, remember, that "high-level Chinese government officials" had intruded into the American political process. The committee's Democrats, with whom the Senator thought he'd cleared the statement, quickly formed a solid wall of opposition and refutation. They were led by Senators John Glenn, Carl Levin and Robert Torricelli. We hope Senator Glenn enjoyed his ride in the space shuttle, but it now appears that Senator Thompson's conclusion was exactly on target.

The Los Angeles Times report Sunday, citing access to Mr. Chung's grand jury testimony (and almost certainly with the help of disgusted sources in the FBI or Justice Department), said Mr. Chung met on August 11, 1996, in Hong Kong with General Ji, who asked him to serve as a conduit for Clinton-Gore contributions. Investigators have identified a $300,000 wire transfer days later to Mr. Chung's Hong Kong bank account sent at General Ji's behest. The General told Mr. Chung, "We like your President." (By May 1998, shortly after Mr. Chung had begun cooperating with Justice's investigation, the FBI put him and his family under armed 24-hour guard at various Los Angeles hotels.)

The Times account is a compelling addition to this story, but it wasn't necessary to wait until this week's momentous arrival of Zhu Rongji to realize that the U.S.'s ability to do business with China was seriously off the rails. Our Micah Morrison detailed in these pages (February 26, 1998) the campaign-related dealings of Macau's Ng Lap Seng, a shadowy figure with ties to the Asian criminal underworld and high reaches of the People's Liberation Army. Mr. Ng sent more than $1 million to accounts controlled by Clinton restaurateur-fund-raiser Charlie Trie. Together, the Thompson Report noted, they collaborated in a scheme to funnel "hundreds of thousands of dollars in foreign funds" to the Democratic National Committee. Mr. Ng since has received new honors and appointments from the Chinese government.

No matter who was President this week, he would be required to deal with Mr. Zhu on a wide array of sensitive concerns—China's bid to WTO membership, its troubling human-rights practices, its relationship with volatile North Korea, its insistence that Taiwan be left undefended, its spying at Los Alamos, and the matter of most favored nation trading status for a nation, whatever its government, that has more than a billion citizens. Yet if Mr. Clinton, say, presses for Congressional assent to a WTO agreement, will this be an honest assessment of U.S. interests, or a payoff for General Ji's timely help in getting re-elected?

What's more, the institutions of our government have aligned themselves to cover up this question. In sentencing Mr. Chung last December, U.S. District Judge Manuel L. Real remarked that he was "surprised that the Attorney General has eschewed appointment of a special prosecutor." And as a result of its uncompromising stonewall for the President in the Thompson hearings through the impeachment trial, there is no single Democrat who retains enough standing or credibility to help a President whose foreign policy is collapsing daily.

Yet in fact, Bill Clinton is the President, and his disregard for the implications of his own recklessness, waved off and even defended by the Democratic Party, now leaves him to face China without the reservoir of authority that attends a normal Presidency. We'll know by week's end the political value of affability.

April 12, 1999

Review & Outlook

Zhu Knows

Bill Clinton certainly knows how to make friends fast. Judging from the $300,000 contribution from the head of China's military intelligence to the Clinton-Gore re-election campaign, by 1996 Beijing had overcome whatever reservations it might have had about a candidate who vowed not to "coddle tyrants." As Prime Minister Zhu Rongji found out last week when Mr. Clinton shot down China's bid for WTO membership, however, getting the President you want is not enough. What's important is a President who can deliver.

Zhu Rongji

The irony here is that the associations and assistance that helped return Mr. Clinton to the White House now help render him impotent to push through any agenda. With regard to China, America has two compelling interests: first, to do its best to see that China continues to wean itself off the Communist system in the direction of more economic and political openness; second, to ensure that in the interim stages China's newfound wealth does not become the source of increased belligerence. This, after all, is what distinguishes engagement from acquiescence.

After a meeting in which Mr. Clinton attached what proved to be unacceptable conditions for WTO membership, Mr. Zhu sagely cited an unfavorable "political atmosphere." In other words, Congress, the media and the public were upset at reports that China meddled in U.S.

election campaigns and stole sensitive nuclear technology. Such episodes are bound to break out now and then, moreover, as long as China remains a Communist power that violates the rights of its citizens, lobs missiles off Taiwan in a fit of pique and increasingly sees U.S. forces in the Pacific as unwelcome. Mr. Zhu's bland denials of wrongdoing to the contrary, it was his government that a year ago promoted Ng Lap Seng—the shadowy figure who helped transmit $1 million in Chinese donations to the Clinton campaign—to posts with the Chinese People's Consultative Conference in Beijing and the Preparatory Committee for the Macau Special Administrative Region.

Especially under such circumstances, promoting normal trade relations requires the expenditure of a considerable part of political capital by American leaders. Mr. Clinton's problem is that he has no such credibility. Congress, to be sure, is an obstacle. But it is the nature of Congress to incline in this direction—just ask George Bush—because it is a collection of parochial interests. Likewise it is in the nature of presidents to seek the broader national interest. Yet instead of pushing China on its commitment to openness, Mr. Clinton chose to scuttle Beijing's WTO bid on the reef of overtly protectionist conditions.

Only a year back everyone thought the MFN issue had been put aside forever. This present difficulty is not simply a matter of Chinese missteps, or even a function of the Clinton fund-raising entanglements with China. It is instead a function of a larger irresolution, the inevitable offspring of a foreign policy born less of vital interests than of interest groups, not to mention the empty threats now coming home to roost. That may be one reason that when it comes to dealing with problem regimes, people look to men and women with a reputation for toughness: Richard Nixon with China, Ronald Reagan and Margaret Thatcher with Mikhail Gorbachev, John Paul II with the leadership of his native Poland.

Engaging dangerous powers is always tricky. When that power happens also to be the world's most populous nation, one still committed to Communist rule, the shoals are all the more treacherous. The easy way out is simply to view the enormous contradiction that constitutes a modernizing China as either all black or all white, whereas the American interest clearly lies in distinguishing between the two, often amid a cacophony of conflicting social, political and economic passions. This in turn requires not only judgment, but a public credibility built on past action that will see a leader through the tough calls. Having been sent home nearly empty-handed, perhaps even Mr. Zhu now appreciates the real price of character in an American President.

Editorial Feature

Mopping Up Whitewater

BY MICAH MORRISON

LITTLE ROCK, Ark.—Presented with a check she signed in 1983 with the notation "Payoff Clinton" in her handwriting, Susan McDougal told her latest jury here that the money was for

a land purchase in the hamlet of Clinton, Ark. Never mind that among the documents prosecutors introduced were a list of loans noting one "B Clinton" and a sheet of interest calculations ending with the figure "$5081.82"—the exact amount of the putative Clinton, Ark., check.

Yesterday Ms. McDougal's trial ended with the jury unable to agree on criminal contempt charges, and acquitting her of obstruc-

Susan McDougal

tion of justice. The Clinton camp's elation at this outcome was no doubt diminished a few hours later when Judge Susan Webber Wright cited the president himself for civil contempt for "willful failure" to follow her instructions to testify truthfully in the Paula Jones case. Independent Counsel Kenneth Starr still has three more trials on deck and owes a final report, but these mop-up decisions attest that Whitewater is winding down in the legal arena. What remains is a tissue of lies and evasions still frustrating Mr. Starr's search for the truth about whether the Clintons participated in banking fraud schemes and then used the powers of the presidency to abort investigations.

Mr. Clinton is of course still president, though held in contempt in the Jones case and impeached over issues involving Monica Lewinsky. For others involved in Whitewater, the Clintons have been, as Ms. McDougal's former husband, the late James Mc-Dougal, once observed, "like tornadoes moving through people's lives." Ms. McDougal served 18 months for civil contempt and four months (before being released on medical grounds) on her 1996 fraud conviction in a $300,000 loan scheme. Then-Arkansas Gov. Jim Guy Tucker and James McDougal were convicted on other fraud charges at the Whitewater trial, a major milestone in Mr. Starr's inquiry. Mr. McDougal died in prison in 1998 while serving time on the charges.

On the other side of the controversy Whitewater figure David Hale, a witness against the president, last month faced a county prosecution a few blocks away for making false statements to state insurance regulators, but escaped with only a 21-day jail sentence. No one in Arkansas had ever been prosecuted on such charges before, and Mr. Hale says the case was ginned up as payback for his cooperation in the Whitewater probe. The charges were first raised in the tense period of the McDougal-Tucker case by a local prosecutor who made no secret of his yearning for higher political office. Mr. Hale was a key witness in the McDougal-Tucker trial. In a plea bargain with Mr. Starr, he served 24 months in federal prison for fraud charges involving his small business investment company, which had loaned the $300,000 to Ms. McDougal.

The latest charges against Ms. McDougal arose because she had refused to answer grand jury questions in Mr. Starr's probe of Bill Clinton. Mr. Starr's original mandate, of course, was to investigate Whitewater, the real-estate development company owned by the McDougals in partnership with Bill and Hillary Clinton. Ms. McDougal refused to answer whether Mr. Clinton knew about the $300,000 loan and whether he testified truthfully at her trial. Called as a defense witness at that trial and testifying via videotaped deposition, President Clinton had said he was not aware of the $300,000 scheme and that he had never received a loan from the McDougals' S&L, Madison Guaranty. The president's 1996 trial testimony was contradicted by Mr. Hale, and later by Mr. McDougal, who changed his testimony following his conviction on multiple fraud counts. Their all-important claim: that they had met with then-Gov. Clinton to cook up the $300,000 loan.

At the just-concluded trial, Ms. McDougal finally did offer answers to the questions. She testified that she "never discussed" the $300,000 loan with Mr. Clinton and that to her knowledge he had testified truthfully at her 1996 trial. But Ms. McDougal's credibility, already strained by her felony Whitewater convictions and civil contempt jailing, was further undermined by her preposterous lie about the "Payoff Clinton" check going to pay off a land loan in Clinton, Ark. The only apparent motive for this fairy tale would be to cover up for the Clintons in the face of new evidence that they indeed were beneficiaries of illegal loans.

Prosecutors introduced two key checks at the trial: one, for $27,600, from Madison Guaranty, payable to Bill Clinton; and a second—the "Payoff Clinton" check, for $5081.82—signed by Ms. McDougal and payable to Madison Guaranty. The $27,600 check, the prosecution said, was a loan to Mr. Clinton to retire the balance of an earlier $30,000 loan to Whitewater from Madison Bank, a separate McDougal-controlled entity. The check, however, was not endorsed by Mr. Clinton before its deposit at Madison Bank.

The $5081.82 "Payoff Clinton" check was combined with a nominee loan for $25,000 by Mr. McDougal to a Madison associate. The $25,000 check and the $5081.82 check paid off the principal and interest of the $27,600 Clinton loan. Prosecutors supported the theory of the Clinton loan with other evidence: FBI testimony about a Madison employee who saw Mr. Clinton's name on a printout of outstanding loans; minutes of a Madison Bank board meeting; the list of S&L borrowers noting "B Clinton"; and the sheet of monthly interest calculations with "$27,600" written at the top and "$5,081.82" at the bottom.

Nothing can be proved beyond a reasonable doubt at this point, but the new evidence in the "Payoff Clinton" loan scheme meshes with the general pattern of fraudulent practices detailed in the 1996 trial and the original Resolution Trust Corp. criminal referrals issued in 1992 and 1993, which named the Clintons as possible beneficiaries of illegal practices. Ms. McDougal's current trial also revealed other new details, including confirmation that the Office of

Independent Counsel had drawn up a draft indictment of Mrs. Clinton—presumably related to fraud at Madison Guaranty in the Castle Grande land deals.

Later this year, Whitewater and the Washington coverup will get another examination when former Associate Attorney General Webster Hubbell goes on trial on charges related to Mrs. Clinton and Castle Grande. But while new evidence accumulates at every trial, an impeached president holds power in the Oval Office. Finding the truth about the Clintons is rapidly passing out of the domain of the courts and into the hands of history.

Mr. Morrison is a Journal editorial page writer.

Editorial Feature

Does Clinton
Have an
'Enemies List'?

By WILLIAM McGURN

Maybe the Internal Revenue Service has learned more than we give it credit for. When congressional investigators looked into the Nixon White House 25 years ago, they found more than enough evidence to support John Dean's charges that the president had directed associates to compile an enemies list of people who were to find themselves the subject of IRS tax audits after the election. Less noted is the committee's finding that Nixon had largely been frustrated in these attempts. In other words, the IRS had resisted the Nixon effort to politicize it.

Today the situation has reversed itself. In the Nixon days, we had a president calling upon the IRS for audits that never materialized. In the Clinton days, by contrast, we already have a large number of audits of people and groups who might reasonably be described as Clinton foes, from Paula Jones, the Heritage Foundation and the Christian Coalition to Oliver North's Freedom Alliance, the National Rifle Association and five foundations associated with then-Speaker Newt Gingrich. We further have an IRS desperate to prevent the release of information that would help tell us whether such audits were in fact random or taken from some new enemies list.

The latest wrinkle came late last month, when the IRS delivered 8,000 pages of material to the Landmark Legal Foundation. In January 1997, Landmark filed a Freedom of Information Act request for some simple information: the names of anyone who had requested audits or investigations of 501c(3) tax-exempt organizations. Yet even after a federal district court twice ruled against it, the IRS is still playing games. Most of the names and organizations on the 8,000 pages provided have been blacked out, with no legal explanation given. Whether the IRS will be free to continue to refuse releasing the requested information or delay any real response until after Bill Clinton has left office is now up to Judge Henry H. Kennedy Jr., who will meet this morning with both sides' lawyers to discuss the status of the case.

Judge Kennedy has been here before. The IRS first tried to avoid coming up with the information by claiming Landmark would have to pay tens of thousands of dollars for the search, fees typically not charged for public-interest nonprofits. In October 1998, Judge Kennedy rejected the IRS claim. But the IRS shifted, now claiming that Landmark was not entitled to the material because it was privileged tax return information. This, of course, is absurd: Landmark is after information about the accusers, not the accused. Again Judge Kennedy found against the IRS, though he put off Landmark requests for depositions of IRS officers and for an index giving a case-by-case explanation of any document withheld. That the IRS has now responded with the pertinent information mostly blacked out suggests an agency determined to abuse Judge Kennedy's patience.

Landmark's president, Mark Levin, says he needs to know two things to ensure that the IRS has complied with the request. First, he wants to know what the IRS searched. Landmark staffers have gone through most of the documents, the bulk of which consist of correspondence to and from members of Congress. There are no phone messages or logs, no e-mail, and only a handful of notes originally requested, and Mr. Levin's suspicion is that the search may have been confined to the correspondence of the IRS legislative affairs office. Indeed, his question gets to the integrity of the discovery process. Unless Landmark is permitted to depose IRS officials about where they searched and why, there is no way to verify that the IRS complied with the law.

Equally important is that the IRS be compelled to give a reason when it declines to provide a given document or name. We can all imagine a legitimate basis for withholding the name of, say, a chief financial officer for some nonprofit who has become a whistle-blow-er. Surely, however, what's called for here is a case-by-case explanation, not a blanket dismissal. Remember, Landmark is not asking for any tax or financial information about the audited parties. It's not even asking which parties were audited. All it wants to know are the names of those who might have fingered these groups for investigation.

We don't know whether those audited were targeted in a Nixon-like quest by Clinton officials or sympathizers bent on settling scores—though it is interesting to note that the name that Landmark says comes up most frequently in the 8,000 pages is Democratic Rep. Henry Waxman. What we do know is that in America people have a right to know their accusers, especially when the accusation affects their livelihoods. In a May 1997 memo to the heads of all agencies, no less than Janet Reno reminded administrators that the principles of open government "include applying customer-service attitudes toward FOIA requesters, following the spirit as well as the letter of the Act, and applying a presumption of disclosure."

Clearly the attempt by IRS officials to keep the requested information out of Landmark's hands by dragging their feet and blacking out names is hard to reconcile with Miss Reno's "presumption of disclosure," much less her directive on "customer-service attitudes." It might all lead you to conclude that the IRS has more than demonstrated it no longer deserves the benefit of the doubt. You might even begin to wonder, what's it trying to hide?

Mr. McGurn is a member of the Journal's editorial board.

Clinton in Contempt

Bill Clinton's legacy—and in the face of an ongoing Independent Counsel probe, his legal position as well—suffered another blow on April 12, 1999. In a historic judicial rebuke, U.S. District Judge Susan Webber Wright found the President in contempt of court for providing "intentionally false" testimony in the Monica Lewinsky case.

The contempt citation, like Mr. Clinton's impeachment, had its origin in the sexual harassment suit brought against the President by Paula Jones, a former Arkansas state employee. In a January 1998 deposition before Judge Wright, President Clinton claimed that he had never been alone with or had sexual relations Ms. Lewinsky, a witness called by the Jones lawyers. Judge Wright's rebuke was stinging: "The record demonstrates by clear and convincing evidence that the president responded to plaintiff's questions by giving false, misleading and evasive answers that were designed to obstruct the judicial process."

Judge Wright's finding was not the end of Mr. Clinton's troubles. Independent Counsel Kenneth Starr was weighing whether to indict him after he left the Presidency on criminal charges of perjury and obstruction in the Lewinsky case. Mr. Starr would soon step down. His replacement would be among the last independent counsels. With the bruising impeachment battle over, a consensus had developed in Congress not to renew the controversial Independent Counsel Statute.

In May, Rep. Chris Cox's Select Committee on U.S. National

Security published a detailed report on Chinese espionage coups. The panel had been formed to investigate reports that donations to the Clinton-Gore campaign by the Democratic Party's largest 1996 contributor, Bernard Schwartz, head of Loral Space & Communications, had influenced White House decisions on technology exports to China. Detailed, thorough, and with some startling conclusions—including that China had "stolen design information on the United States' most advanced thermonuclear weapons"—the Cox Report nevertheless failed to have much impact.

The Journal suggested this was due to Mr. Cox's failure to connect the dots. The story of China espionage and the intersection of political donations and intelligence failures remained cloudy. The committee "can be forgiven for soft-pedaling campaign finance in the interest of bipartisanship," the Journal wrote, "though this means the report stops short of complete understanding and real accountability. The details we do not yet know, but what is altogether too clear is the climate and culture were set from the top of the administration."

Review & Outlook

Someone Has to Do It

The consensus around Washington seems to be that after Ken Starr, there won't be another Independent Counsel law. So we guess that means we were right to oppose its creation in 1978, as was Justice Scalia's lone dissent against the law in 1988, as indeed was Ken Starr, who opposed it then and does so now. Having both opposed the law then and defended Mr. Starr from his critics, we feel entitled to the benefit of perspective on 20 years' experience with this statute.

Kenneth Starr

We recall taking Ray Donovan's side when he asked: "Where do I go to get my reputation back?" We continued to express concern throughout the investigations of Ed Meese, Alexia Morrison's chase after Ted Olson and of course Lawrence Walsh's never-surpassed Inspector Javert performance in Iran-Contra. Back then we had the IC critic's chair pretty much to ourselves. So it may come as no surprise that we're bemused by the Beltway mob suddenly trying to drive the Independent Counsel into the wilderness.

If the Clinton years have taught the American body politic anything at all it is that keeping the Presidency accountable is dirty work, but somebody has to do it. Our fear is that when Congress lets the law lapse, it is going to simply walk away from the subject and the Beltway will acquiesce. The same, hard question will stand: Who should police the Presidency?

It's generally conceded that without an Independent Counsel, this oversight function will largely revert to the Justice Department. We're going to say some harsh things here about Justice, but not without a necessary preface: Bill Clinton is sui generis, unique. Few serious observers, especially among the active judiciary, doubt that Bill Clinton's abuse of the nation's governing institutions has been relentless and unprecedented. The Chief Justice essentially told the President's lawyers not to bother appealing their several losses on feckless privilege claims. The language of Judge Susan Webber Wright's contempt citation this week is agog with incredulity: "It appears that the President is asserting that Ms. Lewinsky could be having sex with him while, at the same time, he was not having sex with her."

What Bill Clinton taught us is that the Presidency's implied powers and authority are greater even than most had imagined. A determined President can get away with a lot. This is not always a bad thing. Even the Founders conceded implied powers, acknowledging the realities of national leadership. FDR's leadership in war comes to mind. But the Clinton Presidency, with no evident interest in leadership, has made its legacy the obvious need for accountability. But where among our institutions should that accountability reside?

There is no hope of arriving at an answer until there is some broad admission of the ruin Mr. Clinton has brought to the Department of Justice. Absent a Justice you can trust, no oversight is possible under our system.

The Clinton assault on Justice began on day one, when he appointed Webster Hubbell, a crook, as Associate Attorney General. Though he fired all 93 U.S. Attorneys at one swipe, the best and brightest Democratic lawyers of Mr. Clinton's generation never had a chance to serve Justice in his Presidency. They were passed over for cronies and compliant affirmative action appointees like Janet Reno. The record since is appalling.

Most famously, Ms. Reno refused to appoint an Independent Counsel to look into 1996 campaign violations involving the President and Vice President, rejecting the counsel of not only FBI Director Louis Freeh but Charles La Bella, her own handpicked Public Integrity investigator on campaign finance. The whole episode has made a mockery of the notion of independence and brings us squarely against the inherent conflict of interest in letting Justice police the Presidency. The vaunted Public Integrity Section? The National Law Journal reported last month that Public Integrity hasn't filed a report to Congress as required by law since 1996. Justice's violations of the Vacancy Act enraged even Senator Robert Byrd. Its investigation into the illegal involvement of the Teamsters and other unions in the 1996 election is inexplicably stalled. The "unproven" Filegate scandal tainted the FBI's integrity.

All this said, we are perfectly willing to entertain the possibility of Justice serving at least as the clearinghouse for accusations of Executive misconduct. Among other things, the highly successful and thoroughly unfair assault on Mr. Starr shows that a prosecutor standing alone cannot really defend himself in the public arena. And if the buck can be passed to an Independent Counsel, other institutions will tend to shirk their duty.

This does not merely concern the "professionals" at Justice. Duty also means that the relevant oversight committees of Congress do their jobs—when it matters, not after Justice is overrun by a praetorian guard. The media, more powerful than ever, needs to distinguish between dogged pursuit of malfeasance and the spectacle of simply seeing if someone can survive the media bonfire, which now burns past midnight. Finally, there are our two political parties.

As Madison envisioned, these factions police each other. But party politics in a civilized nation isn't a blind Faustian bargain, either. When the Nixon Presidency began to fall outside the acceptable historical boundaries, Republicans of stature said so, avoiding dangerous stresses on the system. This did not happen during the Clinton years. Historians will have to sort the reasons for the Democratic phalanx around this Presidency, with not a single of their Senators voting disapproval.

If this precedent holds, if political survival is now the trump value in our government—a "permanent campaign" above all else—then we strongly doubt that anything will be solved by merely ringing down the curtain on the last Independent Counsel. In this the electorate has a responsibility. Beyond some point, we all have to recognize that as well as the Founders' system has served us, they knew that its success ultimately depends on the basic instincts of civic responsibility of the individuals whom voters choose to govern them.

Editorial Feature

What's Wrong With Wright

The long-awaited opinion arrived in Washington last week with the feel of an ammunition drop at a long-abandoned battlefield. Judge Susan Webber Wright found President Clinton guilty of some of the same charges brought by the House managers in the Clinton impeachment trial but never conclusively established in a judicial ruling.

For constitutional scholars scrounging among the debris, it was a movable feast. A federal judge was holding a president in contempt of court: an historic moment. The opinion was loaded with barbed language and findings of willful misconduct. Yet the most intriguing line may be the most innocuous: "It was during the President's televised address that the Court first learned the President may be in contempt of court."

Rule of Law

By Jonathan Turley

This one line could prove the most controversial part of Judge Wright's opinion and the issue upon which her own role in the crisis will be judged. It isn't the content but the date of Judge Wright's decision that is troubling.

Judge Wright makes clear that the date of the opinion was no judicial snafu of poor timing or indecision. Judge Wright noted that Mr. Clinton's contempt was obvious and hardly required "extended analysis." Yet she decided to withhold judgment as the impeachment battle unfolded and finally ended with acquittal. At the very moment in history where an independent court ruling was most needed, she decided to remain silent.

The reference to the president's speech gives a specific date upon which his possible contempt was apparent to the court: Aug. 17, 1998. That was the evening of the president's televised message. It was also before any referral by Independent Counsel Kenneth Starr to the House for impeachment.

For more than six months, Congress would debate the president's conduct in the Jones deposition and his claims of technical compliance with the truth. If the president's intentional false testimony was clear and didn't require "extended analysis," why then did Judge Wright take an extended period to issue her conclusions? Judge Wright explained that "the Court determined that it should defer to Congress and its constitutional duties prior to this Court addressing the President's conduct in this civil case." The purpose of this deference is unclear; the court was not assisting Congress but withholding material information from it.

Susan Webber Wright

Federal courts have a constitutional duty to rule on legal questions without concern for the political consequences. Exercising judgment as to the best time to release an opinion can be the most political act of all for a federal court. This may be why courts have historically shown "deference to Congress" by ruling on legal matters related to impeachment without delay—leaving the merits of impeachment to Congress to decide with a complete record.

Judge Wright was correct about one thing: a timely ruling would have had an effect on the impeachment process. In showing intentional and willful acts by the president, she relied on many of the same exchanges and transcripts presented by the House managers— and contested by White House counsel—during the Senate trial. At some points, the opinion is indistinguishable from portions of the prosecution's argument. If Judge Wright had resolved these questions before the trial, some of the president's arguments to Congress couldn't have been plausibly maintained and the core issues placed in sharper relief for the public.

Mr. Clinton testified before the grand jury that his deposition in the Jones case was technically true and that he did not lie in his answers before Judge Wright. This became a common refrain in the White House defense in the impeachment trial. The White House actually used a videotape of Judge Wright to suggest that she also found the definitions of sexual relations ambiguous and unclear.

Mr. Clinton insisted in his case before Congress that, while he was not helpful, he was lawful in his testimony, never obstructed the proceedings, and complied with his technical obligations as a witness. The president's lawyers further emphasized, with considerable success, that Judge Wright had found that the information in the deposition wasn't material or relevant to the case due to her subsequent dismissal of the action.

Judge Wright makes fast work of these arguments in her contempt decision, finding that

• the president's deposition testimony "was intentionally false";

• his statement to the court that the Lewinsky affidavit was "absolutely true" was in fact "misleading and not true";

• "the President's sworn statements in this civil lawsuit [were a] willful refusal to obey this Court's discovery Orders";

• the president chose to "employ deceptions and falsehoods in an attempt to obstruct the judicial process"; and that

• "the Court did not rule that evidence of the Lewinsky matter was irrelevant or immaterial" and the President withheld information "deemed by this Court to be relevant to plaintiffs' lawsuit."

If this opinion had been issued in August or indeed at any time in 1998, it might not have changed the outcome of the Senate trial but it would have materially advanced the debate. The White House suggestion that this was simply a clever manipulation of words by the president would have been replaced with the finding that this was a simple act of contempt for both the federal court and federal law. The suggestion that the question of falsity could be only answered by "getting into the President's mind" would have been answered by a court expressing little such difficulty.

Judge Wright's decision to delay her ruling had precisely the effect that she wanted to avoid: she became involved in the crisis through an act of omission or, perhaps more aptly, an act of acquiescence. By remaining mute for months, Judge Wright allowed the president to plausibly maintain arguments of technical legality despite her conclusion that the violations were easily established.

If Judge Wright had ruled on the contempt issues in 1998, the court would have left the significance of the ruling to Congress to resolve in the impeachment context. Instead, the court allowed Congress to speculate on a legal judgment that should have been part of the record for its political judgment. Issued long after its greatest relevance had passed, her contempt finding against President Clinton will remain a curious example of how justice delayed is justice denied. Read in the aftermath of the trial, the opinion's outrage appears strikingly ironic: more of a requiem than a ruling.

Mr. Turley is a professor at George Washington University Law School.

REVIEW & OUTLOOK

Clinton's China Policy

A friend working with Chinese college students in Beijing called this week to discuss the rioting against the American embassy there. He said that when President Clinton's apology for the Belgrade bombing was finally shown on Chinese television, many of the students said they found the apology "insincere." They didn't believe it.

Bill Clinton's China policy was a hash before his ambassador in Beijing endured several days of stoning. Chinese Premier Zhu Rongji came to Washington expecting to close a deal on entry to the World Trade Organization. It didn't happen. Besides the already difficult politics of WTO admission, he arrived amid burgeoning allegations of Chinese espionage at our nuclear weapons facilities. Events such as these make it clear that managing our relationship with China would be difficult under the best of circumstances. It is a foreign-policy challenge of enormous complexity that has required the sustained concentration of recent administrations. As readers of these columns are aware, at the center of our complaint against Bill Clinton has been the charge that by abusing the authority of his office in various ways, he has undermined the authority of that office. He has weakened the Presidency's ability to exercise fully its assigned task of shaping and representing this nation's interests. The pervasive doubts about his intentions in Kosovo are but one example.

The mess in China, though, offers an opportunity to view the decline of this relationship precisely within the context of a Presidency misusing its office. This week's news peg for that abuse is the testimony before the House of former Clinton fund-raiser Johnny Chung, who has described receiving $300,000 from China's number one intelligence official to help re-elect Mr. Clinton in 1996. This, too, is a "relationship."

Indeed, in our view any clear understanding of the current state of U.S.-China relations depends not so much on the activities of Secretaries of State, National Security Advisers or Trade Reps as it does on the following individuals and organizations: Ron Brown, Joseph Giroir, Mark Middleton, the Lippo Group, Ng Lap Seng, Charlie Trie, John Huang, Maria Hsia and Janet Reno. They, too, were formulators of Mr. Clinton's China policy.

AP Photo/H.B. Hays, USIA

U.S. Ambassador to China Jim Sasser

Back in August 1993, former Little Rock Rose Law Firm chairman Joe Giroir incorporated the Arkansas International Development Corp. to bring Indonesia's Lippo Group together with American companies seeking to do business in China. This is the culture of penny-ante deal-making that would soon migrate directly to China, culminating as direct appeals for Clinton campaign funds.

Exactly one year after the Giroir Arkansas incorporation, Commerce Secretary Ron Brown embarked on a six-day trade mission to China. "We are not ideological or philosophical about this," he said. "We are relentlessly pragmatic, bottom-line oriented." New Orleans-based Entergy Corp. then signed a $1 billion memorandum of understanding with the Lippo Group and the North China Power Group to manage and expand a power plant outside of Beijing.

In February 1995, an Arkansas insider named Mark Middleton, who had been working in the White House as an aide to Chief of Staff Mack McLarty, left his job there to pursue a career as an Asian dealmaker, where he worked closely with Mr. Giroir, by now also transplanted to Asia.

September 1995: At a White House meeting among President Clinton, Mr. Huang, Mr. Giroir, Lippo Group scion James Riady and senior Clinton adviser Bruce Lindsey, a decision was reached to dispatch Mr. Huang to the Democratic National Committee as a top fund-raiser.

A month later, Mr. Trie, a Little Rock restaurateur, and his partner, Macau businessman Ng Lap Seng, organized a reception for Commerce Secretary Brown at Hong Kong's Island Shangri-La Hotel. (Between 1994 and 1996, Mr. Ng, a shadowy figure with ties to the triad organized crime underworld and the Communist regime in Beijing, funneled more than $900,000 to accounts controlled by Mr. Trie and visited the White House 10 times.)

The Island Shangri-La event, which surfaced in a December article in The Wall Street Journal, was attended by wealthy businessmen from Hong Kong, Macau and China, who said they felt the event's organizers had pressured them to make political contributions. The faxed pretext for the dinner was an opportunity to meet Secretary Brown. The article reported that "Messrs. Trie and Middleton, who often work together and even shared office space and use the same cellular telephone on visits to Hong Kong, arranged for some of the Asians they met on earlier trips to meet Mr. Clinton."

In February 1996, Charlie Trie escorted mainland Chinese arms merchant Wang Jun to a White House reception for donors. A month later, China fired missiles over the Taiwan Straits to intimidate the island nation during democratic elections. Also that month, President Clinton approved the transfer of satellite-export licensing from the State Department to the Commerce Department, over State's objections. The transfer had been sought by, among others, Loral Space & Communications Chairman Bernard Schwartz, a major Clinton donor.

In August 1996, Clinton donor Johnny Chung would meet in a Macau abalone restaurant with General Ji Shengde, the head of China's military intelligence. According to Mr. Chung's testimony, General Ji provided him with $300,000 to donate to the Clinton-Gore campaign and the Democratic Party. Mr. Chung kept most of the money for himself.

Now, bear in mind that this is still before the end of Mr. Clinton's first term. At this juncture, one might ask: What were the Chinese supposed to make of these people? Or of this American government? What did Slobodan Milosevic think?

By October, with election a month off and the press unraveling the fund-raising operation, Mr. Huang was suspended from the Democratic National Committee. More details poured out in the ensuing months—the Thompson Committee hearings and final report, the indictments of Charlie Trie and Maria Hsia, the federal charges against Johnny Chung.

Ultimately, both the Director of the FBI and the prosecutor brought into the Justice Department to investigate recommended to Janet Reno that she appoint an independent counsel to pursue these matters involving the President. Repeatedly, the Attorney General refused to do so. Again, all this gets followed in the world's foreign offices.

Even now, however, with Johnny Chung's admissions before Congress, there is an instinct to regard it as mainly a story about U.S. campaign-finance abuses. Surely that is not what is at stake here. Our relations with China are now symbolized by the pocked walls of the American embassy. In recent years, anyone attempting to shape an appropriate U.S. policy toward China has had to grapple with the Hong Kong handover, Taiwan, North Korea, the treatment of political dissidents and practicing Christians, Tibet, most favored nation status, the WTO, China's nuclear-weapons transfers to unfriendly nations and not least the existence of several discrete power centers in the Chinese Communist Party. It is simply not credible to argue that a President could hope to represent the interests of the United States in anything so sensitive as this complex relationship while he or his minions were simultaneously inviting his negotiating partners in China or their surrogates to finance his survival in office.

So now, when the President of the United States publicly apologizes for a mistake to the people of China, 20-year-old students in Beijing say they doubt his sincerity. The U.S. does indeed need a coherent and credible policy toward China. But it will have to wait.

REVIEW & OUTLOOK

The Banquo Report

A ghost sat at the end of the table yesterday as the Cox Committee served up a Chinese menu of espionage coups. As inexplicable as the American security blunders seemed, the diners kept averting their eyes from the Clinton campaign finance scandal.

It is of course true that the first security breaches occurred under earlier administrations, including Republican ones. And also true that there is important work to be done redressing failed procedures, and that this enterprise will be helped by a bipartisan recognition of the problem. Indeed, Energy Secretary Bill Richardson, one of this Administration's adults, has by all accounts made a credible start with this project. The Cox Committee can be forgiven for soft-pedaling campaign finance in the interests of bipartisanship, though this means the report stops short of complete understanding and real accountability.

Christopher Cox

All nations support spies, after all, and by the law of averages they will sometimes succeed. Despite earlier leaks to the contrary, the report makes clear that carelessness with military secrets clearly reached a crescendo in the Clinton years. We know, in particular, that the discovery of the Los Alamos leak first came to light in 1995, when the CIA received a document detailing China's use of U.S. designs in their latest warheads. We know that the Justice Department repeatedly refused the FBI permission to wiretap Wen Ho Lee, suspected of providing China with much of the information. We know too that the Energy Department, which has authority over U.S. nuclear laboratories, briefed then-deputy national security adviser Sandy Berger about the problem in 1996.

Which is to say, in the midst of the President's re-election campaign, not to mention in the wake of the Senate Banking Committee hearings on Whitewater. We're told that President Clinton himself was not let in on the secret until 1998. If true, this is itself reason enough for Mr. Berger to be sacked. We further know that Mr. Lee himself was not fired until this newspaper and the New York Times published stories about the leaks. And that no corrective plan was put into place until last fall, which is to say more than three years after wholesale spying was detected.

All of this, as the Marxists were wont to say, was no accident. There was, first of all, the peculiar environment the White House allowed to be created with talk of a "strategic partnership" with China, and with the late Ron Brown ferrying corporate fat cats over to China to ink their multimillion-dollar contracts. From his National Security Council post, Mr. Berger, a former China trade lobbyist, sat in on the weekly campaign strategy meetings where fund raising was discussed. These appearances already show an aura of carelessness.

But worse, from the first, campaign finance and espionage have been intertwined. Indeed, the Cox panel itself was convened in response to a request from Newt Gingrich, who wanted a committee to investigate reports whether contributions to Mr. Clinton's 1996 re-election campaign by Bernard Schwartz, head of Loral Space and Communications and the Democratic Party's biggest contributor in 1996, influenced subsequent White House decisions on technology exports to China. Mr. Clinton himself happily approved waivers allowing space launches even though he'd been warned about the potential threat to national security, and later acceded to requests from Hughes Electronics to transfer export approval authority to Commerce from the State Department. And the report concludes that Loral and Hughes knowingly and illegally passed sensitive information to the Chinese without first securing required licenses.

Around the same time, money for the Clinton campaign was coming from Liu Chaoying, daughter of China's retired senior military officer and a lieutenant colonel in the People's Liberation Army in her own right. The report concludes that Miss Liu's transfer of $300,000 to Democratic fund-raiser Johnny Chung in 1996 "was an attempt to better position her in the United States to acquire computer, missile and satellite technologies." There are many more of these stories, for example the financing for fund-raiser Charlie Trie from Ng Lap Seng of Macau. We know that Al Gore passed the hat at a Buddhist temple, and a bigwig PLA gunrunner sipped coffee with the President at the White House. But the report merely says it was unable to interview witnesses who took the Fifth Amendment or fled the country, so "no significance should be attributed, one way or the other" to its lack of findings on campaign finance. Many of the fleeing witnesses landed in China, where they became at least implicit bargaining chips in negotiations with Mr. Clinton.

Still worse, it is not clear where bribery ended and extortion began. John Huang was transferred from his perch at Commerce to fund raising in the Oval Office after a September 13, 1995, meeting in the Oval Office with the President, Lippo scion James Riady, senior Clinton aide Bruce Lindsey and Arkansas/Jakarta businessman Joseph Giroir. This looks like the beginning of a Chinese fund-raising conspiracy, but Attorney General Janet Reno has steadfastly refused to appoint an independent counsel to find out despite the urging of FBI Director Louis Freeh and her own handpicked investigator Charles La Bella.

Ms. Reno's own Justice Department investigation has secured cooperation from Mr. Chung and Mr. Trie, and a plea bargain with Mr. Huang is reportedly impending. This is either progress or completion of a coverup. Reports of the Huang agreement say Justice will specify that there is no evidence that he engaged in espionage or any violations of national security laws.

Meanwhile, Carl Cameron of Fox News Channel has obtained interesting leaks of wiretap transcripts between Mr. Chung and Robert Luu, a Los Angeles lawyer who, Mr. Cameron reported, represented Chinese intelligence. Mr. Luu told him not to worry too much about the contributions, but "the important thing is not to touch Hughes and Loral." And in a discussion of concocting a cover story blaming contributions not on the Chinese government but on "princelings" — the privileged children of China's elite, Mr. Luu says, "Chairman

Jiang agreed to handle it like this. The President over here also agreed.'" Fox reported the White House denial of any such agreement.

There is plenty of reason to believe, in short, that Chinese political contributions to Mr. Clinton importantly intersected with spectacular intelligence failures by his Administration. The details we do not yet know, but what is altogether too clear is the climate and culture were set from the top of this Administration. As we asked when the President stumbled into a war he still does not have the will to win, does character matter yet?

June 16, 1999

REVIEW & OUTLOOK

Starr's Mandate

At this juncture, the news that Independent Counsel Kenneth Starr is sticking to his mandate and will issue a final report on the Clintons would appear to be no news at all. But to some commentators Mr. Starr remains a clear and present danger to the Republic, and so the campaign to delegitimize the Independent Counsel continues unabated among the co-dependents.

In point of fact—facts still mattering in most legal and press circles—Mr. Starr is bound by law to issue a final report. The Clintons are the perfect example of why he should do so. If news reports are correct and Mr. Starr has decided not to indict the Clintons after the President leaves office, few legal avenues remain open to him after the two trials scheduled for Arkansas insider Webster Hubbell. A final accounting would give the public, and history, its only chance to view all the evidence available to the Independent Counsel.

Mrs. Clinton, of course, is squarely within Mr. Starr's mandate. His original instructions from the special three-judge panel of the U.S. Court of Appeals instructed him to investigate any violations of federal criminal law involving Mr. and Mrs. Clinton, Madison Guaranty S&L, the Whitewater Development Co., and Arkansas lender David Hale's Capital Management Services. Mr. Hubbell's latest trial, now slated for August, appears likely to disclose new details about Mrs. Clinton's role in these matters.

While a normal prosecutor is indeed supposed to shut up if he decides not to indict, the whole thrust of the Independent Counsel law has been that when an allegation concerns high officials, there may be some things that the public should know, even if you don't have a criminal violation that you think can be proven beyond a reasonable doubt.

Against this, the argument seems to be we should tell less, and the public should know less, about Hillary precisely because she's now seeking high office. This we-don't-want-to-know isn't journalism as we learned it, but does seems to be the logical outcome of a lot of high-minded press thumb-sucking in recent years.

REVIEW & OUTLOOK

Watching the Watchdog

When the Independent Counsel statute washed over the falls yesterday, it took an awful lot of high dudgeon with it. The statute was born in the Nixon years on a wave of tut-tutting over the need to create some Olympian public figure, a prosecutor purified of base motive, who would operate "independently" of a Justice Department in thrall to a politically indiscriminate President.

We said then it was a bad idea. We thought that the system of checks and balances put in place by the Founders was still the appropriate place to seek protection against abuse of power by the Executive. Oversight insulated from politics seemed difficult, if not impossible.

That has proven to be the case, though the reformers might not have predicted that a liberal President's supporters—Carville's army—would so unapologetically drag an Independent Counsel into Washington's media muck and hold his head under water. Now, 21 years later, perhaps it will be possible for all parties to keep their focus on what was the problem then and remains the problem now: the integrity of the Department of Justice.

Kenneth Starr

Yes, nearly everyone is agreed now that the device known as "independent" counsel had insurmountable flaws. But the problem it tried to address remains: How do you watch the watchdog? Who takes responsibility for the Attorney General, who just announced that she will hold full power over special investigations of public officials? In theory, the power of prosecuting serious malfeasance rests with the Executive, and that is probably necessary for an orderly government. But can we really expect the Justice Department to police the White House to which it reports?

Again, we assume there is now a rough political consensus around this issue. Liberals hadn't the slightest doubt that Richard Nixon was leaning on John Mitchell. They constantly professed to worry about the same thing during the Reagan Administration, targeting Ed Meese the moment he arrived in town. Conservatives vented at Judge Walsh's Iran-Contra odyssey, but liberals cheered his openly political election-eve indictment of Caspar Weinberger in 1992 and his baseless prosecution of Elliott Abrams. Today few doubt any longer that Ms. Reno is an adjunct to the Clinton-Gore political operation. Just yesterday we have the spectacle of Justice's former No. 3 and first Reno overseer, Webster Hubbell, pleading to another felony.

It would help, we think, if there were a better understanding of the problem posed here. The problem is not merely that the Executive is powerful. It is a powerful bureaucracy, and a bureaucracy's greatest power is to ensure that nothing happens. The Castle Grande case at the center of the Hubbell plea was a scam through Madison Guaranty back in Arkansas, but the obstruction of the Madison investigation—the decision to do nothing about it—was in Washington. This was what former Treasury official Roger Altman's heads up to the White House was about, and the investigation that RTC investigator Jean Lewis was yanked off of by the bureaucracy.

The lesson and the legacy of the Starr investigation into the Clinton Administration is that a legal stonewall conducted by a Presidency will succeed. We assume all sides will acknowledge this as well. Indeed it obviously continues today in Webb's latest plea, which merely involves conduct prior to the Clinton Presidency. Ken Starr was never able to tie the White House directly into any of these events because a President is surrounded by many aides and well-wishers, who don't always have to be told what to do.

The Clintons, of necessity, have the stonewall down to a science, starting with the incipient Senator's $100,000 commodities scam, successfully withheld until the statute expired. Then, before the Kendall and Bennett spincyclers arrived, we witnessed the Senate Whitewater hearings in which a parade of public officials from the White House, Treasury and federal agencies claimed in front of TV cameras that "to the best of their recollection" they remembered nothing. Has there been a more embarrassing spectacle in the postwar history of public service?

When the press and Congress tried to find out what the sudden Travel Office firings were about, they were stonewalled. Then Justice obediently prosecuted Billy Dale. When Vincent Foster killed himself, the White House counsel told Justice's investigating prosecutors to get lost. Filegate's 900 raw FBI files? Yawn, "an honest bureaucratic mistake." The campaign-finance players fled to China. The reason that a big breakthrough came about sex-

Janet Reno

ual behavior was that this was the one thing the President couldn't delegate.

Now, after all this, we have this week's news coverage dryly describing Attorney General Reno's new, self-designated investigative powers. She will appoint—and re-move—special prosecutors. She will veto their indictments or appeals or major investigation decisions.

What is likely to happen now is exemplified by Justice's China investigation. It is petering out all over the map. The Justice task force's investigation into the ties between China and the 1996 Clinton campaign contributions has been a catalog of lapses.

Career prosecutor Charles La Bella was handpicked by Ms. Reno to take over the probe in mid-1997. He prepared a 96-page memo indicating that President Clinton and Vice President Gore were subjects of the investigation and that as a result an independent counsel must be named. FBI Director Louis Freeh endorsed his report. Attorney General Reno ignored it; indeed she never even called Mr. La Bella to discuss his memo. Mr. La Bella left after a year. In the year since, Justice has secured a few plea bargains of dubious value with some players in the campaign finance probe and bungled the tax-fraud trial of Maria Hsia, a fund-raiser with ties to Mr. Gore.

Amid such limpid prosecution, defense attorneys for the fund-raising players have seen little need to press their clients to cooperate more fully with the investigation. We now hear that John Huang will cop a plea; he of course attended the famous Sept. 13, 1995, Oval Office meeting where the campaign fund-raising conspiracy was hatched. Don't hold your breath waiting to find out if Ms. Reno's Justice ever asked about it.

And this is not the only instance of the black hole at Justice. What about the investigation of the Teamsters laundering of Clinton-Gore campaign funds? Congress called off its own investigation a year ago after receiving promises of a federal prosecution, but nothing much has happened.

Whatever became of Justice's investigation of the Intriago case, involving tens of thousands of illegal monies sent to the Clinton campaign by a Venezuelan banker and his Miami attorney, both visitors to the White House? A federal judge ruled Friday that Saudi businessman Abdul Raouf Khalil owed BCCI's defrauded depositors $1.2 billion. Reno Justice didn't pursue this result; it's the work of District Attorney Robert Morgenthau, independently elected by the voters of Manhattan.

To deal with the watchdog question, the Founders gave us three branches of government. The Judiciary has done its part, but it is up to the Congress to hold Ms. Reno accountable. It has manifestly failed, and such are the vapors of Washington that Judiciary Chairman Orrin Hatch now considers himself a Presidential candidate. As of today, Congress can no longer shuck off its oversight tasks on an independent counsel.

Congressional Republicans did finally stand up to oversight by impeaching the President, of course, and the conventional wisdom held that this was a political disaster. But Democratic pollster Celinda Lake now says, "Democrats paid a big price" for their defense. On the issue of values, Democrats now lag the GOP by 19 points, as against six points as recently as 1994. Her Republican partner in the joint Battleground Poll, Ed Goaes, says, "Short range, the Republicans were damaged by the impeachment process. Long range, it appears that we have gained a great deal by what

Congressional members did on impeachment." Values, of course, promise to become the big issue of the impending Presidential campaign.

The wisdom of the Founders, in short, may prevail even in this supposedly cynical cyber-age. When the Executive tries to traduce the rule of law, it's up to Congress to stand up to the duties the Constitution gives it.

The 2000
Campaign Begins

On June 16, Vice President Al Gore officially launched his bid for the Presidency. Speaking to a crowd in his hometown of Carthage, Tennessee, he promised a tough fight "for America's families." Speaking to local reporters a night earlier, Mr. Gore condemned Bill Clinton's behavior in the Lewinsky affair, calling it "inexcusable."

The Journal welcomed Mr. Gore to the race, noting that he "seems to be self-consciously struggling with the burden of separating himself from the boss he has served so slavishly for seven years." But the Vice President's condemnation of Mr. Clinton was something new. "We don't remember hearing this at the time, or during that notorious post-impeachment pep rally on the White House lawn. But if Mr. Gore wants to critique the Clinton years, we welcome him to what should be a rich vein of campaign themes."

Mr. Gore's announcement was soon followed by one from Hillary Rodham Clinton. On July 7, on a farm outside Oneonta, New York, Mrs. Clinton announced the "listening tour" that would launch her bid to represent in the United States Senate a state she had never lived in. "I'm going to be listening very hard," Mrs. Clinton told the more than 200 reporters and 30 television crews. "I'm going to be learning a lot."

"Hand it to her," wrote Journal contributing editor Peggy Noonan. "Hillary Clinton had a spectacular day yesterday as she stood on the edge of a rolling field on Sen. Daniel Patrick Moynihan's upstate farm and announced that she may announce. It was as deft and clever a political presentation as I've ever seen, a marvel of spin and more. She was poised, articulate, both cool and warm and—a first for her—modest. She was in fact a natural."

In Washington, the independent counsel probe into the Clintons went on. Mrs. Clinton faced possible indictment for false statements in the White House Travel Office affair. Both Clintons remained vulnerable to fraud and conspiracy charges in the Whitewater land scandals. And the President faced possible indictment for perjury and obstruction in the Lewinsky affair after he left office. The matter of the President's perjury before a grand jury on August 17, 1998, "remains very much unresolved," Prof. Gary McDowell wrote in the Journal. "Since April, when Judge Susan Webber Wright found the president in contempt for lying in the Paula Jones sexual harassment lawsuit, the matter of Mr. Clinton's 'other' perjury before the grand jury has dangled ominously above what is left of his administration. Lying under oath before a federal grand jury is certainly as serious a matter as lying under oath in a deposition in a pending civil suit."

REVIEW & OUTLOOK

Gore's Chore

Vice President Gore formally joined the race for the White House yesterday, and we wish him luck. All the more so since he seems to be self-consciously struggling with the burden of separating himself from the boss he has served so slavishly for seven years.

It's no coincidence, for example, that the veep chose last night to tell a TV interviewer he was privately appalled at President Clinton's behavior during the Lewinsky fiasco. We don't remember hearing this at the time, or during that notorious post-impeachment pep rally on the White House lawn.

But if Mr. Gore now wants to critique the Clinton years, we welcome him to what should be a rich vein of campaign themes. For openers, he might start with the bill that passed Congress this week to rein in frivolous lawsuits from the Year 2000 computer glitch problem.

The Senate passed a version of this legislation, 62-37, joining a House bill that passed earlier this year. The White House is threatening a veto, which tees things up perfectly for Mr. Gore to break from his boss's fealty to the trial lawyers.

Even if he didn't invent the Internet, Mr. Gore has certainly invented himself as the Digital Pol, someone who understands the high-tech New Economy. Or at least that's the image he tries to project when he's out in Silicon Valley raising campaign cash. Here's his chance to prove it.

Of course, this would mean rebuffing the part of his political coalition Mr. Gore would rather not brag about, i.e., Bill Lerach and friends. Mr. Lerach is the San Diego lawyer who's made a fortune suing high-tech companies merely because their stock prices fall. He then funnels much of that extorted fortune into the hands of politicians, mostly Democrats, who pass laws that make it easier for him to sue more companies. He and his fellow carnivores are waiting to sue everyone in sight over any Y2K problem, real or imagined.

Which is why the industry united to urge Congress to pass these very modest protections. Alas, this bill does nothing for million-dollar spilled-coffee judgments. It's limited solely to Y2K problems. It includes a cap of $250,000 for punitive damages, as opposed to actual damages, for companies with fewer than 50 employees. And it gives companies 90 days to fix a problem before the vultures can pounce.

Keep in mind the Year 2000 problem is hardly the result of corporate greed or malfeasance. It's an accident of the calendar and the digital world in which ones and zeros rule. But this means nothing to the trial lawyers, who have successfully lobbied the White House to issue its veto threat.

So where's Mr. Gore now that Silicon Valley really needs him? Here's an easy call, a chance to repay John Doerr, Steve Jobs and the other Valley pals who've helped give him his hip, high-tech gloss. Mr. Gore also has partisan cover on this one, as 12 Democrats (including liberals Chris Dodd of Connecticut and Patty Murray of Washington) joined 50 Republicans in voting for the Senate bill.

Andrew Grove, the Intel chairman, put it squarely in a Washington speech last week. He said a veto is a vote against the high-tech industry, and that "Gore's reputation is already somewhat tarnished by the Year 2000 issue."

The White House strategy now is to use its veto threat to pry concessions out of the House-Senate conference. Mr. Clinton could then sign a bill so watered down that even the trial bar wouldn't mind, and Mr. Gore would be able to claim he kept everybody happy. We hope the high-tech community is smart enough to keep the pressure on.

This of course has been the Clinton Way—having it both ways, using rhetoric to obscure the truth, be all things to all voters. If Mr. Gore really wants to distinguish himself from the worst of Clintonism, he'll have to do better than denounce sex with interns, six months too late. He'll need to separate himself from the Clinton way of lying, and Y2K is a good place to start.

June 4, 1999

Editorial Feature

Victory Would Be Hillary's Best Revenge

A Republican senator running for re-election next year recently reacted this way to Hillary Rodham Clinton's now probable New York Senate campaign:

"Can't you get her to run against me?"

Think of the benefits, added this savvy GOP pol. He could immediately fire his fund-raisers. A couple of national mass-mailings would bring in more than enough campaign cash. The chance to beat the First Tiger Lady would unite otherwise fractious Republicans from Jerry Falwell to Christie Whitman.

Potomac Watch

By Paul A. Gigot

And victory would make him a national GOP celebrity.

That widely shared sentiment says more about Mrs. Clinton's political ambition than all of the canned public Democratic applause she's now hearing. In private, many Democrats are worried about her candidacy. It's Republicans who are pleased, if also dumbfounded at her audacity.

"I continue to be astonished that she's going to run," says one operative charged with re-electing a GOP Senate. "There's a virtual certainty that if she runs it hurts everything else Democrats want to do." No Democrat can afford to say this on the record, of course. And the First Lady's media friends have stayed quiet, perhaps to encourage what everyone understands would be a reporter's dream—two presidential races for the price of one.

The exception is The New Republic, which has trashed her candidacy as loudly as it's promoting Al Gore's—and which is no coincidence, comrade. Its editors know Mr. Gore has enough problems without adding Hillary's.

Any Democrat not inhaling James Carville's exhaust can tell you the risks:

She'll suck money and attention away from other viable Democrats, especially those challenging vulnerable GOP incumbents. Sens. Slade Gorton of Washington and Spence Abraham of Michigan, both likely to have women as opponents, should be especially pleased that the First Feminist will have first call on national liberal cash.

Hillary Clinton

Hillary's run also makes it harder for Mr. Gore to establish his own identity. The point isn't that the vice president won't be his own man. It's that Hillary's political prominence will remind everyone of the controversies of the last eight years.

This can't help a candidate whose standing already suffers from national Clinton fatigue. About half the country says the veep is too close to Mr. Clinton, and 52% say they're less likely to vote for him if Saturday Night Bill campaigns actively for him. Like it or not, Hillary would be Mr. Gore's de facto running mate. Her stumping this week as part of "Women for Gore" was an implicit payback for the veep assuming this burden.

My guess is that Mrs. Clinton's scandals would hurt her less in New York than many Republicans hope (even when Ken Starr's final report includes copious detail about her scandal role). Her bigger problem would be her liberalism and her cool, condescending public persona.

Given all of this, the most interesting question is, Why even take such a gamble? Why not leave Washington gracefully, take a job that keeps you in the limelight (say, the Red Cross) but out of the line of fire, and return to politics after the passions of the 1990s recede into misty nostalgia? Sure, Mrs. Clinton wants to be president and so needs to show she can win votes in her own right. But she could do that more easily in 2004 in Illinois, a state where she has genuine roots, against a weaker Republican than Mayor Rudy Giuliani in New York, a state where she's a carpetbagger. No, the only way to comprehend a run in 2000 is as part of a compulsive, almost maniacal attempt at political vindication. Her candidacy only makes sense as an In-Your-Face dare to the country to validate the First Couple's years in office.

Her friends say that, even more fiercely than her husband, she believes the pair have been unjustly maligned. In their first term Whitewater cost her the chance to become Eleanor II, and in the second Monica forced her to become the role model she never wanted to be, a national Tammy Wynette. More even than Bill, she holds grudges and wants revenge.

Victory in 2000 would erase the stain of impeachment and scandal, repudiate her critics, and give her the chance to build the New Progressive era that she put up with philandering Bill in order to create.

Understood this way, her candidacy is a monumental act of political vanity that raises the stakes in 2000 even higher than they already are. And it fits the strategy of the past year, when her husband has put victory in 2000 above any second-term accomplishment. It also puts her own fortunes above her party's, but that's always been the Clinton way. The party, c'est moi. And, who knows, maybe Republicans will be stupid enough to help her. The best news Mrs. Clinton could get would be a late (September 2000) and vicious GOP primary between Mr. Giuliani and Long Island Rep. Rick Lazio that saps their resources and tarnishes the winner. And that could happen. On the other hand, the Clintons had better hope that Americans, and especially New Yorkers, don't begin to view them as the house guests from Arkansas who entertained us for a while but grew tedious and now refuse to leave.

REVIEW & OUTLOOK

The Icon Lady

What befits an icon most? Nowadays it's the prospect of draping oneself in high political office. More than 300 reporters showed up to welcome First Lady Hillary Clinton to the politics of New York State,

Hillary Clinton

as she began her "listening tour" to ponder a possible Senate candidacy. We would like to welcome her as well. We recall during the first-term debate over her health-care initiative how much energy went into arguing over whether she was the "functional equivalent" of a government employee and therefore beyond several federal laws. It surely will be healthier all around to have Hillary Clinton finally functioning as an officially certified professional politician.

The early reviews of her out-of-town tryout with Pat Moynihan were good, marveling at how deftly she handled the day of photo shoots and batting-practice questions from reporters. That said, the fundamentals of this candidacy continue to be cause for wonder.

For starters, there is the Iron Law of Icons in politics. It holds that once celebrity figures turn into candidates, they slowly sink to earth. If a celebrity candidate starts off with 80% approval, as a Dwight Eisenhower or John Glenn did, they can survive their displacement from the pedestal. But Mrs. Clinton's celebrity is not in the same pure league as, say, Joe DiMaggio. She begins this quest with mediocre poll numbers (the average of all current surveys put her in the low 40s). "The best day that former Miss America Bess Meyerson and Geraldine Ferraro had in running for New York Senator was the day they announced," says Brian Lunde, a former executive director of the Democratic National Committee. "It was largely downhill from there."

There is the matter of the state's ambivalent, touchy Democratic Party, nowhere more so than in New York City. The island's fractious Democrats are like something out of medieval Italy. This is the place, after all, that spawned both Dick Morris and Harold Ickes. Thus, the most vicious media attack on Hillary so far appeared on the cover of the Village Voice, seconded most recently by the liberal Newsday's hyperliberal columnist Jimmy Breslin. Few New York politicos, though, are willing to express their concerns publicly. Rep. Nita Lowey, her own Senate aspirations trashed and left by the side of the road, now sounds like Susan McDougal.

Most New Yorkers look forward to the campaign spectacle of pols from the same party trashing each other. To ensure that the state's voluble Democrats don't bad-mouth her, Mrs. Clinton has transposed several New York enforcers to this campaign from the main Clinton operation. They include Harold Ickes, Terry McAuliffe and Susan Thomases. It's telling that this newcomer to New York politics is calling on the same crowd that was instrumental in the sordid 1996 campaign fund-raising scandal.

New York Democratic consultant Hank Sheinkopf, a senior strategist in the 1996 Clinton campaign, puts her odds of winning at no better than 50-50. This makes the candidacy enormously stressful for New York's already beleaguered Democrats. They've recently been putting forward such hapless candidates as Ruth Messinger and Peter Vallone, but when they lose, New York's resilient liberals manage to plod forward with their diehard base reforming into a globulous whole. But if the icon loses, she could take the creaking New York Democratic idea down with her.

Hillary's money is a more immediate Democratic concern. For six years, the Clintons have been a fund-raising black hole, siphoning into themselves every dollar in the Democratic financial universe. They've made relentless trips to New York City to pick up their percentage of rich Democrats' stock-market gains. Mrs. Clinton's outsized candidacy, most agree, could raise $20 million to $25 million, reducing the flow of funds to more needful Democratic Senate candidates or the Gore campaign.

The late Jim McDougal once described the Clintons as "tornadoes that move through people's lives." New York Democrats may learn the feeling. If she loses, don't expect her to hang around Westchester County to help restore the wreckage.

And of course there is the legacy of the Clinton scandals and unsolved mysteries. So far, Mrs. Clinton has dismissed questions about all this by saying, "We've moved beyond all of that." Maybe that's what they do in Little Rock, but this is New York, whose political culture never moves "beyond all of that."

"As a candidate you have to answer every question," New York Senator Charles Schumer said this week. "Every one." The Breslin column this week was an attack on her "smug deviousness and untruthfulness." The Voice's comprehensive cover story was on the "Hillary Clinton Sleaze Factor."

As the truly iconic New York oracle Yogi Berra once said, "When you come to a fork in the road, take it." Mrs. Clinton isn't at the fork yet. She has only formed an "exploratory committee." For all the hoopla, the filing deadline for the Senate seat isn't until next summer. We wouldn't be surprised if around Christmas she suddenly pulled out, citing personal reasons. The millions raised by her exploratory committee would be available for other political purposes. More than a few New York Democrats would breathe a great sigh of relief. And who knows, with any luck they might be able to get Alec Baldwin to run against Rudy.

Editorial Feature

The Natural

BY PEGGY NOONAN

Hand it to her. Hillary Clinton had a spectacular day yesterday as she stood on the edge of a rolling field on Sen. Daniel Patrick Moynihan's upstate farm and announced that she may announce. It was as deft and clever a political presentation as I've seen, a marvel of spin and more. She was poised, articulate, both cool and warm and—a first for her—modest.

Hillary Clinton

She was in fact a natural.

I watched all morning rapt as CNN and MSNBC went live, and I think I saw some of what the future will hold.

The media presence was huge, a reported 200 journalists, and most if not all seemed transported. "The listening tour" they breathed as they filled time. "Hillary Clinton's listening tour is about to begin." It is of course not a listening tour but a talking tour aimed at defusing bombs and getting good press, but the reporters called it the magical listening tour because—well, because her people told them that's what it is. And if there's one thing her people know it's them people.

It wasn't only a lack of skepticism from the elite press but a presence of enthusiasm. CNN's Bruce Morton said of the day: "It's really the voters' show. . . . The point is to hear what they have to say." But that was not the point, as he surely knew. MSNBC's Chris Jansing made a sad-clown face and said of Mrs. Clinton's candidacy, "It all began in the depths of her depression." Ms. Jansing asked reporter Chip Reid how Hillary was feeling now—excited, nervous? Mr. Reid, reporting from the White House, said he thought the first lady was excited. "She's running on Clinton time," a now-happy Ms. Jansing said of Mrs. Clinton's lateness.

Martin Kettle of London's Guardian newspaper lightened things up just by answering questions. "Why are you here?" he was asked. "Hillary Clinton's a world figyah!" he replied. Does she have star power? "Well she's been well received in Britain—she has a huge stah following!"

Now we saw Mrs. Clinton walking, live, down a lane as she chatted with Sen. Moynihan in full, lanky gentleman-farmer-by-way-of-Harvard button-down shirt and khakis. He introduced her to the press—"Hi, Gabe!"—saying: "I hope she will go all the way. . . . I think she is going to win. . . . I think it will be wonderful for New York."

Then Mrs. Clinton stepped forward—no notes, no text, standing behind a bare standup mike, looking exposed and undefended, a brave woman entering the arena, which is how her people wanted her to look. Surrounded by the huddling press she explained her candidacy.

"The last few months have been quite extraordinary for me," she said. "I'm humbled and surprised to be standing here today." She suggested she had in fact been drafted—hundreds of New Yorkers had come to her, and she listened to their excitement, and soon she too was excited by what she could do with them and for them. They e-mailed and sent notes and phoned. It would not have been gracious to ignore them. And so she will "spend the next few weeks and months listening."

"I care deeply," she said. "I am concerned that we work together to face the challenges that face New York and the people of New York." She'll be "listening hard, trying to figure out how to serve the people of New York."

She said she wants to help improve education and health care, and specifically to help "the crown jewels, the teaching hospitals" of

New York. Her husband has cut their federal funding. She has announced she opposes his move. Just watch, the Republican political consultant Jay Severin said yesterday: Mr. Clinton will announce a plan, she will oppose on the grounds it hurts New York, he will change his mind based on the eloquence of her arguments, and she will call news conferences announcing her triumph.

"I've been a tireless advocate all my life," she said in a note of self-congratulation that was her one mistake of the day. Hearing how she's worked so hard to help us reminded me of how the Clintons are always saying that they've devoted their lives to public service. When politicians say, "I'm in politics," it may or may not be possible to trust them, but when they say, "I'm in public service," you know you should flee.

The press threw softballs, and she neatly hit them deep into left and right, but the carpetbagger issue she hit out of the park. "It's a fair question," she said, conceding the obvious with grace. "I have some work to do to demonstrate that what I'm for is more important than where I'm from." They must have worked for weeks on that one. (Mrs. Clinton did prep sessions in the White House this past weekend, and a Clinton supporter said she was excellent from the beginning.)

She said she takes seriously New Yorkers' legitimate questions about what skills she'd bring to the state and to the Senate. She said in effect that she brings not a lack of ambition but a gift for advocacy.

She was disciplined. A question about Monica got the mantra response: I'm looking forward to meeting with New Yorkers. A question that might have been tough was rendered soft in the phrasing: How will she respond to charges regarding the $100,000 profit in cattle futures? She's looking forward to creating a new future with New Yorkers.

The press was impressed.

Mrs. Clinton right now is doing two important things. First, she is nailing down her base. This means building excitement in the left wing of her party by convincing them that she is one of them and worth fighting for. Thus her blunt attack on vouchers the other day before the National Education Association. A year from now, when it matters, she will speak not as a "progressive" but as a moderate; her base, knowing the game, will not take offense. Yesterday's speech was a departure, but Mrs. Clinton will be talking to the left for the next few months. This will garner renewed criticism, some of it fierce, from those who are not of the left. But that doesn't matter, because of the second thing she is doing.

That is absorbing attacks, every day. For the next nine months or so she'll be playing rope-a-dope, exhausting her foes by taking every blow they can throw. She's doing this now because right now it doesn't matter what is said of her. A year from now, when it matters, if New York's pundits—the Dunleavies and Dowds, the Brookhisers and Breslins—are still attacking her, they will look obsessed and winded. She will look long suffering and glistening. The criticisms of '99 will be but a memory. Reporters will be reduced to covering her latest proposals. She knows this. Her people know this. It's why, right now, they don't mind attacks.

Yesterday was a very good day for Mrs. Clinton because it gave her wall-to-wall great coverage. But that may turn out to be good news for Republicans, in the same way that an alarm clock going off at the right time is good news. It rings, you hear it, you wake up and get dressed and stop dreaming and go to work.

Ms. Noonan, a contributing editor of The Wall Street Journal, is author of "Simply Speaking" (HarperCollins, 1998).

July 9, 1999

Editorial Feature

The Remaking of
Hillary Rodham Clinton

So now we know how Bill Clinton plans to get around the sticky little problem of presidential term limits. His wife is going to run as
Bill, while he morphs into his wife. Down the road this gives them a
shot at another eight years.

Or so it looked this week, the kickoff of the most amusing case of
trading places since Eddie Murphy and Dan Aykroyd swapped chauf-
feurs on film.

Potomac Watch

By Paul A. Gigot

The soon-to-be-former president spent
the week campaigning as the liberal his
wife once admitted to being. He finally
stumped for the poor he's kept at a safe
political distance during seven years of massaging the "forgotten
middle class."

Meanwhile, Hillary Rodham Clinton began her New York Senate
campaign as a born-again moderate, a candidate ardently but mod-
estly "listening" to New Yorkers to discover what in Oneonta's name
to run on. About Mrs. Clinton it was once said, as a compliment, that
she "has the courage of her husband's convictions." Now, as a candidate in her own right for the first time, she's suddenly conviction-
free.

You have to appreciate the audacity. Bill Clinton has always been
expert at reinventing himself—from Hot Springs gadabout to Hope
idealist, from New Democrat to FDR wannabee and back to New
Democrat. Now it's Hillary's turn to exploit America's short atten-

tion span, and she got off to a brilliant start this week.

Her photo-op schmooze with retiring Sen. Daniel Patrick Moynihan was especially rich. This is the same senator who was the most vigorous Democratic opponent of the Clintons' two most notable proposals—health care and welfare reform.

He called the former a misguided attempt to restrict medical choices and the latter a betrayal of Democratic principles. Mrs. Clinton's mentor and policy guru, liberal Marian Wright Edelman, also denounced welfare reform.

But there was Mrs. Clinton Wednesday declaring what a pleasure it was to start her campaign "by listening to probably the wisest New Yorker that we can know of at this time," that is, Mr. Moynihan. And, laying it on really thick, that "it means a great deal to me to stand here with someone whom I admire so much."

As for welfare reform, the first lady now says she was for it all along—except for those excesses pushed by "the Republican Congress." Mr. Moynihan was a gracious if terse host, but the old pol and ever-loyal Democrat must have been laughing silently to himself.

This transformation is of course deliberate election strategy. (Mrs. Clinton is about as spontaneous as Elizabeth Dole.) She knows she can't win an election as an honest liberal, not even in New York, and certainly not against Rudy Giuliani. Nor can she win as the old, condescending Hillary of 1992 who sneered about "baking cookies" and "Tammy Wynette."

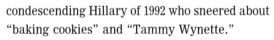

In this sense her new political career is precisely the opposite of the "declaration of independence" from Bill it is advertised to be. Her campaign represents her final and total accommodation to the political life she's made with him.

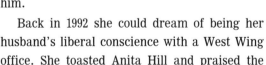

Hillary Clinton

Back in 1992 she could dream of being her husband's liberal conscience with a West Wing office. She toasted Anita Hill and praised the French welfare state (New York Times, April 7, 1990). Then came health care and Whitewater, followed by negative approval ratings and her internal exile through the 1996 election.

Those ratings didn't turn around until her husband's philandering made her into the oldest story in country music, the loyal woman wronged. Her ability to draw 200-plus TV cameras to Davenport, N.Y., this week is a direct result of the celebrity victimhood she once despised.

And now, to top it all off, she's beginning a campaign that sounds like it was co-scripted by her husband, which it probably was. To have a chance to win, in short, she is becoming the ultimate Tammy Wynette, standing not just by her man but also by her man's shifting principles. I liked the old Hillary better. She was more honest.

Daniel Patrick Moynihan

And yet she may win. Judging by their performance this week, the non-Murdoch media will treat her like Audrey Hepburn. They will bend to her wish to ignore her $100,000 commodity tip and other ethical miracles. ("I think we've moved beyond all of it," Mrs. Clinton said Wednesday.) Her friends will dismiss all critics as "Clinton haters."

And the Republicans, those geniuses, may help her too. In a normal state a Hillary run would unite all GOP factions. But New York Republicans—especially Gov. George Pataki and renowned ethicist Al D'Amato—seem bent instead on gaining revenge against Mr. Giuliani for endorsing Mario Cuomo in 1994.

They're quietly backing Long Island Rep. Rick Lazio, whose candidacy would drain the mayor's resources and who might even beat him in a late (September 2000) GOP primary. This is the first lady's dream, and maybe even her expectation.

And why shouldn't it be? If her husband can make a career of beating dumb Republicans, so can she.

REVIEW & OUTLOOK

Asides

Campaign Finance Statement

Tomorrow, FBI chief Louis Freeh will present the Director's Award for Distinguished Service to the Law Enforcement Community to former Justice Department official Charles La Bella, the former head of DoJ's ill-fated campaign finance probe. Attention should be paid.

Mr. La Bella was one of two prominent law-enforcement insiders to recommend that an independent counsel investigate the funding of the 1996 Clinton-Gore campaign; the other was Mr. Freeh. Brought in from the Office of U.S. Attorney in San Diego to inject some credibility into Justice's rudderless probe in 1997, Mr. La Bella was forced out in less than a year. Mr. Freeh, Mr. La Bella told the San Diego Union-Tribune earlier this year, separately came to the same decision to recommend an independent counsel.

Holding a 10-year appointment, the FBI Director is hard to push around. But after being shoved out of Janet Reno's Justice Department, Mr. La Bella was denied appointment as U.S. Attorney in San Diego, despite the recommendation of his predecessor. So even before the Clinton-Reno years at Justice end, it is good to see the FBI giving Mr. La Bella this distinguished service award.

REVIEW & OUTLOOK

The Counterattack Continues

So Linda Tripp is to be prosecuted for protecting herself from the Clinton tong's penchant for punishing its opposition. Before getting into the legalities, let's see if we understand correctly just what the Bill Clinton Amen Chorus thinks Linda Tripp should have done.

When Monica asked her to lie to the Paula Jones grand jury to help the President, they apparently think that Linda should have said, "Sure, I'd be happy to get selective memory, just like all those White House and Treasury big shots who couldn't remember anything important in front of the D'Amato Whitewater hearings. If they can get away with lying, maybe I can too. But Monica, could you ask Bruce Lindsey if I'll get a better deal than Susan McDougal. But yeah, any dame would be happy to lie to protect Bill."

Linda Tripp

Of course, it didn't turn out this way. Instead Linda Tripp, who'd seen the Clinton White House in action from the inside, went to Radio Shack and started taping her phone calls with Monica Lewinsky. She told the truth to a grand jury, and the Clinton counterattack team hammered her hard. She suffered selective leaks of records from her Pentagon personnel file, then the invective and ridicule of reporters and cable blabbers friendly to the President's pre-impeachment cause.

Now comes a selective prosecution under Maryland's anti-wiretap laws. Conclusion: the counterattack continues.

Eventually Ms. Tripp may prevail, but only after a punishing ordeal. After months on pretrial tenterhooks, former Travel Office head Billy Dale was quickly acquitted by a Washington jury. And only last week the American Spectator magazine was vindicated, after a year-long investigation by former Justice Department official Michael Shaheen.

The Spectator, one of the Clinton presidency's most relentless and toughest critics, had to defend itself against charges that it had funneled money through a Hot Springs bait shop owner to David Hale, a key witness against Mr. Clinton in the Independent Counsel's Whitewater prosecution. The widely circulated stories also implicated philanthropist Richard Scaife, a major backer of the Spectator. Many accounts of this affair, replete with baroque details of great wealth and bait-shop conspiracies, were written up in the spirit of Hillary Clinton's famous accusation of a "great right-wing conspiracy" against her and her husband.

There was nothing to it, Mr. Shaheen discovered. But by now, the offensive, based on false accusations, has had its intended corrosive effect on the magazine. So we've had a year-long investigation of how a magazine spent its money reporting stories critical of the President of the United States. That is to say, Clinton tacticians have learned how to use the legal system to bludgeon its press critics.

With something of a post-impeachment reassessment going on, we are learning more about how the legal system has favored the Clinton team. Suddenly, we have the case of Norma Holloway Johnson, chief judge of the Federal District Court in the District of Columbia. The Associated Press reported Saturday that Judge Johnson set aside the normal random assignment of judges, and steered cases involving Webster Hubbell and Charlie Trie to two Clinton appointees. Assigning such politically volatile cases to judges only recently nominated by the President is unprecedented, and yesterday Judge Johnson reportedly explained to her colleagues that she did it because of heavy workloads.

It should be said that Judge Johnson cast a skeptical eye on some Clinton claims when she heard the assertions of special privileges for Secret Service agents. But it now turns out that Judge Johnson was also instrumental in the Linda Tripp indictment. The Maryland prosecutors could not proceed without the evidence of the Tripp tapes, and in receiving them Independent Counsel Kenneth Starr had granted her immunity that would have protected them from both federal and state prosecutors. But Judge Johnson intervened and decided to transmit the tapes to the Maryland prosecutor's office.

We suppose the best outcome for Ms. Tripp would be to plead it out and get on with her life, but it is not clear what kind of a deal she might be offered. In the case of the Democrats who illegally used a scanner in 1996 to steal GOP Rep. John Boehner's cell phone conversation with his colleagues about the Gingrich ethics investigation, two Democratic foot soldiers were allowed to enter a plea and got fined $500 each. Rep. Jim McDermott, who disclosed these tapes to the public, claimed the First Amendment protects the truth, and is now thinking of running for the Senate in Washington.

Linda Tripp is facing 10 years, and a full-blown trial. She did not wiretap, but merely recorded her own conversations, which is entirely legal in many states, even without the consent of other parties. The Maryland law has so seldom been applied that no judicial decisions applying can be found in a standard legal data base. Marna McLendon, one of the Maryland prosecutors involved, declared "the public is watching."

Somehow the same standard is not applied to, say, the release of information from Ms. Tripp's Pentagon files. In another post-impeachment revelation, for that matter, Judge Susan Webber Wright has just ruled that President Clinton should pay $90,000 for extra legal fees incurred by Paula Jones because of the President's false testimony. She said the President "deliberately violated this Court's discovery orders, thereby undermining the integrity of the judicial system." Indeed, perjury is an indictable felony; is the public watching?

In retrospect it's amusing to recall the idea popularized after the impeachment that it was time to "move on." In fact, the last week's events alone make it clear that the legal system is stuffed to bursting with Clinton incidents that continue to undermine this presidency's stature and credibility, and even more seriously to undermine the lofty ideal of equal treatment under the law.

REVIEW & OUTLOOK

Bad Lawyer Joke?

How many lawyers does it take to make the American Bar Association look bad? At this year's annual convention, the answer is two: One President of the United States and one former associate Attorney General.

President Clinton was honored yesterday by the ABA, at whose annual convention he gave the keynote address. His speech came

just 11 days after a federal judge fined him $90,000 for lying to her court and at a time when the Arkansas state court is considering his disbarment. But Mr. Clinton passed up the opportunity to lecture his brother and sister attorneys on legal ethics and instead used the occasion to do what he does best—talk politics, by blasting Republican Senators for not confirming judges swiftly enough. Mr. Clinton knows his audience. Remember—this is the same organization that

Webster Hubbell

abetted the scurrilous campaign against Supreme Court nominee Robert Bork.

Earlier in the convention, the ABA was privileged to hear from another illustrious member of the bar, Webster Hubbell, the former Number Three person in the Justice Department. To be precise, Mr. Hubbell is actually a former member of the bar, from which he tendered his resignation a few years ago after his own little trouble with the law.

Mr. Hubbell, who could have provided illuminating firsthand accounts of "How to Loot Money From Your Law Partners" or "How to Beat the Rap on Hush Money," chose instead to vilify the man who put him in federal prison for 18 months, Kenneth Starr. Talk about a crowd pleaser.

As Gerald Walpin pointed out yesterday in these pages, the ABA's mission is "to increase . . . respect for the law." A laudable goal, indeed, and surely a reason for inviting attorneys of the highest skills and ethical standards as speakers. We know of no more per-jurers or convicted felons scheduled to address the ABA convention this year. But if the ABA is looking to attach its reputation to anoth-er courtroom veteran for next year's convention, we propose O.J. Simpson.

REVIEW & OUTLOOK

Something Happened

We're beginning to think that the epitaph over the eight years of the Clinton administration is going to read, "Honest bureaucratic mistake."

This, of course, was the explanation offered when more than 900 raw FBI files on Republican figures floated into the White House. Now it appears that the scandal over the transfer of nuclear-missile technology to China is about to recede into these same bureaucratic mists.

The Washington press the past few days has been carrying stories  about Robert Vrooman, the former Los Alamos counter-intelligence chief, who now says that suspected spy Wen Ho Lee is the victim of ethnic bias. We doubt it. Still, we have some sympathy for Messrs. Vrooman and Lee. They're the ones out in the open taking the bullets, while the Reno Justice Department and at the top, the Clinton White House, deploy their bureaucracies to deflect responsibility, even the smallest responsibility, away from them and onto others.

Janet Reno

The handling of the Los Alamos Chinese spying case sounds familiar. It sounds like what happened to the campaign-finance investigation, if indeed Chinese espionage and Chinese contributions can be separated.

Wen Ho Lee has been under FBI suspicion at the lab for years. By

1995, the U.S. was actively investigating the possibility that China had obtained data on the W-88 nuclear warhead. In June 1997 the FBI asked the Justice Department for a "FISA warrant," referring to the Federal Internal Security Act, which sets up a federal court that approves such requests, to conduct surveillance of Mr. Lee and his wife. In August, Allan Kornblum, a Justice deputy counsel, said the Bureau had failed to show "probable cause."

Rejections of FISA requests are rare. As to probable cause, an August 5 report by Senators Fred Thompson and Joseph Lieberman lists the FBI's suspicions about the Lees across 18 paragraphs, including: "The FBI learned that during a visit to Los Alamos by (Chinese) scientists from IAPCM, Lee had discussed certain unclassified (but weapons-related) computer codes with the Chinese delegation. It was reported that Lee had helped the Chinese scientists with their codes by providing software and calculations relating to hydrodynamics." A congressional source tells us that two additional reasons to monitor were dropped from the public report for security reasons.

The FBI then made an unprecedented appeal of the denial to the Attorney General. After a meeting about security issues, the head of the FBI's National Security Division told Ms. Reno "we've been turned down" by her department. The Thompson report then states: "Attorney General Reno has said that she does not recall the conversation, but does not deny that it occurred." Nonetheless, another Justice attorney, Daniel Seikaly, ended up with the assignment of reviewing the original turndown, and weeks later concurred with the decision not to monitor the Lees.

The turndown of this wiretap is at the heart of the Thompson-Lieberman report. Both criticized Justice's refusal.

Sen. Lieberman, noting various bureaucratic failures by the FBI along the way, concluded: "I ask why, given the extreme importance of this case to America's national security, [Justice] did not raise this issue to the Attorney General herself, push the FBI harder to make its case, or decide to send the request for a warrant to the court to make the final judgment."

Squaring this circle, Sen. Thompson said Justice "adopted a highly restrictive view of probable cause, even though the showing necessary in a national security context is less than for a criminal investigation." Another report by the President's Foreign Intelligence Advisory Board, led by former Sen. Warren Rudman, raised precisely the same issues regarding these decisions.

Obviously there was a judgment call to be made here. And reasonable people might differ on the call. They might differ, that is, if Justice under Ms. Reno had not by now shown itself to come down routinely on the side of doing nothing or next to nothing in investigations of this sort. As in the campaign finance investigation of illegal foreign contributions to the President's re-election campaign.

Consider the record. As with the Los Alamos case, clearly something illegal was taking place with the Chinese fund raising. But Ms. Reno rejected the advice of both Charles La Bella and Louis Freeh to turn these matters over to an independent counsel. The La Bella episode is especially illuminating.

It would have been one thing if Ms. Reno had simply rejected Mr. La Bella's recommendation. But she and her aides went further, essentially trashing La Bella for his position and pushing him out of federal service. One might reasonably suspect that the lower-echelon lawyers, including those handling the Los Alamos decisions, knew better than to get on the wrong side of any Justice investigations involving China.

Then, after giving "her people" full responsibility for this investigation, and after a few indictments, the result has been no jail time for anyone. Johnny Chung and John Huang got probation. Charlie Trie awaits sentencing.

And it is similarly clear that something happened at the Sept. 13, 1995, Oval Office meeting at which Bill Clinton, Bruce Lindsey, Joe Giroir and James Riady told a nobody named John Huang that he was moving from his Commerce Department job over to fund raising for the DNC. Absent a real inquiry into this crucial meeting's content, we're supposed to conclude that it was John Huang's idea to go all the way to China to break the contribution laws.

In other words, it is at least clear to us that Bill Clinton and Janet Reno have inculcated the Department of Justice with a culture of nonfeasance. Nonfeasance is about not doing what duty requires. And duty, some sense of a higher purpose or judgment, is what we think Senators Thompson and Lieberman are asking for in their report on the Los Alamos case. It is what many had hoped for in the campaign-finance investigation.

But neither Mr. Clinton nor Ms. Reno are inclined to do what they don't want to do. They always have their reasons. Somehow, whether it is national security or the integrity of a presidential election, the electorate is supposed to shrug and get over it.

Perhaps, for another year or so. It will then be the next President's job to remake Justice from a place of constant suspicion about motive to one of respect.

August 30, 1999

Editorial Feature

Clinton's Other Perjury

A year and a day after Bill Clinton lied about the Monica Lewinsky mess to a federal grand jury, the three-judge special court overseeing Kenneth Starr's independent counsel investigation gave the president one more worry. By a two-to-one vote on Aug. 18, judges Peter Fay and David Sentelle refused to terminate Mr. Starr's probe. His "unusually

Rule of Law

By Gary L. McDowell

productive" investigation should be allowed to continue, despite the dissent of Judge Richard Cudahy that the investigation had reached "a natural and logical point for termination" with the impeachment and acquittal of President Clinton.

At one level the decision can be read as simply granting the Office of Independent Counsel the opportunity to clear up a few trifling matters before it files its required report and closes up shop. But when pressed as to whether his office might yet file indictments against either the president or his wife, Mr. Starr declined to comment, leaving open the possibility of something yet to come.

There remains very much unresolved the matter of the president's perjury before the grand jury on Aug. 17, 1998. Since April, when Judge Susan Webber Wright found the president in contempt for lying in the Paula Jones sexual harassment lawsuit, the matter of Mr. Clinton's "other" perjury before the grand jury has dangled ominously above what is left of his administration.

Lying under oath before a federal grand jury is certainly as serious a matter as lying under oath in a deposition in a pending civil suit. And if Mr. Starr is going to tie up his long investigation with no loose ends, an indictment against the president for the multiple counts of perjury alleged by both the independent counsel and David Schippers, the chief counsel to the House Judiciary Committee during the impeachment proceedings, would be properly brought.

It is worth recalling that Mr. Clinton's impeachment wasn't simply a party-line vote; Democrats voted for it, too. And during the heated debates over the president's fate not even his strongest defenders denied that he had lied under oath to the grand jury.

Most took the tack of then-Congressman, now-Senator Charles Schumer of New York: "To me it's clear that the president lied when he testified before the grand jury—not to cover a crime, but to cover embarrassing personal behavior." Democrats argued that such perjury simply didn't rise to the level of being a high crime or misdemeanor as required by the Constitution for impeachment. Yet they still thought that there needed to be "some public consequence for the president's despicable behavior," as Rep. Ronald Berman put it.

Perjury to cover embarrassing personal behavior is still perjury; and such perjury is sufficiently serious a federal crime for Sen. Herbert Kohl to have argued that the president could still be "criminally prosecuted, especially once he leaves office." In Sen. Kohl's view, "his acts may not be 'removable' wrongs, but they could be 'convictable' crimes." Even the most ardent Clinton supporters did not see his acquittal in the Senate as placing the president above the law; in Sen. Barbara Boxer's words, "he remains subject to the laws of the land just like any other citizen of the United States."

But perhaps Sen. John Breaux summed up best what the president would still confront: "There is the court system. There are the U.S. attorneys out there waiting. There may even be the Office of Independent Counsel, which will still be there after all of this is finished."

As the federal government's prosecution of perjurers makes clear, there are plenty of parallel cases. One that was still very much alive during the president's impeachment and trial was that of Dr. Barbara Battalino, formerly with the Veterans Affairs Administration. Dr. Battalino had been indicted in April 1998 by the Justice Department for lying before a federal magistrate. Her crime was simple and straightforward and stunningly similar to that of the president: She had lied to avoid the embarrassment of admitting to a consensual sexual act on Veterans Affairs premises back in 1991. Her formal sentence did not end until this July.

The Battalino case shows how seriously perjury is taken as a matter of federal criminal law. The relevant provisions of the U.S. Code allow for those guilty of perjury to be "fined . . . or imprisoned not more than five years, or both." Under the U.S. Sentencing Guidelines, Mr. Clinton, if indicted and convicted of perjury, would pose an interesting problem for the judge hearing the case. On the one hand, he would be a first offender with no prior convictions and therefore might reasonably expect a degree of leniency that might mean for each count only six to 12 months in jail (or, more likely, in home confinement with an electronic monitor like Dr. Battalino's) and a fine of between $2,000 and $20,000.

On the other hand, he is a public official and the sentencing guidelines are less charitable in those cases: "If the defendant abused a position of public or private trust . . . in a manner that significantly facilitated the commission or concealment of the offense, increase [the punishment] by 2 levels." It would not be surprising to find a judge inclined to throw the book at the president, as Judge Wright put it, "not only to redress the President's misconduct, but to deter others who might themselves consider emulating the President of the United States by engaging in misconduct that undermines the integrity of the judicial system."

Deciding whether or not to seek an indictment is always a matter of prosecutorial discretion. Mr. Starr may well feel that the political controversies surrounding his investigation are such that indicting the president for perjury would itself undermine the public's faith in the judicial process. On the other hand, there are few public servants who have demonstrated as strong a commitment as Mr. Starr to do right as he sees it whatever the costs. Of course, that might mean leaving any indictment to the U.S. attorney after Mr. Clinton leaves office. The statute of limitations will not have expired by the time the president leaves office in January 2001.

And that is what should be especially worrying to the president and his wife as her bid for the Senate heats up. For one way or the other, as another famous non-native New Yorker once said, it ain't over till it's over.

Mr. McDowell is director of the Institute of United States Studies at the University of London. A related article appears on the next page.

Editorial Feature

Perjury? Let the Courts Decide

During the impeachment debate, Democrats' favorite line was that it was the job of the courts, not the Senate, to decide whether President Clinton committed perjury. Here's what some of them had to say last February:

"Rejecting these articles of impeachment does not place this president above the law. As the Constitution clearly says, he remains subject to the laws of the land just like any other citizen of the United States."

— Sen. Barbara Boxer (D., Calif.)

"Whether any of his conduct constitutes a criminal offense such as perjury or obstruction of justice is not for me to decide. That, appropriately, should and must be left to the criminal justice system, which will uphold the rule of law in President Clinton's case as it would for any other American."

— Sen. Joseph Lieberman (D., Conn.)

"For those who believe that the president is guilty of perjury and obstruction of justice—criminal offenses—there is a forum available for that determination."

— Sen. Richard Bryan (D., Nev.)

"Still, President Clinton is not 'above the law.' His conduct should not be excused, nor will it. The president can be criminally prosecuted, especially once he leaves office. In other words, his acts may not be 'removable' wrongs, but they could be 'convictable' crimes."

— Sen. Herbert Kohl (D., Wisc.)

"[T]he legal system, our civil and criminal laws provide the proper venue for a president who has failed in his private character. . . . And in this case, the legal system can and will continue to address the president's personal transgressions."

— Sen. Frank Lautenberg (D., N.J.)

"Offensive as they were, the president's actions have nothing to do with his official duties, nor do they constitute the most serious of private crimes. In my judgment, these are matters best left to the criminal justice system."

— Sen. Kent Conrad (D., N.D.)

"I have concluded that the Constitution was designed very carefully to remove the president of the United States for wrongful actions as president of the United States in his capacity as president of the United States and in carrying out his duties as president of the United States. For wrongful acts that are not connected with the official capacity and duties of the president of the United States, there are other ways to handle it. There is the judicial system. There is the court system. There are the U.S. attorneys out there waiting. There may even be the Office of Independent Counsel, which will still be there after all of this is finished."

— Sen. John Breaux (D., La.)

"[P]unishment for alleged criminal law violations is not up to the United States Congress. That's up to the criminal justice system. After his term is up, less than two years from now, he is like any other American. He would have any other defenses that any other American has. That's the proper forum for that."

— Rep. Zoe Lofgren (D., Calif.)

Editorial Feature

Vetting the Frontrunners: Albert Gore Jr. Occidental and Oriental Connections

BY MICAH MORRISON

CARTHAGE, Tenn.—On his 1998 tax returns under "supplemental income," Vice President Al Gore lists a $20,000 royalty payment from Union Zinc Inc. for the right to mine zinc from his 88-acre farm here in the verdant hills of the Cumberland River valley. In the 25 years he has held the zinc lease, Mr. Gore has earned more than $450,000.

The man who provided Mr. Gore with that farm and mineral lease is of some note as the 2000 presidential race begins. Mr. Gore's father, former Sen. Albert Gore Sr., acquired the land and mineral rights on what appears to be highly favorable terms from Armand Hammer, the late chairman of Occidental Petroleum Corp. Mr. Hammer, an influence peddler of the highest magnitude, trafficked in politicians of all parties and stripes; he pleaded guilty in 1975 to making illegal contributions to Richard Nixon's campaign in the Watergate affair. But the closest and most sustained of Mr. Hammer's connections seem to have been with the elder Mr. Gore and his family. It was the earliest of a number of controversial associations that tarnish the stiff Boy Scout image of Al Gore Jr.

This is not a tale of smoking guns and indictable offenses. Yet voters should know the financial connections of candidates, though they probably will make their decisions on other grounds. And while the candidates will not appreciate questions being raised about the murky areas of their finances, the lessons of the Clinton era suggest that it is better to put matters on the table early, lest they rise

Whitewater-like to haunt a new administration.

The Hammer-staged zinc payments were first disclosed by Charles Babcock of the Washington Post in 1992, as then-Sen. Al Gore Jr. campaigned on the presidential ticket with an Arkansas upstart named Bill Clinton. An Occidental Petroleum subsidiary, Occidental Minerals, had negotiated the generous terms for Occidental's right to mine minerals beneath the land in 1972. The senior Mr. Gore had set his sights on the land as early as 1970, Mr. Babcock reported.

Al Gore

Occidental Minerals purchased the estate from a local widow in 1972; within a year, Mr. Gore Sr. had bought the property and sold it to his son.

The $20,000 annual lease payment amounted to $227 an acre, much more than the $30 an acre Mr. Hammer's company had been paying locally only a few years earlier. Until 1985, Mr. Babcock noted, Occidental paid Mr. Gore Jr. "$190,000 for the lease without mining under the property because it never built a mine in the area." In 1985, it sold the lease to Union Zinc, which began mining operations. The mine has changed hands several times since and is now owned by Pasminco, an Australian company.

Mr. Babcock's 1992 article said the lease payment was the senator's "most important source of income after his salary." In recent years, Mr. Gore's steady zinc profit has been eclipsed by his environmental bestseller, "Earth in the Balance," which has earned more than $1.1 million in royalties, according to the vice president's tax returns and financial-disclosure statements.

After the elder Mr. Gore lost his 1970 Senate re-election bid, Mr. Hammer placed him on Occidental Petroleum's board of directors and named him chairman of an Occidental subsidiary, Island Creek Coal Co.—posts that would bring him more than $500,000 per year.

The senior Mr. Gore died in December. He is survived by his wife, Pauline. The vice president was named executor and trustee of his father's estate, and was given "sole discretion" to manage a trust on his mother's behalf. The vice president's 1998 financial disclosures value the estate in a range between $266,000 and $565,000, including a block of Occidental Petroleum stock listed at a value of between

$250,000 and $500,000. Local property records, however, place the value of Mr. Gore Sr.'s land holdings alone at more than $1.1 million.

Mr. Hammer was generous with the younger Mr. Gore as well, beyond the zinc lease. Occidental Petroleum was one of the largest contributors to Mr. Gore's successful 1990 bid for Senate re-election. The Hammer family and corporations made donations up to the legal maximum in all of Mr. Gore's campaigns, according to Mr. Hammer's former personal assistant, Neil Lyndon, writing in London's Daily Telegraph.

Mr. Hammer was Mr. Gore's guest at the 1981 inauguration of Ronald Reagan. In May 1987, Mr. Gore and Mr. Hammer were in Moscow for a convention of International Physicians Against Nuclear War, a group calling for the abolition of all nuclear weapons. Mr. Hammer received a humanitarian award from the group; Mr. Gore delivered a speech saying conventional arms should be cut along with nuclear weapons. A month later, Mr. Hammer hosted a luncheon for presidential candidate Gore in Los Angeles.

Mr. Lyndon wrote that the younger Mr. Gore regularly dined with Mr. Hammer and Occidental lobbyists in Washington, and that he and his wife, Tipper, attended Mr. Hammer's lavish parties. "Separately and together, the Gores sometimes used Hammer's luxurious private Boeing 727 for journeys and jaunts," Mr. Lyndon noted. The former Hammer aide added that the "profound and prolonged involvement between Hammer and Gore has never been revealed or investigated." Vice President Gore's office did not respond to a request to discuss Mr. Hammer.

Mr. Hammer died in 1990 at 92. The Hammer myth, developed with great care during his lifetime, presented the billionaire industrialist as a generous patron of the arts and a champion of peace during the Cold War. But the reality behind the myth was far different.

In his penetrating 1996 book, "Dossier: The Secret History of Armand Hammer," author Edward Jay Epstein demolished the elaborate biographical backdrops Mr. Hammer and his helpers erected. Drawing on FBI documentation and files from Moscow intelligence agencies, Mr. Epstein told the story of Mr. Hammer's extensive business dealings with the Soviet Union. Mr. Hammer helped develop, and exploited for his business purposes, the image of a benign and profitable communist colossus, at a time when Stalin was murdering millions. Lenin himself, Mr. Epstein documents, told Stalin that Mr. Hammer was a "path leading to the American business world, and this path should be made use of in every way." Mr. Hammer mined asbestos and brokered the production of tractors and pencils for Stalinist Russia. He cut lucrative fur deals. He trafficked in Czarist art, real and forged. He laundered millions for the Soviet Union in sham transactions. Later, Mr. Epstein reports, Mr. Hammer leapt into the big time by acquiring Libyan oil rights for Occidental Petroleum through a combination of shrewd dealing and bribery.

Much of this was not a secret in Cold War Washington, certainly not to J. Edgar Hoover. But Mr. Hammer also collected politicians, among them Albert Gore Sr. In 1950, Mr. Epstein writes, Mr. Hammer made then-Rep. Gore "a partner in a cattle-breeding business, and Gore made a substantial profit." Over the years, as Mr. Gore rose in prominence and went on to the

Gore family values: In an early '50s photo, Sen. Albert Gore Sr., Armand Hammer, Pauline Gore, and the Gore children, Nancy and Albert Jr.

From "The Dark Side of Power" by Carl Blumay

Senate, many favor-seekers traveled to Tennessee to purchase some very expensive cattle. The profits allowed the senator and his family to live in luxury at Washington's Fairfax Hotel. In return, Mr. Gore provided several valuable services to Mr. Hammer, including fending off the FBI.

In 1972, a Hammer operative gave $54,000 in laundered hundred-dollar bills to Nixon fund-raiser Maurice Stans for use in the Watergate coverup. Questioned by the FBI and a Senate committee, Mr. Hammer lied about the money. But his flunkies crumbled under questioning. In 1975, Mr. Hammer pleaded guilty to three counts of making illegal campaign contributions. He spent the rest of his life campaigning for a pardon, which President Bush granted in 1989.

Mr. Hammer also had close ties to two lawyers who later would play important roles in the Clinton administration: Mickey Kantor, who served as commerce secretary, U.S. trade representative and White House damage-control specialist, and Gerald Stern, the Justice Department's special counsel for financial-institution fraud. Mr. Stern was on Occidental Petroleum's payroll as senior general counsel before coming to Washington. Mr. Kantor was a key player as outside counsel to Occidental when his law firm, Manatt, Phelps, Phillips & Kantor, waged a long and ultimately unsuccessful battle to open portions of the California coast to oil drilling.

Mr. Kantor was the 1992 Clinton-Gore campaign chairman and head of the transition team; Mr. Stern, a boyhood friend of Mr. Kantor's, was staff coordinator of the transition team. At Justice, Mr. Stern managed the department's largely fruitless efforts to get to the bottom of the BCCI banking scandal. A decade earlier, before Mr. Stern worked for Occidental, Mr. Hammer had been deeply involved in his own maneuvering to gain control of Financial General Bankshares, a Washington, D.C., bank holding company. When his takeover attempt did not succeed, Mr. Hammer sold his interest in Financial General to BCCI front men in 1981. BCCI was shut down in 1991 amid charges of global bank fraud.

Mr. Gore's lifelong association with Armand Hammer casts some doubt on the popular impression that he was unsullied before accepting the vice presidential nomination on Bill Clinton's ticket. In fact, some of the most controversial figures in the Clinton scandals came into the administration from the Gore camp. Craig Livingstone, the central player in the appearance of hundreds of FBI files at the White House, is a former Gore advance man. Nathan Landow, who entertained former White House volunteer Kathleen Willey while apparently trying to suppress her story about the president's sexual advances, was a Gore fund-raiser, and remains one today. Mr. Landow has denied any wrongdoing in the Willey matter and no charges were brought against him.

And Mr. Gore had his own, independent connections with some of the Asian figures made famous by the Clinton scandals. His notorious appearance at a 1996 fund-raiser at the Hsi Lai Buddhist temple in California—where $65,000 was funneled to the Clinton-Gore effort through the use of Buddhist monks as conduits—followed a decade-long association with fund-raiser Maria Hsia, who staged the temple event. A Senate Governmental Affairs Committee report identifies Ms.

Hsia as "an agent of the Chinese government." The six-volume report details the Gore connection with Ms. Hsia, as well as a lengthy relationship with campaign-finance figures James Riady and John Huang.

The dry committee report is engagingly retold for the nonobsessive in Bob Zelnick's useful 1999 biography, "Gore: A Political Life." "Gore and the Buddhists went back a long way," Mr. Zelnick notes, "and always at the center of the relationship was money for the Tennesseean and his campaigns." Ms. Hsia, Mr. Riady and Mr. Huang were instrumental in bringing then-Sen. Gore to Taiwan in January 1989 under the auspices of a lobbying group they had formed a year earlier, the Pacific Leadership Council. Mr. Riady's Lippo Group provided the seed money for the trip; Mr. Huang handled the itinerary.

Following Sen. Gore's 1989 trip, Ms. Hsia and the Pacific Leadership Council "helped run numerous fund-raising events on his behalf," the Senate Governmental Affairs Committee reported, "organizing Asian-American and Indo-Americans in Tennessee for Gore's re-election." Ms. Hsia, an immigration broker, "enlisted Senator Gore's office in trying to help her arrange business deals—on a commission basis—between Tennessee businesses and Taiwanese business contacts."

While offering few details, the Governmental Affairs Committee's final report stated that Ms. Hsia had been "an agent of the Chinese government, that she acted knowingly in support of it, and that she has attempted to conceal her relationship" with it. Ms. Hsia is currently under indictment in the Buddhist Temple scheme; her attorney has denounced the charges as "absolutely false."

Ms. Hsia also was no stranger to Peter Knight, the sometime Washington lobbyist who is Mr. Gore's current senior fund-raiser. In his book, Mr. Zelnick reports that Mr. Knight and Leon Fuerth—Mr. Gore's longtime national security assistant—urged Mr. Gore in 1988 to accept Ms. Hsia's invitation to Taiwan. Mr. Knight's interest, Mr. Zelnick suggests, was to develop the Asian-American community both on his boss's behalf and to further his own career as a lobbyist.

In 1996, Mr. Knight signed on as campaign manager of the Clinton-Gore re-election effort. As the campaign-finance scandal unraveled, Mr. Knight and Mr. Landow—the Democratic fund-raiser involved in the Kathleen Willey affair—were widely criticized for squeezing a $100,000 donation out of the impoverished Cheyenne and Arapaho tribes of Oklahoma and attempting to extract business concessions from them.

Mr. Landow told the Washington Post that he met with the tribes only to be "polite" and did nothing improper in seeking further business with them related to mineral rights in a long-running land dispute with the federal government. These days, he is back in action on Mr. Gore's behalf, helping raise $50,000 at a Maryland event in May. The vice president's office did not respond to a request for details on Mr. Landow's current role in the Gore campaign. Mr. Knight told the Post that he himself had only minimal contact with tribal representatives; according to the Post, his lobbying firm had been seeking a $100,000 retainer and a $10,000-a-month fee from the tribes in the land dispute.

Mr. Knight came under congressional scrutiny as well for his lobbying efforts on behalf of Molten Metals Technology, a Massachusetts toxic-waste cleanup firm that donated $90,000 to the Democrats in 1996. In a separate probe, the House Commerce Committee referred to Attorney General Janet Reno questions about a $1 million fee Mr. Knight received after lobbying federal officials to move the Federal Communications Commission headquarters to a building complex controlled by Tennessee developer Franklin Haney, a Gore family friend and Knight client. No charges were brought in either matter. In a separate prosecution, Mr. Haney was acquitted in July on 42 counts of making illegal contributions to Mr. Gore and other politicians.

Mr. Gore also raised eyebrows in May with the appointment of former Rep. Tony Coelho to run his presidential campaign. Among hardened political professionals, the move was taken as a sign that the Gore campaign will not overly trouble itself about the ethical quandaries of big-time money raising. In 1989, Mr. Coelho beat a hasty retreat from Congress as scandal clouds gathered around him.

The immediate cause of his departure was an undisclosed financial relationship with financier Michael Milken. But Mr. Coelho by that time had become infamous as a pioneer of the hardball political shakedown, threatening business and political action committees for "donations" with the reminder that congressional Democrats were in a position to punish their enemies and reward their friends.

It was politics as blood sport, and Rep. Coelho pursued it with a vengeance. One friend that reaped the reward was the savings-and-loan industry. Mr. Coelho raised millions for the Democratic Party from S&L owners, including hosting parties aboard a Potomac yacht named the "High Spirits," owned by Vernon Savings & Loan of Texas. He rewarded his S&L friends in 1987 by helping to gut a House reform package, prolonging a debacle that cost the taxpayers more than $200 billion. Vernon's owner eventually was convicted of looting the S&L, and Mr. Coelho was forced to reimburse the conservators for the use of the yacht.

Does any of this matter to the 2000 presidential race and a possible Gore administration? In many respects, Al Gore and George W. Bush have similar histories as sons of prominent politicians. But unlike his putative presidential opponent, Mr. Gore has not relied on his father's connections in cutting deals leading to great personal wealth. He has, however, toiled at the feet of not only Bill Clinton but Armand Hammer, another master of transient morality, and his taste in associates tends to raise doubts about his clean-cut persona. This of course is no disqualification from serving as president. The charitable voter would recall the words of that political sage Mr. Dooley: "Politics ain't beanbag."

Mr. Morrison is a Journal editorial page writer.

All About Scandals

After five years as Independent Counsel, Kenneth Starr stepped down in October 1999, citing the "intense politicization" of his work. "The wiser course, I believe, is for another individual to lead the investigation," Mr. Starr wrote in a letter of resignation.

In an article for the Journal, Mr. Starr defended his probe and analyzed the institutional limitations on the Office of Independent Counsel. "The investigation has resulted in the convictions of 14 people," Mr. Starr wrote, "including a sitting governor of Arkansas, the business partners of the president and first lady, and the former associate attorney general of the U.S. Yet more remains to be done."

Mr. Starr was succeeded by Robert Ray, an experienced federal prosecutor. Mr. Ray, the Journal observed, "will face a big decision of his own: Whether to indict Mr. Clinton for perjury once he is no longer President. The issue here is whether Mr. Clinton will be held accountable for his 'other perjury.' Federal Judge Susan Webber Wright in Arkansas has addressed the first perjury, which was in her court during Paula Jones's civit suit. Judge Wright worried about the precedent set by Mr. Clinton's behavior, and so held him in contempt of court and ordered him to pay an additional $90,000 to lawyers for Mrs. Jones. But there is another perjury, even more serious because it took place before a federal grand jury and after extensive preparation by counsel."

In Washington, new evidence continued to emerge about the Justice Department's mishandling of the investigation into the 1996

Clinton-Gore re-election effort. "Congressional veterans couldn't recall ever seeing anything quite like it," the Journal noted on September 30. "Last Wednesday, four current or retired FBI agents appeared before a Senate oversight committee to testify in detail how Justice Department officials had blocked and subverted their efforts to investigate the campaign finance scandals of the 1996 Clinton-Gore ticket."

In New York, U.S. Attorney Mary Jo White mounted a prosecution of former International Brotherhood of Teamsters political director William Hamilton for an elaborate campaign-finance fraud scheme. A jury convicted Mr. Hamilton of all counts in the scheme to funnel $885,000 to the re-election campaign of then-Teamster president Ron Carey. "Testimony at the trial included accounts of illegal money-laundering schemes involving the AFL-CIO, the Democratic National Committee and liberal activist groups," the Journal noted. "Having won this stunning conviction, Ms. White must now decide whether to pursue higher-ups—notably Mr. Carey and Richard Trumka, the treasurer of the AFL-CIO—who were implicated by evidence offered at the trial."

REVIEW & OUTLOOK

Obstruction of Justice Department?

Congressional veterans couldn't recall ever seeing anything like it. Last Wednesday, four current or retired FBI agents appeared before a Senate oversight committee to testify in detail how Justice Department officials had blocked and subverted their efforts to investigate the campaign finance scandals of the 1996 Clinton-Gore ticket.

The country can't rule out that it might be dealing with an "Obstruction of Justice Department," was Chairman Fred Thompson's conclusion after the agents had finished, and their Justice supervisors had their chance to respond. FBI agents testifying in public against their superiors in the Department of Justice is explosive stuff. But with a few notable exceptions, such as the Washington Times and Fox News Channel, press coverage of the story has been minimal or nonexistent. So we're going to take some space here to tell this fascinating tale.

The tension traces back to the Justice Department's investigation into the sources of the Clinton-Gore campaign fund-raising abuses. FBI agent complaints about the limits that Justice's Public Integrity Section placed on them date back some two years. "I am convinced the team at DoJ is, at best, simply not up to the task," said I.C. Smith, a now-retired 26-year Bureau veteran who ran its Little Rock, Ark., office, discussing an August 1997 memo he had written to Director Louis Freeh. "The impression left is the emphasis is on how not to prosecute matters, not how to aggressively conduct investigations leading to prosecutions." Mr. Freeh didn't respond directly to Agent Smith's letter, but within three months he unsuccessfully urged Janet Reno to appoint an independent counsel to probe the Clinton-Gore campaign.

Still, there had to be some reason to account for the agency's sense of nonmovement in the Justice Department. A strong illustration of it emerged from the agents' testimony last week.

The agents testified that Laura Ingersoll, then head of the campaign finance task force set up by Justice, and Lee Radek, the head of Public Integrity, for four months blocked their request to ask a judge for a warrant to search the Little Rock office of Clinton fund-raiser Charlie Trie. Agents sifting through Mr. Trie's trash found that vital records subpoenaed by Senator Thompson's committee were being shredded. They also had an informant who had seen Mr. Trie bring in "duffel bags full of cash" to the Democratic Party. But their request to main Justice for a warrant was turned down for four months. It wasn't granted until Charles La Bella

Janet Reno

replaced Ms. Ingersoll; by then newspapers were uncovering the relevant evidence first. Eventually Mr. La Bella himself was sidelined and forced to leave Justice after he joined Mr. Freeh in recommending an independent counsel.

Agent Smith said he was "astounded" by the torn-up Trie documents. According to the agents' search-warrant affidavit, they included torn photocopies of six checks from Asian contributors to President Clinton's legal defense fund, travel records for Ng Lap Seng, the mysterious Macau tycoon who wired $1 million to Mr. Trie, statements from Chinese banks, Democratic National Committee donor lists and a Federal Express record showing that Mr. Trie had sent two pounds of documents to the White House in May 1997. Some of the documents indicated that the White House was keeping Mr. Trie informed of the investigations against him.

However, the Asian checks to the legal defense fund were dismissed by Justice. "Ingersoll indicated, in so many words, 'we will not pursue this matter'," Agent Smith told Director Freeh on a separate occasion.

Ms. Ingersoll also refused the FBI's request to seek a search warrant, saying the agents hadn't found "a smoking gun." In July 1997, the Little Rock agents convinced Public Integrity attorneys to approve a "car stop" after an unidentified man was seen removing documents from Mr. Trie's home and taking them to the home of Maria Mapili, Mr. Trie's business manager. But Ms. Ingersoll withdrew approval for the search after learning that the man was W.H. Taylor, Mr. Mapili's lawyer. Mr. Taylor was also a personal attorney for chicken tycoon Don Tyson while he was under investigation by an independent counsel.

FBI agent Daniel Wehr testified that he was "scandalized" when he was told at a briefing by Ms. Ingersoll they should "not pursue any matter related to solicitation of funds for access to the President." He said, "The reason given to me was that that's the way the American political process works." Ms. Ingersoll says she must have been misunderstood.

Agent Roberta Parker testified that she became so frustrated that she kept three, 200-page spiral notebooks documenting her complaints about Justice. She turned the notebooks over to FBI officials in response to a House subpoena. Ms. Parker said the notebooks were not turned over to the House and when they were returned to her last month, 27 pages covering the Trie search-warrant controversy had been ripped out of one of them. Senator Thompson says the notes are "the only detailed, contemporaneous record" of the disputes between FBI and Justice and he will conduct his own investigation into what happened to them.

Today, Justice's campaign finance probe remains technically active, though Senator Thompson thinks that may be only so Justice can deny him access to certain documents. The major players from John Huang to Charlie Trie to Ms. Mapili have all struck plea bargains with Justice. "After all the wrongdoing, nobody's going to jail," Senator Joseph Lieberman dryly noted. Senator Lieberman, the only Democrat to attend the hearing, said the search warrant refusal was clearly an "error" and "arouses so much suspicion." Senator Thompson concluded that Justice officials have "done everything in the world at every juncture and every step to direct the finger of suspicion toward them."

The agents' remarkable testimony in fact elicited an angry public response from the President last Friday. At the annual White House press picnic, he fell into an extraordinary 10-minute interview with Paul Sperry, the bureau chief of Investor's Business Daily. Mr. Sperry asked Mr. Clinton on a rope line when he was going to hold his next formal news conference. Mr. Clinton asked why, and Mr. Sperry said "the American people have a lot of unanswered questions." When Mr. Clinton asked "Like what?" Mr. Sperry told him "questions about illegal money from China and the campaign finance scandal." President Clinton exploded in anger over the agents' testimony and told the reporter that "the FBI wants you to write about that rather than write about Waco."

According to an account of the incident by James Grimaldi of the Seattle Times, Mr. Clinton "blew up" and claimed "the only person who has been linked to money from China" is former Republican National Committee head Haley Barbour. He said his campaign had given Justice's campaign task force "every shred of evidence, and they haven't found a thing." Photos taken of the incident show a red-faced Mr. Clinton wagging his finger about a foot in front of Mr. Sperry. On Monday, a White House spokesman said, "The President does not regret making those comments" and Mr. Sperry says Press Secretary Joe Lockhart personally told him he would never be invited back to the White House.

The White House's touchiness on the campaign finance probe has to be seen in the context of other developments this month—the unpopular clemency for the Puerto Rican terrorists, the revival of the controversies surrounding Waco, and even the difficulties over the Clintons' New York mortgage. Senator Arlen Specter, for instance, announced he will lead a bipartisan probe of the Justice Department's handling of high-profile cases such as the Waco disaster and its refusal to wiretap the phone of suspected Chinese nuclear spy Wen Ho Lee.

What these revelations demonstrate is that Senator Thompson is showing some Congressional initiative, precisely the form of oversight we hoped would emerge in the wake of the independent counsel statute's expiration. There isn't going to be another impeachment, but it's clearer than ever that the most significant institutional damage to result from this period is the subversion of Justice.

The formation of serious policy, for example on China, can't proceed because of this rot. What emerges from these FBI accounts is a portrait of not merely a botched investigation but of an active coverup.

REVIEW & OUTLOOK

Mr. Ray's Decision

Ken Starr is leaving as independent counsel for the Clinton presidency, the advance reports have it, to be replaced with Robert Ray, who has served as an aide to both Mr. Starr and Independent Counsel Donald Smaltz. This puts a central question before the nation: What is left for the law to do with Bill Clinton?

The House impeached the President, and the Senate voted not to remove him. The initial reporting on Mr. Ray suggests that his office will try to tie up loose ends, pursuing the intimidation of Kathleen Willey and the Travel Office firings. The seriousness of those matters notwithstanding, Mr. Ray will face a big decision of his own: Whether to indict Mr. Clinton for perjury once he is no longer President.

The issue here is whether Mr. Clinton will be held accountable for his "other perjury." Federal Judge Susan Webber Wright in Arkansas has addressed the first perjury, which was in her court during Paula Jones's civil suit. Judge Wright worried about the precedent set by Mr. Clinton's behavior, and so held him in contempt of court and ordered him to pay an additional $90,000 to lawyers for Mrs. Jones. She wrote of the need "to deter others who might themselves consider emulating the President of the United States by engaging in misconduct that undermines the integrity of the judicial system."

But there is another perjury, even more serious because it took place before a federal grand jury and after extensive preparation by counsel. This is the testimony that was the subject of the famous leaks in Bob Woodward's latest book—including a protest about the planned testimony from presidential attorney Bob Bennett, "It's insanity." The serious legal implications of this testimony have received scant attention, though they were spelled out on these pages by Gary McDowell on Aug. 30. The point is that Mr. Clinton testified before the grand jury on the Lewinsky matter on Aug. 17, 1998, and the statute of limitations will not have run out by Jan. 21, 2001, when he will be a private citizen without the protections of the Presidency.

At that point Mr. Ray will have to decide whether to indict citizen Clinton. It may sound strange for him to bring a rather belated indictment, except that is what leaders of Mr. Clinton's own party repeatedly urged. Consider this remarkable set of quotations from Democratic Party leaders during the impeachment debate:

"President Clinton is not 'above the law.' His conduct should not be excused, nor will it. The President can be criminally prosecuted, especially once he leaves office. In other words, his acts may not be 'removable' wrongs, but they could be 'convictable' crimes."

— Sen. Herbert Kohl (D., Wisc.)

"Rejecting these articles of impeachment does not place this President above the law. As the Constitution clearly says, he remains subject to the laws of the land just like any other citizen of the United States."

— Sen. Barbara Boxer (D., Calif.)

"Whether any of his conduct constitutes a criminal offense such as perjury or obstruction of justice is not for me to decide. That, appropriately, should and must be left to the criminal justice system, which will uphold the rule of law in President Clinton's case as it would for any other American."

— Sen. Joseph Lieberman (D., Conn.)

"For those who believe that the President is guilty of perjury and obstruction of justice—criminal offenses—there is a forum available for that determination."

— Sen. Richard Bryan (D., Nev.)

"[T]he legal system, our civil and criminal laws provide the proper venue for a President who has failed in his private character. . . . And in this case, the legal system can and will continue to address the President's personal transgressions."

— *Sen. Frank Lautenberg (D., N.J.)*

"Offensive as they were, the President's actions have nothing to do with his official duties, nor do they constitute the most serious of private crimes. In my judgment, these are matters best left to the criminal justice system."

— *Sen. Kent Conrad (D., N.D.)*

"[P]unishment for alleged criminal law violations is not up to the United States Congress. That's up to the criminal justice system. After his term is up, less than two years from now, he is like any other American. He would have any other defenses that any other American has. That's the proper forum for that."

— *Rep. Zoe Lofgren (D., Calif.)*

"I have concluded that the Constitution was designed very carefully to remove the President of the United States for wrongful actions as President of the United States in his capacity as President of the United States and in carrying out his duties as President of the United States. For wrongful acts that are not connected with the official capacity and duties of the President of the United States, there are other ways to handle it. There is the judicial system. There is the court system. There are the U.S. attorneys out there waiting. There may even be the Office of Independent Counsel, which will still be there after all of this is finished."

— *Sen. John Breaux (D., La.)*

Resolving this President's perjury is a matter of principle. That said, however, let us acknowledge plainly that there are two competing principles in play here. The first is the dignity of the presidential office. It would be impugned by putting the just-impeached President in the dock. Against this there is the principle, a matter of faith grasped at every level of American life, that no one is above the law.

In considering whether to indict Bill Clinton for his perjury, Mr. Ray will have to strike a balance. But there can be no doubting that his primary job as an officer of the federal court is upholding the rule of law. Doing nothing would do damage to this most fundamental idea. The issue of dignity can be weighed in other forums—for example by an application to Mr. Clinton's successor for a presidential pardon.

October 19, 1999

Editorial Feature

Scandal Decisions: Indict Clinton? Free Archie?

BY MICAH MORRISON

The beast is back.

Yesterday a special judicial panel named former Assistant U.S. Attorney Robert Ray to succeed battle-scarred Kenneth Starr as Whitewater independent counsel. An endgame is not quite in sight for the scandals that have stalked the Clinton administration, though several fateful decisions are looming.

Robert Ray

The biggest question Mr. Ray faces is whether to indict Mr. Clinton after he leaves office for lying to a federal grand jury. Both Mr. Starr and David Schippers, the chief counsel for the House Judiciary Committee during the impeachment proceedings, alleged that Mr. Clinton committed multiple acts of perjury in his Aug. 17, 1998, testimony in the Monica Lewinsky matter. Article One of the House impeachment resolution charged the president with "perjurious" testimony to the grand jury about his relationship with Ms. Lewinsky, his attempts to influence witnesses, and statements he made under oath in a civil deposition in the Paula Jones sexual harassment lawsuit.

Mr. Clinton's legal peril deepened considerably in April, when U.S. District Judge Susan Webber Wright determined that he had indeed lied in the the Jones lawsuit. Charging the president with contempt, Judge Wright fined him $90,000 for providing "false, misleading and evasive answers" in the sworn deposition. Judge Wright castigated the president for "engaging in conduct that undermines the integrity of the judicial system"; Mr. Clinton repeated the substance of this testimony to the grand jury, after extensive opportunity for reflection and consulation with counsel. A judge who views the case the way Judge Wright did might be inclined to throw the book at him, with a fine of up to $20,000 and the possibility of a year in jail or under home confinement. He also faces possible disbarment.

The 39-year-old Mr. Ray has a reputation as an aggressive prosecutor. After a stint with the U.S. attorney for the Southern District of New York, he went to work in 1995 for Independent Counsel Donald Smaltz, who was investigating former Agriculture Secretary Mike Espy. Mr. Ray won convictions of Tyson Foods executives Jack Williams and Archie Schaffer in tough cases. He joined Mr. Starr's staff in April. Mr. Smaltz praised Mr. Ray as "a very experienced prosecutor who is trial savvy and has good leadership abilities."

The appointment puts Mr. Ray in the crosshairs of the brutally effective Clinton attack machine. The White House immediately went on the offensive. Spokesman Joe Lockhart compared Mr. Starr to a garbage peddler and called Mr. Ray's appointment "dubious."

A perjury prosecution is not the only worry for the Clintons. Mr. Ray will supervise a continuing probe into an alleged attempt to silence Kathleen Willey, a former White House volunteer who accused the president of making an improper sexual advance. Mr. Ray also must decide whether Hillary Clinton broke any laws in the White House Travel Office affair.

If Mrs. Clinton continues her run for a Senate seat in New York, her legal work is likely to come under scrutiny too. Mr. Ray must produce a final report on the entire Whitewater affair, including the Clintons' dealings with Madison Guaranty Savings & Loan. Mrs. Clinton was a key figure in that investigation, and at one point she was the subject of a draft indictment drawn up by Mr. Starr's office. The draft indictment is believed to have focused on her work on the fraudulent Castle Grande land deals, a Madison project riddled with illegal insider transactions. Questioned under oath about Castle Grande, Mrs. Clinton suffered repeated memory loss.

Down in Little Rock, there's been a lot of grumbling about the Clintons lately. The political class is asking why the president helped Hillary in New York by offering clemency to 16 Puerto Rican terrorists but won't pardon Arkansas's own Archie Schaffer, the Tyson Foods executive convicted of violating the Meat Inspection Act by giving an improper gift to Mr. Espy. Don Tyson, the powerful chairman of Tyson Foods, was granted immunity from prosecution in exchange for his cooperation and a guilty plea by the corporation to one count of providing an illegal gratuity. Mr. Tyson turned out not to be a particularly helpful witness, and the full reach of his influence remains one of the mysteries of Whitewater. Mr. Espy was acquitted of all charges in December.

Congress also is gearing up for another look at several controversies of the Clinton era, particularly the Justice Department handling of the campaign-finance affair. The Senate Governmental Affairs Committee has heard testimony from FBI officials about the reluctance of top Justice officials to probe the campaign-finance case, and last week Sen. Arlen Specter received approval for a new probe into Justice's handling of campaign finance, Chinese espionage and the Waco disaster. Meanwhile Rep. Dan Burton presses on with investigations into avenues of illegal funding, despite taking a terrible beating from the Clinton machine.

By Clinton-era standards, it has been a quiet few months on the scandal front. Over at the White House, the president's damage-control team used to joke about "feeding the beast"—satiating the hunger of the media and congressional committees for facts about the scandals. But on the evidence of nearly seven years of investigations and prosecutions, the biggest and toughest beast in the jungle is Bill Clinton. So far, Mr. Ray and the new congressional probes just look like fresh meat.

Mr. Morrison is a Journal editorial page writer.

Editorial Feature

What We've Accomplished

By Kenneth Starr

On Monday a superb career prosecutor took over as Whitewater independent counsel. The investigation has resulted in the convictions of 14 people, including a sitting governor of Arkansas, the business partners of the president and the first lady, and the former associate attorney general of the U.S.

Yet more remains to be done. Why? Partly because of factors beyond our control: an inability to reach an agreement with the Justice Department and the institutional limitations of independent counsels.

While on my way to Little Rock for the first time, just after my swearing in, I got a call from Attorney General Janet Reno, who graciously pledged that the Justice Department would be helpful and that she would do all she could to protect the independence of the investigation.

I expected the investigation would be fairly quick—several months, a year at most. To an outsider, the subject of the investigation—matters related to Whitewater Development Co. and Madison Guaranty Savings & Loan—looked straightforward. And I wasn't starting from scratch; I inherited the work of Robert Fiske, the "regulatory special counsel" appointed by the attorney general after a law authorizing independent counsels had expired but before Congress reauthorized it.

When I got to Little Rock, though, I found that the work went far beyond a real-estate transaction once upon a time. Mr. Fiske and his staff had been investigating cases of bankruptcy fraud, various tax matters and apparent irregularities in a gubernatorial campaign. These were not the main Whitewater/Madison issues, but they did involve people who held information highly useful to the investigation. Prosecutors often follow seemingly tangential leads in hopes of gaining the cooperation of key witnesses.

Mr. Fiske, like any federal prosecutor, had the authority to take the investigation in whatever direction seemed promising. I soon found that I did not. The Ethics in Government Act tightly limits the jurisdiction of independent counsels, who must get the blessing of the Justice Department before advancing onto new terrain. Indeed, with Justice's approval, our mandate grew to cover matters related to the firing of White House Travel Office employees, the accumulating of FBI files in the White House, the congressional testimony of a former White House Counsel, and Monica Lewinsky.

The investigation was slowed further by litigation over the authority of the independent counsel. Example: In June 1995, a grand jury indicted then-Gov. Jim Guy Tucker in one of the matters Mr. Fiske had investigated. The trial judge held that we lacked jurisdiction, even though the Justice Department had specifically authorized us to continue the investigation. The Eighth Circuit Court of Appeals reversed this ruling, but the defendants appealed again. Not until February 1998 did Mr. Tucker enter a guilty plea. Mr. Tucker was not unique. In the modern litigate-to-the-hilt legal culture, we were forced to defend our jurisdiction at every turn.

Neither ordinary federal prosecutors nor special counsels like Mr. Fiske are hamstrung by these sorts of jurisdictional defenses. That's one reason why, in my April testimony before the Senate, I recommended against reauthorizing the independent counsel law.

We were also slowed by the nature of what we were investigating: convoluted financial frauds, not simple whodunits. The evidence sometimes proved elusive. Important documents came to light long after we had sought them—in the White House book room, in a Little Rock attic, even in an abandoned car.

A crucial witness, Susan McDougal, served 18 months in jail to avoid testifying before a grand jury—and President Clinton, through his public statements, appeared to be encouraging her unlawful silence. Other witnesses suffered selective amnesia when we questioned them. Still other witnesses invoked dubious privileges—executive privilege to cover conversations with the first lady, for instance, and the never-before-imagined Secret Service privilege. We nearly always prevailed in these cases, but only after extensive litigation.

And although for a time we enjoyed a productive and collaborative relationship with the Justice Department, just as Ms. Reno had promised me, our relations soured over the last 18 months of my tenure. At times, political appointees in the department actively interfered with our investigation. (I hasten to add that the department's excellent career lawyers never did.)

Of course, the Lewinsky matter changed the landscape in a great many ways, some of which I have only recently recognized. In Federalist 65, Alexander Hamilton wrote that an impeachment is likely to ignite the public's "animosities, partialities, influence, and interest." That prediction, penned in 1788, became reality in 1998 and 1999. From the start, I knew that this job, done diligently, wasn't going to win me any popularity contests. And I was right. The partisan attacks, which began early in my tenure, escalated a thousand-fold last year.

I once believed that this partisan assault was a purely personal hardship. I came to realize that the impact is larger. It has hindered the investigation. Consider: About 5% of all federal criminal trials end with a hung jury, when jurors cannot reach a unanimous verdict. In this investigation, 75% of trials have produced hung juries. In the first of these, in 1996, the jurors apparently had a good-faith dispute over the evidence. But in our two trials earlier this year, some people entered the jury room with agendas. Even judges sometimes appear to be swayed by politics. In such cases, we have almost always prevailed in a higher court. But the appeals consume time and resources.

Regrettably, the independent counsel's work is not yet complete. We completed the Little Rock investigations, and we made a great deal of progress toward a final report. But there are still important decisions to be made. Because of the public's apparent distrust, these are decisions that I could not prudently make. That's why, after thorough consultation with my colleagues in the office, I decided to resign.

Ideally, the office would close and the Justice Department would take over all pending matters. If a matter raised a conflict of interest, as some presumably would, the attorney general would assign it to a special counsel like Mr. Fiske. The department, however, rejected this approach, so the Independent Counsel office must continue—in the superb hands of Robert Ray.

I depart with a handful of regrets. We should not have sought or accepted additional jurisdiction from the Justice Department. There were strong reasons for doing so—often the new matter involved evidence with which we were already familiar—but in retrospect it was a mistake. Moving beyond Whitewater/Madison slowed our progress, increased our costs, and fostered a damaging perception of empire building.

I regret, too, that I did not try harder to explain myself and our work to the public. I believed, as my ethics adviser put it, that an independent counsel is above all a prosecutor, and prosecutors in our system speak only in court. But we were subjected to assaults that ordinary prosecutors never face. I should have answered them.

And I keenly regret that I cannot finish the job I undertook five years ago. But I do not for a moment regret my appointment or my tenure as independent counsel.

Holding federal office is a humbling experience and a high privilege. I did not seek this responsibility, but I have done my best to uphold the public interest in each and every decision.

It has been my privilege to work with scores of diligent, highly skilled lawyers and investigators. When I think back on what we accomplished together—the facts we uncovered, the strategic decisions we made, the indictments we brought, the indictments we decided not to bring, the record we built—I am gratified.

Mr. Starr, a former federal judge and solicitor general, was Whitewater independent counsel.

REVIEW & OUTLOOK

Asides

What Trie Got

After pleading guilty to a felony in the 1996 Democratic fund-raising scandal, Bill Clinton's friend Charlie Trie was fined $5,000 and sentenced to four months' home detention and four years' probation. The judge actually had to stiffen the sentence beyond the Justice prosecutors' pitch for simple probation. At this rate, guys will be volunteering to take the campaign-finance fall, assuming the stakes are high enough.

Editorial Feature

Swap Schemes: Campaign Finance On Trial

BY MICAH MORRISON

A federal jury in New York will soon decide whether former International Brotherhood of Teamsters political director William Hamilton is guilty of a conspiracy to embezzle $850,000 in union funds to illegally aid the 1996 re-election effort of then-Teamster President Ron Carey. The arcane case has received scant media attention, but a wakeup call may be on the way. A conviction of Mr. Hamilton could open the door to a criminal conspiracy prosecution that would rock the Democratic Party.

Mary Jo White

U.S. Attorney Mary Jo White brought a five-count indictment against Mr. Hamilton, charging him with conspiring to divert funds from the Teamsters' treasury, embezzlement of union funds, mail fraud, wire fraud and false statements. Two conspirators, former Carey campaign manager Jere Nash and liberal activist Michael Ansara, pleaded guilty to siphoning union funds and testified for the government at the trial.

The case is not about the technicalities of campaign-finance laws. At issue is the misuse of Teamster funds contributed by the rank-and-file to sway an internal election.

"Money poured out of the Teamsters' General Treasury Fund like water from an open faucet," Robert Rice, Ms. White's lead prosecutor, told the jury. Under federal law, it is illegal to use money from a union treasury to promote the candidacy of anyone running for union office. Union dues, in other words, could not be used to fund Mr. Carey's campaign against James Hoffa, son of the legendary labor leader.

But it is legal to use union money to make certain other types of political contributions. For example, donations to issue-advocacy groups that lobby voters and contributions for get-out-the-vote drives are permitted.

Mr. Hamilton reported to Mr. Carey and was in charge of Teamster political donations. The prosecution charges that he and his alleged co-conspirators cooked up a series of swap schemes to generate and conceal illegal donations to Mr. Carey. Mr. Hamilton donated Teamster funds to voter-education and -mobilization groups that had been enlisted in the alleged scheme. In return, the prosecution says, these groups or their friends made donations to the Carey campaign or retired debts owed by the campaign.

Mr. Rice told the jury that in the early fall of 1996, "$885,000 poured out of the Teamsters' General Treasury Fund under the guise of political contributions to four organizations." In exchange for those contributions, "$325,000 from other sources was kicked back to benefit the Carey re-election effort."

A parade of witnesses detailed the serpentine schemes. The services of top officials of the Clinton-Gore re-election effort, the Democratic National Committee and the AFL-CIO were enlisted, according to trial testimony. Some of the fund-transfer allegations cited during the trial involve Terry McAuliffe, today a senior Democratic Party fund-raiser and in 1996 head of the Clinton-Gore re-election effort; Mr. Carey, whose 1996 re-election to head the Teamsters was later voided due to the scandal; and AFL-CIO Secretary-Treasurer Richard Trumka, who asserted his Fifth Amendment privilege when questioned by government investigators. While these men have not been charged, evidence introduced by Ms. White's team suggests that the conspiracy to violate election laws reached much higher than Mr. Hamilton.

One of Mr. Hamilton's alleged co-conspirators, political consultant Martin Davis, approached top Democratic Party officials as part of the scheme, Mr. Rice told the jury. Mr. Davis went to Mr.

McAuliffe in search of money. "McAuliffe put Davis in touch with Laura Hartigan, the finance director of the Clinton-Gore committee," Mr. Rice said. "Laura Hartigan, in turn, put Davis in touch with Richard Sullivan, the finance director of the Democratic National Committee." Mr. Davis pleaded guilty to conspiring to funnel union funds and agreed to cooperate with the prosecution. But as Mr. Hamilton's trial neared, Mr. Davis apparently had second thoughts; he did not appear as a witness. His plea bargain with the government is now "under review," Mr. Rice said.

Mr. Hamilton's attorney, Robert Gage, opened a three-pronged defense last week. First, all the Teamster contributions were made in good faith to "legitimate organizations" that had "important relationships with labor," Mr. Gage told the jury in his opening statement. Second, 1996 was a tumultuous election year, and Democrats were desperate to defeat "the Gingrich Congress." Finally, the conspiracy was executed by Mr. Nash and Mr. Davis, not his client.

Mr. Gage plays a tricky political card in the courtroom. His first witness was Sarah Weddington, the matronly Texas lawyer who fought Roe v. Wade to the Supreme Court. A character witness, she played no part in the alleged swap schemes. Smiling broadly at the seven women on the jury, she declared that Mr. Hamilton was "one of the most honest people I've ever known."

But juries are notoriously fickle, and the pander on abortion and Mr. Gingrich may not go over well. Out of the jury's presence, Judge Thomas Griesa summed up the case: The issue is "whether Mr. Hamilton approved certain contributions . . . in order to procure contributions indirectly for the Ronald Carey campaign."

The defense has yet to rest its case. But if the jury puts the swap notion foremost in its deliberations, Mr. Hamilton could be looking at a serious problem. And Ms. White, a rising star in Democratic Party legal circles, would be looking at one of the toughest decisions of her career: whether to proceed with a conspiracy case against some of the most powerful figures in her own party.

Mr. Morrison is a Journal editorial page writer.

REVIEW & OUTLOOK

Asides

Starry Eyed

Some unreported news from the impeachment vindication front: A three-judge federal appeals court recently ruled that Ken Starr had not, contrary to White House propaganda, illegally leaked grand jury secrets. Clinton lawyer David Kendall then filed for a rehearing before the entire D.C. Circuit. He lost, 11-0.

Meanwhile, FBI Director Louis Freeh recently sent Mr. Starr a remarkable thank you letter that predictably has been ignored in the press. FBI men and women "have all been greatly impressed with your sacrifice, persistence, and uncompromising personal and professional integrity," Mr. Freeh wrote on Oct. 19.

"In all of your many dealings with FBI personnel, Divisions, Field Offices and Headquarters elements, we have been continuously impressed with your integrity and professionalism. You have always respected the truth, and have never engaged in any misleading or evasive conduct or practice. Your single objective has been the promotion of justice and the safeguarding of the judicial process."

Enough said.

REVIEW & OUTLOOK

Where's Janet?

Looks like we have company. For some time, we have covered the battle waged by the Landmark Legal Foundation to get the IRS to explain why an extraordinary number of think tanks and organizations that might reasonably be described as Clinton opponents suddenly found themselves audited in the mid-1990s. To determine whether this was an astounding coincidence or part of a more sinister effort to use the IRS to go after political enemies, the Landmark people have sought the answer to one question: Who asked the IRS to investigate whom?

Theirs has been a largely solitary battle, fought over tedious legal terrain. Even so, they have managed to extract some telling nuggets the IRS and its politician friends would as soon not have you know. The growing stench is attracting some of our colleagues in the Fourth Estate, notably the Associated Press, Fox News and ABC News.

This week, for example, the AP baldly stated that "officials in the Democratic White House and members of both parties in Congress have prompted hundreds of audits of political opponents in the 1990s. The audit requests ranged from the forwarding of constituent letters and newspaper articles alleging wrongdoing to personal demands for audits from members of Congress." Former Rep. David Skaggs (D., Colo.) was named as one of the latter, fingering the Heritage Foundation and Citizens Against Government Waste. Both found themselves the subject of audits within two months of the IRS's getting Mr. Skaggs's letter.

The IRS position is incredible. It says letters from politicians asking that someone be audited are confidential tax-return information. But then it makes sure that such requests track through the case files. It is hard for us to understand why the officer looking into whether the Heritage Foundation should be audited would need to see that Congressman Skaggs wanted just such an audit. Republicans, to be sure, also have played this game, but we don't know yet know the degree because the IRS refuses to release the information. What we know is that there are a raft of conservative outfits complaining about audits and no corresponding complaints from liberal ones.

Indeed, at this stage we don't know whether forwarding possible targets on to the IRS is just another thing Congressmen do, or whether there was a campaign among outfits to get constituents to write letters to their Congressmen suggesting audits of their political enemies, which would then be forwarded on (thus providing the Congressmen with cover). We don't even know the nature of those hundreds of communications between Congress and the IRS and the White House and the IRS that have not been released. In short, not least of the scandals here is that going on three years after Landmark first filed its FOIA request, we have yet to move out of the discovery phase. It is hard to reconcile this stonewalling on the part of the IRS and its attorneys at the Justice Department with Janet Reno's May 1997 memo to all agency heads about the imperative for "following the spirit as well as the letter of the [Freedom of Information] Act, and applying a presumption of disclosure."

Specifically, there remain three unresolved issues that would reveal much about what was going on at the IRS.

• Landmark wants to ask an IRS official about 114 relevant case files, which have inexplicably gone missing. The Justice Department is dead set against it, and has asked the judge to say no.

• Landmark wants to ask the IRS official who handled the FOIA request for "any" information about third party audit requests why he did not include the Commissioner's files in his search. The Justice Department again says they can't have it.

• Finally, Landmark has asked for a key tape recording of a San Francisco meeting in which IRS official Terry Hallihan is alleged to have talked about the shredding of files and ways to conceal the fact that audit requests came from a Congressman. At first the IRS denied the tape existed; now it says that it was the personal tape of an employee, which anyway has been recorded over with music and another meeting. Justice is asking the judge to say Landmark can't have this, either.

Those who remember Watergate know that Richard Nixon complained bitterly about his enemies, and many times told aides to have these people audited. How many times during the Clinton impeachment hearings did the likes of Richard Ben Veniste, Marty Meehan, Liz Holtzman and Lawrence Tribe tell us that sex was nothing compared with the scandal of politicizing the IRS? As Congress rightly appreciated in 1974, this constituted a grave abuse of power and a direct assault on the First Amendment. Less well known is that a Congressional investigation determined that the IRS largely resisted Nixon's attempts to politicize it—much to Nixon's evident frustration.

Unlike Nixon's foes, however, it is a matter of record that many of Clinton's enemies were audited. And that politicians were instigating such audits. If the First Amendment means anything, surely it means that an American has a right to agitate for his views without having it result in the IRS looking over his books. What is it that Janet Reno and Justice so desperately do not want us to see?

November 22, 1999

REVIEW & OUTLOOK

Ms. White's Conviction

On Friday the U.S. Attorney for the Southern District of New York, Mary Jo White, did what Attorney General Janet Reno has so conspicuously failed to do for the past three years: bring home a significant conviction in a campaign-finance case. While "reformers" clamor for more campaign-finance laws, the ones on the books are not enforced. Worse, the flag of "campaign finance" is offered as a cover for all sorts of otherwise illegal activity, such as stealing money from your fiduciaries.

Mary Jo White

This defense did not work in the trial of William Hamilton, former political director of the International Brotherhood of Teamsters. A Federal jury convicted him on all counts in a conspiracy to embezzle $885,000 in union funds to aid the 1996 re-election effort of then-Teamster President Ron Carey. Testimony at the trial included accounts of illegal money-laundering schemes involving the AFL-CIO, the Democratic National Committee and liberal activist groups. Having won this stunning conviction, Ms. White must now decide whether to pursue higher-ups—notably Mr. Carey and Richard Trumka, the treasurer of the AFL-CIO—who were implicated by evidence offered at the trial.

"Trial testimony revealed that several other individuals participated in the conspiracy that looted the Teamster treasury," current

Teamster President James P. Hoffa said in a statement issued after the convictions. "We urge U.S. Attorney Mary Jo White and the Justice Department to pursue these individuals to the fullest extent of the law." Mr. Hoffa further noted that the funds in question have not been returned to the Teamster treasury, saying he has directed the union's attorneys to prepare "appropriate legal action" to recover them. So the Teamsters may bring a triple-damages suit against the AFL-CIO, or at least its treasurer. Trial testimony also included references to roles played by other prominent unions in parts of the conspiracy, most notably Gerald McEntee's American Federation of State, County & Municipal Employees and Andy Stern's Service Employees International Union.

Also implicated by trial testimony is Terry McAuliffe, all-purpose Clinton-Gore fund-raiser. Just last week, Mr. McAuliffe hosted a $200,000 fund-raiser for the Gore campaign in honor of Tony Coelho, the Gore campaign chief. Last week we also learned, through a Freedom of Information Act action by ABC News, that Stephen Potts, director of the Office of Government Ethics, wrote a letter to the White House complaining about its statements on his office's view of the now-canceled arrangements under which Mr. McAuliffe would back the Clintons' home purchase. It seems the President lied in saying the ethics office had ruled this was not a gift under government rules. The crowd now at the top of the vice president's 2000 campaign suggests that a Gore administration would continue the law-enforcement practices of the Clinton administration.

Mr. McAuliffe's efforts to aid Mr. Carey—finding a donor for his campaign in return for larger Teamster contributions to the Democratic Party—did not succeed in moving money. Richard Ben-Veniste, his lawyer, says his client did no wrong. But it would be instructive to learn if a jury agrees; the conspiracy laws can be broadly construed.

The Hamilton verdict establishes that money definitely did move from the Teamster Treasury to the Carey campaign. In his opening statement, lead prosecutor Robert Rice detailed the involvement of Mr. Carey and Mr. Trumka. Mr. Hamilton asked Mr. Carey to approve a $150,000 contribution to the AFL, which had not then requested the money. The next day Mr. Trumka submitted a request for the $150,000 and told an accountant that some money might be coming in, which should be sent to the activist group Citizen Action. Carey approved the $150,000, which ended up at Citizen Action. Then $100,000 was sent to another body, the November Group, where it was used to reduce fees owed by the Carey re-election campaign.

The prosecution presented a parade of witnesses testifying to various aspects of the elaborate swap schemes and ruses that generated the illegal donations for Mr. Carey. Phone messages, faxes, phony invoices and a cascade of hefty checks formed the basis of the paper trail. As Mr. Rice said, "Money poured out of the Teamsters' General Treasury Fund like water from an open faucet."

Ms. White has to determine whether the leaders of organized labor can be allowed to play this way with their members' money. By the way, in the Beck decision, the Supreme Court has ruled that union members that do not agree with political contributions by their leaders are entitled to refunds on their dues; days after taking office, the Clinton administration rescinded Bush administration Labor Department regulations setting up procedures to enforce this rule. Beck, like campaign finance, is a law Clinton Justice has simply decided to ignore.

Mr. Hamilton's attorneys have pledged to appeal, but he might be wiser to cooperate. He faces as much as 30 years in prison and over $1 million in fines and restitution when he comes for sentencing before U.S. District Judge Thomas Griesa.

The burden of deciding how far to carry this case, though, now rests with Ms. White. Will she proceed with a broad criminal conspiracy case against some of the most powerful figures in both organized labor and the Democratic Party? Her resounding victory in the Hamilton case is reason to press on, and it would be reassuring to learn that even in the Clinton administration there are prosecutors professional enough to go where the evidence leads them.

The Most Corrupt Administration Ever

The year 2000 opened with hard-fought primary battles in both the Republican and Democratic camps. One of the GOP candidates, Sen. Orrin Hatch of Utah, hit a nerve with a televised address condemning the Clinton-Gore administration. Sen. Hatch detailed a litany of improper and illegal practices. "After assessing the investigations, indictments and numerous top-level resignations covering a gamut of departments in this administration, we have to confront the possibility—however sad, however tragic—that when those investigations are finally over, this administration may be remembered as the most deceitful and corrupt in our nation's history."

The New Hampshire primary presented the first of many twists and turns in what would prove to be a tumultuous political year. It also signaled an election-year theme, the Journal noted. "Bill Clinton was the 800-pound gorilla in the New Hampshire primary. More precisely, the issue of presidential character is the election's 800-pound gorilla."

In March, an associate of Vice President Gore, Maria Hsia, was convicted of five felony counts in the Buddhist Temple affair, an illegal fund-raiser that had come to symbolize the wrongdoing of the 1996 campaign finance scandal. Reports of a long-suppressed Justice Department memo into the campaign finance affair also began to appear in the press. The memo, by former Justice Department campaign finance task force head Charles La Bella, bitterly took top Justice officials to task for refusing to appoint an independent counsel to investigate President Clinton, Vice President Gore and other senior administration figures.

As Sen. Hatch had noted, the character of the Clinton Administration was reflected in a long series of scandals and questionable practices. One serious question was whether the Internal Revenue Service was auditing opponents of the White House. The Journal supported efforts by independent organizations to get to the truth. The IRS should "explain why an extraordinary number of think tanks and organizations that might reasonably be described as Clinton opponents suddenly found themselves audited in the mid-1990s."

Questions about the Administration's impact on the institutions of government also arose when the Chief U.S. District Court judge for the District of Columbia came under scrutiny for directing five scandal-related prosecutions to judges appointed by President Clinton. And as the Independent Counsel sought to wrap up his investigation, speculation mounted about the possible indictment of Hillary Rodham Clinton in the Whitewater and Travel Office affairs.

Editorial Feature

Will Mrs. Clinton Be Indicted?

BY BARBARA K. OLSON

Hillary Rodham Clinton's transformation from her husband's campaign manager and chief apologist to a politician in her own right moved closer to fruition this week. On Tuesday, two 26-foot moving vans lumbered onto Old House Lane in Chappaqua, N.Y., to disgorge Mrs. Clinton's possessions into her new home. The White House insisted that the Clintons had paid their own moving bills and delivered their own furniture. But it was hard not to doubt this assertion, given that White House secretary Carolyn Huber, a former assistant at the Rose Law Firm, was in charge of unpacking in Chappaqua. Ms. Huber, remember, had earned her 15 minutes of fame by "discovering" missing Whitewater billing records in a White House residence room Mrs. Clinton was using.

One of the more remarkable election campaigns in this nation's history thus moves from its "listening" phase onto less gossamer footing. At least the first candidate will now have an ostensible residence in the state she seeks to represent in Congress. But Mrs. Clinton's legal problems aren't over. The independent counsel investigation, which Kenneth Starr in October turned over to veteran New York prosecutor Robert Ray, continues. Last week Rep. Steve Buyer (R., Ind.) one of the House impeachment managers, speculated that Mrs. Clinton is running for office in order to avoid prosecution. "It insulates her because Republicans are now saying the independent counsel can't go out and indict the first lady because of the impact that that's going to have on Republicans," Mr. Buyer said.

Whatever Mrs. Clinton's motives, Democrats seem determined to see her win. On Tuesday the Washington Post reported that the first lady had raised hundreds of thousands of dollars in soft money that goes into a special Democratic Party account designed to skirt federal campaign-finance limits. This is a sure sign that campaign adviser Harold Ickes, who orchestrated Bill Clinton's fund-raising abuses in 1996, is hard at work again. Sen. Robert Torricelli, chairman of the Democratic Senatorial Campaign Committee, told reporters that his party would do—and spend—"whatever is required to win" the New York Senate race.

Moving day: She's a New Yorker, but her legal problems may not be over.

AP Photo/Bridget Besaw Gorman

An indictment of Mrs. Clinton would certainly complicate that effort. Although not much is known about where Mr. Ray is headed, speculation continues in Washington—and in New York—that the independent counsel's office has considered and is still considering an indictment. I know firsthand that there is plenty of evidence of misconduct by Mrs. Clinton. For several years, as a House congressional committee chief investigator and later as general counsel to the Senate's assistant majority leader, I investigated the first lady's role in numerous Clinton scandals. She responded under oath to 26 questions presented by our committee. What might an indictment of Mrs. Clinton look like? Here are some possibilities:

● **The Travel Office firings.** In spite of her denials, we now know that Mrs. Clinton was the driving force behind the firing of seven career employees in the White House Travel Office in 1993. The Clintons had every right to make these personnel moves, but they had no right to smear the people they were firing, to drag the FBI into the rationalization for their decision, or to press a Justice

Department prosecution of Billy Dale, fired head of the Travel Office, whom a jury acquitted after a few minutes' deliberation. And Mrs. Clinton could be indicted for concealing her role in the affair and lying repeatedly to the House committee and federal investigators about it.

● **The FBI files.** There is ample evidence that the first lady had a larger role than she has been willing to acknowledge in hiring Craig Livingstone, the former nightclub bouncer recruited to head the White House Office of Personnel Security. Mr. Livingstone and his assistant Anthony Marceca requisitioned hundreds of confidential personnel files on Republicans from the FBI, which the FBI dutifully shipped to these White House political operatives.

The full use to which the White House put these records has never been disclosed, but there is some indication that they may have been combed for data to include in the infamous White House database. That operation involved the merging of Democratic Party political records with sensitive and confidential White House information to create a resource bank for future political operations. Several sources have made it clear that the White House database was a pet project of Mrs. Clinton's from the beginning. Her efforts to hide her role in this scheme could lead to indictments for perjury and obstruction of justice.

● **Whitewater.** Mr. Starr apparently concluded that he had no legal authority to seek an indictment of a sitting president. But Mr. Clinton could yet face indictment after his term ends for lying and perhaps for helping to fleece a federally insured savings institution. And if anything, Mrs. Clinton—who has testified in the Whitewater inquiry six times—had a more direct and incriminating role in that scandal than her husband. The evidence is overwhelming that she worked more intensively on Whitewater matters than she ever admitted.

The billing records onto which Ms. Huber stumbled had been subject to congressional and independent counsel subpoenas for months. They might have been among the documents in White House deputy counsel Vince Foster's office the night of his death. When those billing records were finally examined, they showed that Mrs. Clinton's involvement in the underlying savings-and-loan misconduct while she was a lawyer at the Rose firm in Arkansas was much greater than she had stated.

Her possible role in hiding these records from the investigators is an important area of vulnerability as we saw in the indictment of Webster Hubbell, which identified Mrs. Clinton more than 30 times as the "1985-86 billing partner." Moreover, her conduct—and that of her chief of staff, Maggie Williams and White House counsel Bernard Nussbaum—in collecting and concealing records from Foster's office has also never been satisfactorily explained, and could be part of a perjury and obstruction of justice indictment.

Mr. Hubbell pleaded guilty to evading taxes on income he received during the period he was to be cooperating with the independent counsel. The money was labeled "hush money" by the U.S. Court of Appeals for the District of Columbia and an indictment for conspiracy to obstruct justice would follow against Mrs. Clinton if she were linked to those funds.

- **Obstruction of justice in the Lewinsky matter.** Mr. Clinton undoubtedly concealed his affair with Monica Lewinsky from his wife as well as his advisers and lawyers. Once the scandal was out in the open, however, there is no doubt that Mrs. Clinton was a key operator in developing the corrupt legal strategy and the vicious public relations war the White House waged to keep the president in office. We know that Sidney Blumenthal and James Carville, both close to the first lady, were instrumental in the efforts to discredit Ms. Lewinsky and Mr. Starr, respectively. We don't know how far Mr. Starr and Mr. Ray have gone to investigate these efforts to impede their investigation. But conduct far less questionable has been prosecuted in the past.

Sen. Torricelli's determination to do "whatever is required to win" Mrs. Clinton's Senate race is reminiscent of Mr. Clinton's statement to Dick Morris when the Lewinsky scandal broke that he would "just have to win." As anyone who has followed the Clintons will know, this is their longstanding modus operandi. And as I learned in writing a book about Mrs. Clinton, victory at any expense has been a bedrock element in her lifelong drive for political power. Mrs. Clinton has found that a take-no-prisoners approach to legal obstacles works, and that she can get away with it. It will be interesting to see whether Mr. Ray and his prosecutors have the evidence and prosecutorial resolve to teach her otherwise.

Ms. Olson is a Washington lawyer and author of "Hell to Pay: The Unfolding Story of Hillary Rodham Clinton" (Regnery, 1999).

Editorial Feature

The Most Corrupt Administration Ever

BY ORRIN HATCH

These are excerpts from a televised address by the senator, a Republican presidential candidate, airing this week in New Hampshire and Iowa:

We need to look at what happened right after the Clinton-Gore administration's re-election in 1996. In fact, even before the campaign was over, the revelations started. More word of attempts by the administration to politically misuse the power of federal agencies like the FBI, the Secret Service, the Immigration Service and even the Census Bureau. Disturbing allegations that the IRS was retaliating against political opponents of the administration. Questionable practices or abuses of power at the Commerce Department, the Interior Department and Housing and Urban Development. . . .

And then came still more revelations . . . including allegations of the misuses of government power to raise millions upon millions in illegal campaign contributions. Not just that the Lincoln bedroom had a political purpose and a price. Not just that the White House was open to suspicious characters—despite official warnings—who purchased access to the president and various federal departments with their checkbooks. Even beyond that, the White House saw frequent visits by a bagman for the Riady family of Indonesia [which is] tied to Chinese business and government interests and—hard as this is to believe—another fund-raiser who was indirectly tied to a high official of the Chinese army. . . .

The administration's answer was a frightening echo of the Watergate scandal: "Everybody does it." But the fact is, that isn't true. No administration in our history has ever had a political fundraiser in such a high position in government who was so closely tied to foreign interests, allowed him not only repeated access to the White House but [to] CIA briefings and top-secret clearances, and then made him privy to the United States' positions in trade negotiations. The administration had also altered those positions in ways that were favorable to these foreign interests. And, finally, all this occurred as allegations cropped up of missile technology transfers and a massive breach of U.S. nuclear secrets by the Chinese government. . . .

Faced with an astonishing range of allegations about illegal activities, from perjury by administration officials before Congress to damaging missile technology transfers and even theft of nuclear secrets, the Justice Department did not pursue corruption but thwarted its own lead attorney in the investigation as well as FBI Director Louis Freeh. After refusing to follow the dictates of law and appoint an independent counsel to thoroughly investigate the illegal fund-raising . . . the department arranged highly questionable, even sweetheart, plea bargains with key wrongdoers who might have provided damaging testimony. . . .

After assessing the investigations, indictments and numerous top-level resignations covering a gamut of departments in this administration, we have to confront the possibility—however sad, however tragic—that when those investigations are finally over, this administration may be remembered as the most deceitful and corrupt in our nation's history.

Just ask yourself: What other administration has ever, to this extent, used the awesome power of the White House and federal departments to assure its political survival even when this meant politically intervening with civil and criminal investigations? What administration refused to hold accountable so many officials and political allies—most of them lawyers—for casually defying congressional committees with the false testimony of chronic memory loss? What other administration seemed to get away with diligently fighting and discrediting not just a court-appointed independent counsel investigating corruption, but even punishing one of its own Justice Department lawyers, Charles La Bella, for urging vigorous investigation? And what other administration has so callously defied subpoenas and held back documents and, when forced to disclose them, routinely released them on Friday afternoons—and then all but openly gloated at their ability to thwart any real media attention? . . .

The first step in putting all this right and setting out to rescue the democratic process is reasserting this: There is an antidote to all the blab, falsehood and duplicity of modern political campaigning. It's the biggest breakthrough, the greatest technological marvel ever invented in politics. It's called the truth. The power of the truth. Telling the simple unvarnished truth. And counting on the people to recognize it, feel its magnetic pull, signal their approval and rally to its support. . . .

I am disturbed that the current front-runner in the race for the Republican nomination for the presidency doesn't really want to speak to this issue. And the second-place candidate in the polls wants to make simplistic charges about "special interests" and calls for even more rules and restrictions on political speech and activity that would make it impossible for an opposition party to raise the issues of corruption. We must point out how "the corrupt system" is really about a unique and historic brand of wrongdoing by a new class of elitist liberals and political power-seekers who appear to think themselves above the people and unaccountable to them.

Editorial Feature

Pertinent Question: Will GOP Duck Clinton Character?

By Robert L. Bartley

With Sen. Orrin Hatch hovering at 1% in the polls, nothing he says or does is likely to have a big impact on the outcome of the

Orrin Hatch

Republican primaries. Yet when he challenges the front-runners to speak up on the Clinton administration's ethical failures, they should start thinking about the November election.

The Hatch challenge came in his 28-minute paid TV broadcast on local stations in Iowa and New Hampshire, excerpted on this page Jan. 13. "At the center of the national crisis of morale and trust," Sen. Hatch said, "is probably the worst breach of faith with the American people by a federal administration in our history." Yet the Republican front-runner "doesn't really want to speak to this issue," while his leading opponent talks only of "special interests" and campaign finance rules.

"We must point out how 'the corrupt system' is really about a unique and historic brand of wrongdoing," he continued. We confront "a new ethos in politics that says whenever a politician wants to halt a corruption investigation, he not only stonewalls the probe but claims a vast conspiracy against him and then launches embittered political attacks on law enforcement authorities and congressional committees." And, "Defenders of the administration say: 'This isn't

Watergate.' And, you know, they're right. It's worse than Watergate."

However Sen. Hatch finishes in Iowa and New Hampshire, any eventual GOP nominee will have to decide whether he should campaign by holding Democrats responsible for the ethical standards of the Clinton administration. So far the issue has been the proverbial unmentioned elephant in the corner of the GOP campaign. Yes, everyone talks vaguely of restoring dignity to the presidency. But when the Journal's Dorothy Rabinowitz queried the candidates last spring after the impeachment vote, she was told the feeling at Bush headquarters was that it was "time to move on." John McCain seems more outraged by currently legal campaign contributions than by already illegal ones.

Yet the issue of presidential character has dominated the last eight years of our national life, with Travel Office firings, a White House suicide, disappearing billing records, campaign contributions from the Chinese military, botched national security investigations and on and on. And Democrats almost to a man have been complicit in the coverup.

None more so than the likely nominee, Vice President Al Gore. He has his own connections with many of the suspicious parties that predate the appearance of Bill Clinton in Washington, and has populated his campaign staff from the party's hardball wing. Will we see Republican ads featuring the vice president intoning "no controlling legal authority," or asserting that impeachment was "a great disservice to a man I believe will be regarded in the history books as one of our greatest presidents"?

Perhaps the moment merely hasn't arrived. Gov. Bush spent the primary season developing an issues platform, rather than appearing to run an anti-Clinton campaign to avenge his father's defeat. His people suggest that there will be plenty of time for the character issue when the nomination is settled and the contest is with a Democrat.

Perhaps, but in the last two GOP campaigns a different logic prevailed. Raising a character issue involves "going negative," risking the wrath of pundits and other high-minded souls. Besides, there's a feeling that the voters (1) want to forget about Monica Lewinsky and Paula Jones, (2) feel that talk of Chinese spies, billing records and the like only reminds them of Monica and Paula, and (3) are anyway so disgusted with it all they will vote against Democrats without being reminded of why they should.

So in 1996 Bob Dole hesitated to raise the ethics issue until the middle of October, when it seemed a matter of desperation rather than conviction. In 1998, with an impeachment inquiry already under way, the congressional campaign masterminded by Newt Gingrich didn't broadcast ads on ethics except in a few districts in the last week of the campaign. This was not enough to have an impact, just enough to allow critics to call the issue discredited. In both cases, restraint did not keep Democrats from running ads telling lies about Republican positions on Medicare and other issues—not considered as "negative" as ads telling the truth about presidential character.

So Sen. Dole was roundly defeated, and Speaker Gingrich's Republicans lost seats. When the House nonetheless voted up a bill of impeachment, the political seers predicted that fire and brimstone would fall on the House managers who talked of ethics and even sex on national television. But the impeachment managers somehow seem politically healthy in the impending election. Indeed, standing up for morality has been a political plus.

So Sen. Hatch may be doing his party a favor by reminding the eventual nominee what needs to be said. When properly reminded, a good many Americans are likely to agree with him:

"We also have to acknowledge the bold, steady, instinctive use of all the modern means of communication to dissemble, mislead and fool the people as well as to cover up official corruption. Such actions really are something new and something terribly dangerous. This routine practice of political deception to hide an inner falsity—this institutionalization of the cynical deceit that you've not done anything wrong if you can talk your way out of it—is the real cultural legacy of this administration. And is at the heart of what disturbs us about the corrosion in our political system."

Mr. Bartley is editor of the Journal.

REVIEW & OUTLOOK

Judicial Discretion

A few days ago, the Associated Press's Pete Yost reported on one of the lingering ghosts of the Clinton scandals: "Addressing a growing controversy, federal judges in the nation's capital killed a rule that enabled the chief judge to send prosecutions against friends and supporters of President Clinton to his judicial appointees." In the normally well-cloaked world of judicial procedure, this is a very big deal. As far as we can make out from a large database search, the AP story was picked up by next to no major news outlets.

Norma Holloway Johnson

Last month, Rep. Howard Coble, chairman of the House Judiciary subcommittee on courts and intellectual property, reported that Chief U.S. District Court Judge Norma Holloway Johnson directed five scandal-related prosecutions in Washington to judges appointed by President Clinton. Cases are usually assigned on a random computer-selected basis. Rep. Coble is seeking a judicial inquiry into Judge Johnson's conduct.

This past summer, the Associated Press also disclosed that Judge Johnson had directed cases against Presidential pal Webster Hubbell and fund-raiser Charlie Trie to Clinton appointees. Judge James Robertson was assigned the Hubbell case in April 1998. Judge Paul Friedman was assigned the Trie case in January 1998. Later, Judge

Friedman was assigned the cases of campaign finance figures Maria Hsia and Pauline Kanchanalak.

The jury was seated this week in Ms. Hsia's trial, which begins next Monday. She figured prominently in the famous 1996 event featuring Vice President Gore at a Buddhist temple in California, about which Mr. Gore famously announced, "I did not know it was a fundraiser." The Gore-Hsia financial relationship, dating back to 1989, is elucidated in the current issue of Fortune magazine.

The matters newly revealed last month include the assignment of the case of Mark Jimenez, a fugitive from the Justice Department's campaign-finance probe, to Judge Friedman (who, it should be noted, drove the internal review that had resulted in abolishing the discretionary assignment rule). And hearings regarding Miami businessman and Democratic fund-raiser Howard Glicken were assigned to Judge Henry Kennedy, a 1997 Clinton appointee.

Mr. Glicken was charged with illegally soliciting a $20,000 campaign contribution and pleaded guilty. Judge Kennedy received a letter on Mr. Glicken's behalf from Vernon Jordan six days before the sentencing. Mr. Jordan noted that Mr. Glicken was an "active member in the Democratic Party" and requested "leniency." Mr. Glicken received a fine, probation and community service. Mr. Trie escaped with a slap on the wrist. The Hsia and Kanchanalak cases of course are pending.

In a letter to the U.S. Court of Appeals requesting an investigation, Rep. Coble asks: "Did Judge Johnson abuse her discretion" and "should she have allowed the normal random case-assignment to occur?" In an August letter to the Washington Times late last year, Judge Johnson defended her actions. It was her responsibility to "move the docket as expeditiously as possible," she wrote. She noted that District Court rules authorized the chief judge to assign complex cases to other judges when circumstances warrant.

Ironically, Judge Johnson herself issued the famous ruling denying President Clinton an executive privilege claim to prevent testimony by the Secret Service. Executive privilege, like the chief judge's ability to rationalize the court's case flow, were essentially prudential practices. Both now are casualties of the practices of the past seven years.

March 3, 2000

REVIEW & OUTLOOK

Mr. Gore's Scandal

Maybe now Senator Bill Bradley will get a response to his demand that Al Gore explain his appearance at a 1996 fund-raiser at a Buddhist temple in Hacienda Heights, California. Yesterday, a federal jury convicted Clinton-Gore fund-raiser Maria Hsia of five felony counts in the temple scheme and related events.

Here's the Vice President on the subject Wednesday evening, debating Mr. Bradley in Los Angeles just hours before the Hsia conviction came in: "I agree with Bill Bradley and John McCain on the need for campaign finance reform . . . I don't accept PAC contributions in this race. I called two years ago for the elimination of so-called soft money from campaigns. . . . If you will entrust me with the Presidency, I will put this in the highest priority category and make it happen."

In the meantime, a jury convicted Ms. Hsia of causing false election statements to be filed with the Federal Election Commission regarding fund raising at the Hsi Lai Buddhist Temple, the Hay-Adams Hotel in the capital, and the Century Plaza Hotel in Los Angeles. But it is the Gore temple event that resonates.

At Ms. Hsia's trial, evidence was presented that more than $100,000 was raised by the Vice President's appearance at the temple luncheon. Nuns were used as unwitting dupes in the conduit scheme to funnel funds to the Democrats. Clinton fund-raiser John Huang testified that Ms. Hsia passed him an envelope with $100,000 in checks. "I just took it with me and went with my wife to the airport," Mr. Huang told the court.

The tack taken by Mr. Gore, and others, on this subject is to offload the blame onto some vague entity called "special interests" who "taint" everyone with their money. No, this matter is about real people with real names. The big question outstanding in this scandal to which Maria Hsia was a party is the relationship of the President and the Vice President to the principal fund-raisers. The second big issue is the nature and means of the scandal's coverup. In every previous instance, investigations and prosecutions have hit a stone wall as they neared the President and Vice President. Two recent example are particularly relevant.

At the Hsia trial, Mr. Huang echoed Mr. Gore's lame, early description of the Buddhist temple event as "a community outreach event." Later in his testimony, Mr. Huang said that fund raising became mixed into the community event because of Mr. Gore's "tight" schedule, but that Mr. Gore "wasn't aware of the change." Mr. Huang has already cut a deal with the Justice Department, receiving one year of probation, a fine and community service.

Maria Hsia

Another of the Justice Department's wrist-slapped plea bargainers, Charlie Trie, was up on Capitol Hill this week testifying, if you can call it that, about his role in the scandal. Mr. Trie, recall, is the Clinton Arkansas crony who consorted with Macau gangsters, showed up at the White House with bags of cash and fled the country when the heat rose. Mr. Trie pleaded guilty last year and is serving a four-month home detention sentence.

Listen to this: "All of my mistakes were my own doing and not encouraged by President Clinton or anyone else," Mr. Trie told the House Government Reform Committee. He said the donors he brought to the White House "just wanted to go to events with important people and to get the opportunity to have our picture taken with the President of the United States." The White House line has been that these weren't fund-raisers. But Charlie Trie did allow to the committee that "It was . . . well known that it cost $50,000 to attend a coffee."

In 1998, Senator Fred Thompson's Governmental Affairs Committee voted out a report identifying Mr. Trie, Mr. Huang and Ms. Hsia as three of six individuals in the campaign finance scandal with ties to Beijing. Two others were James and Mochtar Riady, the money men behind many figures in the Clinton scandals. The Riadys "had a long-term relationship with a Chinese intelligence agency," the Thompson report noted. Ms. Hsia was identified as an "agent of the Chinese government," a charge her attorney has denounced as "absolutely false."

In Wednesday night's debate, Mr. Gore said, "I think we've talked about the issue of campaign finance reform in response to a previous question, but we can't talk about it too much." This doubtless could prove true in the months ahead. House Government Reform Committee Chairman Dan Burton noted during Mr. Trie's testimony that former White House aide Mark Middleton and Arkansas businessman Ernest Green are still under investigation. Kenneth Starr's successor, Independent Counsel Robert Ray, must soon settle a host of outstanding issues, the most important of which is whether to indict a President for perjury and obstruction of justice after he leaves the White House.

The Justice Department, fresh off victories in the Teamster election-fraud case and the Hsia trial, now faces important decisions about moving up the food chain. As Senator Thompson said yesterday of the Hsia conviction, "I don't know who's more surprised, me or the Justice Department."

And finally there is John McCain, who last time we looked was gaining ground when beating the drum of the Clinton-Gore scandals. He spent a tough week turning Bob Jones and Warren Rudman into household names. Maybe he should spend the weekend doing the same for Maria Hsia.

March 13, 2000

REVIEW & OUTLOOK

Learned His Lesson?

"I made a mistake, and I think the importance of making mistakes is what you learn from them," Vice President Al Gore said last week of his famous visit to the Buddhist Temple. "What I learned from it was the need for campaign finance reform."

So much for that, the presumptive Democratic Presidential nominee suggests. We need a batch of new campaign finance laws, he asserts, though others may see the problem as following and enforcing the laws already on the books. The week produced another flood of revelations depicting an ongoing coverup, obstruction of justice at the White House, and the deep and personal involvement of the Vice President and presumptive presidential nominee.

Al Gore

Indeed, with Tom Brokaw incredulous and the editors of the New York Times huffing about Janet Reno's Justice Department, we may even be headed into another of the periodic ethical firestorms that have marked the Clinton administration since the initial Whitewater allegations. Which may be precisely what the spinmeisters intended, since the Whitewater history proves the firestorms surge, but then subside. This comes at an ideal time, after the super-Tuesday campaign wrap-up and with the start of a congressional recess. In the face of an impending book by Impeachment Counsel David Schippers discussing the long-suppressed La Bella memo, pre-emptively leaking an edited version now may make it "old news" when the campaign begins in earnest.

Not that Friday's Los Angeles Times scoop by reporters Bill Rempel and Alan Miller is not damaging enough. It reports that the memo by former Department of Justice campaign-finance task-force leader Charles La Bella accused Justice Department top brass of using "intellectually dishonest" double standards, "gamesmanship" and "contortions" in justifying their refusal to appoint an independent counsel to investigate, among others, Mr. Gore. One wonders what the full version says.

The New York Times followed with another revelation, that the U.S. Attorney in Los Angeles was undertaking an investigation of Mr. Gore's Buddhist Temple fund-raiser, until ordered off the case by Lee Radek, the head of Justice's Public Integrity Section. Mr. Radek wrote that since the case had independent counsel implications, "your office should take no steps to investigate these matters at this time." It now appears that Mr. Radek then turned around and argued to Ms. Reno that the incident did not require the appointment of an independent counsel, and that she took his advice against Mr. La Bella, FBI chief Louis Freeh and other top Justice advisers.

The principal beneficiary of these decisions was Vice President Gore, now the standard-bearer for the Democratic Party and the Clinton historical legacy. Mr. Gore "may have provided false testimony," the La Bella report concludes, about his involvement in and knowledge of shady White House fund raising. He told investigators that he attended fund-raising sessions concerning "soft money," the unrestricted cash that flowed largely to television advertising by the Democratic National Committee and state party organizations. But he insisted these sessions did not raise "hard money"—funds going directly to the Clinton-Gore re-election effort.

The hair-splitting distinction is a legacy of our misguided campaign finance laws, of course, but is well understood by attorneys briefing Mr. Gore. His account was quickly contradicted by records, and has been shifting ever since. Confronted with notes and memos about a November 1995 meeting at the White House where hard money was discussed, Mr. Gore said he couldn't recall those conversations and memos. The latest explanation to surface comes in an FBI memo saying, "The Vice President also observed that he drank a lot of iced tea during meetings, which could have necessitated a restroom break."

The Vice President's account is now further undermined by the documents revealed in the L.A. Times. It turns out former White House chief of staff Leon Panetta told FBI agents that Mr. Gore was "attentively listening" to the hard-money discussion and "walking through the papers" at the November meeting. According to the Times, "These documents also indicate that the task force obtained photographs from that meeting showing Gore looking at papers that he did not recall reviewing."

Ms. Reno twice ruled that this evidence did not meet the threshold required for the appointment of an independent counsel, though much more stringent standards were applied in the case of lower-ranking officials. The L.A. Times reporters wrote that those benefiting from the double standards included not only the Vice President and President, but First Lady Hillary Rodham Clinton and former White House aide Harold M. Ickes, mastermind of her Senate campaign.

"It is the first indication that the task force was considering Mrs. Clinton's conduct in the fund-raising scandal," the reporters wrote. She and Mr. Ickes met with trustees of the Clinton legal defense fund to discuss contributions of money Charlie Trie had received via Macau. Although the illegal money was returned, Mr. La Bella argued that the President, the First Lady and Mr. Ickes may have violated a fiduciary responsibility in failing to alert the DNC, where Mr. Trie was a major fund-raiser.

Also on Friday, U.S. District Judge Royce Lamberth unsealed documents suggesting that the White House may have concealed thousands of e-mail messages under subpoena by Justice Department and congressional investigators. A White House contractor told the court that some of the e-mails deal with, among other things, "Vice President Al Gore's involvement in campaign fund-raising controversies." Back during the Watergate scandal, concealing items under subpoena was called an obstruction of justice.

Interest in Clinton administration abuse of the legal process waned when the House impeachment resolution was swept under the Senate rug. There seemed little remaining means of redress. Legal redress is one thing, but political redress another. Clearly Mr.

Clinton and those around him see the Gore candidacy as a vehicle of vindication for impeachment. But John McCain, becoming a national phenomenon on the strength of his anti-Clinton appeal, made clear that Clinton ethics are by no means dead as a political issue. After Friday's revelations, Governor Bush issued a perfectly proper statement, but he has never succeeded in making himself heard on the ethics issue. A full-throated and often-repeated condemnation would be the best thing he could possibly do to bring McCain voters into his camp.

In terms of legal redress, avenues are not completely closed. For one thing, the impeachment clause does not apply merely to Presidents but to "all civil Officers of the United States"—which is to say, an Attorney General who refuses to enforce the law. Instead, the Senate has just approved the elevation of the judge who presided over the John Huang wrist-slap without asking whether prosecution and defense were in collusion.

With Mr. Huang facing no real compulsion to provide evidence and Charlie Trie using his congressional testimony to apologize for causing problems for President Clinton, it's hard to follow a legal trail to the Oval Office, where the Clinton ethical transgressions start. The coverup has been successful, except that the President has not been able to avoid involvement in one particular. To wit, personal perjury.

Both Independent Counsel Kenneth Starr and Counsel Schippers alleged that Mr. Clinton committed multiple acts of perjury in his Aug. 17, 1998, testimony in the Monica Lewinsky matter. Article One of the House impeachment resolution charged the President with "perjurious" testimony to the grand jury about his relationship with Ms. Lewinsky, his attempts to influence witnesses, and statements he made under oath in a civil deposition in the Paula Jones sexual harassment lawsuit.

Last April, U.S. District Judge Susan Webber Wright determined that he had lied in the Jones lawsuit. Charging the President with contempt, Judge Wright fined him $90,000 for providing "false, misleading and evasive answers" in the sworn deposition. The Arkansas Bar has requested that Mr. Clinton defend himself against a motion for his disbarment; the deadline for a response is March 16. During the impeachment proceedings, the point that the President could after all be indicted for perjury after he left office was pressed by a retinue of Democrats—for example Senators Joseph Lieberman, John Breaux, Kent Conrad, Herbert Kohl, Richard Bryan, Frank Lautenberg and Barbara Boxer.

Whether to take their advice is the biggest question facing Mr. Starr's successor, Independent Counsel Robert Ray, and his prosecutorial discretion will depend partly on whether or not the ethics concerns fade or rise as the Presidential campaign proceeds. Perjury and obstruction of justice are not minor matters; the country should hear what Mr. Gore and Mr. Bush have to say about them. It is still not too late to prove that even Presidents are not above the law.

March 20, 2000

Editorial Feature

Another Clinton Victim: The Integrity of the Federal Courts

Justice is supposed to be blind, deciding the law without favoritism. But there is a gradual accumulation of evidence that points in a contrary direction—that when criminal cases important to President Clinton were assigned and decided in the federal district court in Washington, D.C., Justice lifted her blindfold and politics controlled. The cloud of suspicion can be removed only if the D.C. federal court system and Congress thoroughly investigate and make public their findings. Let's look at some of the facts. When I was a special consultant to Kenneth Starr's Office of Independent Counsel, the OIC often found its investigation delayed and disadvantaged by lower-court rulings subsequently reversed on appeal.

Rule of Law

By Ronald D. Rotunda

When the Department of Justice brought its campaign-finance prosecutions, it also ran into a series of adverse rulings, also reversed on appeal. The trial judges who made a series of errors were all members of "the Magnificent Seven," a label the Clinton appointees gave themselves (until Mr. Clinton added an eighth judge in 1998).

Normally, criminal cases are supposed to be assigned randomly. However, we now know that when criminal prosecutions were brought against Webster Hubbell and others with close ties to Mr. Clinton, Chief Judge Norma Holloway Johnson of the U.S. District

Court in Washington, D.C., secretly bypassed the traditional random assignment system, passed over more experienced judges, and assigned the cases to the Magnificent Seven. When her colleagues discovered what she had done, some of them disclosed this information to the press. In a stunning rebuke, they last month took away her power to tamper with judicial assignments. But the damage was already done.

Judge Johnson assigned the Hubbell case to Judge James Robertson. She assigned to Judge Paul Friedman the campaign-finance case against Charlie Trie, the campaign-finance case against Democratic fund-raiser Maria Hsia, and the false-statements case against Thai lobbyist Pauline Kanchanalak. These Clinton-appointed judges then issued rulings that crippled the prosecution; in all these cases, various panels of the D.C. Circuit reversed. Do you detect a pattern here?

Norma Holloway Johnson

In the case of Ms. Hsia, Judge Johnson asked the Justice Department to ask her to assign the case to Judge Friedman. Then she used that request as her justification to make the special assignment. Some people launder money; others launder requests. I have never heard before of a judge playing such cat-and-mouse games in an apparent effort to hide her motives.

Judge Johnson assigned the case against Democratic fund-raiser Howard Glicken to Judge Henry H. Kennedy Jr., a 1997 Clinton appointee, claiming that it was "complicated or protracted," although Mr. Glicken's lawyer announced, when Mr. Glicken was charged, that he would plead guilty. She assigned the case against Miami fund-raiser Mark Jimenez to Judge Emmet G. Sullivan, a 1994 appointee.

One case in particular stands out, the prosecution of Webster Hubbell for income tax evasion. Parties not particularly close to Mr. Hubbell—but close to the president—paid Mr. Hubbell nearly $1 million. In return, Mr. Hubbell, who was in prison at the time, appeared to do no work. A cynic might call the payments hush money.

Judge Robertson, who presided over this case, had worked in and donated money to, President Clinton's 1992 campaign. In the Hubbell tax-fraud prosecution, Judge Robertson ruled that he could ignore the ruling of the three-judge panel of the D.C. Circuit and hold that the OIC did not have jurisdiction to prosecute Mr. Hubbell and the other defendants, and that it could not use tax documents subpoenaed from Mr. Hubbell. Judge Robertson used incendiary language, calling the OIC's tactics (which other circuits had approved) "scary." The D.C. Circuit agreed with these other circuits and reversed.

At the time, the OIC did not know that Judge Johnson had manipulated the assignment to get the case before Judge Robertson. I went back to the transcripts after this information became public and saw Judge Robertson's comments in a new light. The transcript reads as if Judge Robertson had decided that the case was not going to trial; he just had not decided why.

At the hearing of May 8, 1998, OIC counsel asked Judge Robertson to set a trial date, which is standard operating procedure. The judge responded that he normally does that but it would be "arbitrary" to do so here, "when we're looking at the kinds of motions that I'm sure are coming." In other words, the judge refused to set a trial date because of motions not even filed; that is not standard operating procedure. The OIC attorney replied that he had already talked to defense counsel and they were prepared to find a mutually agreeable date, to which Judge Robertson answered, apparently in surprise: "Oh." He still refused to set a date.

At the June 2, 1998 hearing, the judge again questioned whether "it makes sense for us to set a trial date," and he volunteered that any date will be written "in sand here if there are, heaven forfend, interlocutory appeals." The defendants are not entitled to interlocutory appeals but the prosecution is, so once more it appeared that the judge had already decided that there would be no trial.

On July 1, three business days after oral argument, Judge Robertson issued a lengthy written opinion. This is an extraordinarily brief time in which to formulate a decision and write it up, unless the judge had made up his mind in advance.

Perhaps it was happenstance that Judge Johnson secretly assigned the Hubbell case to Judge Robertson, a Clinton appointee. Perhaps Judge Robertson's statements in the transcript do not indicate that he, from the very beginning, had prejudged the matter and decided there would be no trial. But then another eyebrow-raiser occurred: It was discovered that Clinton-appointed judges on the D.C. district court were holding monthly caucuses from which other federal judges were excluded.

Four non-Clinton judges in the D.C. court, appointed by both Democrats and Republicans, were so upset that they anonymously told the press they questioned the propriety of these caucuses. One was quoted as saying: "We all come with political viewpoints but we try to leave politics behind. Unfortunately, the Clinton appointees have gone off on their own."

Monica Lewinsky and Linda Tripp have been called victims of the Clinton presidency. Perhaps the Clinton presidency will claim as its greatest victim the reputation of the federal courts for integrity and impartiality.

Mr. Rotunda is a professor of law at the University of Illinois.

REVIEW & OUTLOOK

The 'Crime-Fraud Exception'

In a recent scene from "The Sopranos," the popular HBO Mafia series, one of Tony Soprano's capos calls him about a murder witness: "Tony, you know that witness who thinks he saw what you and I know didn't happen? Well, he now says he forgot what he thinks he saw."

Because of conversations like that, the legal concept of "attorney-client privilege" has what is called the "crime-fraud exception." If you are planning a caper at the Ravenite Social Club, you can't make your conversations immune from inquiry just by having your lawyer in the room. Yesterday Judge Royce Lamberth ruled that the "crime-fraud exemption" applied to certain conversations in the White House Counsel's office pertaining to the use of government records to trash the reputation of Kathleen Willey. Indeed, Judge Lamberth ruled that President Clinton personally committed "a criminal violation of the Privacy Act."

Kathleen Willey

Ms. Willey, recall, is the former White House aide who went on "60 Minutes" to accuse the President of groping her near the Oval Office after she requested a job promotion. The day that her interview aired in March 1998, senior White House officials held a meeting, with President Clinton on the phone from Camp David. At the White House were Counsel Charles Ruff and deputy counsels Cheryl Mills and Bruce Lindsey. The White House admits that the President concurred with the recommendation that friendly letters Ms. Willey had written him would be released from her employment file. The idea, or "spin," was that the letters would distract attention from Ms. Willey's charges.

Now, the Privacy Act is a law passed in 1974 in reaction to the misuse of government files by the Nixon White House. Chuck Colson, a Nixon aide then, went to prison for two years for misusing a single FBI file. Too bad Mr. Colson didn't have the benefit of the legal opinion Clinton mouthpieces were spreading yesterday, that the Act doesn't apply to the White House. At a press conference yesterday, the President says the law never crossed his mind. But Judge Lamberth found that plaintiffs in his court established "that the White House and the President were aware that they were subject to the Privacy Act, and yet chose to violate its provisions."

The plaintiffs in the suit are individuals contending that their privacy rights were violated when the Clinton White House gathered some 900 FBI files on Republican appointees; they are represented by the conservative activist firm Judicial Watch. Independent Counsel Robert Ray recently reported that there was "no substantial and credible evidence" that senior officials or the First Lady were involved in seeking the files. But he noted that his office "did not investigate alleged violations of the Privacy Act of 1974 because such offenses are excluded from the jurisdiction of an independent counsel."

That is to say, criminal violations of the Privacy Act would have to be prosecuted by Janet Reno's see-no-evil Justice Department. The alternative is to seek redress through civil suits like the one in Judge Lamberth's court. Judicial Watch has pressed interrogatories exploring whether the Administration has abused government records in trashing its political opponents.

After all, what else was the White House Willey meeting about? James Carville has testified that Mr. Clinton called him after Ms. Willey's interview and said "there was some letters that she had written and his lawyers were considering making them public and what did I think about it?" Terry Good, the director of White House records, testified that he asked his staff to pull the Willey letters after Cheryl Mills told him the President's Counsel wanted the letters. Mr. Clinton himself testified before the grand jury that "when everybody blew it up, I thought we would release." Mrs. Clinton also got into the act. An official Justice Department response in the Filegate case notes that in a phone conversation between Mrs. Clinton and Clinton aide Sidney Blumenthal they "agreed the letters should be released."

In one of a spate of silly Clinton defenses going on just now, columnist Richard Cohen writes of Mr. Ray's findings, "so much for Filegate," and asks that we and others apologize to the Clintons. Whether files were "ransacked" may yet be established by the Judicial Watch suit, as well as a separate Privacy Act suit filed by Linda Tripp, whose employment records were released by the Pentagon.

Whether or not the President initiated the acquisition of FBI files, he clearly sets the tone of the White House, where the smear is a standard tactic. FBI files on former Travel Office chief Billy Dale were specifically sought seven months after he was fired. He was trashed on national television by Clinton lawyers, then indicted on embezzlement charges, but acquitted by a jury in less than two hours. During the impeachment trial, Rep. Lindsey Graham noted that Mr. Clinton told Mr. Blumenthal that Monica Lewinsky was a "stalker-type person" shortly before stories to that effect appeared in the press. Mr. Good also testified that Ms. Mills asked him to pull "anything and everything that we might have in our files relating to Linda Tripp."

Now we have the case of the intimidation of potential witnesses in the matter of e-mails that were not delivered in response to subpoenas. Six Northrop-Grumman employees who worked under White House contract testified before Congress that they were ordered not to tell anyone about e-mails discovered missing in a computer error. Betty Lambuth, the on-site Northrop manager, said a White House official told her that if anyone talked "we would lose our jobs, be arrested and put in jail." Many of the e-mails in question were to Vice President Gore's office, and now reportedly also include previously undisclosed e-mails between Monica Lewisky and grand jury witnesses Betty Currie and Ashley Raines during the investigation leading to impeachment.

We don't know how long "The Sopranos" will run, but this Administration will last until next January 20.

Editorial Feature

Clinton Revisionism

BY MICAH MORRISON

The Whitewater investigation by former Independent Counsel Kenneth Starr won convictions of 14 figures associated with Bill and Hillary Clinton. Those felons included Webster Hubbell, Mrs. Clinton's former law partner and President Clinton's associate attorney general, who went to prison on fraud and tax evasion charges; former Arkansas Gov. Jim Guy Tucker, Mr. Clinton's successor, forced from office when he was convicted of fraud and conspiracy; and the Clintons' former Whitewater Development Co. business partners, James and Susan McDougal, convicted on multiple bank fraud and conspiracy charges.

Back in Arkansas, that is, the Clintons had close personal, political and business relationships with a substantial number of people then in the midst of committing felonies. With Mrs. Clinton's miraculous $100,000 commodity trading profit and an illegal $300,000 loan to Whitewater partner Susan McDougal at the heart of the Arkansas bank fraud, the Clintons themselves fell into the ambit of reasonable doubt.

As a candidate, Mr. Clinton successfully lied about marijuana use, his Vietnam draft deferment and an affair with an Arkansas chanteuse named Gennifer Flowers. In a sign of things to come, candidate Clinton's team wheeled out a vicious attack on the Arkansas crooner, portraying her as a lying gold digger, though in fact she had been truthful.

The Clintons brought many of the same habits and cast to Washington. Mr. Hubbell reigned at the Justice Department, and controversy erupted around the firings at the White House Travel Office. Article I of the House impeachment resolution charged Mr. Clinton with "perjurious" testimony before a grand jury probing obstruction of justice in the Monica Lewinsky matter, including attempts to influence witnesses, and in statements made under oath in the Paula Jones sexual harassment civil deposition. Later, U.S. District Judge Susan Webber Wright found the president in contempt for providing "false, misleading and evasive" answers in the Jones case.

This record bears some repeating now, since an effort is under way to write it out of history. The most serious of several efforts at Clinton revisionism comes from Jeffrey Toobin, a staff writer for the New Yorker and legal-affairs analyst for ABC News. In his recent book, "A Vast Conspiracy: The Real Story of the Sex Scandal That Nearly Brought Down a President," Mr. Toobin argues that Mr. Clinton was a "good guy" brought down by a dishonest media and zealots working under Mr. Starr. Mrs. Clinton's famous charge of a "vast right-wing conspiracy" has the "unmistakable ring of truth," Mr. Toobin writes. Mr. Clinton's opponents were motivated by "hatred," "opportunism" and "greed."

A second volume making the revisionist case is "The Hunting of the President: The Ten-Year Campaign to Destroy Bill and Hillary Clinton," by journalists Joe Conason and Gene Lyons. It focuses largely on the Arkansas end and on media coverage of the president's problems, and it comes to basically the same conclusion as Mr. Toobin. The hunters of the president "perverted the law and debased the media" in pursuit of a "ratings-driven coup d'etat." Mr. Starr, an "ambitious partisan," is the chief villain. The New York Times, the Los Angeles Times, the Washington Post and the editorial page of this newspaper, including this writer, take a drubbing.

To anyone who remembers Mr. Starr's record of convictions, these efforts seem well worth ignoring. But signs abound that this line of thinking is being taken seriously. No less a personage that the Washington bureau chief of the New York Times, Michael Oreskes, wrote in a recent review of a book by Peggy Noonan on Hillary Clinton that Ms. Noonan (a contributing editor to this page) failed to take on the argument by Mr. Toobin that the president, "while flawed and foolish, was really a good guy, besieged by overzealous opponents who did far worse things." The influential New York Times columnist Anthony Lewis, writing in the New York Review of Books about the two volumes, echoes the charge that Mr. Starr's "attempt to drive Clinton from office" brought the country "close to a coup d'etat."

The notion that skepticism about the Clintons' morality and truthfulness is born of "hatred," too, is subtly invading public discourse. Only last Sunday, for example, the front page of the New York Times carried a headline saying that out-of-state contributors to Rudolph Giuliani's Senate campaign "loathe" Hillary Clinton. They have "seethed" through the Clinton years, the story explains. Well after the jump from the front page, the article mentions that Mrs. Clinton gets about the same proportion of her money from out of state, but the Times reporter makes no allusions about her contributors' motives—which might include wanting something from her husband's administration. Similarly, no one speaks of the speaker of the House being brought down by "Gingrich haters," or a Supreme Court nominee being rejected by "Bork haters."

Those of us who have spent years chronicling the Clintons were scarcely surprised when he became the second president in U.S. history to be impeached; nor are the narratives of half-truths, omissions and attacks offered up by Messrs. Toobin, Conason and Lyons particularly original or enlightening. Impeachment, as Alexander Hamilton recognized in Federalist 65, is bound to ignite intense "animosities, partialities, influence and interest." Our commentary, collected in five bound volumes and continuing, has had many critics and equally effusive praise.

Throughout that commentary, one phrase recurs: abuse of power. It's a theme the Clinton revisionists miss. And with few notable exceptions, the press largely missed the import of scandal stories of the early Clinton years, failing to connect the dots. Those years provide the essential context of the Clinton impeachment: real corruption in Arkansas, years of political warfare in

Washington as Congress faced off against a brutal and largely effective White House attack machine, serious malfeasance at the Justice Department, and stonewalling from the Oval Office. By the time presidential perjury and obstruction of justice appeared in the vehicle of an intern named Monica Lewinsky, the die was cast.

Mr. Toobin misses this context by focusing on Washington and largely ignoring the Whitewater mess in Arkansas. He is at sea amid complex financial crime, for example throwing up his hands over the $300,000 Susan McDougal loan, portions of which wound up in accounts benefiting the Whitewater Development Co. Mr. Toobin calls the loan "something of a mystery." But in his eagerness to smear prosecutors on Mr. Starr's team, Mr. Toobin does pause long enough in Arkansas to attack Deputy Independent Counsel Hickman Ewing Jr. as an unbalanced religious fanatic, a tremendous slur against a distinguished public servant. The rest of Mr. Starr's team fares little better. They "generally fell into one (or both) of two categories," Mr. Toobin writes: "the unemployable and the obsessed."

Mr. Lewis echoes these attacks. There "were few respected lawyers with prosecutorial experience left when the office got to the Lewinsky challenge," he writes. Americans should not forget "the abuses committed by Starr and his people."

A more dispassionate view of Mr. Starr's prosecutors and the impeachment case comes from Richard Posner in "An Affair of State: The Investigation, Impeachment, and Trial of President Clinton." Mr. Posner, chief judge for the Seventh U.S. Circuit Court of Appeals, writes with care and precision. Mr. Starr, he notes, fought a losing public-relations battle "with the White House's slander machine." The president's own lawyers "were part of a campaign of slander directed against the Independent Counsel's office." While faulting Mr. Starr's team—and also the Supreme Court—on some points, Judge Posner establishes the independent-counsel staff as thorough, reliable and experienced. Prosecutors, he notes, "are aggressive people; if they were not, our crime rate would be even higher than it is."

After learning from Linda Tripp that it was likely that Mr. Clinton had obstructed justice, Mr. Starr's team used "typical hardball prosecutorial methods to try to nail him for these crimes," Judge Posner writes. "They had been frustrated by Webster Hubbell's refusal (as they thought) to cooperate with them; now they saw what seemed to be the explanation, a kind of underground railroad running from the government in Washington to Revlon in New York along which Clinton and Vernon Jordan whisked potential witnesses against Clinton out of reach of investigators."

Ms. Lewinsky, while pressuring the president to find her work, had been offered a job at Revlon after a recommendation by Mr. Jordan. Tax records show that in 1994, after leaving the Justice Department and while under investigation by Mr. Starr, Mr. Hubbell received consulting fees from 15 companies, including $100,000 from the Riady family—key players in the 1996 campaign-finance scandal—and $62,000 from Revlon. Mr. Hubbell has never fully explained what work he did for the money. In the end, the Starr team may have "jumped to conclusions too soon," Judge Posner notes. But it was "a natural inference" from matters already under investigation. "Where there is smoke, there is usually fire."

Mr. Toobin rarely raises his narrative voice above switchblade level. In "Hunting the President," Messrs. Conason and Lyons tell a full-throated Arkansas tale. Alas, it's one full of sound and fury, signifying nothing.

Fierce defenders of the president, Messrs. Conason and Lyons string together Arkansas tales and media critiques recycled from columns in their home publications, the New York Observer and the Arkansas Democrat-Gazette. The president can do little wrong, and his enemies are legion: right-wing zanies, Mr. Starr and "important journalists and news organizations succumbing to scandal fever."

In their zeal to defend the president and attack his opponents, the authors focus on the trees but fail to see the forest. Raucous and competitive by nature, the media pursued Clinton conduct—belatedly, in the view of this page—on recognizing that it was a hell of a story. James and Susan McDougal were corrupt. Federal investigators did uncover crimes at Madison Guaranty Savings & Loan, owned by the Clintons' business partners, the McDougals. Mr. Clinton did lie about his relationship with Gennifer Flowers, foreshadowing future troubles. The CIA did operate out of Mena airfield in western Arkansas, and so did a kingpin cocaine dealer. Tawdry, awful things did happen in Arkansas, fueling journalistic suspicions. The authors dismiss all this as bad faith on the part of the media.

Closer to home, "Hunting the President" spends some time attacking this page's coverage of the Clinton scandals, but gets a number of the details wrong. Stephens Inc. chairman Jackson Stephens, for example, did not meet with Journal editor Robert L. Bartley to complain about the paper's coverage, as the authors twice state. And this writer never was "swaggering" around a Hot Springs fishing camp carrying "semiautomatic pistols" or "making noisy public displays" of dislike toward President Clinton in "public places"—or anywhere else, for that matter. If the authors had bothered to check this claim—advanced by a Tarot-dealing Hot Springs astrologer—they would have been told it was false.

Arkansas psychics aside, "Hunting the President" reinforces the revisionist narrative advanced by Mr. Toobin and Mr. Lewis: that Mr. Clinton was done in by a conspiracy perhaps vast, certainly right-wing and maybe even criminal. The missing piece here, of course, is Mr. Clinton's own conduct. Mr. Clinton's problems always seem to be the fault of someone else: his enemies in Arkansas, the GOP Congress, Mr. Starr, right-wing conspirators.

The book wars over impeachment doubtless will continue for a long time, but the last chapters of the Clinton scandal saga have yet to be written. Mr. Starr's successor, Robert Ray, has indicated that he may indict Mr. Clinton for perjury and obstruction in the Lewinsky-Jones matter once Mr. Clinton has left office. Mr. Toobin's book dismisses the criminal case against Mr. Clinton. By contrast, Judge Posner's volume says that Mr. Clinton is "guilty of serious crimes"—obstruction of justice in discussions with Ms. Lewinsky about filing a false affidavit, as well as perjury in the Jones deposition, in testimony before the Starr grand jury and in responses to congressional questions.

Indeed, much has yet to be revealed about the conduct of the Clinton presidency and the activities of those who opposed him.

A true history of Bill Clinton's wild ride to impeachment and beyond likely will have to wait some time, until tempers have cooled and participants have departed the public stage. Meanwhile, for the latest in the greatest fin de siecle political drama in U.S. history, pick up a newspaper. Preferably this one.

Mr. Morrison is a Journal senior writer and co-editor with Robert L. Bartley of the five-volume series, "A Journal Briefing: Whitewater."

May 1, 2000

Editorial Feature

Secrets Aren't Secure On Clinton's Watch

By Oliver "Buck" Revell

The State Department has experienced yet another major security lapse—the loss of a laptop computer belonging to its Bureau of Intelligence and Research. The computer apparently contained "code word" material that is more sensitive than even "secret" documents. Yet officials did not promptly report the loss. Last week, Secretary of State Madeleine Albright took some belated disciplinary action, but sources and methods used in the analysis of weapons proliferation intelligence could be at great risk.

This is part of a disturbing trend of security lapses in the Clinton administration. In December, an intelligence officer assigned to the Russian Embassy in Washington was expelled from the U.S. after he was discovered operating a listening device in a seventh-floor conference room at the State Department. No one has yet explained how the "bug" was planted in such a sensitive location or who planted it.

The problem extends far beyond the State Department. The Central Intelligence Agency was severely embarrassed when it found out that its former director, John Deutch, had placed highly classified information on his personal computer and then used this computer to send and receive unsecured e-mail. This made all of the data contained in the computer subject to compromise. Once again, this breach of security was not promptly reported.

It gets much worse. The apparent loss to the People's Republic of China of highly classified data on American nuclear weapons from one or more of our national laboratories is one of the most egregious security breaches in our history. We still don't know much about these security lapses. Are those responsible for espionage within the Energy Department still there? What damage has already been done? What we do know is disturbing. An initial assessment by the U.S. intelligence community determined the following:

• China obtained by espionage classified U.S. nuclear information that probably accelerated its program to develop more advanced nuclear weapons.

• China obtained at least basic design information on several modern U.S. nuclear re-entry vehicles, including the Trident II.

• China obtained information on a variety of U.S. weapon designs, including the neutron bomb.

The administration has been lax in correcting these lapses. Senior officials at the Justice Department denied the FBI's request to search the laptop computer belonging to Wen Ho Lee, a Los Alamos nuclear scientist—even though Mr. Lee had signed a waiver allowing a search any time. Even in the unlikely event that evidence obtained in the search was held to be inadmissible in court, it's vitally important to prevent sensitive information from being transmitted or compromised.

Then we have the sorry spectacle of Chinese influence-peddlers and, in at least one instance, a Chinese military official being paraded into the White House to meet President Clinton in return for significant campaign contributions. I cannot recall a single instance in my 35 years of government service when senior National Security Council staffers would have hesitated to inform their superiors of intelligence about a foreign government's attempt to influence our political process. But that is exactly what happened with information developed by the FBI concerning illegal campaign contributions by intermediaries of the Chinese government.

The Cold War may be over, but there can be no doubt that our adversaries are many, and they have increasingly effective methods to penetrate even our most closely held secrets. We need a vigorous program at all levels of government to protect classified information. Unfortunately the Clinton administration has failed at this task. The president and his aides have not upheld their oaths to "preserve and protect" our country against "all enemies, foreign and domestic." I can only hope the next president, whether Al Gore or George W. Bush, sets a higher standard.

Mr. Revell, a former associate deputy director of the FBI, is the author of "A G-Man's Journal: A Legendary Career Inside the FBI" (Pocket Books, 1998).

May 5, 2000

REVIEW & OUTLOOK

The Get-Lost Virus

"Concealing subpoenaed evidence is a crime. In my judgment, the White House obstructed justice, and we're just trying to find out who did it."

Rep. Chris Shays, Wednesday

Rep. Shays opposed President Clinton's impeachment, one of only five House Republicans to do so. But Rep. Shays believes something's rotten in the White House's failure to turn over hundreds of thousands of e-mails in response to subpoenas by Congress and independent counsels authorized by its own Justice Department. It's hard not to wonder.

Al Gore

The first three White House witnesses at this week's hearing by Rep. Dan Burton said, "I don't recall . . ." "I don't remember" or "I have no specific recollection . . . ." a total of 32 times. White House impeachment lawyer Cheryl Mills quoted Robert F. Kennedy and said "nothing you discover here today will feed one person, give shelter to someone who is homeless . . . or offer justice to one African-American or Hispanic juvenile." Her memory then failed her nine times in response to questions about the e-mails.

Mr. Shays is right. It's obstruction of justice, which conceivably is considered legal now in most media circles. At last Saturday's White House Correspondents dinner, reporters roared as President

Clinton joked about his stonewalling tactics: "Over the past few months, I've lost 10 pounds. Where did they go? Why did I not produce them to the independent counsel?"

Thus the legacy grows. The White House learned of the technical glitch that led to the missing e-mails in 1998. A February 1999 memo from Karl Heissner of its Office of Administration said, "we may not want to call attention to the issue" by notifying Congress. He concluded: "Let sleeping dogs lie." Later, White House lawyer Kate Anderson scratched out all references to the e-mail problem in a proposal for computer funds it sent to Congress. Now, the White House claims it didn't reconstruct the e-mail because it had "limited resources available" because of Y2K efforts.

What is clear is that the White House never moved to recover any of the e-mails until this March, when the Justice Department opened a criminal investigation into allegations by five Northrop-Grumman contract employees that they had been ordered by White House aides not to reveal the e-mail problem.

Federal Judge Royce Lamberth has ordered the White House to conduct a rapid search of the e-mail and of related hard drives, noting that the Clinton Administration had "political incentives" to drag out any search. He has rejected the White House's timetable for its search and told it to consult with FBI experts on how to get it done.

The one press organization that never threw in the towel on this story or others like it is the Associated Press. Its coverage has been invaluable, though you somehow need access to the wire service to keep up. One source, with an AP search engine, is at www.drudgereport.com. Among AP's reporting for just the past week:

• In an unprecedented move, a five-judge oversight panel has named an outside prosecutor to investigate why Norma Holloway Johnson, the chief federal judge in the District of Columbia, ignored the normal court rotation and assigned six separate Whitewater and Clinton campaign fund-raising scandal cases to Clinton-appointed judges.

• Details of the memo by Justice investigator Charles La Bella recommending an independent counsel for the 1996 Clinton-Gore fund-raising scandals came out in Senate testimony. Mr. La Bella concluded that "the vice president may have given false statements" when he said he didn't know his fund-raising phone calls had illegally channeled money into "hard money" accounts. White House aide Harold Ickes sent Mr. Gore 13 memos referring to "hard" money. Mr. Gore claims he never read any of them.

• A memo from a White House computer specialist revealed that a large quantity of e-mail for aide Sidney Blumenthal was deleted from his personal computer just after President Clinton was impeached. White House officials also discussed deleting the messages to Mr. Blumenthal from their permanent archives as well, but now say the matter was "routine." Mr. Blumenthal was accused of using his job to spread rumors about Clinton opponents.

The missing e-mail includes all traffic sent from and to Vice President Gore's office between 1994 and 1998. During that time, the Vice President made his "no controlling legal authority" fund-raising calls from the White House, attended the infamous Buddhist temple event and attended White House meetings on "hard money" for which he says he must have been in the bathroom at crucial moments. The e-mail might yield information on all those events.

It's quite a spectacle to see Washington authorities have to play hide-and-go-seek with the White House in the middle of a Presidential election. But the November election is no game. Serious issues from Social Security reform to missile defense are at stake. The American people deserve to know what the Clinton-Gore Administration is trying to conceal before the vote.

In 1996, Ross Perot warned voters that if Bill Clinton won re-election they would have to endure a lengthy impeachment battle, and he was right. Now, in 2000, we are asked to ignore potential scandals that may be lurking behind the White House curtain and instead elect this Administration's loyal, involved Vice President.

The e-mails should be examined by responsible legal authorities and the investigation of Judge Johnson concluded before the vote this November. The alternative is holding a vote, then telling the electorate to go lump it after they no longer have the constitutional power to do anything about it.

Campaign
Finance Scandals

In June, the head of the Justice Department's campaign finance task force urged Attorney General Janet Reno to appoint a special counsel to investigate whether Vice President Gore had lied about his knowledge of the Buddhist Temple affair. The recommendation—the latest push by law enforcement officials since the earliest days of the scandal to secure an independent investigation—sent shock waves through the Justice Department and the Gore campaign. Justice's newest task force head, Robert Conrad, had interviewed the Vice President in April about the temple affair and concluded that he may have been giving evasive and untruthful answers. In March, a Gore associate, Maria Hsia, had been convicted of channeling illegal contributions in the temple scandal.

Pressure on the Justice Department in the campaign finance probe, presumably from the White House and its allies, was intense. FBI Director Louis Freeh warned Ms. Reno of the pressure in a series of memos and asked Justice to step aside in favor of an independent prosecutor. "A surfeit of newly released documents from the Justice Department make it clear that Ms. Reno became Mr. Gore's guardian angel," the Journal noted, "standing between her man and his accusers at every turn, even against senior members of her own staff."

The documents also revealed the FBI's concept of the origin of the scandal. Mr. Freeh reported a "criminal investigation that has taken us into the highest reaches of the White House." His "core group investigative plan" was "based on a theory that most of the alleged campaign abuses flowed from an all-out effort by the White House and the DNC to raise money."

In Little Rock, meanwhile, a committee of the Arkansas Supreme Court voted to disbar President Clinton. The charge was "serious misconduct"—lying before a federal judge in the Paula Jones sexual harrasment case.

REVIEW & OUTLOOK

Who Is Richard Trumka?

Good news for Al Gore: It looks like the fix is in on the Big Labor fraud scandal that threatens top players from the 1996 Clinton-Gore re-election effort, the Democratic National Committee and the AFL-CIO. Last month, the International Brotherhood of Teamsters filed a civil-racketeering suit against its former president, Ron Carey, and other ex-officials, seeking $3 million in damages for ripping off the union. U.S. Attorney Mary Jo White paved the way for the civil suit late last year when a federal jury found former Teamster political director William Hamilton guilty of fraud and embezzlement in the case.

Richard Trumka

Close followers of this subject immediately noted who was missing from the civil suit filed by current Teamster President Jim Hoffa. It didn't name the high-ranking union and DNC officials who were implicated during presentation of the government's case at the Hamilton trial. These officials include AFL-CIO Secretary Treasurer Richard Trumka and Terry McAuliffe, today a senior Democratic Party fund-raiser and in 1996 head of the Clinton-Gore election team.

Mr. Trumka is one of the most powerful figures in the American labor movement and his record in the Hamilton affair is troubling. The official Justice Department line is that the criminal side of the Hamilton probe is continuing. But Mr. Trumka has been throwing his weight around, a signal to Reno Justice, perhaps, that this Friend of Al may be too big to indict.

Mr. Gore's links to the union are tight. Last year, the Vice President received an unusual primary endorsement from the AFL. In January, Mr. Trumka traveled to Iowa to publicly back Mr. Gore against Bill Bradley. In February, the AFL gave the Teamsters $500,000 to finance their strike against Overnight Transport; columnist Robert Novak recently reported that inside the labor movement the payment is referred to as "reparations" for AFL participation in the Teamster fraud scheme. In April, despite strong statements from Mr. Hoffa and leaks predicting vigorous civil action against union higher-ups in the Hamilton conspiracy, the Teamster president filed a tepid lawsuit; Mr. Hoffa appears to have decided that his best interests rest with Mr. Gore and Mr. Trumka.

The Hamilton case tried in federal court in Manhattan was not about arcane technicalities of campaign-finance laws. At issue was the looting of the Teamsters' treasury by Mr. Hamilton and co-conspirators to fund Mr. Carey's successful re-election campaign. A federal monitor later found fraud and overturned the election. "Money poured out of the Teamsters' General Treasury Fund like water from an open faucet," the prosecutor told the jury in the Hamilton trial.

Evidence introduced by Ms. White's prosecutors suggests that a criminal conspiracy reached higher than Mr. Hamilton. The prosecution noted that Mr. Trumka was a player in two schemes that went before the jury. In one, according to testimony by a Hamilton co-conspirator, Mr. Trumka and two other top labor leaders agreed to make $50,000 donations to Mr. Carey, illegal under labor law.

In the second, Mr. Trumka allegedly helped launder $150,000 in AFL funds to Mr. Carey through Citizen Action, a consumer advocacy group. Mr. Trumka has denied any wrongdoing, but asserted his Fifth Amendment privilege when questioned by government investigators. The AFL-CIO's code of conduct says that no officer who takes the Fifth can hold office, but President John Sweeney waived it for Mr. Trumka. Citizen Action is named in the Teamster civil suit.

Mr. McAuliffe, the Democratic Party fund-raiser and one-time financier of the Clintons' Westchester homestead, worked with a key Hamilton co-conspirator, Martin Davis. Mr. Davis pleaded guilty to conspiring to funnel union funds and agreed to cooperate with the prosecution, but apparently got cold feet on the eve of the trial and did not testify. Mr. Davis, Mr. McAuliffe, Mr. Trumka and Mr. Carey hold the keys to unlocking the secrets of the fraud conspiracy.

According to testimony at the Hamilton trial by a former DNC finance director, Mr. Davis and Mr. McAuliffe attempted to carry out a scheme in which the DNC would find a donor to Mr. Carey and in return the Teamsters would donate money to Democratic groups. Under federal law, it's illegal to use money from a union treasury to promote the candidacy of anyone running for union office, which would have been the effect of the McAuliffe-Davis swap. Mr. McAuliffe's lawyer, Richard Ben-Veniste, says his client was not involved in any wrongdoing and cooperated fully with the investigation.

What Mr. Gore gets from all this is pretty clear—union backing in his battle with George W. Bush. What Mr. Hoffa wants from Mr. Gore also is fairly clear—an end to federal oversight of his corruption-plagued union. What remains unclear is how much of the politicized game-rigging we've seen at the Justice Department during the Clinton years would continue into a Gore Presidency. The Hamilton case, withering on the vine, is not a promising sign. A criminal indictment against higher-ups in the Hamilton affair would be.

May 24, 2000

REVIEW & OUTLOOK

Truth and Consequences

A CBS-New York Times poll released over the weekend said that 66% of the American people thought that Bill Clinton would run for the Presidency again if he could. This is the President who on the

subject of his constitutionally limited two terms in office languidly says, "Most days I'm OK about not being on the ballot." Well, it turns out that most Americans have had about enough of the I'm OK, You're OK Presidency: Some 57% responded that they wouldn't think of voting for him if somehow his lawyers pulled off a next time. In any event, the White House's lawyers have been busy elsewhere.

Bill Clinton

On Monday, a committee of the Arkansas Supreme Court voted to disbar the President. The charge is "serious misconduct"—lying before a federal judge during a deposition in the Paula Jones sexual harassment case. His attorney, David Kendall, blames the President's newest problem on "partisan mudslinging." In fact, the incident was referred to the committee by U.S. District Court Judge Susan Webber Wright, in whose presence the President lied, and yes, by a complaint from a conservative legal group. Last April Judge Wright ruled that the President was in civil contempt for giving "intentionally false testimony" and fined him $90,000.

The reason lawyer Kendall can hoist up the "partisan mudslinging" charge is that people tend to think it's all a Washington story. In truth, a lot of Mr. Clinton's big legal losses have come from the folks back home. The disbarment action now goes before a Pulaski County circuit court judge in Little Rock. If the judge decides to disbar the President, Mr. Clinton can appeal to the Arkansas Supreme Court. Beyond this matter, Arkansas has been the venue for significant Whitewater convictions by Arkansas juries under Kenneth Starr, for Judge Wright's contempt ruling, and for a statewide corruption cleanup.

Like it or not, Arkansans can't free themselves from the Clinton school of politics. The following, for instance, is from the legal brief the President's lawyers filed to the disciplinary committee: "Many categories of responses which are misleading, evasive, nonresponsive or frustrating are nevertheless not legally 'false,'" including "literally truthful answers that imply facts that are not true."

Speaking of partisan mudslinging, this brings us to Mr. Starr, the former Independent Counsel. No one needs a tutorial in what he's been accused of. Some of these accusations have also found their way into court, and Mr. Starr has been winning lately. Last week, a federal judge in Little Rock in three separate orders threw out complaints by foes of the independent counsel charging him with misconduct.

Of former witness Julie Hiatt Steele's complaint against the Starr office, U.S. District Judge John Nangle found "absolutely no evidence that [Mr. Starr] ever directly or impliedly asked her to lie." This rebuke of Ms. Steele's much publicized complaint went virtually unnoticed. Similarly, Judge Nangle found no evidence that the Starr office had tried to suborn perjury as charged by former Clinton aide Stephen A. Smith. The judge also threw out a complaint lodged against Mr. Starr by a lawyer from Connecticut.

Also last week, news surfaced hither and yon of a 1996 memo written by FBI Director Louis Freeh. It warned of intense political pressure on Justice, presumably from the White House, in the campaign-finance scandal; the Freeh memo asked the department to step aside in favor of an independent counsel.

Mr. Freeh's memo, written to FBI Deputy Director William Esposito, recounts a conversation that Mr. Esposito had with the head of the Justice Department's Public Integrity Section, Lee Radek, and a subsequent conversation Mr. Freeh had with Attorney General Janet Reno. Mr. Freeh wrote to Mr. Esposito that he had advised "the attorney general of Lee Radek's comment to you that there was a lot of 'pressure' on him . . . regarding this case because the attorney general's job might hang in the balance (or words to that effect)."

Mr. Radek has said since that the memo has "no basis in fact." Yesterday, however, FBI General Counsel Larry Parkinson told the House Judiciary Committee that Mr. Esposito's account could in fact be confirmed; FBI Assistant Director Neal Gallagher was in the room at the time of the Radek-Esposito meeting, Mr. Parkinson said, "and essentially corroborates the account that is described in the Director's memo."

There is a connecting thread in much of what we've recounted here: the question of whether someone is, or is not, telling the truth. In the poll cited earlier, Mr. Clinton's job rating remained high, at 59%. There is comfort in that result. Then asked whether Mr. Clinton has more honesty and integrity than most others in public life, 70% said no.

June 14, 2000

Editorial Feature

How Reno Let the Big Fish Get Away

These excerpts on the investigation of the Clinton-Gore fund-raising practices are from FBI Director Louis Freeh's memorandum of Nov. 24, 1997, to Attorney General Janet Reno. They were released last week under subpoena to the House Committee on Government Reform, headed by Rep. Dan Burton. The headings in the text are from the committee's summary of the Freeh memo, which can be found at http://www.house.gov/reform.

Louis Freeh

Highest Reaches of the White House

"Because this criminal investigation has taken our investigators into the highest reaches of the White House—including an examination of many specific actions taken by the President and Vice President—we have had to assess the potential application of the Independent Counsel statute virtually every step of the way."

Covered Persons Being Investigated by the Task Force

"It should be noted that, in the current administration, even the most senior White House staffers (such as former Deputy Chief of Staff Harold Ickes) are not 'covered persons' under the statute. The 'covered persons' provision includes individuals working at the Executive Office of the President who are paid at or above level II of the Executive Schedule (currently $133,600). Although Congress clearly intended to capture a significant number of high-level White House officials within the 'covered persons' provision, most of the current officials have avoided coverage simply by accepting a salary below level II."

Investigative Plan

"The core group [including the President, Vice President, and top White House and DNC officials] investigative plan was based on a theory that most of the alleged campaign abuses flowed, directly or indirectly, from the all-out effort by the White House and the DNC to raise money. It was this consuming quest for campaign cash . . . that led to the transfer of John Huang from the Department of Commerce to the DNC to begin the aggressive solicitation of Asian Americans. It led to the ambitious plan for White House coffees, overnights, and other perks for large donors. It led to the telephone solicitations by the President and the Vice President and the attempted merger of the WHODB and DNC databases. While that does not mean the core group members necessarily are culpable for the criminal violations the investigation uncovers, neither should they be immune from intensive investigative scrutiny.

"While the DOJ prosecutors in charge of the Campcon investigation did not formally object to this investigative [core group] plan, they also did not embrace it. From the beginning, there was a fundamental disagreement about how the investigation would proceed. The FBI. . . wanted to focus intently on the core group, on the theory that many of the apparent campaign abuses flowed, directly or indirectly, from the core group's all-out effort to raise money. In contrast, the prosecutors wanted to focus on the opportunists, with a 'bottom up' strategy that might or might not lead eventually to the core group."

"[The bottom up approach] did neglect some of the larger issues. With the exception of the White House fund-raising calls, begun belatedly in September 1997, there has never been a concentrated investigation of the core group and its fund-raising efforts. In fact, DOJ did not assign a prosecutor specifically to the core group activities until July, after Director Freeh ordered an aggressive plan to interview all relevant core group and DNC officials and to become more persistent on subpoena compliance issues."

Flawed Investigation

Cautious Approach to Investigating Covered Persons:

"From the outset, the DOJ attorneys in charge of the Task Force have proceeded very cautiously before authorizing any investigative step that might involve a 'covered person.' Unlike a normal investigation, where agents and attorneys simply follow all logical investigative leads, the DOJ attorneys have been extremely reluctant to venture into areas that might implicate 'covered persons.' This reluctance has led to a flawed investigation in several ways."

Partitioned Investigation:

"First, the Task Force has partitioned its investigation, focusing on individual persons and events without effectively analyzing their relationship to the broader fund-raising scheme."

Incorrect Dispositive Factual Assumptions:

"Second, the Task Force attorneys sometimes have made dispositive factual assumptions without investigating to see if those assumptions are accurate. For example, the attorneys concluded in the spring of 1997 that Vice President Gore's White House fund-raising calls were not worth investigating because they all involved solicitation of 'soft money' (a factual assumption that turned out to be incorrect). The White House coffees are a second example; until very recently, there still has been no serious investigation of the coffees, primarily because the DOJ attorneys had assumed—incorrectly—that they all occurred in the 'private' White House space."

Lengthy Legal Analysis

"Third, important investigative areas, such as the serious allegations raised by Common Cause, have never been pursued because they have been tied up in lengthy threshold legal analyses within the Department."

Separation of IC Analysis from Investigation:

"The Department has also walled off the day-to-day investigation from much of its Independent Counsel legal analyses. Most decisions regarding IC issues are still handled by DOJ attorneys who have only limited involvement in the ongoing investigation. While obviously these issues deserve the careful scrutiny of experienced Public Integrity attorneys, the separation between the legal analysts and the front-line investigators (both agents and attorneys) has been unusually rigid. Ironically, this separation became even more pronounced following the September shake-up of the Task Force. Until at least mid-October, the new Task Force heads, Chuck La Bella and Jim DeSarno, had no meaningful role in the Department's handling of Independent Counsel-related matters. As a result, the investigative approach to those matters has suffered from lack of coordination."

FBI Cut Out of Deliberative Process Regarding IC Decisions: "Beginning in September, however, the nature of the weekly [Campcon] meetings changed markedly, and there no longer was any meaningful discussion of IC-related issues. While the FBI has very recently received several DOJ drafts on pending IC matters, FBI officials have not had any significant role in the deliberative process."

Common Cause Allegations

No investigation:

"To this day, there has been no decision on whether the allegations [that the Clinton/Gore campaign (as well as the Dole campaign) engaged in an illegal scheme to circumvent the federal campaign financing laws] should be investigated by the Task Force or referred to the FEC."

President Controlled DNC:

"[The Campcon Task Force] has obtained substantial evidence that the President and his key advisers controlled virtually all aspects of the DNC fund-raising efforts."

IC for Common Cause Allegations:

"The Justice Department has weighed in on the legal issue, at least initially concluding that this scheme was simply an act of 'coordination' between the Clinton/Gore campaign and the DNC. In her April 14 letter to Congress, the Attorney General stated that the FECA 'does not prohibit the coordination of fund raising or expenditures between a party and its candidates for office.' The Common Cause response, which appears to be supported by the evidence, is that this is not a case about mere 'coordination.' Instead, it argues, the case is about a scheme in which President Clinton and his top advisers raised and spent millions in direct support of his candidacy, and used the DNC as a mere conduit."

"On their face, the Common Cause letters present serious allegations of potential campaign violations . . . . Because the allegations clearly involve the President, they should be investigated by an Independent Counsel. Moreover, the Attorney General should seek the appointment of an Independent Counsel immediately, for two reasons: (1) the Department has had the allegations for more than a year; and (2) there is virtually no chance that the allegations could be resolved in the course of a limited preliminary inquiry."

Vice President Gore's Telephone Solicitations

Delayed Investigation:

"While Vice President Gore admitted in March 1997 that he had made fund-raising calls from his West Wing office at the White House, the Task Force did not undertake any serious investigation of these calls until July."

VPOTUS'S Participation and Knowledge:

"The evidence tends to show that the Vice President was an active participant in the core group fund-raising efforts, that he was informed about the distinctions between 'hard' and 'soft' money, and that he generally understood."

Seek an IC:

"If the Attorney General decides not to seek an Independent Counsel on the broader fund-raising scheme, she still should refer the matter of the Vice President's telephone solicitations. Even on the narrowly focused issue presented by the existing preliminary inquiry, there appears to be a technical violation of Section 607."

President Clinton's Telephone Solicitations

Seek an IC:

". . . the Attorney General should also seek the appointment of an Independent Counsel with respect to the President's telephone solicitations. Like those of Vice President Gore, the President's fund-raising calls were part of the alleged scheme to circumvent the campaign financing laws, regardless of where the calls took place or how the money is characterized. . . . An Independent Counsel should be appointed to investigate this scheme, and the President's solicitations should be part of that investigation.

Editorial Feature

Reno Stonewall: Third Time a Charm?

The striking thing about the latest recommendation of an independent investigation of Al Gore and his Buddhist Temple hijinks is how quickly it leaked. Capitol Hill sources report that the attorney general—"visibly perturbed over the premature disclosure," as the AP described her at her weekly briefing Friday—is ordering an internal investigation of the leak.

Thinking Things Over

By Robert L. Bartley

So the indomitable Ms. Reno will strap a polygraph around Robert J. Conrad Jr., who brought her the same bad news the third time around as the latest head of her own campaign finance investigation. The leak aside, Mr. Conrad's recommendation was a show of courage, given the fate of the two previous messengers. His predecessor, Charles La Bella, was pretty much hounded out of the department. FBI Director Louis Freeh cannot be fired, but has had to endure a lot of bad-mouthing and petty harassment.

Rather than pinpointing a culprit, Ms. Reno is likely to learn that the final year of an administration is when the bureaucrats you've been sitting on start to leak. I saw it firsthand during the Ford administration, when GOP national security officials upset with detente blew up the Vladivostok summit agreement. Some Ford administration insiders still blame my articles for defeat, but out of it eventually came Ronald Reagan and a tougher foreign policy.

Ms. Reno has manifestly been sitting on the Justice Department to stop the campaign finance investigation, with the sole crutch of Lee Radek of the Public Integrity Section. It turns out that even Robert Litt, whom our sources had identified as a political obstacle, came to agree with the Freeh-La Bella-Conrad conclusion. We will start to learn whether Ms. Reno can stonewall one more time when she appears before Sen. Arlen Specter, who said he would summon her before his Judiciary subcommittee tomorrow. So far she has been able to face down congressional tormentors, relying on the immunity of femininity and illness, at one point fainting in church.

Janet Reno

Both she and Congress, too, were able to hide behind the independent counsel law, which relieved them of responsibility while setting up an investigator the president was free to attack in the political arena. Editorially this newspaper opposed the law, pointing out that many independent investigations—Teapot Dome, Watergate and even the initial Whitewater appointment of Robert Fiske—were chartered without it. Historically, the way the system worked was that Congress, the press and the public created enough of a political furor to force appointment of an independent investigator. These investigators were harder to attack politically, because the president and attorney general did have the de jure power to fire them—but at a political price, as Richard Nixon discovered with the Saturday Night Massacre.

We are now back at square one and will see whether Sen. Specter, scarcely a GOP hatchetman, and the rest step up to their responsibility of oversight. Their principal power is to make sure the issue does not go away between now and November. Mr. Gore affects Clintonesque chutzpah in complaining that the twice-delayed investigation now comes up only four months before an election. Ms. Reno laughably says she doesn't want "to interfere with the democratic process."

That is to say, leaking the facts to voters is the bureaucracy's ultimate defense of the rule of law. Mr. Gore has played a "limited, modified hangout," releasing the transcripts of Mr. Conrad's examination. The vice president repeatedly asserted that at the Buddhist Temple he was the only person in the room who didn't understand it was a fund-raiser. He took a similar position on presidential coffees. The Congress can make sure he and surrogates such as Ms. Reno repeat this constantly for the next four months. The voters can decide on its credibility.

More may also happen. Weigh the potential effect if, say, Mr. Conrad and his team resigned in protest, a la Elliot Richardson that Saturday night. It's entirely conceivable that Clinton & Gore might decide that the path between here and November would be smoother with an independent investigation than without.

Al Gore

If Ms. Reno faces down political options, Congress also has legal ones. For starters, the Constitution provides for impeachment not only for presidents but for "all civil Officers of the United States." Society did not seem to enjoy its recent education in this process, but second thoughts have started to set in. Also, Congressman Dan Burton, rough and ready chairman of the Government Reform and Oversight Committee, made a point in conjunction with his release of the Freeh and La Bella memos. "After this election, assuming we get a new attorney general, I think I will be sending criminal referrals."

Chairman Burton singled out the attorney general; in refusing to appoint a counsel when the law demanded it, "she broke the law and obstructed justice." The threat is scarcely unprecedented; two attorneys general were convicted in the Watergate coverup. John Mitchell was convicted of conspiring to obstruct justice, and served 19 months in jail. Richard Kleindienst received a suspended sentence after pleading guilty to a misdemeanor charge of misleading Congress.

Rather than single out an ailing woman, Chairman Burton suggested he would also refer President Clinton and Vice President Gore: "I am confident and certain that they knew, especially the president, that illegal campaign contributions were coming in from foreign sources." These threats of course seem politically farfetched, the law and the facts notwithstanding, but they do add credence to Mr. Clinton's more immediate legal jeopardy.

Robert Ray, who succeeded Kenneth Starr and retains jurisdiction over matters referred to him, is studying whether to indict the president for perjury in the Paula Jones case, an offense for which he has already been cited for contempt by Judge Susan Webber Wright and faces disbarment proceedings in the state of Arkansas. Sentiment seems to be swinging in the direction of asking Mr. Clinton to show some responsibility for what he has put the nation through. The latest Wall Street Journal/NBC poll found that 64% of respondents disapproved of the president as a person. Some 54% of respondents agreed he should be disbarred.

All of which is to say, Congress and the Republicans cannot claim to be powerless before Ms. Reno's stonewalling. With the independent counsel law gone, their responsibility is clear. If justice continues to be corrupted, some of the blame will rest on Sen. Specter and his colleagues.

June 29, 2000

Editorial Feature

Al Gore,
Environmentalist and
Zinc Miner

BY MICAH MORRISON

*"The lakes and rivers sustain us; they flow through the veins of the
earth and into our own. But we must take care to let them flow back out
as pure as they came, not poison and waste them without thought for
the future."*

— AL GORE,
"EARTH IN THE BALANCE"

"He taught me how to plow a steep hillside with a team of mules.
He taught me how to clear three acres of heavily-wooded forest with
a double-bladed axe. . . . He taught me how to stop gullies before they
got started. He taught me how to drive, how to shoot a rifle, how to
fish, how to swim. We loved to swim together in the Caney Fork
River off a big flat rock on the back side of his farm."

— AL GORE ON HIS FATHER,
SEN. ALBERT GORE SR.,
FROM ALGORE2000.COM

CARTHAGE, Tenn.—On his most recent tax return, as he has the
past 25 years, Vice President Al Gore lists a $20,000 mining royalty
for the extraction of zinc from beneath his farm here in the bucolic
hills of the Cumberland River Valley. In total, Mr. Gore has earned
$500,000 from zinc royalties. His late father, the senator, introduced
him not only to the double-bladed ax but also to Armand Hammer,
chairman of Occidental Petroleum Corp., which sold the zinc-rich

land to the Gore family in 1973.

It also seems that zinc from Mr. Gore's property ends up in the cool waters of the Caney Fork River, an oft-celebrated site in Gore lore. A major shaft and tailings pond of the Pasminco Zinc Mine sit practically in the backyard of the vice president's Tennessee homestead. Zinc and other metals from the Gore land move from underground tunnels through elaborate extraction processes. Waste material ends up in the tailings pond, from which water flows into adjacent Caney Fork, languidly rolling on to the great Cumberland.

Messy Business

Mining is intrinsically a messy business, and Pasminco Zinc generally has a good environmental record. But not one that would pass muster with "Earth in the Balance," Mr. Gore's best-selling environmental book. As recently as May 16, the Tennessee Department of Environment and Conservation issued a "Notice of Violation." It informed Pasminco that it had infringed the Tennessee Water Quality Control Act due to high levels of zinc in the river.

Those zinc levels exceeded standards established by the state and the federal Environmental Protection Agency. A "sample analysis found that total zinc was 1.480 mg/L [milligrams per liter], which is greater than the monthly average of .65 mg/L and the daily maximum of 1.30 mg/L." Pasminco "may be subject to enforcement action pursuant to the Tennessee Water Quality Control Act of 1977 for the aforementioned violation," the notice stated.

This was not the first time Mr. Gore's mining benefactor had run afoul of environmental regulations. In 1996, the mine twice failed biomonitoring tests designed to protect water quality in the Caney Fork for fish and wildlife. Mine discharge "failed two acute tests for toxicity to *Ceriodaphnia dubia*," a species of water flea, according to a mine permit analysis by Tennessee environmental authorities. "The discharge of industrial wastewater from Outfall #001 [the Caney Fork effluent] contains toxic metals (copper and zinc)," the analysis stated. "The combined effect of these pollutants may be detrimental to fish and aquatic life."

Tests for The Wall Street Journal by two independent Tennessee laboratories, conducted in September 1999 and this month, showed trace amounts of zinc and other metals in the Caney Fork that were in compliance with federal standards. But soil tests revealed what one lab called problematic "large quantities" of heavy metals in the riverbank soil downstream of the Caney Fork effluent. In both sets of tests, samples of water and soil were provided to the labs by the Journal.

Soil samples drawn from the mine effluent and downstream "contained large quantities of Barium, Iron, and Zinc, as well as smaller amounts of Arsenic, Chromium and Lead," Warner Laboratories found in September. "The soil from each of these sites seems to have some problems according to our findings. The levels of Barium, Iron and Zinc far exceed any report limit [a detection threshold within the testing system] and it should be noted that these results are extremely high compared to typical soil found in a populated neighborhood."

Tests conducted in June by the Environmental Science Corp. found similar traces of heavy metals in the water and soil. The report found the soil samples to contain relatively high levels of "Barium, Iron, Zinc, and several of the other metals, including Aluminum, Calcium and Magnesium." The ESC report also noted traces of cyanide in some water and soil samples.

Pasminco is not required to test soil along the banks of the Caney Fork. Both labs, while noting anomalies in the soil, believe the results do not warrant concern as environmental hazards. The water and soil clearly are not, however, "as pure as they came," as Mr. Gore demands in "Earth in the Balance."

A 1998 study by the Environmental Working Group, a Washington-based organization, criticized the zinc-mining operation for purchasing a toxic waste that included sulfuric acid and reselling it as fertilizer. The mine buys acid waste from steel plants, uses it as purification agent in zinc processing, and then sells the waste to fertilizer companies, according to a report in the Tennessean, a Nashville newspaper. Most soil scientists say the procedure is safe.

Tennessee environmentalists disagree. "Clearly, when you spread those types of chemicals around on a farm or on the land, you're going to get a lot of runoff," Brian McGuire, executive director of Tennessee Citizens Action told the Tennessean. "So it's going to get into the water. We're poisoning ourselves."

A Pasminco official noted that the mine has had few violations and works to uphold a "very strict standard" of environmental quality. The Gore campaign did not respond to requests for comment. But some Tennessee residents say Mr. Gore becomes testy when questioned about the zinc mine. Tom Gniewek, a retired chemical engineer from Camden, Tenn., has studied the zinc mine for years and tried to question Mr. Gore about it at town-hall meetings. "He gets real angry," Mr. Gniewek says. "Instead of answering the question, he attacked my motives and accused people like me of vandalizing the earth."

Mr. Gore's original purchase of the zinc-rich land is of some interest as well, shedding light on his long relationship with Mr. Hammer, the former Occidental Petroleum chief. A controversial influence peddler who trafficked in politicians of all stripes and parties, Mr. Hammer pleaded guilty in 1975 to providing hush money in the Watergate scandal.

Mr. Hammer cut a wide swath across Washington from the 1930s until his death in 1990 at 92. His controversial career was marked by decades of profitable business dealings with the Soviet Union, which were closely watched by the FBI. He leapt into the big time by acquiring Libyan oil rights for Occidental Petroleum through what biographer Edward Jay Epstein has characterized as a combination of shrewd business dealings and bribery. After his 1975 conviction, Mr. Hammer spent the rest of his life campaigning for a pardon, which President Bush granted in 1989.

Mr. Hammer cultivated close relationships with many politicians, but he was closest to Mr. Gore's father, a U.S. senator from 1953 until 1971. Mr. Hammer's Occidental Minerals snapped up the zinc-bearing property in 1972. The senior Mr. Gore's farm is on the opposite bank of the Caney Fork. Mr. Hammer paid $160,000, double the only other offer, according to the Washington Post, which first disclosed details of the arrangement during the 1992 presidential campaign.

According to deed documents in Carthage, a year later Mr. Hammer sold the land to the senior Mr. Gore for $160,000, adding the extremely generous $20,000 per year mineral royalty. Ten minutes after that sale, the former senator executed a deed selling the property, including the mineral rights, to his son, the future vice president, for $140,000. Albert Gore Sr. told the Post he kept the first $20,000 royalty for himself, evening up the father-son transaction.

The purpose of the sale appears to have been transferring the annual $20,000 payment from Mr. Hammer to the young Mr. Gore.

Gore Zinc Bounty

Mine and tailings pond

Al Gore Homestead

Rick Seymour for The Wall Street Journal

The Post reported that the "$20,000 a year amounts to $227 an acre, much more than the $30 an acre Occidental Minerals, part of Hammer's oil company, paid the senior Gore and some neighbors a few years before the 1973 arrangement."

In 1992 then-Sen. Gore told the Post that although he had been working for "slave wages" as a newspaper reporter, he quickly came up with a $40,000 down payment from two previous real-estate investments. In 1974, the zinc mine began annual payments of $20,000 to Mr. Gore, an important source of income to the young politician for many years.

After the senior Mr. Gore lost his 1970 Senate re-election bid, Mr. Hammer named him chairman of Island Creek Coal, an Occidental subsidiary, and appointed him to the board of directors of Occidental Petroleum. The late Mr. Gore's estate is conservatively valued at $1.5 million, including a block of Occidental stock worth between $250,000 and $500,000. The vice president is executor and trustee of his father's estate, with "sole discretion" to manage a trust on his mother's behalf.

As Albert Gore Jr. rose through the political ranks, Mr. Hammer continued to assist him. The Hammer family and corporations made donations up to the legal maximum in all of Mr. Gore's campaigns, according to Mr. Hammer's former personal assistant, Neil Lyndon, writing in London's Daily Telegraph. Mr. Gore regularly dined with Mr. Hammer and Occidental lobbyists in Washington, Mr. Lyndon wrote. "Separately and together, the Gores sometimes used Hammer's luxurious private Boeing 727 for journeys and jaunts." The former Hammer aide noted that the "profound and prolonged involvement between Hammer and Gore has never been revealed or investigated."

Mr. Hammer was famous for his dealings with the Soviet Union, and received a humanitarian award in Moscow in 1987 from International Physicians Against Nuclear War. Mr. Gore, who had been elected to the Senate in 1984, delivered a speech to the same convention, saying conventional arms should be cut along with nuclear weapons. As vice president, Mr. Gore became the Clinton administration point man on relations with Russia.

More Hypocrisy

Mr. Gore would be well served to get the facts out about his relationship with Mr. Hammer, beginning with the zinc bounty. The issue is bigger than whether there is a pollution problem in Tennessee. When Mr. Gore's zinc riches are at stake, he appears unwilling to live by the standards he sets out for others in "Earth in the Balance."

His record of uncompromising environmental rhetoric seems another instance of the kind of hypocrisy that has dogged his campaign for months. He's been accused of being a slumlord for providing substandard housing to a tenant on a rental unit adjoining his farm. A well-remembered 1996 speech to the Democratic National Convention, invoking his sister's death by lung cancer and attacking the tobacco industry, also contributed to his reputation for slippery sanctimony when his close ties to Tennessee tobacco were revealed. And of course Mr. Gore has been sharply criticized for posturing on campaign finance reform while under investigation for possible fundraising crimes in the 1996 campaign.

No mention of the zinc mine appears in "Earth in the Balance," on Mr. Gore's campaign Web site or in his speeches. At this point the story of the Tennessee farm, the zinc mine, the politician and the influence peddler is largely one of cant and hypocrisy. This is not a hanging crime in the political world, but the vice president, among others, might note that Bill Clinton's problems also began with a murky land deal and a shady financier.

Mr. Morrison is a senior editorial page writer at the Journal.

July 17, 2000

Editorial Feature

Malicious Discretion at Justice

You don't have to be a "Clinton-hater" to smell something fishy about the prosecution of Charles Bakaly III, formerly spokesman for Independent Counsel Kenneth Starr. The New York Times says trying him on criminal contempt of court charges is "unduly punitive

Thinking Things Over

By Robert L. Bartley

and extreme." Julian Epstein, Democratic House Judiciary counsel, brands it "a terrible prosecution."

Does it cross the bounds of "hate" to draw the obvious conclusion? To wit: This is the latest instance of the Clinton administration abusing the judicial process to settle scores and hound its critics. That is to say, the latest evidence of the corruption of the rule of law by Janet Reno's Department of Justice.

Charles Bakaly

Mr. Bakaly is accused of not playing square with investigators probing whether he was the source of a Times story saying that Mr. Starr's office had concluded it had legal powers to indict a sitting president. A three-judge panel of the D.C. Circuit court ruled that whatever the sources of the story, it contained no illegal leaks. The case against Mr. Bakaly rests on lawyerly pushing and shoving about what he was or was not obligated to tell the investigators. Normal discretion would conclude no harm, no foul; but Ms. Reno has unleashed the prosecutorial pit bulls.

To top it off, the case is being heard by Judge Norma Holloway Johnson, whose hotheaded opinion on the "leaks" was unanimously overturned by the appellate court. And without a jury, a circumstance prosecutors arranged by picking charges with only a six-month sentence, though disbarment could follow. Judge Johnson is herself under investigation by a five-judge panel on why, as chief judge of the district court, she bypassed random selection procedures and steered Clinton scandal cases to Clinton-appointed judges.

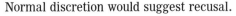

Normal discretion would suggest recusal.

But then, this is Clinton-era justice. Ask Billy Dale, whom Ms. Reno's pit bulls pursued for embezzling to justify the White House Travel Office firings. A D.C. jury threw the charges out peremptorily, but a message remained for any bureaucrat with the temerity to stand up to a Clinton whim.

Or ask The American Spectator, which found FBI agents detailed to investigate it because of an Arkansas psychic's inference that some of the money it spent reporting in Arkansas went to bribe David Hale to testify adversely about the president. The charge was as cockamamie as it sounds, according to an official study by Michael Shaheen, a storied Justice Department careerist. But no press watchdog even sounded an alarm about an arm of government investigating how a bona-fide publication spent its money reporting stories critical of the president.

The Linda Tripp wiretapping prosecution was a state action, but it came after Maryland Democratic legislators petitioned prosecutors, and after Judge Johnson provided crucial help in releasing the tapes to local prosecutors. Predictably, it proved unsustainable.

Contrast these cases with the prosecutorial discretion Mr. Starr's successor just displayed about Mrs. Clinton's role in the Travel Office firings. In 1994, Mrs. Clinton had White House Associate Counsel Neil Eggleston file answers to General Accounting Office interrogatories. Her answer was that while she was aware of a review of the Travel Office, "she had no role in the decision to terminate the employees."

Mr. Ray's official report concludes, "with respect to Mrs. Clinton, there was substantial evidence that she had a 'role' in the decision to fire the Travel Office employees." It details her frequent conversations with those immediately responsible, "which produced a momentum to take immediate action." In short, Mrs. Clinton's role was prime mover and her GAO response a lie. Still, Mr. Ray declined a prosecution he deemed unsustainable: "The evidence was insufficient to prove to a jury beyond a reasonable doubt."

Mr. Ray is also studying whether to indict President Clinton after he leaves office for his lies in the Paula Jones case. Indeed, the president's guilt has already been adjudicated in Judge Susan Webber Wright's contempt citation. The president's goose is cooked if Mr. Ray applies anything like the standards used to prosecute Mr. Bakaly.

While pursuing Mr. Bakaly, Ms. Reno is exercising maximum discretion not to pursue wrongdoing outlined by FBI Director Louis Freeh and Charles La Bella, former head of her own campaign funding task force. A third recommendation to charter an independent investigation of Vice President Gore's truthfulness in the fund-raising investigation now sits on her desk, forwarded by the current head of her task force, Robert Conrad. Since Justice is now investigating the leak of that recommendation, the Bakaly prosecution is a warning to Mr. Conrad and his staff.

This is not merely a matter of passing scandal. The foundations of our free society rest on the rule of law, the principle that laws apply to both high and lowly, that this is a government of laws rather than men. Clinton-Reno justice breeds a cynicism that eats at these foundations.

Last week the CATO Institute held a symposium on the rule of law. Sen. Fred Thompson, the Tennessee Republican who had a front-row seat at both Watergate and Whitewater, gave an outstanding speech. Despite scandals from Teapot Dome to Iran-Contra, "there was never any feeling that the system had broken down," he said. "I believe it's pretty fair to say that we pretty well protected the rule of law for about 200 years."

In the current administration, "one might be tempted to conclude that there was virtually a continuous undermining of the rule of law." Many of the cases do remain ambivalent, but the Freeh and La Bella recommendations do not. "These memoranda are powerful and shocking documents. We see these career law-enforcement officials practically begging the attorney general to do the right thing." Ms. Reno's rejection is a clear breach of the rule of law "of historic proportions. It will undoubtedly contribute to the cynicism and skepticism that has become so prevalent in our society today, especially among our young people."

"Leaders, I believe, still have the responsibility of reminding the American people of what is at stake," Sen. Thompson said. This responsibility should especially be weighed by Republicans as they plan a feel-good convention in Philadelphia and generally hesitate to raise scandal issues obviously weighing on the minds of voters. Times are good now, the senator said, but in the next crisis we will need leaders and a system the public trusts. "That to me is the most important issue facing us today, and how we resolve it will play a large part in determining our destiny as a nation."

REVIEW & OUTLOOK

The Big Stall

Whether Al Gore or George W. Bush moves into the White House next January, you almost have to wonder how many people in Washington are going to be unhappy when the moving vans carry the current residents away. For the past seven years, no matter what other normal activities the Clinton Presidency may have been engaged in, it seems that some constant, smothering haze of controversy or ill will has hung over the city. So enured are the locals to all this that they barely notice anymore when yet another passel of Clinton lawyers rolls across the sidewalk in yet another intractable legal dust-up.

Royce Lamberth

Ask Royce Lamberth. The federal district judge is becoming the Judge Roy Bean on the frontier of Clinton jurisprudence, the fellow whose lot in life it now is to sit and listen to lawyers in the Clinton government explain why this or that piece of evidence or documents can't be found, can't be produced, or how they can't get the computers to work, can't explain why the lawyers in here yesterday misspoke, and so on.

And so yesterday, with a U.S. Justice Department lawyer named James Gilligan standing before him, Judge Lamberth spoke in the blunt dialect of his native Texas: "You weren't going to admit that until it was drug out of you in this hearing."

"This" is any clear expression from the Clinton lawyers of how long it would take the White House to restore the thousands of e-mails the White House claims got lost in the computer ether somewhere. What were the e-mails conceivably about? Oh nothing— Monica, Whitewater, Al Gore, the White House fund-raising operation.

Judge Lamberth has been wrestling with the estimates delivered by the lawyers of the e-mails' recovery operation, ranging from a few months to several years. Accordingly he's been taking testimony on this since last Thursday from White House employees who've broken out of the White House compound.

Two former White House computer specialists, Sheryl Hall and Betty Lambuth, took the stand in Judge Lamberth's court to testify on the hundreds of thousands of White House e-mails that weren't searched in response to subpoenas. The computer glitch was discovered in May 1998, but the White House kept mum until the Washington Times broke the story in February. Judge Lamberth is presiding over a lawsuit by Reagan-Bush appointees who contend their privacy rights were violated by the White House's collection of their FBI files.

Ms. Hall was formerly the chief of White House computer operations, who testified that the missing e-mails included information on the FBI files, 1996 Clinton-Gore fund raising, the Lewinsky scandal and the Commerce Department trade missions. Ms. Hall is suing the White House, claiming she was demoted after she protested the White House's illegal creation of contributor data bases for the Democratic National Committee.

Betty Lambuth was the head of a Northrop-Grumman computer task force at the White House. She backed up Ms. Hall's testimony. She and two other Northrop employees say that after they uncovered the missing e-mails "we were told that if any of us spoke out about them, we would lose our jobs, be arrested and thrown in jail." White House aides have denied making these threats.

In her first affidavit in February, Ms. Hall predicted the Clinton Administration would find ways to delay production of the e-mails until it leaves office. She and Ms. Lambuth testified that it would take only four to six weeks for five workers to restore the e-mails.

Since the problem was made public five months ago, the White House has failed to produce a single e-mail. In April, the recovery figure given to Judge Lamberth by the White House was 170 days. Gregory Ekberg, the independent auditor hired by the White House to review its retrieval efforts, told an incredulous Judge Lamberth that he was never told of the judge's April order for the White House to produce e-mails immediately. He said the only deadline he received was to finish the job by the end of this year. Meanwhile, White House technicians gave testimony claiming that all their recovery efforts are failing.

Judge Lamberth will take more testimony later this week. It is generally believed that the largest chunk of missing e-mail is to and from Vice President Gore's office. Last week, Robert Conrad, the former prosecutor now in charge of Justice's campaign-finance task force, recommended an independent counsel for Mr. Gore. So there is some incentive here for the Clinton government's lawyers to do whatever they have to do until the clock runs out. When the clock runs out, the moving vans will come and go. What will linger in the air for a long time is the particular kind of work this White House made federal lawyers do on its behalf.

July 21, 2000

REVIEW & OUTLOOK

The Riady Connection

One month before the 1996 Presidential election, Washington reporters for this newspaper broke the story of Asian commercial interests—notably Indonesia's Lippo Group, controlled by the Riady family—contributing millions to the Clinton-Gore re-election effort. Today, with less than four months to go to the 2000 elections, the Riady connection and questions of corrupt influence still resonate.

Attorney General Janet Reno has vehemently opposed an independent inquiry into White House fund raising ever since 1996. This is clearly shown in the voluminous Justice Department memoranda painstakingly unearthed by Rep. Dan Burton's investigative committee.

In four years of detailed memos to Ms. Reno, FBI Director Louis Freeh repeatedly argued for an independent counsel to probe a "core group," including President Clinton, aided by a floating cast of "opportunists." Charles La Bella, the campaign task force head at Justice, observed that the scheme had the markings of a "loose enterprise" conspiracy. He joined Mr. Freeh in calling for Ms. Reno to appoint an independent counsel. Mr. La Bella later left the embattled task force post, his Justice career in ruins.

Robert Conrad is the latest in a series of Justice task force heads. Last month he recommended that a special prosecutor investigate Vice President Al Gore for possible crimes related to fund raising. Mr. Conrad also is studying whether to indict Lippo head James

Riady on campaign-finance violations. The issue haunts this campaign. As Mr. Gore revs up his own bid for the Presidency, Rep. Burton revealed earlier this week that a videotape from a December 1995 White House coffee captures the voice of Mr. Gore telling a donor that "we ought to show Mr. Riady" some of the soft-money television ads that are an element of the finance scandal from the Clinton-Gore 1996 re-election bid.

In March, Mr. Conrad led a team to Jakarta to request Indonesian Attorney General Marzuki Darusman's assistance in investigating the Riady connection. Mr. Darusman told the Journal the investigators were "very anxious" to get to the bottom of it all.

Al Gore

Advocates of a special prosecutor and the loose enterprise theory have focused on a key White House meeting on September 13, 1995, when the enterprise likely was set in motion. At the meeting was President Clinton, then-Commerce Department official John Huang, Mr. Riady, senior Clinton aide Bruce Lindsey and Arkansas businessman Joseph Giroir. Now some of these figures, as well as key players from other sectors of the Whitewater scandal, are turning up in Indonesia in a new Riady-financed venture.

To many, perhaps most, it may seem as if the Clinton coverup has succeeded. But Mr. Riady and some of his associates are still open to prosecution. Nor should silence fall over the court of public opinion. Somebody should be asking Mr. Riady some tough questions. To wit, is the "loose enterprise" rewarding its own for keeping quiet about Bill Clinton?

The new venture is AcrossAsia, a holding group for the multimedia arm of the Lippo Group. AcrossAsia debuted last week on Hong Kong's recently organized Growth Enterprise Market stock exchange. The Riady family controls 78% of AcrossAsia through a Cayman Island trust. As our Jay Solomon reported from Indonesia, among those profiting from AcrossAsia are former Arkansas Governor Jim Guy Tucker, convicted in the Whitewater scandal; Mr. Giroir; and Dwight Harlan, an Arkansan who played a role in one of the Whitewater schemes.

In 1996, Mr. Tucker, then the sitting Governor of Arkansas, was convicted of fraud and conspiracy charges in a prosecution that also saw the conviction of the Clintons' former Whitewater Development Co. partners, James and Susan McDougal. In a second case, Mr. Tucker pleaded guilty to fraud in arranging a sham bankruptcy in a cable-television deal.

Mr. Tucker later was hired as a consultant for a Lippo affiliate and with his wife was an investor in K@belvision, a fiber-optic network trying to bring the Internet to Indonesia. K@belvision is controlled by the Riadys through AcrossAsia. Mr. Tucker now runs the cable group and has a 1.5% stake in the holding company, worth roughly $40 million at last Friday's stock market debut.

Mr. Giroir is one of the most interesting figures in the background of the Clinton scandals. A storied Arkansas wheeler-dealer and long-time associate of the Riadys, he also holds a 1.5% stake in AcrossAsia. Mr. Giroir was a former managing partner of the Rose Law Firm, working with the young Hillary Rodham and Webster Hubbell, among others. According to Congressional testimony, Mr. Giroir was at the center of efforts to move Mr. Huang—a former senior official of the Lippo Group—from the Commerce Department to the Democratic National Committee. Mr. Huang later pleaded guilty to campaign finance violations and received a wrist-slap one year of probation from Justice.

Mr. Tucker's employee, Mr. Harlan, has an equity stake in K@belvision and was the figurehead president back in Arkansas of Castle Sewer & Water, one of the scams in Kenneth Starr's successful prosecution of Mr. Tucker and the McDougals. Mr. Harlan was not charged with any crimes and testified for the prosecution, identifying documents.

Mr. Riady also raised suspicions in Washington of a possible hush-money payment after reporters ferreted out news that he had provided a $100,000 payment to Mr. Hubbell, the disgraced former Associate Attorney General, when Mr. Hubbell was under pressure to cooperate with Mr. Starr. Mr. Hubbell pleaded guilty in 1994 to fraud and went to prison for 18 months. The $100,000 payment came after Mr. Riady and Mr. Huang attended meetings at the White House and also met with Mr. Hubbell.

In 1997, Senator Fred Thompson's investigative committee voted out a report identifying Mr. Riady and Mr. Huang as among those involved in the campaign finance scandal having ties to the Communist regime in China. The principals have denied the charge and Democrats on the Thompson committee contended the evidence was inconclusive.

Perhaps it is all a great big coincidence, but we doubt it. It's time someone took a much closer look at Mr. Riady and AcrossAsia, both in Asia and here at home.

REVIEW & OUTLOOK

'Loose Enterprise'?

"I never worried about what Webb Hubbell would say," President Clinton told Justice Department campaign-finance task force head Robert Conrad in April. "If he wanted to say something bad about me, he'd have to make it up."

Webster Hubbell is the former Associate Attorney General of the United States and Arkansas crony of the President and First Lady who pleaded guilty to fraud in 1994 and went to prison for 18 months. Two independent counsels—Robert Fiske and Kenneth Starr—saw Mr. Hubbell as one of the keys to the Clintons' Whitewater dealings and sought the truth from him in the manner prosecutors do, with high-stakes pressure and cajoling. At the same time, supporters' money rained down on Mr. Hubbell, most notably in the form of a $100,000 payment from another Clinton insider, James Riady of Indonesia. Mr. Hubbell said nothing to implicate the Clintons.

Mr. Clinton's interview with Mr. Conrad, released by the White House Monday, again raises questions of corrupt influence that haunt this Presidency and the 2000 campaign. Was the $100,000 Lippo payment hush money to keep Webb Hubbell silent? Was Mr. Riady at the center of what former Justice task force head Charles La Bella called a suspected "loose enterprise" criminal conspiracy to shred campaign finance laws?

The Whitewater investigation merges with the campaign-finance probe in the figure of James Riady, with Justice examining campaign contributions from Mr. Riady's $12 billion conglomerate, the

Lippo Group.

The President's answers to Mr. Conrad sound a familiarly evasive note. Take the possible hush money payment. Circumstantial evidence that something was going on is strong. Mr. Riady met with Mr. Hubbell—then under tremendous pressure to cooperate with Mr. Starr—on the morning of June 23, 1994; in the afternoon, Mr. Riady saw the President in the White House. Four days later, a Lippo entity cut Mr. Hubbell a check for $100,000.

Mr. Conrad asked Mr. Clinton, "Do you have any recollection of a conversation with Mr. Riady concerning Webster Hubbell in the days before a Riady-controlled entity paid him $100,000?"

Webster Hubbell

"No, sir, I don't," the President said, and then began to establish wiggle room: "You know, let me say this. It's possible that he could have said to me, 'I'm going to help Webb Hubbell, you know, I know Webb Hubbell and I want to try to help him,' because everybody knew that I knew him well, that he had been here working. And so if, in fact, I did meet with him then, if that, in fact, did happen, and if—. But I don't remember it, but might have met with him. If, in fact, I met with him it wouldn't surprise me if he'd said that, something like that in passing. But I do not remember him doing that."

Mr. Clinton also was asked about $1 million Mr. Riady purportedly pledged to funnel to Democrats in the 1992 campaign. Mr. Riady allegedly offered the money to Mr. Clinton during an August 1992 car ride. As a foreign national, Mr. Riady is barred from contributing to U.S. campaigns.

Here again Mr. Clinton's memory failed him. If Mr. Riady had offered the money during the car ride, the President told Mr. Conrad, "I'm surprised I don't remember it. I mean, but I, I—. You asked me what I remember. I can't remember any specific thing. I know that I saw him sometime in '92 after I became the nominee, and I know he said he was going to help us. If he said he was going to give us $1 million, which he might have done, I just don't remember it."

For four years, FBI Director Louis Freeh has urged Attorney General Reno to appoint an independent counsel precisely because figures such as Mr. Riady and Mr. Hubbell are so close to the President. In memos to the Attorney General, Mr. Freeh has argued that a "core group," including top White House officials, aided by a floating cast of "opportunists," set out to illegally funnel money to Clinton-Gore campaigns and other entities. The wink-and-nod payment to Mr. Hubbell through Mr. Riady strikes us as precisely what Mr. La Bella meant by a "loose enterprise." Mr. La Bella, we should note, was forced out of Justice after joining Mr. Freeh's calls for an independent counsel.

Advocates of a special prosecutor and the loose enterprise theory have focused on a key White House meeting on September 13, 1995. At the meeting was President Clinton, then-Commerce Department official John Huang (a former senior Lippo Group executive), Mr. Riady, senior Clinton aide Bruce Lindsey and Joseph Giroir, an Arkansas businessman with close ties to Lippo. After the meeting, Mr. Huang was sent to a new post at the Democratic National Committee. He later pleaded guilty to campaign-finance violations and received a wrist-slap one year probation from Justice.

It remains to be seen what Mr. Conrad will accomplish. But at least he seems to be asking some of the right questions. To the President he said, referring to Mr. Huang and the now-notorious Clinton fund-raising pal Charlie Trie, "The two people most responsible for [illegal 1996 contributions] were the two people that were in that position because of their relationship to you. Would you agree with that?"

The President angrily retorted, "Is this guilt by association, sir? What do you want to say?"

We would say there is reason to believe a conspiracy existed to evade and break the law. If that doesn't matter, then the law itself doesn't matter.

The Permanent Campaign

In August 2000 the Republican and Democratic parties convened and chose George W. Bush and Vice President Al Gore as their respective presidential candidates. Mr. Bush chose Dick Cheney, a former Secretary of Defense and an experienced Washington hand, as his vice-presidential running mate. Mr. Gore chose Senator Joseph Lieberman, a respected moral spokesman for his party.

The Gore choice was telling. "What Mr. Gore so desperately wants now is moral and political separation from his boss," the Journal wrote. "He knows that Dick Cheney's speech to the GOP convention last week was a direct hit, linking him like a Siamese twin to the scandals and deceptions of the last eight years: 'Somehow we will never see one without thinking of the other.' He also knows his Clinton ties are killing him among culturally conservative voters across the country: in the South, among married women and parents, and with those over age 65."

It remained to be seen whether Mr. Gore had his boss's touch for politics. "Mr. Clinton's gift to history is the 'permanent campaign,'" wrote Journal editor Robert L. Bartley. "As Napoleon taught the world to move beyond mercenary armies to the total mobilization of societies for war, President Clinton has transcended the old-fashioned political campaign. Under the precedent he has established, the campaign is no longer for a few weeks every other fall. Instead, campaign tactics and campaign mores suffuse every moment, every act of governance."

As the campaign unfolded, Democrats urged that the scandals surrounding the Clinton-Gore White House be left in the past. But new acts in the drama kept unfolding. In late August, Attorney General Reno for the third time rejected a recommendation that an independent prosecutor be named to investigate Mr. Gore's role in the 1996 campaign finance scandal. The request had come from her own campaign finance task force head, Robert Conrad, who believed Mr. Gore may have been lying about his role in the Buddhist Temple affair.

In September, Independent Counsel Robert Ray, Kenneth Starr's successor, issued a summary statement of his office's analysis of the Clintons' Whitewater land deals and actions later taken in Washington: "the evidence was insufficient to prove to a jury beyond a reasonable doubt that either President Clinton or Mrs. Clinton knowingly participated in any criminal conduct." That is "not to say there is no evidence," the Journal noted, but that "the coverup worked." In another autumn scandal development, the Wen Ho Lee espionage case, born out of the campaign finance scandal, collapsed, leaving more questions than answers. "It is abundantly clear that Mr. Lee was up to no good," the Journal wrote, outlining some of the evidence against him.

REVIEW & OUTLOOK

Big Bill

Every now and then there's a scene in a movie involving a pool party and a fat guy. Everyone's sitting around the side of the pool socializing, when the fat guy gets up on the diving board and starts bouncing up and down. Sometimes he's holding a fat cigar. Everyone stops to watch the fat guy jumping on the diving board and obviously they're wondering if the guy is going to catapult his corpus into the pool. And of course the fat guy does exactly that, driving a huge wave of water onto all the guests who scatter screaming in dumbfounded disbelief. How cheesy can you get?

Bill Clinton

Well, Bill Clinton, the President, has just belly-flopped into the GOP convention. He's managed to get the whole place talking about him. He's got the Republican nominee talking about him, the nominee's father, a former U.S. President, talking about him, and now yesterday even the nominee's sainted mother was talking about him.

Man, this is fat-guy heaven. It's all about him. It's all about Bill Clinton. President, politico, pundit—it hardly seems to matter which hat Bill Clinton's wearing at any given moment; the personas all seem to, well, blur.

We happen to indeed believe that the simple answer to what Mr.

Clinton has been up to the past week is unbound self-centeredness, even by the normal standards of mammoth presidential psyches. Mr. Clinton, however, is not merely one of the weekly shouters on "The McLaughlin Group" but a two-term President in the last months of his tenure in office. At this twilight moment few historians of the Presidency would likely call these Clintonian interventions "presidential," though conceivably it is the fading twilight itself that has brought on all this braying at the opposition.

Some readers might think the foregoing a bit harsh; this is, after all, the President of the United States. Consider, though, what's been said.

This is the Clinton crack that set off President Bush and Barbara Bush: "I mean, how bad could I be? I've been governor of Texas; my daddy was President; I own a baseball team. They like me down there; everything is rocking along hunky-dory. Their fraternity had it for eight years, give to ours for eight years."

Then there was this on the Supreme Court to the trial lawyers' convention on Sunday, after first noting that Dick Cheney's South Africa vote "takes your breath away." What really worried him, said the President, are "the people now whom I've tried to put on the court of appeals who are African-American and Hispanic who are being held in political jail because they can't get a hearing from the Republican Senate."

On Fox TV Tuesday, the day John McCain and Condoleezza Rice spoke, the President got into a riff about the GOP darkness descending on the elderly, the environment and abortion: "What they want to do is to seem safe and reliable and compassionate and inclusive. They're not going to be up there saying, 'Vote for us, our favorite Supreme Court judges are Justice Thomas and Justice Scalia, and we're going to repeal Roe v. Wade,' but that's what's going to happen."

And finally came the President's assessment of the state of his wife's candidacy for the open New York Senate seat: "Everybody that always hated me all those years and were so mean to me, they've transferred all their anger to her now. It's almost as if they've got one last chance to beat me." He also added that "it wasn't her idea to run"; she was goaded into the race by some New York Democrats.

All this in less than a week. In the past six days, Mr. Clinton has made at least eight political appearances. The biggest looming ahead is the Democratic Convention in Los Angeles, and on the available evidence it appears there's a good chance that Bill Clinton will hit L.A. like some political black hole, siphoning into himself all the event's available oxygen and energy, and along with it Al Gore's candidacy. He speaks Monday.

It is impossible to imagine that either the Gore campaign or other high-level Democrats are happy with the President's recent hyperactive assaults on the opposition. You can't say they weren't warned. These are classic Clinton improvisations, executed for reasons of self-interest. The most recent victim of this exercise was Israel's Ehud Barak. Ask all of his lawyers about it. And if this belly-flopping into the campaign pool keeps up, you can ask Al Gore about it in November.

August 8, 2000

REVIEW & OUTLOOK

Gore's Clinton Fatigue

So once again Democrats are calling in the symbolic moral caval-
ry to save them from Bill Clinton's legacy. By making Connecticut
Senator Joseph Lieberman his running mate, Al Gore has picked

Joe Lieberman

someone as far away from his president as he
could go and still stay within his own party.

Mr. Lieberman, we readily admit, is one of
our favorite Democrats. He's a political grown-
up who takes ideas seriously. Despite an overall
liberal voting record (1998 Americans for
Democratic Action rating: 80%), the man who
rescued the Senate from Lowell Weicker in 1988
has also shown an ability to think for himself.

He's sympathetic to education vouchers, is
on record as agreeing with George W. Bush on
private Social Security accounts and missile defenses, supports cutting capital-gains taxes and opposes assisted suicide. In the 1980s, he
was a rare Democrat who backed Ronald Reagan's raids on Libya
and Grenada and attacked the War Powers Act. It's a sign of Mr.
Gore's predicament, down 17 points in the polls, that he is turning to
Senator Lieberman despite these glaring contradictions with his own
history and agenda.

What Mr. Gore so desperately wants now is moral and political
separation from his boss. He knows that Dick Cheney's speech to the
GOP convention last week was a direct hit, linking him like a Sia-

mese twin to the scandals and deceptions of the last eight years: "Somehow we will never see one without thinking of the other." He also knows his Clinton ties are killing him among culturally conservative voters across the country: in the South, among married women and parents, and with those over age 65.

As a moral spokesman, Mr. Lieberman is the closest thing Democrats have to an anti-Clinton. He has teamed with Bill Bennett to denounce Hollywood for its violence and misogyny, much as Tipper Gore did in the 1980s before her husband reined her in. He's certainly an amusing counterpoint to all of those David Geffen-Hugh Hefner bashes celebrating Mr. Clinton next week in Los Angeles.

But Mr. Lieberman is best known as the first prominent Democrat to rebuke Mr. Clinton during Monica-gate. "Such behavior is not just inappropriate, it is immoral and it is harmful, for it sends a message of what is acceptable behavior to the larger American family, particularly to our children," he said, in a soundbite Mr. Gore hopes to see often on TV this week.

We don't doubt Mr. Lieberman's sincerity. But the ironic effect of that 1998 rebuke was to help Mr. Clinton and his fellow Democrats survive the scandal. Here's how liberal Washington Post reporter Robert Kaiser described Mr. Lieberman's calculus on Feb. 13, 1999, after the Senate failed to convict Mr. Clinton:

"After the elections, Lieberman was more forthcoming about the political motivation for his Sept. 3 speech. The president's August confession, he said, was a threat to the Democratic Party. 'We had worked so hard,' he said, to demonstrate that Democrats had learned 'the difference between right and wrong . . . and to re-establish the party's connection to mainstream values.' And because 'Clinton himself was at the center of this transformation, I feared that . . . we were in danger as a party.'"

Mr. Lieberman told Mr. Kaiser that "I don't want to be too self-inflating here," but that his rebuke had provided political cover to even the most pro-Clinton Democrats, who could say, "'I agree with Joe Lieberman,' and it seemed to help."

Mr. Gore is hoping this symbolic inoculation will get Democrats past one more election, but count us as skeptics. For one thing, Mr. Lieberman voted with every other Senate Democrat to acquit the president, so even his moral authority is tainted by Mr. Clinton.

As for Mr. Gore, his ethical problems go well beyond guilt by association to include Buddhist Temples, White House coffees that raise money but somehow aren't fund-raisers, and "no controlling legal authority." Voters may fairly ask why Mr. Gore has decided to distance himself from the man he called "one of our greatest presidents" only when an election looms.

For months now we've read that voters don't care about the Clinton scandals, that "Clinton fatigue" is a myth, and that impeachment doesn't matter. Someone forgot to tell the voters. Now, with his Lieberman selection, Mr. Gore is all but admitting that his boss could cost him the election. This is the price of putting your ethics in a blind Clinton trust.

August 11, 2000

REVIEW & OUTLOOK

How Different?

Clearly one reason that Al Gore picked Senator Lieberman as his running mate is the expectation that a man with one of Washington's cleanest reputations will, as Macbeth hoped, wash away the stains of the Clinton years. So we will put again the blunt question asked by Dick Cheney in his acceptance speech last week:

"Does anyone, Republican or Democrat, seriously believe that under Mr. Gore, the next four years would be any different from the last eight?"

When Vice President Gore was asked by Tom Brokaw the other night about Sen. Lieberman's criticism of the President, he replied he agreed but, "I think honestly, Tom, that most people are ready to move on."

Al Gore

We also agree. The question then before the voters is, Would a Gore Presidency qualify as "moving on"?

To explore the answer to that question let's go back to the start of Mr. Gore's prominence in the nation's political life, when he, like Sen. Lieberman, was chosen by the nominee as a clean face for the ticket. Sen. Gore was represented to the voters as a fresh voice of the baby-boomers' generation, unlike President Bush and four years later Sen. Dole, the last presidential candidates of the generation that fought World War II.

So he won. Then what happened?

Let's assume for the sake of discussion that notwithstanding such Gore legacies as the long history with former Soviet agent Armand Hammer and Occidental Petroleum, the new vice president entered the White House a relative political virgin. In the years since, he's been pretty badly infected with something—at best unseemly, at worst beyond the law.

The conventional wisdom just now is that Mr. Gore has to get out from under "Clinton's shadow." Maybe so, but Mr. Gore casts shadows too, the result of his own real presence at various administration scandals.

The most famous are the various fund-raising scandals—the Buddhist temple event, the White House strategy meetings and the Vice President's money calls from the White House—all of it denied in the most preposterous, Clintonian language.

He thought the temple fund-raiser was "community outreach." The FBI report said he told them he wasn't privy to the White House soft-money talk because "he drank a lot of iced tea during the meetings, which could have necessitated a restroom break." And of course for those calls, there was "no controlling legal authority."

This stuff makes the "meaning of is" seem almost ingenuous. What's more, it is all Mr. Gore's doing, not Bill Clinton's. He made these shadows.

So now, as his mentor did some eight years ago, Al Gore has chosen to associate himself with one of the Senate's Democratic straight arrows. On the basis of experience, one may reasonably ask: Will Al Gore contaminate Joe Lieberman?

As we noted yesterday, Sen. Lieberman is already and unhesitatingly trimming centrist Democratic positions he once supported. Social Security privatization now troubles him. His support for school vouchers for all schools has faded, replaced by a union-approved enthusiasm for charter public schools, a stance that abandons Orthodox Jewish schools' hope for vouchers. Incredibly, Al Gore, who has done nothing other than trash vouchers, announced all of a sudden yesterday, "If I was the parent of a child who went to an inner city school that was failing . . . I might be for vouchers, too." We guess this means the Gore-Lieberman ticket has got some sort of arcane Buddhist defense in place on this tough issue.

But this Gore statement on vouchers is suggestive of the argument we wish to make here. There is no chance that Sen. Lieberman is going to cleanse Al Gore, any more than Al Gore cleansed Bill Clinton.

It is pretense to think so, but it is exactly this pretense that voters will be asked next week and afterward to believe.

Editorial Feature

Titan of the Media Age

LOS ANGELES—When Bill Clinton strides out on the podium at Staples Center tonight, we will all be witnessing a figure of historical fascination—a media-age Napoleon, perhaps, or Alexander.

Mr. Clinton's gift to history is the "permanent campaign." As Napoleon taught the world to move beyond mercenary armies to the total mobilization of societies for war, President Clinton has transcended the old-fashioned political campaign.

Thinking Things Over

By Robert L. Bartley

Under the precedent he has established, the campaign is no longer a few weeks every other fall. Instead, campaign tactics and campaign mores suffuse every moment, every act of governance. And, like Alexander severing the Gordian Knot, for him it has worked. He won a second term as president, overcame suspicions and scandals that would topple other mortals, fought off an attempted impeachment. Tonight he appears as a victor.

In the media age battles are not waged with bayonets, of course, but with spin. Yet in his arena, President Clinton has been cool and decisive in the heat of combat. Longtime Washington hands were agape with awe when he seized the opportunity to rout the Gingrich Republicans by vetoing an emergency resolution to keep the government open, then blaming them for closing the government. During this crisis he also first met Monica Lewinsky, but when her crisis eventually struck he was bold. "We'll just have to win it, then," he declared when Dick Morris reported that polls showed an apology would not wash. He called up the heavy Hillary artillery, which had already dispatched Gennifer Flowers in the 1992 campaign, to propound a "vast, right-wing conspiracy." He reacted to a House impeachment vote with a rally on the White House lawn, with Vice President Al Gore proclaiming that his boss "will be regarded in the history books as one of our greatest presidents."

While the President took some hits, the success of his campaign is measured in the currency of a new household word, "Clinton-haters." No one has ever suggested a "Gingrich-hater," a "Bork-hater" or a "Nixon-hater." Yet even those adult enough to know better readily accept an elocution designed to suggest that criticism of Mr. Clinton is motivated by "hate." The phrase adroitly changes the subject from Mr. Clinton's alleged transgressions to the motives of his critics. Republicans in impeachment are "partisan," while Democratic defenders are not. Kenneth Starr is animated by animus against  Mr. Clinton's libertine habits, not by devotion to the rule of law. By contrast, I suppose, James Carville's $100 bill in the trailer park was motivated by "love."

So as the nation prepares to watch Mr. Clinton tonight, let me say for the record that I and my colleagues on the editorial page of The Journal do not hate Mr. Clinton. We have of course covered his scandals exhaustively; our "Whitewater" books reprinting our Clinton coverage now total five volumes; choice excerpts are currently posted on OpinionJournal.com.

Our motivation has been simple: We early on decided that Clinton character was the big story of the 1990s, as President Reagan's rescue of the economy and triumph over Communism was the big story of the 1980s. So we set out to cover the story in a way that most of our competitors have not; Mr. Clinton and his supporters do not appreciate this, but the reaction suggests that a good many readers do.

That said, I certainly agree with Sen. Bob Kerrey's observation that Mr. Clinton is an "unusually good liar, unusually good." The capacity to lie without shame has been this president's most powerful weapon, the key to his dominance of the spin wars. The lies have served him well on big things. In 1992 he campaigned as a New Democrat, by the way evincing some sympathy from our columns. In 1993, he and his wife proposed to socialize 14% of GDP. By 1996 he was running for re-election on welfare reform. By 1999, he was rejecting the centrist Medicare reforms proposed by his own Breaux Commission, better to keep the issue alive for this fall. A seamless morph.

The Clinton lies have been even more central on the small things—personal scandals such as the draft, the $100,000 commodities coup, the Whitewater land flips, the Travel Office firings, the Rose Law firm billing records, the 1992 tax return omitting the gift from Jim McDougal when he assumed the Whitewater debts, the solicitation of no-show jobs for Webster Hubbell. On such matters we've learned that the presidency is a powerful office, protected by layers of deniability, directions dispensed by winks and nods, the willingness of minions to sacrifice, in the case of Mr. Hubbell and Susan McDougal, even serving jail time.

If you click into OpinionJournal.com and read the reprint of Micah Morrison's 1997 article, "What Did the President Know When?", you will come away with little doubt that the Asian fundraising scandal was hatched in an Oval Office meeting on Sept. 13, 1995. Here Mr. Clinton, James Riady and their top aides dispatched John Huang to his fund-raising post at the Democratic National Committee. FBI Director Louis Freeh and Justice investigator Charles La Bella recommended an independent investigation of this apparent conspiracy, but were rebuffed by Attorney General Janet Reno.

The damage to the Justice Department and rule of law has been staggering. There is said to be a pending indictment of Mr. Riady; I wonder if it includes the President as a co-conspirator? Yet in truth, at best it would be difficult to penetrate the walls of the Oval Office and prove this case in a court of law or even conclusively in the court of public opinion. In Watergate, it took the testimony of President Nixon's own counsel, John Dean, backed up by tape recordings.

So in the case of President Clinton, we are left with the sordid spectacle of Paula Jones, Monica, the $850,000 settlement, what the meaning of "is" is, a president found guilty of contempt by a judge and facing disbarment in his home state. It is "only sex," the president's defenders explain. No, it is about many other unbridled appetites and many other lies. It surfaces with sex because that's one area where he has to take direct and individual responsibility, one thing he could not delegate.

When the president speaks tonight, the real issue will be whether his success becomes the model for future American politics, whether the slash-and-burn permanent campaign is here to stay. Al Gore seems to have learned his lessons well; and Joseph Lieberman bids to become the latest in a long list of figures diminished by getting too close to the fire. Perhaps Bill Clinton will win his ultimate vindication with the triumph of Al and Hillary. But then, Napoleon and Alexander, despite their splashing successes, did not fare well in the end.

August 23, 2000

Editorial Feature

Abusing the INS

By David P. Schippers

Democratic presidential candidate Al Gore has been talking a good game recently about integrity in politics. But that's not how he always plays it.

In June 1998, as part of our oversight investigation of the Justice Department, my staff and I, reporting to the House Judiciary Committee, were looking into the White House's use of the Immigration and Naturalization Service to further its political agenda. The most blatant politicization of the agency had taken place during the 1996 presidential campaign, when the Clinton-Gore administration pressured the INS into expediting its Citizenship USA program to grant citizenship to tens of thousands of aliens the White House considered likely Democratic voters.

Al Gore

The handling of this pressure campaign, the end result of which was the circumvention of long-established policies at the INS, was left to Mr. Gore. He and his office were responsible for keeping the pressure on, a job they did admirably, as e-mails we recovered clearly showed.

The White House's INS campaign started early in the election year, but ran almost immediately into a roadblock: Commissioner

Doris Meissner didn't want to speed up the naturalization process and she warned the White House that such a move might be viewed as politically motivated. Undaunted, the White House asked Douglas Farbrother of Mr. Gore's recently formed National Performance Review staff to look into removing barriers to citizenship.

As early as March 1996, Mr. Farbrother was reporting his efforts and results to Mr. Gore's office. Mr. Farbrother met with both INS and Justice Department officials in March, asking them to delegate broad authority to the local managers, waive "stupid rules" and recruit local people to process alien applications. Mr. Farbrother reported to Mr. Gore that unless those reforms were implemented, the backlog wouldn't be "processed in time."

At one point Mr. Farbrother sent an e-mail updating Elaine Kamarck, an official in the vice president's office. Ms. Kamarck responded in all uppercase type: "The president is sick of this and wants action. If nothing moves today, we'll have to take some pretty drastic measures."

A week later Mr. Farbrother sent a lengthy e-mail directly to the vice president lamenting that district directors weren't being given enough discretion to produce one million new citizens by the registration cutoff day. "Unless we blast INS headquarters loose from their grip on front-line managers, we are going to have way too many people still waiting for citizenship in November," he wrote. He added: "I can't make Doris Meissner delegate broad authority to her field managers. Can you?" Mr. Gore answered: "Will explore it. Thanks."

By the end of March, Ms. Meissner had seen the light and delegated authority. By April 4, 1996, Ms. Kamarck was able to report to the president that everything was in place to naturalize over one million aliens in time for them to vote in the 1996 election.

For aliens to obtain citizenship, federal regulations require that their application be accompanied by a complete set of fingerprints. Fingerprint cards are sent to the FBI to determine if the applicant has a criminal or arrest record. An application may be denied if the alien has a serious criminal record or if he falsely denies ever having been arrested. The FBI fingerprint check is an essential and critical part of the naturalization process since it is the only method of preventing violent felons, dope peddlers and other criminals from obtaining citizenship.

It was in this area that Mr. Gore's pressure caused the biggest breakdown. To save time, FBI arrest records weren't inserted into the aliens' files, and as a result aliens with criminal records were granted citizenship. Even those files with fingerprints skipped through the system: Just prior to the voter-registration deadline a box was discovered in the Chicago INS office containing nearly 5,000 FBI arrest reports that had never been cross-checked against aliens.

Later, when it was discovered that thousands more FBI reports were never processed, the Clinton-Gore administration sought to convince the public that the foul-up really didn't really harm the process. They cited statistics showing that the rejection rate of 17% was just about what it had always been. But the INS numbers didn't take into account the thousands of aliens who weren't rejected, but would have been under normal procedures. If the traditional process had been followed, the rejection rate in the summer of 1996 would have easily exceeded 30%.

In the end, the White House got their one million voters and re-election. The U.S. got 75,000 new citizens who had arrest records when they applied; an additional 115,000 citizens whose fingerprints were unclassifiable and were never resubmitted; and a final 61,000 who were given citizenship without even having their fingerprints submitted so that no check was possible. Those numbers were developed by the accounting firm of Peat Marwick as a result of an audit of the 1996 Citizenship USA program.

In June 1998, we undertook to again pick up the investigation of the program. Our interest intensified when we heard that a similar plan may be in the works for the 2000 presidential election. Among other things, we wanted to find out if the criminals who were given citizenship in 1996 were continuing their criminal activity in the two years since. My staff pulled out about 100 of the most violent or serious crimes that were committed by aliens prior to naturalization and documented by arrest records.

Of those 100 records, some 20% showed arrests for serious crimes after the subject was given citizenship. The charges included murder, rape and child sexual abuse. Based on those results, we resolved to ask for updates on every arrest record. Had we been given enough time to put together evidence and witnesses, Citizenship USA might even have figured in Mr. Clinton's impeachment trial.

This is not what I call "integrity." Rather, this is just one more example of the Clinton-Gore administration's two working mottoes: "The end justifies any means," coupled with "win at any cost."

Mr. Schippers, chief counsel to the House Judiciary Committee during the Clinton impeachment trial, is author of "Sellout: The Inside Story of President Clinton's Impeachment" (Regnery, 2000).

REVIEW & OUTLOOK

Three-Ring Scandals

Scandal surrounding the Clinton-Gore White House should be "put behind us," Democrats urge. Of course—does anyone want more of this stuff? Still, those who forget history are doomed to repeat it. Besides, the Gore scandals aren't just history. Everytime you look up, out comes the next act. This past week has been quite a circus.

Let's see. For the third time, Attorney General Janet Reno rejected the advice of her campaign finance task force to appoint an independent counsel to investigate Vice President Gore's role in the 1996 campaign scandals. Mr. Gore's campaign greeted the news with a classic Clinton-style blame-everybody-else defense (something Mr. Gore himself apparently isn't ready to put behind us), issuing another pious call for campaign finance reform.

FBI Director Louie Freeh wrote to Attorney General Reno in 1997 arguing for an independent counsel to probe Mr. Gore: "The Vice President was a very active, sophisticated fund-raiser who knew exactly what he was doing; his own exculpatory statements must not be given undue weight. If the Attorney General relied primarily on those statements to end this investigation, she would be inviting intense and justified criticism."

Indeed, many of Mr. Gore's statements on the Buddhist temple and other fund-raising scandals—the "no controlling legal authority" and "iced tea" defenses—are simply preposterous. Whether or not an independent counsel would indict or invoke prosecutorial discretion, rehashing these statements would be an embarrassment. But Ms. Reno has spared Mr. Gore a third time.

The potential here is apparent in another of the week's events. Carol Elder Bruce, the independent counsel appointed to probe Interior Secretary Bruce Babbitt, issued her final report. While Ms. Bruce found insufficient evidence to convince a jury that Mr. Babbitt intentionally lied to Congress about his rejection of an Indian casino license, she concluded there was "circumstantial evidence" that he had lied. Mr. Babbitt himself admitted to a grand jury that some of his sworn statements "were not entirely accurate or at least constituted 'overstatement.'"

Indeed, the Minneapolis Star-Tribune reports that prosecutors and FBI agents on Ms. Bruce's team were so divided last year about whether to indict Mr. Babbitt for perjury that she had to hire an outside consultant for perspective. Her report notes that then-White House Chief of Staff Erskine Bowles was so concerned by Mr. Babbitt's written misstatements to Senator John McCain that Mr. Bowles summoned him to the White House to tell him personally "that lying to a United States Senator was unacceptable and serious business."

Ms. Bruce did conclude that there was "no evidence of a quid pro quo" linking hefty campaign contributions to Democrats from Indian tribes with Interior's decision to reject the request of a competing tribe to open a Wisconsin casino. Her decision not to prosecute strikes us as a sound exercise in discretion by a prosecutor, but no great endorsement of a public official.

As a third event, we have the great Gore e-mail hunt—subject of a Judicial Watch case that this week was being argued in federal Judge Royce Lamberth's courtroom in Washington. In 1993, it was announced that Vice President Gore's office e-mails were to be archived by White House computers. Oops!—somehow or other, most were not.

It's understandable, of course, why some folks in the White House would want to simply put e-mail behind them, along with the rest of the past. Consider that in 1997, Congressional searches of the Vice President's office e-mail turned up evidence that it had blatantly politicized the granting of citizenship before the 1996 election, as reported on this page Wednesday by Judiciary Committee Counsel

David Schippers.

When Congress subpoenaed the White House for e-mails on campaign fund raising and the Lewinsky scandal it got nothing—even after the computer glitch was discovered. The Justice Department has admitted to Judge Lamberth that it "misled" him about the e-mail searches, and the grand jury convened last month by Independent Counsel Robert Ray is looking into why subpoenas covering e-mail were ignored by the White House. Even now, no outside party has been allowed to search the e-mails—a full six months after their existence was revealed.

This week, Mark Lindsay, who as director of management for the White House has charge of 2,500 employees there, admitted that an affidavit from a White House computer specialist stating that all e-mails had been archived simply wasn't true. Then Justice's attorneys invoked executive privilege to avoid having Mr. Lindsay discuss any conversations he'd had with President Clinton on the missing e-mails. Yesterday, Justice suddenly dropped the privilege argument and Mr. Lindsay claimed there had been no such conversations. So, what's being hidden? We all now know how Justice misused legal arguments during the Lewinsky scandal—causing delays that prevented the timely production of evidence of Presidential perjury and obstruction of justice.

So the Justice Department has now given Mr. Gore yet another pass on his 1996 fund-raising scandals, while getting in the way of Judge Lamberth's attempt to get at the truth of Mr. Gore's missing e-mails. Among the scandals that may yet take center ring in this apparently endless circus is the behavior of Ms. Reno herself.

September 19, 2000

REVIEW & OUTLOOK

The Wen Ho Lee Diversion

The Wen Ho Lee case ended last week with the former weapons scientist pleading guilty to a single felony charge, with the President of the United States distancing himself from his own Justice department, and now with Asian-American activists charging that the Lee case was the product of racism. This has the look of a classic fiasco. We're not so sure, though, that the case didn't end just about the way Bill Clinton would have liked—in a fog of non-conclusions. Before our jovial President saunters away from another stinkpile, it might be worth putting this affair in its proper context.

Wen Ho Lee

Incredible to behold, "Wen Ho Lee" somehow became a household name in the United States. To the casual viewer, the storyline ran that a sole Chinese-American computer scientist at the Los Alamos National Laboratory, Wen Ho Lee, managed to become the conduit for passing some of the nation's most sensitive nuclear weapons data to China's government. Lee himself participated in his inflation, appearing on "60 Minutes" last August to proclaim his innocence. By then, needless to say, he had become an ethnic martyr.

Let's review the actual timeline on the Lee affair:

Start with the atmosphere of unseriousness about security that pervaded the administration. Early on, Rep. Frank Wolf held hearings into the White House's slovenly process for issuing security clearances to its own personnel. Russian intelligence managed to place wiretaps in one of the most presumably secure floors of the State Department, with sensitive laptop computers disappearing. There was as well the gaudy cast of characters rolling through the White House for campaign-contribution coffees and photo-ops— Macau gangsters, Chinese arms dealers, Johnny Chung and Charlie Trie, who later fled to China.

At an amazing press conference on Dec. 7, 1993, Energy Secretary Hazel O'Leary unveiled the DOE's "openness initiative." "The Cold War is over; we're coming clean," she said. She announced that 32 million pages of classified documents were now subject to review and possible release to "put the United States out in front as a nation willing to share." She joked: "During the Cold War, I would have been arrested for what I said."

No wonder Wen Ho Lee thought the rules had changed. They had.

Indeed, in mid-1997, Attorney General Janet Reno turned down the FBI's request to put a wiretap on Wen Ho Lee, whom they'd been investigating for years. Given the stakes here, and the by-the-books use of a wiretap under such circumstances, the request should have been a routine slam dunk. But Ms. Reno blocked it. Her justification: The evidence against Lee was too fragmentary.

We know, however, that Wen Ho Lee copied sensitive data onto 10 computer tapes, a warehouse of information. Seven of those tapes are still missing. He repeatedly failed polygraph tests. A prima facie case was obvious; the wiretap was warranted. In the event, he entered a guilty plea to one count and promised to cooperate with investigators over the next year.

The Hazel O'Leary "willing to share" national security policy ended in January 1999, with the release of the Cox Report, asserting: "The PRC thefts from our National Laboratories began at least as early as the late 1970s. Significant secrets are known to have been stolen, from the laboratories or elsewhere, as recently as the mid-1990s. Such thefts almost certainly continue to the present."

Exactly two months later, the Energy Department announced that it had fired Los Alamos computer scientist Wen Ho Lee. Quickly, Lee ended up carrying responsibility for the whole sieve of data leaking out of Los Alamos.

On March 19, 10 days after the Wen Ho Lee firing and two months after the Cox Report, President Clinton was asked at a news conference whether any of these Los Alamos security breaches took place on his watch. The President replied: "To the best of my knowledge, no one has said anything to me about any espionage which occurred by the Chinese against the labs during my presidency."

This is almost certainly a false statement. A New York Times story the next day notes "different accounts" of when Mr. Clinton was informed of China's espionage. A House committee was told Mr. Clinton was briefed in 1998. But in the weeks prior to the March 19 news conference, White House aides said National Security Adviser Sandy Berger had briefed the President in July 1997.

According to the Times, NSC spokesman David Leavy "said that since the completion of [the Cox] report, Berger and other aides had refreshed their recollections. 'After the Cox committee process, we've remembered more,' Leavy said."

Also at his March 19 news conference, Mr. Clinton hotly denied that his administration suppressed reports of Chinese spying to avoid association with reports of laundered Chinese contributions to the 1996 Clinton-Gore campaign. "That is not true," the President asserted.

Our view of this "fiasco" would run like this:

With the issuance of the Cox Report, it was obvious that the administration faced a massive security embarrassment involving the very nation alleged to have funneled money into the President's re-election. And so to divert attention from a genuine fiasco, the Clinton brain trust found a scalp, a fall guy, in Wen Ho Lee.

We may never know the truth about Lee's activities or guilt (of a piece with the Chinese contributions), but the notion, allowed to run for a year, that somehow this one man constituted the Los Alamos breakdown was preposterous; it was a diversion. Now the chase has ended in a predictable plea bargain, and the "investigation" will soon disappear into the mists, carrying with it this presidency's responsibility for what happened at the Energy Department on its watch, as with so many other security lapses.

As we've learned, however, even embarrassments can be turned to political advantage. Rendering the whole affair into mush the day after the plea agreement, the President said, "It's very difficult to reconcile the two positions—that one day he's a terrible risk to the national security, and the next day they're making a plea agreement for an offense far more modest than what had been alleged."

But yesterday, just four days later, a report appears in the New York Times, in which government sources lay the primary blame for the Wen Ho Lee case on FBI Director Louis Freeh: "The FBI sold Janet Reno a bill of goods," says a voice from the shadows. Director Freeh, with Charles La Bella, is the one administration official in the Justice Department who recommended that Janet Reno appoint an independent counsel to investigate Bill Clinton's and Al Gore's fund-raising activities in the 1996 campaign.

Looking at this from top to bottom, it would appear that the one thing the Clinton administration has shown the energy and skill to protect is itself.

REVIEW & OUTLOOK

The Coverup Worked

"This office determined that the evidence was insufficient to prove to a jury beyond a reasonable doubt that either President Clinton or Mrs. Clinton knowingly participated in any criminal conduct." With these words, Independent Counsel Robert Ray issued a summary statement on his office's analysis of the Clintons' Whitewater land deals and actions later taken in Washington. The first conclusion to be drawn from all this is that the coverup worked.

Robert Ray

In itself Whitewater is an ancient land deal in Arkansas, of course, but attempts to cover up its embarrassment continued into the Clinton White House and indeed until today. The heart of the problem was a corrupt savings and loan, Madison Guaranty, owned by Clinton Whitewater partners James and Susan McDougal. It collapsed at a $73 million loss to taxpayers. At the time of their Whitewater partnership, the Clintons may or may not have known what Mr. McDougal was up to, but by the time Bill ran for President the debacle was clear enough. Just as Bill could have settled the Paula Jones case, the Clintons could have chosen to out the Whitewater mess and move on, for example by waiving privileges, as Jimmy Carter did over his peanut farm or Ronald Reagan did over Iran-Contra.

Instead, the Clintons and their lawyers established an ethos of stonewalls, shady statements, slick lawyering, witness intimidation, and rhetorical assaults on public servants. The key players either kept quiet or were completely discredited by a brutal White House attack machine. The walls were dented by the early, successful prosecutions of the McDougals and Arkansas insider Webster Hubbell, once the number three man at the Department of Justice. But Mr. Hubbell kept his mouth shut. Susan McDougal did hard time without talking; finally questioned by prosecutors, she said more than 40 times that she was unable to recall business dealings related to Madison and Whitewater. Questioned in 1996 by federal investigators about her own work for Madison, Mrs. Clinton said 99 times in a two-hour interview that she couldn't recall.

Jim McDougal decided to cooperate late in the game but died in prison, his potential testimony tarnished by fraud convictions. Arkansas insider David Hale was smeared from the outset. Investigators such as the Resolution Trust Corp.'s Jean Lewis, not to mention Kenneth Starr, were subjected to a character assassination rarely seen in public life.

The result was a series of investigations yielding evidence "insufficient to prove to a jury beyond a reasonable doubt." This is not to say no evidence. Consider, for example, the matter of whether Bill Clinton ever caused anyone to borrow from Madison for his benefit. Evidence described in Mr. Ray's statement consisted of two checks, one made out to "Bill Clinton" and the other with a memo line saying "Clinton payoff." Both bore bank stamps rather than Mr. Clinton's endorsement. This was deemed insufficient evidence to persuade a jury beyond a reasonable doubt that Mr. Clinton had lied in denying personal benefit from Madison.

Fair enough, we suppose. Mr. Clinton is after all President of the United States, and a jury would surely take into account the gravity of any finding of Presidental perjury. Even more so since the case would likely be tried in the District of Columbia. The D.C. jury pool greatly overrepresents not only blacks but government employees, both groups among whom the President is especially popular. While officially prosecutors are not supposed to consider likely jury predilictions in deciding whether to bring cases, it is only human to do so.

Yesterday's statement was limited only to matters already in the public record. Mr. Ray will file a more complete report, including grand jury materials, with the Special Division supervising the independent counsels. Presumably this will be released after relevant parties have had an opportunity to comment, but this will not happen until after the election. We can speculate that it will detail such matters as what part the late Vincent Foster Jr. played in the coverup, and whether the Clintons' 1992 tax return properly accounted for the gift from Mr. McDougal when he assumed their share of the Whitewater debts.

Obviously Mr. Ray is intent on winding up his investigation in an orderly and credible fashion, taking at least some procedural steps toward applying the rule of law to a sitting President. He has succeeded in meeting his timetable this year, with a finding on the FBI files in March, the Travel Office affair in June, and now Whitewater. This clears the deck for a decision of historic proportions in late January: whether to indict ex-President Clinton for perjury and obstruction of justice in the Lewinsky matter.

The orderliness of Mr. Ray's tenure should restore confidence in the independent counsel process, and he should be given some credit for this. This was a man, remember, who was instantly accused when it was leaked in the midst of the Democratic National Convention that he had impaneled a new grand jury to probe possible perjury in the Lewinsky matter. The White House and its allies launched a stinging assault, blaming Mr. Ray for the leak. Days later, a federal judge apologized for accidentally disclosing the news to a reporter. No apologies were forthcoming from the White House.

Mr. Ray's job is to decide, as prosecutors do every day in more mundane matters, about criminal charges. Ordinary citizens are perfectly free to make their own political judgments, and we're sure that future generations will make a historical judgment. The finding of insufficient evidence to persuade a jury beyond a reasonable doubt is understandable. But it is by no means an exoneration of the Clintons for their conduct in either Whitewater or the White House.

Election Day 2000

With Election Day just weeks away, the presidential race was neck and neck. In New York, the unlikely candidacy of Hillary Rodham Clinton had climbed to a narrow lead in some polls. In the final days of the national campaign, with polls see-sawing, a 24-year-old citation against George W. Bush for driving while intoxicated surfaced in the press, propelled by Bush opponents.

But no one was prepared for the strange outcome as election night stretched to dawn. "So victory for the most important office in the world turns on maybe a thousand votes in Florida," the Journal wrote. "For the moment at least, the tumult of partisan politics has been shouldered aside by sheer historical drama." But the tumult would quickly return, and the drama would continue for weeks, the fate of the presidency hanging in the balance.

Editorial Feature

Who Is Harold Ickes?

By Micah Morrison

As the Senate was voting not to remove Bill Clinton from office after impeachment by the House, Hillary Clinton signaled her seriousness about running for the U.S. Senate. She summoned Harold M. Ickes Jr. to a secret meeting at the White House. That day, her cam-

Harold Ickes

paign began. To this day, Mr. Ickes remains by her side. Despite the low-key title "adviser," he is the dominant behind-the-scenes figure in the campaign.

The secret meeting that launched Mrs. Clinton's candidacy is recounted in Washington Post reporter Peter Baker's new book, "The Breach: Inside the Impeachment and Trial of William Jefferson Clinton." Mr. Ickes doesn't get much attention in the book, but New Yorkers ought to take a close look at the mastermind of the Clinton Senate campaign. A vote for Hillary is a vote for Harold. Should Mrs. Clinton win, she and Mr. Ickes will be poised to take over the New York Democratic Party.

Mr. Ickes is a New Yorker par excellence, though his career there is reminiscent of some of Mrs. Clinton's Arkansas friends. As a Razorback, Mrs. Clinton had problems with a miraculous $100,000 profit in cattle futures, the Castle Grande land scheme, the Rose Law Firm billing records. In moving her residence to New York, she has put herself in the hands of a skilled labor lawyer and former deputy White House chief of staff with a history of representing unions, some of them with eyebrow-raising ties to organized crime.

The son of Harold M. Ickes, FDR's secretary of interior, the younger Mr. Ickes toiled for years in the vineyards of the left wing of Democratic Party politics. In 1977, he joined the influential Long Island law firm of Meyer, Suozzi, English & Klein. Interviewed yesterday, Mr. Ickes expressed surprise that he would be the subject of a newspaper article. "You're doing an article about me? Why?!" He defended his record and at times controversial client list. "I'm head of our firm's labor department," Mr. Ickes said. "We have a lot of labor clients."

There is no evidence of ethical impropriety by the law firm, and Mr. Ickes has never been charged with a crime. But the combative lawyer has tangled with law-enforcement authorities and congressional investigators over many issues—union cases, the Whitewater investigation, the 1996 campaign-finance scandal.

From 1983 to 1991, one of Mr. Ickes's major clients was Local 100 of the Hotel and Restaurant Workers International. In 1992, Local 100 settled a civil racketeering suit charging that the union was controlled by the Colombo and Gambino crime organizations, two New York-based Mafia families. In the settlement, Local 100 President Anthony "Chickie" Amodeo resigned and the union was placed under federal trusteeship.

According to published reports, during a 1985 interview by investigators, at which Mr. Ickes was present, Mr. Amodeo said he had known Paul Castellano, boss of the Gambino family, for more than 40 years. In 1983, investigators secretly recorded Mr. Castellano and Mr. Amodeo discussing payoffs. Mr. Castellano was taped saying that Local 100 "was my union and I don't want anything happening to it." He was gunned down in 1985. His successor as head of the Gambinos, John Gotti, was convicted of the murder in 1992.

Bill Cunningham, managing partner of Meyer Suozzi, says the firm "stopped representing Local 100 in January 1992." The firm was "absolutely not" aware of any ties between Local 100 and organized crime. Contrary to published reports, he said, Mr. Amodeo "did not answer any questions in Harold's presence about Paul Castellano."

Mr. Ickes hit the political big time with Bill Clinton. He managed

Mr. Clinton's 1992 primary race in New York and ran the Democratic National Convention that year. In 1993, he resigned from his law firm and went to Washington in 1994 as deputy White House chief of staff. According to his 1994 federal disclosure statement, Mr. Ickes had other clients that can be shown to have links to organized crime.

One was the New York City District Council of Carpenters, charged in a 1990 civil racketeering suit with being controlled by the Genovese crime family. The union later agreed to federal oversight. "Our firm represented the Carpenters," Mr Ickes said yesterday. "I didn't personally represent them."

As head of his law firm's labor department, Mr. Ickes presumably played some role in representing New Jersey Teamsters Local 560, also noted on his federal disclosure statement. The union was accused in a 1986 racketeering suit with using murder and beatings to silence opposition to union boss Anthony "Tony Pro" Provenzano, a member of the Genovese crime family. The charges resulted in the appointment of a trustee to run the union. "I was deliberately very broad on the disclosure," Mr. Ickes said. "But I never personally had a thing to do with them. Again, our firm represented them."

Mr. Ickes's union connections went with him to Washington. Among them was Arthur Coia, president of the Laborers International Union of North America. "Our firm continues to represent LIUNA," Mr. Ickes said. In the mid-1990s, Mr. Coia and LIUNA were the subject of a Justice Department probe for links to organized crime. A draft civil complaint said Mr. Coia has "associated with, and been controlled and influenced by, organized crime figures," and that he "employed actual and threatened force, violence and fear of physical and economic injury to create a climate of intimidation and fear."

LIUNA gave over $1 million to Democrats in 1994 and congressional investigators documented more than 120 contacts between the president and Mr. Coia, including an exchange of golf clubs. Mrs. Clinton was scheduled to address the union in February 1994, as the Justice Department was about to move on its civil case. She deferred the address for a year.

Mr. Ickes was involved in Mr. Coia's relations with the White House. "As deputy chief of staff, I handled a lot of matters and Arthur was a person I dealt with," Mr. Ickes said. "I helped set up, and attended, meetings."

The Justice case was never filed. A settlement for a voluntary cleanup of the union was reached in 1995 and many figures linked to organized crime resigned. Mr. Coia retired early this year, agreeing to plead guilty to one count of tax fraud in exchange for a fine and probation.

At the White House, Mr. Ickes's first major assignment was to run the damage control effort against the Whitewater probe. He was soon a focus of attention himself, summoned in March 1994 to testify before Congress about his knowledge of improper administration contacts concerning the Resolution Trust Corp. probe of Madison Guaranty Savings & Loan. That investigation eventually formed the basis of Independent Counsel Kenneth Starr's successful prosecution of the Clintons' Whitewater business partners, James and Susan McDougal, and Arkansas Gov. Jim Guy Tucker, for bank fraud.

Mr. Ickes's power appears to have reached a zenith in the 1996 campaign-finance scandal. Federal investigators place him at the center of a conspiracy to shred the campaign-finance laws.

In a 1998 report to Attorney General Janet Reno seeking an independent counsel, Justice Department campaign-finance task force head Charles La Bella identified Mr. Ickes as the "Svengali" of a shrewdly constructed criminal enterprise. The "campaign finance allegations do not represent the typical criminal matter," Mr. La Bella wrote. "Rather, they present the earmarks of a loose enterprise employing different actors at different levels who share a common goal: bring in the money."

Each aspect of the sprawling campaign finance scandal—the White House coffees, illegal Asian money, the Buddhist Temple affair, soft and hard money, Lincoln Bedroom sleepovers, access to the president, payments for "photo opportunities," flights on Air Force One and Two, participation in trade missions, contacts with unions, membership in various Democratic National Committee forums and related entities—was linked by "certain common themes" and the "conduct of certain figures," Mr. La Bella reported. He focused on Mr. Ickes, who "assumed the role of Svengali, assuming power—with the imprimatur of the president—to authorize DNC and Clinton/Gore expenditures, award media contracts and direct every aspect of the DNC and Clinton/Gore activities related to the re-election effort."

Mr. Ickes dismisses the La Bella report. "Mr. La Bella never proved anything," he said. "I viewed him as an outright partisan with a vendetta against the Clinton administration."

Despite repeated efforts by Congress, Mr. La Bella, Federal Bureau of Investigation Director Louis Freeh and others, Ms. Reno turned down all requests for an independent counsel in the campaign-finance matter. In 1998, Mr. Ickes returned to legal practice, running Meyer Suozzi's Washington office and a lobbying firm, Ickes & Enright. In January 1999, Ms. Reno declined to appoint an independent counsel to investigate whether Mr. Ickes had lied to Congress about intervening in a strike on behalf of the Teamsters, major contributors to Mr. Clinton. A month later, Mrs. Clinton began her campaign for the Senate.

From the unions to Whitewater and campaign-finance practices, Mr. Ickes's true role, performed brilliantly, has been as consigliere to the dark side of the Clinton presidency. The great question before New York voters is whether the Ickes style, so successful for the Clintons, will be a template for the future of their state.

Mr. Morrison is a senior editorial page writer for the Journal.

October 30, 2000

Editorial Feature

Ken Starr's Vindication

Al Gore's partisans still profess not to understand the "embell-ishments" issue. All politicians embellish. Ronald Reagan, in particular, was famous for not letting factual detail get in the way of a good story line. Why should the vice president get tagged over Texas fire non-visits, inventing the Internet and the rest?

Simple, the embellishments issue is the character issue in drag. People (and the press) are not really comfortable catch-

Thinking Things Over

By Robert L. Bartley

ing Mr. Gore lie about big things—Social Security and his fictitious lock box, for example. But they feel great tagging him on the little things, like where he actually went in Texas. With Reagan, everyone could laugh at the little fibs because everyone under-stood that whatever his faults the Gipper was a man of charac-ter.

With the baby-boomer generation character no longer matters, we've been solemnly and repeatedly instructed. And throughout the impeachment debate we were instructed that it was only sex. That Independent Counsel Kenneth Starr was a sex-crazed religious nut. That the House impeachment managers were committing political suicide.

But lo and behold: We are now in the final week of a presidential campaign. The nation is at peace, more or less, and the incumbent administration has presided over the "miracle economy." But the vice president is fighting for his political life.

The reason for this is anything but mysterious. From the convention to this final week, the character issue has shaped the whole campaign. Mr. Gore's strategic dilemma has been to consolidate the Clinton constituency while separating himself from Bill Clinton personally. The Lieberman choice and the Tipper smooch produced a post-convention surge precisely because they provided separation.

The strategy was meanwhile to consolidate the base by moving left on the issues, hence the "populist" attacks on oil companies, drug makers and the like, plus a laundry list of everything the government was going to buy for you.

Yet as the campaign wore on, and particularly when the public got a close look at the candidates in debate, Al Gore looked less like Joe Lieberman and more like Bill Clinton. That is, the public recognized that the Clinton issue was never only about sex, but started long before Monica Lewinsky became a household name. The issue was truthfulness, accountability, acceptance of personal responsibility—in a word, character.

That Mr. Gore had the Clinton brazenness without the Clinton charm was no surprise to those of us who've been keeping score. The vice president was himself deeply implicated in the Buddhist temple expedition, the "no controlling legal authority" defense, the post-impeachment celebration of "a man I believe will be regarded in the history books as one of our greatest presidents." Janet Reno had to stiff three different investigators who recommended a Gore independent counsel. The administration even now is withholding from Congress documents about the secret deal Mr. Gore struck with his Russian buddy Victor Chernomyrdin to give Russia a pass on certain arms sales to Iran. Committees of both Houses have threatened to subpoena the documents if not released by noon today.

So as the campaign reaches its final frenzy, Mr. Gore is again seeking to avoid identification with Mr. Clinton's works and ways. After an uncomfortably public debate, the president of the United States agreed not to stump the linchpin states for his vice president. Mr. Clinton campaigned in New York on behalf of his wife's Senate candidacy, though skipping the World Series, where Rick Lazio's campaigners circulated photos of Mrs. Clinton in a Yankees cap. Gov. Gray Davis, whose 2004 presidential ambitions would not be served by a Gore victory, invited the president to get out the California vote.

The Gore hope of consolidating the left with populism, in the meantime, hit a rock named Ralph Nader. Mr. Gore mouths populism, but the left is unpersuaded of his sincerity. An editorial in the Nation recommends: "In states where either Gore or Bush has a commanding lead, vote Nader. In the states too close to call, vote Gore." Over the weekend Mr. Gore found himself stumping to curb Nader inroads in Wisconsin and Minnesota.

In the last weeks of the campaign, by contrast, Gov. Bush has dropped much of his initial reticence on the character issue and become increasingly forthright. He closed the third debate: "I'd like to conclude by this promise. Should I be fortunate enough to become your president, when I put my hand on the Bible, I will swear to not only uphold the laws of the land, but I will also swear to uphold the honor and the dignity of the office to which I have been elected, so help me God."

Last week in Pittsburgh, he noted that a leader should be predictable: "He doesn't change personalities, say, for a different debate." He continued: "And finally, a leader must uphold the honor and the dignity of the office to which he had been elected. In my administration, we will ask not only what is legal, but what is right. Not just what the lawyers allow, but what the public deserves. In my administration, we'll make it clear there is the controlling legal authority of conscience. We will make people proud again, so that Americans who love their country can once again respect their government."

The election doesn't take place for another eight days and the polls remain tight; Mr. Gore could still eke out a victory. His labor allies will spur turnout, and more of his black supporters may come to the polls. Perhaps his new Social Security ads will scare grandmothers, and perhaps the Naderite left will ultimately come home. But more likely, on recent momentum, Mr. Gore will have lost Bill Clinton's "New Democrat" appeal on the issues, without escaping the taint of

Bill Clinton's spins and lies.

In the last week of the campaign the character issue is alive, well and even growing. Bill Clinton has taught us that presidents can get away with a lot, using the powers of the office to disdain the truth, destroy enemies and deny all accountability. He's taught us, that is, that the office is too powerful to be entrusted to someone without a strong sense of internal restraint.

Learning this lesson depended on someone finding the courage to bell the cat. This campaign has revolved around the issue of character, and while the ultimate outcome won't be known until next week this is already an extraordinary development. Kenneth Starr, Henry Hyde and the other House managers can count it as their vindication.

REVIEW & OUTLOOK

What's It All About?

The electorate didn't know much about George Bush when this campaign began, and it knew mainly that Al Gore was Bill Clinton's loyal Vice President. We now know about as much about these men as we are likely to learn before tomorrow morning, including a night on the town 24 years ago.

Is it enough? It's never enough. There is no certain way to know who will measure up to the U.S. Presidency. Over the next four years, the President is going to be responsible for something beyond the battles of this campaign, beyond prescription drugs and Social Security.

In terms of a President's probable success, we suspect it helps greatly if a leader is in tune with the spirit of the times. FDR was the right leader for a Depression and a world war. And in our view Ronald Reagan saw the time was at hand to win the Cold War and, by paring back the government, he released the gathering winds of a U.S. economy that was fast organizing itself into an efficient, modern engine of global commerce.

We don't know whether history will say the same of George Bush or Al Gore, but as daily observers of the political and economic currents we feel qualified to have a view of how each fits into the world that awaits him.

The thumbnail version of our view is that this editorial would read differently had the Democratic nominee been Bob Kerrey, Bill Bradley, Evan Bayh or Milwaukee Mayor John Norquist. These men are New Democrats, the party movement which argued that Democratic liberalism needed to integrate with the political and social realities of the late 20th century. The core reality is that government's broad reach is receding, a historic and appropriate decline, as the information age dispersed the power to make socially vital decisions into the hands of individuals.

In terms of the spirits animating the United States in the year 2000, George W. Bush and these four Democrats, whatever their differences, are singing from the same hymnal. None of these four would have campaigned as Al Gore has against special interests as "rats in the barn," or against the antique notion of "Big Oil."

Most important, not one of them, nor indeed any woman who shared their politics, could hope to win the nomination of the Democratic Party in 2000. Al Gore is the nominee because the campaign that Al Gore has run most accurately reflects the static worldview of the Democratic Party's most important constituencies.

Labor is the most prominent and most interesting, because it seems least able to come to terms with a changing world. Mr. Gore's most important party support base, ensuring his nomination last summer over Bill Bradley, was John Sweeney, head of the nation's public-sector unions, who succeeded Lane Kirkland as president of the AFL-CIO. Mr. Kirkland was an industrial unionist but most importantly for our argument, he was a genuine internationalist. Had someone such as Mr. Kirkland succeeded him, we believe the unions would have worked toward a modus vivendi with the global economy. Instead, the insular Mr. Sweeney supported the mobs in the streets of Seattle, who are commanding the world to stop.

Similarly, the teachers' unions have shown themselves unable to react to the manifest catastrophe of black education in the U.S., just as the modern world is demanding and rewarding basic numeracy and literacy. Their intractability in turn freezes the party's nominee, who is left to propose the irrelevancy of more classrooms.

Any honest assessment of the Democrats' striking alienation from the forces pulling American society forward and outward must acknowledge that rationalizing the party's institutional structures and allegiances was never going to be easy. Change has come quickly the past 20 years—for example, erecting and blowing up dot-com empires overnight. The GOP is hardly by nature an engine of change but had the benefit of the Reagan captaincy at a crucial juncture. George W. Bush candidly admits this reality.

The great hope was that Bill Clinton was the man for the needed Democratic transition. He was not. President Clinton did not bring his party into the 21st century. He left it behind. His party's most serious reformers, which included Joe Lieberman, assumed that he would extend the party's base beyond its traditional allegiances. Welfare reform was one such example, embodying the historic shift away from government paternalism and toward individual responsibility.

After that achievement, the party as an institution never really moved again. Mr. Clinton devoted the best years of his life as President mainly to his own needs, personal and political, relentlessly raising money for himself, enrolling his Vice President in the effort. When the rule of law and reason intervened against acts that were illicit or illegal, he deployed the Presidency against the rule of law, enrolling his Vice President in that effort.

Mr. Clinton's inability to truly act in the interest of any goal outside his own needs was revealed even at this late hour, as last week he told an admiring interviewer that electing Al Gore is "the next best thing." Al Gore has run a campaign, filled with enemies, that is perfectly suited to the party and politics Bill Clinton left for him.

And Al Gore has left it to George Bush to run on everything that's left. It is quite a lot. As an idea, Mr. Bush's politics, which he chose to call compassionate conservatism, has at least attempted to fashion a political bridge to the foreseeable future. It is a bridge that allows thoughtful liberals to believe, or hope, that the best qualities of their legacy will find a place in a world that is obviously going to be run less by governments and more by individuals making their own choices.

It's a politics that admits the world has changed. Whatever else we may wish for in a potential Presidency, the person seeking it ought to reflect, in his words and his ideas, that he is enough his own man to be able to embrace this basic reality.

November 6, 2000

Editorial Feature

Touring Cyberspace With DUI Story

My journalism career stretches from hot lead to the World Wide Web. I'm nostalgic for the smell of the former, but the latter has its compensations. This was much in evidence on our Opinion-Journal.com this weekend as we covered the revelation that George W. Bush paid a fine for drunk driving 24 years ago.

The Wall Street Journal publishes every business day, which most of the time is fine by everyone. But now and again a story will break over the weekend and our crack commentator-reporters itch to give the world the benefit of their wisdom. In the olden days, which is to say until the launch of OpinionJournal three months ago, they just had to wait until Monday morning.

Thinking Things Over

By Robert L. Bartley

The D-Dubya-I story broke after deadlines Thursday night and this time around our editors were able to get out an initial reaction in Best of the Web Today at 1 p.m. Friday. At 4:11 Peggy Noonan posted her thoughts, warning that the Gore partisans would likely follow up this true story with worse but false charges and urging Gov. Bush to confront it directly in a "serious and thoughtful speech." The public would understand that he didn't volunteer the facts because of his daughters: "It's something that all of us grown-ups are facing these days: how to be candid with our kids and yet not corrupt them with our candor, not damage them with an implicit message of 'I smoked dope and lived to tell the tale; so can you.'"

By 7:03 Friday night, John Fund posted the news that Tom Connolly, the flamboyant Democratic activist going on TV as the source of the story, was in fact merely a front. The original source was Probate Judge William Childs, who'd been pushing the story in a Portland courthouse, before Mr. Connolly and lawyer John De-Grinney, a Republican who described the inci-dent as "Pearl Harbor politics."

The Portland Press Herald found several other sources who said Judge Childs had been spreading the story. It was picked up by reporters in court for a high-profile arson case,

who went to Mr. Connolly for the records. On Sunday the paper reported that Rebecca Wyke, the deputy secretary of state in charge of the records, said that Mr. Connolly did not contact her office but that Judge Childs called to confirm the record on Nov. 2.

Judge Childs did not do anything an ordinary citizen could not have, but judges are of course supposed to refrain from partisan activity. The appearance of a judge as the font of this last-minute hit is reminiscent of the judicial mores so evident in the Clinton admin-istration—in a "heads-up" of the original Whitewater referral, in Webster Hubbell dispatched to oversee the Justice Department, in the spurning of investigators' recommendations of an independent counsel for Al Gore.

It's at least conceivable that Judge Childs was free-lancing rather than acting at the behest of the Gore campaign. But another Fund column on Sunday's OpinionJournal ran through the reasons such suspicions are natural and the denials are without much credibility. The Gore campaign has a cast of self-described "killers"; Mr. Gore himself once described his political tactics as "rip the lungs out of anybody else who's in the race."

Chris Lehane, the press secretary sent out to issue the denial, was author of "Communications Stream of Conspiracy Commerce," the preposterous 331-page White House report exposed by our Micah Morrison in 1997. It purported to show that all unfavorable media coverage of Clinton scandals traced back to philanthropist Richard Scaife. Gore media consultant Bob Shrum has a history of intensely negative ads, while campaign manager Donna Brazile was forced to resign from the 1988 Dukakis campaign after spreading a rumor that the senior George Bush was involved in an extramarital affair.

There is also the history of last-minute hits against conservative figures that started with the campaign against Supreme Court nominee Robert Bork. Independent Counsel Lawrence Walsh indicted Caspar Weinberger and others on the eve of the 1992 election. Clarence Thomas was almost derailed by Anita Hill. Newt Gingrich's conversations were recorded by a cell-phone scanner run by Democratic activists who much resembled Mr. Connolly. Founded or not in this instance, suspicions are natural.

Other Web commentators were also active over the weekend, though I think I can say no one else had the Noonan-Fund punch. National Review Online showed its usual energy with a raft of reports. The pro-Gore commentators, led by a tittering dispatch by Gary Kamiya at Salon, zeroed in on a conversation between Gov. Bush and Wayne Slater, Austin bureau chief of the Dallas Morning News.

Mr. Slater said that he'd asked the governor whether he'd been arrested after 1968, when he joined the National Guard and reported an earlier arrest over a college prank. He said the governor replied "No," then said, "Wait a minute, let's talk about this." At this point spokeswoman Karen Hughes cut off the conversation.

The 1976 "arrest" fell somewhere between a speeding ticket and a recitation of Miranda rights. But the episode described above is in no way comparable to Bill Clinton, after taking an oath and in defiance of the apparent advice of his counsel, bantering under cross-examination over what the meaning of "is" is. Nor is it comparable, for that matter, to Al Gore telling FBI investigators he didn't know the Buddhist Temple fund-raiser was a fund-raiser and that he missed incriminating conversations because he'd had too much iced tea.

Voters seem to be adding it up pretty much the same way. The early polls mostly say the revelation has had little to no effect; Mr.

Bush seems to be holding a lead that averages about six percentage points. No second shoe dropped overnight Saturday, and the story seems to be fading from the headlines. In olden times, we might have missed it entirely—and I'm sure there's a school of thought that would say so much the better.

Yet it's only natural that those of us in the commentary business would want our say, and in a timely fashion. And I think the episode was revealing. Surely Gov. Bush would have been wiser to have admitted it back in the spring, when some of us suggested he get out any unfavorable history. Better his daughters learned from him than, as they inevitably would, from the media. Even so, the governor admitted his mistake, with no finger-wagging, no iced tea defense, no invocation of lacking "controlling legal authority," and with no more than a whiff of a vast conspiracy.

It would be a relief, that is, to have a president who can admit a mistake with a modicum of dignity.

REVIEW & OUTLOOK

Moment for Leadership

So victory for the most important office in the world turns on maybe a thousand votes in the state of Florida. For the moment at least, the tumult of partisan politics has been shouldered aside by the sheer historical drama.

The television networks awarded Florida to Al Gore in the early evening, then took that back. They then awarded it to George Bush in the early hours of the morning, then took that back. This led Vice President Gore to call Governor Bush to concede, then call back to rescind his concession. So a recount is under way with Mr. Bush narrowly in the lead, and the results are not expected to be final until today. If the count is close enough, the outcome could depend on absentee ballots postmarked by Election Day but trickling in over the next week.

To continue the drama, the Republican Party has held the Congress, but by even narrower margins than before. In Missouri, John Ashcroft conceded the election of a dead man to a Senate seat. Hillary Clinton became the first First Lady to become a Senator, winning handily over the brain-challenged New York State Republicans. Mr. Gore leads in the national popular vote, so that if Mr. Bush's lead in Florida holds, he's likely to win the Electoral College and become President though more voters may have chosen his opponent.

Is this an election, or what?

The drama is surely intense, but the plot is hard to follow, or even discern. The only meaning that can be attributed to this outcome is that the collective electorate can't make up its mind. We suddenly start getting quite unaccustomed pangs of sympathy for our much-belittled politicians. What is the Beltway supposed to do when the nation refuses to give directions or issue instructions?

For all the grumbling about a choice between a tarnished Vice President and an inexperienced Governor, this was in our view a pretty good campaign. Important issues were joined, not least on Social Security, supposedly the untouchable "Third Rail" of American politics. By the campaign's end, it was abundantly clear that Governor Bush was offering a vision of an American people who would live under a smaller national government, and Vice President Gore was promising to thwart any such downward shift in government's role. In almost equal measure, the electorate chose each vision. However eloquent or forceful your neighbor may be for one or the other vision, the American body politic isn't ready yet to commit itself decisively to either.

The Founding Fathers, of course, designed a system that would be slow and resistant to change. Their purpose was to force advocates to persuade more than a passing majority, but to forge something nearer consensus on important issues. It will be fascinating to watch how an essentially tied election will play in this process. Probably it means further division and bickering, but in chastening both sides it could conceivably lead to a search for common ground.

The system the Founding Fathers devised reminds us to look beyond today to history. The Electoral College, by allotting each state a vote equal to its Representatives plus its two Senators, gives some weight to geography when the popular vote advantage is marginal. The last time this was decisive was back in 1888. By and large, in our view, it has served us well; the winner-take-all system in most states encourages a two-party system. And it has practical advantages—if the Florida recount seems burdensome, imagine a national one.

We will have opportunities for legal challenges. But in the close election of 1960, Richard Nixon was statesmanlike enough to discourage Earl Mazo, then a reporter and later his biographer, from pursuing the story that the election had been stolen in Illinois and Texas. Similarly, Vice President Gore's call to Governor Bush, if premature, was a gracious act. In this spirit, we hope and trust, the final result will be determined.

We can also hope, though without so much trust, that the brush with history will ennoble our politicians. On both sides of the partisan aisle, they too must be tired of the gotcha politics that have so marked the Clinton years. There is important business to be done. Despite the campaign, for example, thoughtful Democrats must know that we have a narrowing window of opportunity to reform Social Security. We would add doing something about missile defense to this list. These are of course Governor Bush's issues, and if he should emerge from the recounts, he has a record of trying to build consensus. If in the end Vice President Gore emerges as President, his interest will lie in the "Third Way" politics of successful left-of-center governments in Europe.

Lacking instructions from the voters, that is, it will be up to our politicians to take matters into their own hands, exercising some leadership and assuming some responsibility.

Trying to
Steal an Election

Election Day 2000 did not mark the end of the battle for the Presidency. For more than a month, a fierce legal and political fight, unprecedented in U.S. history, would be waged for Florida's 25 electoral college votes.

The drama began on election night. In the early evening, television networks awarded the pivotal state to Al Gore, then took it back and later projected George Bush as the winner. Still later, the networks moved Florida moved into the "too close to call" column, though Mr. Bush appeared to maintain a narrow lead. Mr. Gore called Mr. Bush to concede the election in the pre-dawn hours, then called back and withdrew his concession.

Whoever won Florida would claim an electoral college majority and thus the presidency. George Bush led his opponent by a few hundred votes. Teams of high-powered lawyers descended on Florida and the world watched as a rapid and overlapping series of pitched battles over vote recounts made their way through state and federal courts. Two machine counts favored Mr. Bush, but Mr. Gore challenged the results, pressing for hand recounts in several heavily Democratic counties. "It's becoming clearer by the day that Al Gore's decision to contest the Florida presidential election results has opened up Pandora's box," the Journal noted.

On Nov. 17, the Florida Supreme Court blocked Florida's secretary of state, Katherine Harris, from certifying Mr. Bush the victor by 930 votes, following the counting of overseas ballots. The Journal called the action an "ominous sign." The court's injunction has "achieved the rare trifecta of overruling all three branches of Florida government at once"—Ms. Harris, an elected executive officer; the Florida legislature, which had mandated the certification deadline; and lower court rulings, which had upheld Ms. Harris's powers.

The United States Supreme Court reluctantly stepped into the fray on Dec. 4, instructing the Florida High Court to reconsider its ruling. But Mr. Gore pressed on, filing more appeals and pressing recount efforts. On Dec. 12, the Supreme Court moved decisively, ruling that the Florida High Court's interventions favoring Mr. Gore were unconstitutional.

On Dec. 13, Mr. Gore conceded. George W. Bush was President-elect.

November 13, 2000

REVIEW & OUTLOOK

Pandora's Politics

It's becoming clearer by the day that Al Gore's decision to contest the Florida presidential election results has opened up Pandora's box. We can only assume the vice president and his fellow Democrats will enjoy living with the demons they've unleashed.

Two counts by machine in Florida have so far favored George W. Bush, not counting the absentee ballots from overseas that could go either way. Yet now Mr. Gore wants a third count, this time by hand and only in heavily Democratic counties. The Bush campaign has sought an injunction to stop this, on the sensible grounds that hand counts allow partisan election officials to "determine the intent of the voter," as the Florida statute puts it.

Put bluntly, the Gore campaign expects that Democratic vote canvassers will find more Democratic votes than nonpartisan machines already have. Any doubt about this should have vanished on the weekend as the nation watched poll officials in Palm Beach County make up the counting rules as they went along.

At first the panel members adopted a "sunlight test," but then for their own obscure reasons they decided to look at the condition of the "chad"—the part of the ballot that would fall off were it properly punched. So we all learned the momentous distinction between a "hanging chad" and the merely "swinging chad," not to mention the "pregnant chad" versus the always vexing "dimpled chad." Once again Mr. Gore is betting on no controlling legal authority.

Not surprisingly, these delphic Democratic chad inspectors found that Mr. Gore had picked up 19 votes, and that this in turn justifies a hand count of the entire Democratic county. Any guess how many votes Mr. Gore will pick up by the time all four Democratic counties have been hand counted? If it is just enough votes to win, look for the Gore campaign and its media echo chamber to then demand that Mr. Bush pack it in.

Keep in mind that this third recount is not based on a single allegation of vote fraud. Instead, it is based on Gore lawyer Warren Christopher's contention that only these four (conveniently Democratic) counties in Florida had "real irregularities," notably that some 19,000 votes were double-punched for president. But in solidly Republican Duval County, some 26,000 votes were also disqualified on Election Day for double-punching or failing to punch hard enough.

Are these ballots also going to be hand counted? And by GOP canvassers? They certainly should be, as statistical economist Edward Glaeser notes nearby. And we'd expect Mr. Bush to make exactly that request if the Democratic-run hand counts miraculously show Mr. Gore ahead, whatever deadline might have passed. While we're at it, let's have a hand recount of the whole country, with United Nations observers overseeing every state elections board. A country that acts like the Philippines deserves to be monitored like it.

The Gore campaign argues that it just wants a fair vote count. But asked Saturday if the vice president would accept even a hand count that went against him, Mr. Christopher refused to answer, saying the campaign was pursuing "various options." There's no other way to interpret such a statement except as an intention by the Gore team to litigate or obfuscate until they finally get a vote count they like.

Meanwhile, other Democrats are playing the race card. The NAACP dispatched itself to Florida to hold a five-hour public hunt for anecdotes of voter intimidation. These will then be shipped off to that great symbol of national trust, Attorney General Janet Reno. The intent is to coax a Justice Department intervention on civil-rights grounds, which could further tie up the Florida vote. Never mind that a huge black turnout last Tuesday of 16% exceeded the 14% African-American share of the Florida population.

Watching all this has left us more than a little depressed. We keep recalling President Clinton's famous remark to Dick Morris when the Monica Lewinsky scandal first broke. Mr. Morris had taken a poll and found that if the president publicly admitted his behavior he might have to resign. Mr. Clinton replied, "We'll just have to win then." This same anything-goes ethos is now being applied to election law.

The question we'd ask other, more conscientious Democrats is whether this is really the kind of politics they signed up for. The Clinton years have been tough on the Democratic Party's reputation for probity, as Election Day showed. The political benefits of prosperity were cancelled out by voters who wanted to restore some moral accountability to government.

There have been a few signs that at least some Democrats care about more than hanging on to power. Senators Bob Torricelli and John Breaux have warned the Gore campaign about a long legal challenge, only to be rebuked by Mr. Gore's flacks. Former Labor Secretary Robert Reich has echoed the senators on TV.

And Bill Bradley, who challenged Mr. Gore in the primaries, told the Washington Post that "When the votes are counted, that should be it. It is a perilous course to try to delay in the expectation that things will be turned around by lawyers. Unless there is something fraudulent or a flagrant violation of law, this should end on Nov. 17." They all said this, of course, before the Gore hand-count gambit became clear.

We are about to find out if we still are a nation of laws, or if the law can be manipulated to steal even the Presidency.

November 13, 2000

Editorial Feature

Let the
High Court Count

This is beginning to feel familiar. I spent a lot of time with a Constitutional crisis way back when I was a boy wonder, being thrust into Watergate in my second year running this newspaper's editorial page. Over a quarter-century and many milestones later, here I am writing again about the presidency held in the balance.

The only winner in this month's dead-heat election, indeed, has been the reputation of Richard M. Nixon. Even liberal commentators, or anyway some of them, have been recounting his acceptance of John F. Kennedy's dubious victory in 1960. He not only declined to challenge the results in Illinois and Texas, but discouraged his friends in the press from probing plausible voting outrages there. The Republic should not be put through that, the bete noire of all liberalism decided.

Thinking Things Over
By Robert L. Bartley

Times have changed, and we now have Al Gore's crew thrashing about for an avenue to overturn George Bush's initial victory. A recount steadily if mysteriously eroded his margin in Florida, but not quite by enough. The threat of court action over a ballot misdesigned by the Democrats themselves met with hoots of derision from all quarters—the Washington Post branded Gore campaign manager William Daley's court threats "a poisonous thing to say in these extraordinary and unsettling circumstances."

So now the Democrats have managed to start a third count, though only a partial one calculated to increase their votes without increasing their opponents'. They have asked for a "hand count," meaning that election officials will second-guess the way machines counted punched cards. An incompletely punched slot that shows "sunlight" will now be counted as punched—the AP reports that the Palm Beach recounters changed their precise test twice during their initial session hand recounting four precincts.

Who makes this highly subjective decision is clear enough in the 2-1 vote by which the Palm Beach board decided that they'd found enough errors to justify recounting the whole county. County Judge Charles Burton dissented. The majority consisted of Theresa LePore, the official who designed the butterfly ballot, and County Commissioner Carol Roberts, understood to be contemplating a congressional race on the Democratic ticket. Whether a ballot shows "sunlight," that is, will be decided by partisan Democrats.

Even with the best of intentions, "sunlight" will replace machine readers only in Democratic strongholds. There will be no hand recount, for example, in the GOP stronghold of Duval County, where about 26,000 ballots were invalidated as improperly marked. Since the "sunlight" test can only increase the vote, applying it selectively is a massive double standard. Selective cleaning is considered dubious even with scientific data, as Edward Glaeser of Harvard details nearby. (This article was on OpinionJournal.com on Saturday, when the current round of controversy started; see also John Fund's Political Diary on Palm Beach County.)

Faced with these realities, Republicans have gone to federal district court, asking for an injunction against the hand recount. Judge Donald M. Middlebrooks scheduled a hearing for 9:30 this morning, rather than the Saturday hearing the plaintiffs requested. Judge Middlebrooks was praised by Florida's Republican Senators when he was named to the bench by President Clinton in 1997; early in his career he also was general counsel to Democratic Gov. Reubin Askew.

Republicans will be arguing that the congenital unfairness of a selective recount judged by Democratic officials amounts to an abridgement of Constitutional voting rights, that equal protection of the laws means all votes should be counted the same way. Democrats will argue that the hand count option is provided in Florida law, and that Republicans should have been smart enough to ask for it in Duval County within the 72-hour deadline the law provides. Meanwhile, seven butterfly-ballot suits filed by voters and supported by the Gore campaign proceed in state court; a state judge has issued an injunction banning certification of the Palm Beach County votes.

Both sides are now in the courts; it is too late for a resolution as clean and as honorable as Mr. Nixon provided in 1960. In an 11th Circuit case likely to bear on the hand count dispute, it took almost a year to resolve a 1994 dispute over absentee ballots for the Alabama Supreme Court. The electoral college is scheduled to meet to pick a president on Dec. 18, the votes will be counted Jan. 6 by the president

of the Senate, who happens to be Al Gore, and the new president will take office Jan. 20. The Gore campaign is criticizing the Bush campaign for even thinking about the transition to a new government. Is this a Banana Republic, or not?

One of the things I learned from my first Constitutional crisis is that for these moments the Founders gave us the Supreme Court. The key moment in Watergate was the high court's 8-0 decision that President Nixon had to honor the subpoena for the White House tapes. The decision came after the court agreed to take the case directly, skipping deliberations by the Court of Appeals.

Supreme Court rules specify that a writ for direct appeal can be justified "upon a showing that the case is of such imperative public importance as to justify deviation from normal appellate practice and to require immediate determination in this Court." A case on who will be the next president would clearly seem to qualify. By any logic, indeed, this matter should not and ultimately cannot be decided in district court, let alone in backwater state justice. The rules on direct appeal do seem to require a district court decision, which Judge Middlebrooks could delay if he chooses.

Yet the Supreme Court is the one body with the prestige to lend legitimacy to any decision. Ultimately this is a Constitutional issue, too, not a matter of Florida voting law. There are also practical considerations. Proposals to rerun the election in one county or state, for example, would run into *Foster v. Love*, in which a unanimous Supreme Court held in 1997 that all states must hold national elections on the same appointed day.

Somehow it's fitting that the Clinton era should end with a crisis of legitimacy centering on the rule of law, as Watergate was at some deep emotional level about the passions of Vietnam. But I remember that we did recover from Watergate and went on to restore the economy and win the Cold War. The experience suggests that the sooner this case gets to the Supreme Court, the sooner we can reach a final result and start the healing process.

Editorial Feature

Recount 'Em All, or None at All

BY ED GLAESER

There is a well-known trick among statistical economists for biasing your data while looking honest. First, figure out which data points don't agree with your theory. Then zealously clean up the offending data points while leaving the other data alone. The key to maintaining academic dignity is to ensure that you do nothing to the data other than eliminate errors.

But while this approach may seem to improve accuracy, it actually leads to biased results. If you only clean the offending data points, then you will disproportionately keep erroneous data that agrees with your prior views. This leads many scholars to believe that data that is partially cleaned at the discretion of a researcher is worse than bad data.

This lesson from the ivory tower has a clear implication for the current mess in Florida. Hand counting ballots in only a few, carefully chosen counties is a sure way to bias the results. Even if hand counting is more accurate than machine counting, there is a clear bias introduced because Al Gore chose which counties to hand count. Mr. Gore has selected the state and counties where recounting has the best chance of helping him.

This is exactly the same as cleaning other data selectively. Naturally, if this opportunity for selective recounting becomes the norm, the floodgates will open and any candidate who loses a close election would be foolish not to demand a recount.

The immediate implication of this is clear. If there is to be recounting by hand, it cannot be selective. There needs to be total hand counting, not just within Florida, but across the U.S. in any state that was close. One candidate cannot be allowed just to choose where he wants the data cleaned. If this is prohibitively expensive, or time consuming, then it is better to leave the process unchanged than to introduce the selective recounting bias.

More generally, one of the principal lessons of macroeconomics is that rules generally work better than discretion. This is as true in elections as any place else. Giving candidates influence over how election results are processed does not help democracy to accurately reflect the will of the people. Judicial discretion is not much better, as judges will be responding to cases selectively filed by candidates. Furthermore, judges determining elections will exalt the judiciary to a king-making role it should not have.

While it certainly may be appropriate to ban butterfly ballots for all of eternity, and while reform of balloting procedures seems like a must, it is also clearly wrong to selectively recount certain areas.

Mr. Glaeser is a professor of economics at Harvard University and a visiting fellow at the Brookings Institution.

REVIEW & OUTLOOK

The Railroad

"Seek and ye shall find," says the Good Book. No one puts more faith in this proposition than the Vice President's lawyers: Given the time, they know, Democratic counters in Democratic counties seeking more votes for the Democratic candidate for President will find them. Indeed, Time.com already reports that when helpful election officials in Pinellas County, which went for Al Gore, "removed the chaff from ballots before they were submitted for recount by the machines, Gore-Lieberman picked up an additional 417 votes."

It is hard not to admit the obvious: The Gore campaign is trying to railroad a victory. Nothing captures the true intentions behind this strategy better than the Palm Beach County Canvassing Board's announcement of its 2-1 decision to proceed with a hand count. They held this press conference at 2 a.m. Sunday, in the middle of the night. An excerpt appears below.

Canvassing board member Carol Roberts walked everyone through her math—there could be 1,900 more votes for Mr. Gore out there!—and then voted to go ahead with a full hand count. Ms. Roberts was joined in this 2-1 decision by Theresa LePore, a Democrat, and arguably the 2000 election's single most controversial person: She is the designer of the now infamous Palm Beach butterfly ballot.

Unlike Governor Jeb Bush, who recused himself from the state canvassing board, Ms. LePore refused to do so. Given Ms. LePore's standing among Democrats as the person who cost them the White

House, by what reasonable standard was she permitted to serve on this board?

Even more telling is the exchange before the vote, in which the board chairman, Judge Charles Burton, also a Democrat, asked for an advisory opinion from the state. At a time when the Gore camp rests its case on the letter of Florida's election law on recounts, what does it say that the two Democratic members of the board were so determined not to hear the state's reading of that law? Read Ms. Roberts's frantic efforts to ram through her desired result.

Then when Secretary of State Katherine Harris announced yesterday morning she intended to adhere to the firm deadline mandated by Florida law, the Gore campaign communications director Mark Fabiani leapt immediately to the ad hominem, labeling her decision to follow Florida law the "naked political act" of a "crony." Campaign spokesman Chris Lehane took it further, likening her to a "Soviet commissar."

There's more. Mr. Gore's lawyers in Palm Beach County rest their legal and moral case on what they insist is every citizen's sacred right to vote be honored. Meanwhile in largely Republican Seminole County these same Gore lawyers argue that 4,700 absentee ballot requests be thrown out because GOP officials had (before the election) been allowed to correct a printer's error.

The team of lawyers around Mr. Gore obviously understand the law and its ramifications all too well. In particular they understand that it provides for an Electoral College, sets a deadline for recounts, and does not entertain after-the-fact changes of the rules, whether it be over the counting of ballot "chads" or the tallying of a vote. And so the Gore strategy is staked not on persuading the American public that the Vice President is right, but in casting sufficient public doubt on the system to make the election appear illegitimate, which somehow gives them carte blanche to put every aspect into (legal) play.

There is a certain unavoidable irony in having this spectacle of legal jujitsu created by lawyers for the public official who claimed the defense of no controlling legal authority. It sounded like a strange concept at the time, but it's now clear that Mr. Gore clearly understands its meaning and its uses. Its clear purpose in Florida now is to railroad an outcome.

In the early hours of Sunday morning, the Palm Beach County Canvassing Board voted 2-1 to authorize a manual recount—as well as to ignore a request to first get a reading of Florida law from the state. The exchange of this 2 a.m. press conference, taken from CNN's Breaking News runs as follows:

JUDGE CHARLES BURTON (Chair, Palm Beach County Canvassing Board): Can I inquire of the Department of Elections? Assuming this board were to request an advisory opinion—

CAROL ROBERTS (Palm Beach County Canvassing Board): Excuse me, Mr. Chair—

BURTON: Hold on.

ROBERTS: —but I made the motion and—

BURTON: All right, we will vote on it in a moment.

ROBERTS: Excuse me, but the gentleman said we should be following the laws of the state of Florida. These are the election laws of the state of Florida. And under Chapter 102, I think it's Chapter—it's 102.166. It's under paren. D. Sorry, it's—sorry, it's paren. five. If the manual recount indicates an error in the tabulation which could affect the outcome of the election, the County Canvassing Board shall—this is the law—correct the error and recount the remaining precincts with a vote tabulation system.

That's A. B, request the Department of State to verify the software or manually recount all ballots. Under existing state law, I do not feel that we need to have an opinion to tell us what state law is. The law is very clear. I also believe, Mr. Chair, that we've heard enough people. I really want to call the vote. I have the right to call the vote. And if you'd like to take a vote on calling the vote, I'll make that.

BURTON: All right. Thank you, Commissioner. The Chair would like to recognize one other person from the Department of Elections. Your name, please.

CARRIE CARPENTER (Assistant General Counsel for the Department of State): My name is Carrie Carpenter and I'm Assistant General Counsel for the Department of State and I believe that the Department could be helpful in providing assistance with interpreting the statute that was just read.

The Department is authorized under the elections code to provide advisory—formal advisory opinions on the election laws of the state of Florida. And does so, regularly, whenever the interpretation of a statute is questioned or in doubt, or perhaps if there may be more than one interpretation of a statute. For example, in this particular statute that was just read which reads, "if the manual recount indicates an error in the vote tabulation which could affect the outcome of the election, the County Canvassing Board shall..." and then it lists three things. However, you really don't get to those three options unless that criteria has been satisfied. And an interpretation of that could be helpful because it is my understanding that it is the Department's position that when a manual recount for the entire county is done, it is because the manual recount of the one percent demonstrated some type of error in the equipment, in the machines that were used. And if what this board found today was not an error of that type, but, instead, was an error of voter—of voter error. For example, if a voter did not push a chad completely through, or a voter did some other type of voting error by not following voting instructions and that caused the machine not to properly read the ballot. That is not the type of error that can be attributed to an error with a machine. And, therefore, that would not be a vote tabulation error that would affect the outcome. It would be a voter error that may affect the outcome. And so I believe that we can provide assistance in giving an interpretation, a formal advisory opinion to this board.

BURTON: And just one other quick question. Quick question.

ROBERTS: I'd like to answer—

BURTON: One quick question.

ROBERTS: I'd like to answer her—

BURTON: Please. Assuming we were to ask for an opinion, when could we receive it?

CARPENTER: You could receive it tomorrow.

BURTON: All right.

ROBERTS: Mr. Chair, I was—I was—I was involved in a recount that produced the immediate past senator of the state of Florida. It was the Mac McKay recount. At no time did anyone ever have the allegation that there was anything wrong with the machines. There was a hand manual recount because I was part of that. And that hand manual recount was actually asked for for the same reasons that I am asking for this now. And I believe based on that, and I will tell you that this is not—that was not the only manual hand recount that I have been involved with. I was involved with a manual hand recount of a state representative's race. It was also asked for. Not because there was any question about the machine tabulations, but because there was a question about the error in the actual count. And I still would like to call the vote. I would like to call the vote.

REVIEW & OUTLOOK

The Gore Hurricane

As the legal hurricane of Democratic lawyers raged across Florida for the seventh day, the charitable view of Al Gore would run something like this: If you had served as Bill Clinton's caddy for nearly eight years, loyally defending whatever needed defending, and after exhausting yourself in a long, hard run across the American landscape, and after about a hundred million voters left you in a nose-on-the-wire, dead-heat finish in the Florida swamps for the Presidency of the United States, you too might try to claw and scratch your way a few feet forward to capture the prize.

Al Gore

So the nation accorded Al Gore his week of life beyond the rules that tether mere mortals to a real world in which everyone recognizes that you have either won the game, or you have lost it. As of 7:30 p.m. yesterday in Florida, the clear outlines of this reality for Mr. Gore were beginning to form themselves into a final decision. Florida Secretary of State Katherine Harris, certifying the election results as the law required, announced that George W. Bush had 300 more of the state's votes than Vice President Gore. And of course Mr. Gore's legal hurricane promised to keep blowing in the courts to keep the counts going.

Set aside for a second the obvious Democratic objections to the Harris certification. The reality is that every official count taken so far has called Mr. Bush the winner. On election night, the results counted by the machines gave Mr. Bush a 1,764-vote margin. The entire state subsequently ran an automatic recount by machine, which left Mr. Bush's margin, before any manual recounts, at about 1,060 votes. We now have the 286 vote result.

Beyond these three vote counts, we have the suggestive results from some of the counties that the Gore camp itself insisted on recounting. Most telling is that of Broward County, a heavily Democratic jurisdiction. On Monday, after manually recounting 3,892 ballots in three precincts, the county's officials decided to stop because the effort had produced a net gain for Mr. Gore of four votes, reflecting no significant error in the original tabulation. The vote to stop was 2 to 1, and one of the commissioners voting to stop was county Judge Robert W. Lee, who is a Democrat. Moreover, preliminary checks of votes in precincts around heavily Democratic Fort Lauderdale produced few changes.

After today comes the absentee-ballot count. No serious person has suggested anything other than that most of those votes will be for Governor Bush. That is, on Friday Mr. Bush likely will still lead.

This strange event is well past the point of ever being able to say that any result is definitive in a sense that would satisfy statisticians or lawyers. What seems evident from the foregoing, however, is that Mr. Gore is not gaining enough ground. We have voted and we have counted and recounted, and despite enduring an extraordinary amount of extraordinary litigation, there is no concrete evidence that the Vice President's prospects are any better than they were the morning after the original, formal, legal election.

Yes, it is still possible to surmise that if Florida recounts every vote in every heavily Democratic precinct in the state, enough chads will drop to the floor to push Al Gore's vote count past Governor Bush's and far enough into the lead for the Gore campaign to claim it has won. Maybe. Or maybe not. Or maybe there comes a point when everyone on the beach has to recognize that the great whale lying on the shore, however magnificent, is in fact dead and beginning to stink.

With every passing day that they are in public view, the Gore lawyers are somewhat less edifying than they were the day before. We now have the spectacle of superstar plaintiffs attorney David

Boies arguing that Mr. Gore's hand-count case turns on the notion of whether the Florida Secretary of State's decision was "arbitrary," or, in Mr. Boies's words: "I would think that both arbitrary and discretion have both objective and subjective qualities to them. The court obviously thought it could make an objective determination that she had acted arbitrarily."

Elsewhere in Florida, another trial lawyer, Dexter Douglass, is litigating on Mr. Gore's behalf. In the unlikely event the Gore campaign discloses the contributions for the second election, we're confident it will show the trial lawyers have essentially financed this effort. The grinding litigation style certainly reflects it. And on Monday it emerged that lawyer Alan Dershowitz, whose last legal circus performance was in the O.J. Simpson trial, is representing eight aggrieved Palm Beach voters.

To a cynic, it's all merely partisan warfare without an exit strategy. That's not quite true. It may well be that every principal involved in the Florida recount battle is a Democrat or a Republican, but not all Floridians are behaving like cannon fodder. Circuit Court Judge Terry Lewis, who affirmed yesterday's certification deadline, is a Democratic appointee. Charles Burton, the Palm Beach canvassing chairman who dissented from the original decision to recount the vote there, is a Democrat, as is, we noted above, a Broward County judge who voted to stop the vote there. Pam Iorio, a Democrat who heads the Florida State Association of Supervisors of Elections, admitted in public, "Hand counting is not always the most accurate indicator of voter intent."

We suspect Ms. Iorio knows what she is talking about. We also suspect that Mr. Gore's lawyers intend to try the lock of every door out there to gain hand counts in venues favorable to their client. This in turn will provoke countersuits from the Bush camp. No one would be surprised if eventually the dispute leaped beyond the boundaries of Florida into Iowa or Wisconsin, for further recounts. The vote ended seven days ago, and Mr. Gore, despite all the king's horses and all the king's men, has not regained the lead in a week's time. With every passing day, whatever Mr. Gore hopes to achieve, diminishes.

November 16, 2000

REVIEW & OUTLOOK

Florida's Political Swamp

Legal maneuvering aside, the real question in Florida was whether any of this would get resolved before pure politics overwhelmed and strangled everything in sight. From where we're sitting it appears that the vote down there is disappearing into the Florida swamps.

Yesterday, we prematurely praised the courage of Democratic County Judge Robert Lee for voting against a complete manual recount of Broward County's 588,000 votes. Judge Lee cast the deciding vote on the county's three-member election commission after a sample recount of Democratic precincts added a mere six votes to Al Gore's total. Judge Lee has now suddenly reversed his vote, and Broward will do a full count. The Los Angeles Times headline explained it best: "Broward Judge Feeling Heat From Political Machine."

Democrats were furious with Mr. Lee. The Times quotes Robin Rohapaugh, an aide to Democratic Rep. Peter Deutsch, who has been watching the judge closely: "He has a reputation as a fair judge, but his votes haven't helped us." Looks like somebody got to Judge Lee. He's helping now.

Columnist Robert Novak reports that for Democrats the Broward vote totals have become "the focus for turning apparent defeat into glorious victory." Their strategy is to claim that thousands of Broward voters, mostly senior citizens, didn't apply sufficient pressure on punch cards to record their vote.

As to the recounts themselves, any Florida county is free to come up with its own recount standards to divine the intent of voters. This obviously is an incentive to the kind of subjective chaos TV viewers everywhere witnessed last Saturday night, as the Palm Beach County election commission changed its standards for counting ballots twice during the night.

Yesterday Republicans accused Palm Beach's now-famous county commissioner, Carol Roberts, of physically abusing ballots during the recount to produce de-chadded Gore votes. She said she was "fair and impartial." The notion that Ms. Roberts is actually counting any ballots, insofar as the day before she was shouting to a crowd of Democratic demonstrators that she was willing to go to jail for the Gore effort, is at the least amusing.

Meanwhile, circuit court judge Jorge Labarga ruled yesterday that local officials are free to count "dimpled chad" ballots as valid if they want to. Those are ballots that are only indented but still fully attached to the ballot. "No vote is to be declared invalid or void if there was a clear intention of the voter." Which of course depends on the meaning of the word "clear" to the local county canvassers.

As to Judge Lee's flip-flop, he claims he was moved to reconsider his stance on a hand recount by citing an advisory opinion issued Tuesday by Democratic Attorney General Bob Butterworth, the chair of the state's Gore campaign. But Mr. Butterworth's own office Web page states he will not issue advisory opinions on matters under the jurisdiction of other state agencies: "Questions arising under the Florida Election Code should be directed to the Division of Elections." Now Mr. Butterworth insists he can issue opinions "on anything I want to."

He also apparently feels he can try to influence local officials in charge of counting votes. The St. Petersburg Times reports that last Thursday, Mr. Butterworth got one of his aides to call County Judge Michael McDermott, chair of the Volusia County elections board. The three men then held a conference call in which the Attorney General told the judge he should do a hand recount.

Judge McDermott objected and said to Mr. Butterworth, "I think you should disqualify yourself from this matter." Shortly thereafter, Mr. Butterworth left the conference call, but his aide continued to lobby the judge to do a hand count. Judge McDermott said the call was improper and says "it will probably be the last" time he speaks with the attorney general. Nonetheless, two hours after the call the Volusia County board voted to conduct a hand count.

Attorneys who have worked for previous attorneys general say Mr. Butterworth probably violated his own office's "Government in the Sunshine" manual. It states that Florida's Sunshine law is violated if one official's involvement in "quasi-judicial proceedings raises a presumption that the contact was prejudicial to the decision-making process."

To recap: a) we have a county judge intimidated into reversing his decision on a vote count based on an improper opinion from an attorney general who chaired the Gore campaign; b) that same attorney general has been caught trying to influence an elections board; c) counties are hiring $7-an-hour temporary workers to help with a recount that will be subjective, standardless and surely sloppy.

There is a silver lining. The 11th Circuit Court of Appeals agreed, en banc, to hear the Bush campaign's arguments to halt the manual recounts. Whatever the outcome of that decision, there is now a string running from Florida into the higher levels of the federal courts. We suspect that if the appeals court judges keep pulling on that string to take a close look, someone's house of cards may come tumbling down.

REVIEW & OUTLOOK

Al Gore's Class-Action

Notwithstanding the sound and fury of 24-hour cable and Internet coverage, clearly the punditry is struggling for a legal precedent that makes sense of Florida's contested vote. Let us suggest that this is because they continue to look in the wrong place. The operative guide here is not election law but tort law, specifically plaintiff lawyers' class-action lawsuit. Earlier this week the American Trial Lawyers Association, now an informal subsidiary of the Democratic Party, put out an e-mail asking 500 of their members to volunteer for the Florida campaign. It shows.

Katherine Harris

Keep this in mind in the immediate aftermath of the state Supreme Court's order late yesterday allowing Florida's counties to go ahead with manual recounts, particularly because the order does not stipulate whether the Secretary of State, Katherine Harris, will ultimately have to accept that count. Because if we know anything about the trial lawyers it's that they view the law as mainly a pickax to chop down the opposition and get what they want.

Accordingly they have approached the contest not as though it were a question of discerning the proper meaning and enforcement of the Florida constitution, but a class-action on behalf of voters who have been swindled by some dark power. Which is also why, 10 days after the Floridians cast their ballots, Al Gore has placed his hopes for the White House in the National Law Journal's 1999 Man of the Year: plaintiffs attorney David Boies.

Now Mr. Boies is well known for having slain the Microsoft dragon. Less well known is that his $1.7 billion settlement reached at the same time with the pharmaceutical industry, one of Mr. Gore's famous "special interests," was the largest class-action settlement in history, or that he was involved in suits concerning oil drilling in Alaska, HMOs and even trade auction houses.

David Boies

Here the Boies-Gore assault on Florida invokes the will of the people even as it aims mightily to denigrate any controlling legal authority that gets in the way, whether the Florida constitution itself or any officer who deigns to administer it, such as Katherine Harris.

At the moment, Mr. Gore's Democratic operatives are trying to smear and ruin Ms. Harris's standing as a public official. Mr. Gore learned this technique from President Clinton, whose associates deployed it against RTC investigator Jean Lewis, Kathleen Willey, Linda Tripp and Billy Dale, to name only a few.

Mr. Gore on Wednesday called for elevating "the tone" of the dispute, in the same week that his own top officers had likened Ms. Harris to "a Soviet commissar," a "lackey," a "crony" out to "steal" an election, and in the words of Harvard's eminent professor Alan Dershowitz, a "crook."

Meanwhile, as this paper reported on our front page yesterday, Democrat Bob Beckel, who managed Walter Mondale's 1984 campaign and has close ties with Team Gore's Warren Christopher, announces a plan to start doing opposition research on the nation's electors. He says he's asking around, "Who are these electors, and what do you know about them?"

The squads of trial lawyers that ATLA called forth are smothering the state's vote in litigation. This has the advantage of giving the operation a patina of legitimacy, looking like you are operating inside the system of laws when in fact Florida's procedures are being exploited with the least admirable tactics of the trial lawyer bar:

venue shopping for favorable Democratic counties, court shopping for favorable judicial decisions, and relentless spinning of a press hungry to fill its 24-hour cycle.

If Broward County doesn't produce enough new votes, try Palm Beach County and after that Dade County and if that doesn't work sue to have the whole state recounted until Chicago's Bill Daley manages to produce enough Democratic counters with enough Democratic chads to put Mr. Gore over the top.

In this world, the law is whatever you can get by with saying it is. So when Ms. Harris required Florida counties seeking to get her to reconsider her state-mandated deadline of 5 p.m. Tuesday to provide a legal basis—in writing—this was cast not as fidelity to law but an example of mere arbitrariness!

Indeed, those at the center of the Gore legal hurricane almost never justify what they are doing on its own terms. As this litigation drags on and the public loses patience with the lawyers, the Gore camp takes to the airwaves to shift the burden onto their opponents, suggesting that "If the shoe were on the other foot, you Republicans would be doing the same thing."

As it happens, the evidence inclines to precisely the opposite: In this election Missouri's Senator Ashcroft gracefully conceded to the dubious victory of a dead man; in 1960 Nixon conceded to Kennedy despite the fairly understood cheating of Daley Pere, and, just as important, in 1974 it was a Republican group led by conservative James Buckley that called on then-President Nixon to resign, for the good of his country and his party. By contrast, notwithstanding Mr. Gore's Saturday Night Liveish protestations that he has only the country's interests at heart, where is the evidence of a similar act of political grace?

And so the lawyers proceed, even as Ms. Harris moves closer and closer to a final certification that looks perfectly in accord with the Florida constitution. As the Bush team argued in court yesterday, Mr. Gore and his lawyers "Are not saying 'please enforce a law,' they're saying 'don't enforce the law.'" Should she go ahead and certify the election after counting up the absentee ballots today and tomorrow, she will have completed the exercise of Florida's executive authority and put on the record a result.

And once again, Al Gore and the trial lawyers will simply litigate and spin some more in the hope that the defendant will throw up his hands and offer to settle. It is becoming increasingly hard to see what these tactics are doing in the company of a democratic election.

November 17, 2000

Editorial Feature

The Donkey in the Living Room

By Peggy Noonan

For many years there has been a famous phrase that derives from the 12-step recovery movement. It refers to a thing that is very big, and obvious, and of crucial importance, that people around it refuse for whatever reason to acknowledge. It's called the elephant in the living room.

There is an elephant in the living room in the Florida story. Actually, it's a donkey. And actually, there are a number of them.

When the story of the Florida recounts and hand counts and court decisions is reported on network and local TV, and in the great broadsheet newspapers, the journalists uniformly fail to speak of the donkey in the living room. They give great and responsible attention to the Florida story. But with a unity that is perhaps willful, perhaps unconscious, perhaps a peculiar expression of an attempt at fairness, they avoid the donkey.

You know what the donkey is. The donkey is the explicit fear, grounded in fact, in anecdotal evidence, in the affidavits of on-the-ground participants, and in the history of some of the participants, that the Gore-Clinton Democratic party is trying to steal the election. Not to resolve it—to steal it. That is, they are not using hand counting to determine who won; they are using hand counting to win.

They are attempting to do this through chicanery, and by interpreting various ballots any way they choose. As in, "This ballot seems to have a mild indentation next to the word Bush. Well, that's not a vote. Person might have changed his mind. This ballot seems to have a mild indentation for Gore; the person who cast this ballot was probably old, and too weak to puncture the paper card. But you can see right here there's a mark kind of thing. I think that's a vote, don't you Charley?" "Oh yeah, that's a vote alright."

David Smith

That's how the chads probably got to the floor in the counting rooms. That is one of the increasing number of stories— none of which are ever the lead, all of which wind up on page 11—indicating the possibility of significant vote fraud throughout the election.

Columnists are writing about it—George Will wrote a great column suggesting what is happening in Florida amounts to an attempted coup, and Michael Kelly wrote suggesting Mr. Gore is not a helper of democracy but a harmer of it; the conservative magazines have weighed in, as has this page. You can hear vote fraud discussed on the all-argument political shows on TV and radio.

But it is not reported as news. And it only counts when it's news. And this is most extraordinary because the Republican fear of fraud—the legitimate fear of it—is the major reason the Bush people don't want more hand counts. They do not trust the counters.

This question—the extent of vote fraud in this election, and the fact that the Republicans think it is governing what is happening in

Florida—is not the unspoken subtext of the drama. It is the unspoken text.

Republicans are convinced, and for good reason, that Bill Daley, who learned at his father's knee, and Al Gore, who learned at Bill Clinton's, are fraudulently attempting to carry out an anti-democratic strategy that is a classic of vote stealing: Keep counting until you win, and the minute you "win" announce that the American people are tired of waiting for an answer and deserve to know who won.

Could a political party in this great and sophisticated democracy, in this wired democracy where sooner or later every shadow sees sunlight, steal a prize as big and rich and obvious as the presidency?

Yes. Of course. If the history of the past half century has taught us anything it's that determined people can do anything. What might stop it? If the media would start leading the news with investigations into the prevalence of vote fraud and the possibility that the presidential election is being stolen.

There have been a number of shameful public moments in the drama so far—Mr. Daley announcing that "the will of the people" is that Mr. Gore win, Mr. Gore's own aggressive remarks in the days just after the election, Hillary Clinton announcing, in the middle of what may become a crisis involving the Electoral College, that her first act will be to do away with the college. And there is this Internet column from Paul Begala, who prepped Mr. Gore for his debates with Mr. Bush. He acknowledged that when you look at an electoral map of the United States, you see a sea of red for Mr. Bush, and clots of blue for Mr. Gore.

"But if you look closely at that map you see a more complex picture. You see the state where James Byrd was lynch-dragged behind a pickup truck until his body came apart—it's red. You see the state where Matthew Shepard was crucified on a split-rail fence for the crime of being gay—it's red. You see the state where right-wing extremists blew up a federal office building and murdered scores of federal employees—it's red. The state where an Army private who was thought to be gay was bludgeoned to death with a baseball bat, and the state where neo-Nazi skinheads murdered two African-Americans because of their skin color, and the state where Bob Jones University spews its anti-Catholic bigotry: they're all red too."

It was a remarkably hate-filled column, but also a public service in that it revealed what animates Clinton-Gore thinking regarding their opponents: hatred pure and simple, a hatred that used to be hidden and now proudly walks forward.

It stands in the living room too.

As does the unstated but implicit message of the hatred: that extraordinary means are understandable when you're trying to save America from the terrible people who would put George W. Bush in the presidency so that they can kill more homosexuals and black men and blow up federal buildings and kill toddlers. Really, if Republicans are so bad it's probably good to steal elections from them, don't you think?

I never thought I would wind up nostalgic for the days when I merely disagreed with Democratic presidents. But whoever doubted the patriotism, the love of country, of John Kennedy or Jimmy Carter?

This crew we have now, Messrs. Gore and Clinton and their operatives, they seem, to my astonishment as an American, to be men who would never put their country's needs before their own if there were even the mildest of conflicts between the two. America is the platform of their ambitions, not the driving purpose of them.

Another donkey in the living room: The sense that Republicans are no match for the Democrats in terms of ferocity, audacity, shrewdness, the killer instinct. Republicans seem incapable of going down to the level of Gore-Clinton operatives. They think that you cannot really defend something you love with hatred because hatred is by its nature destructive: It scalds and scars and eats away.

Republicans seem to be losing the public-relations war. The Democrats have David Boies and Bill Daley, each, forgive me, smooth as an enema, in Evelyn Waugh's phrase. The Republicans have James Baker, who seems irritated and perplexed. Perhaps he is taken aback by how the game has changed, how the Democrats he faces now operate by rules quite different, and much rougher, than the ones they played by 20 years ago.

Now the game for the Gore camp is to win any way you can in Florida, and if you can't win delay, and in the delay maybe you'll win when the Electoral College comes together, or maybe at the very least even if someone stops you, you'll have ruined the legitimacy of the man who does win, which will make it easier for you as you wait in the wings for the rematch in 2004.

There are a lot of donkeys in the living room in Florida, and maybe the Bush people should start to talk about them. Maybe that will make them news. It can't hurt. It's a circus down there anyway.

Ms. Noonan is a contributing editor of the Journal. Her OpinionJournal.com column appears on Fridays.

November 20, 2000

REVIEW & OUTLOOK

The Will of the Lawyers

Al Gore has finally found his controlling legal authority. He's counting on the Democratic judges of Florida to win him an election he couldn't win on his own.

And they just might be up to the job. One ominous sign was the Florida Supreme Court's amazing decision on Friday, at 4:30 p.m., to block Florida Secretary of State Katherine Harris from certifying a George W. Bush victory by 930 votes with all overseas ballots counted.

The seven Solomons issued their injunction without even being asked; the Gore team hadn't filed its brief yet. This by itself is

unheard of, barring fraud, which no one alleges here. The court said it wanted "to maintain the status quo," yet it allowed hand recounts in Democratic precincts to continue. So the only status quo being maintained is the part helping Mr. Gore.

The court's injunction also achieved the rare trifecta of overruling all three branches of Florida government at once. It overrode an elected executive officer, Ms. Harris, who was implementing deadlines enacted by an elected legislature. And it overrode Leon County Circuit Court Judge Terry Lewis, who had twice upheld Ms. Harris's use of her discretion.

Al Gore

"A reading of the entire Election Code suggests a legislative intent to balance the desire for accuracy with the desire for finality," Judge Lewis, a Democrat, wrote. "The plaintiffs assert that she has acted arbitrarily in deciding to ignore amended returns from counties conducting manual recounts. I disagree."

As the only judge who had examined the merits, Mr. Lewis was overruled by judges who hadn't heard a single argument. The court's motive Friday was transparently political—to block what it knew was a significant event, namely Mr. Bush's certification as the winner.

We'd like to think these unelected judges will show less partisanship when they address the merits, but the court's makeup and history aren't reassuring. Six of the seven are Democrats and all were appointed by Democratic governors. Somehow this never gets mentioned by the same media that describe Ms. Harris as a "staunch Republican" (to quote Paul Simao of Reuters).

At least four of the judges were also selected by the lawyer who is Mr. Gore's Florida counsel in this very case. He's Dexter Douglass, who was the chief judge picker for former Florida Gov. Lawton Chiles. "They'll know I'm at the table," Mr. Douglass boasted to the New York Times the other day about his Gore role before the Supreme Court today.

As our John Fund reported on OpinionJournal.com, the Florida Supreme Court seems to have a problem with democracy. The judges have shredded Florida's right to ballot initiatives by routinely declaring them "misleading." The court tossed out four separate initiatives against racial preferences. And two months ago it rebuked the state legislature for having dared to put a "preservation of the death penalty" measure on the ballot in 1996.

Two other judges have made in-kind contributions to the Gore campaign. In Democratic Broward County, manual recounters were at first counting ballots only if at least two of the four corners of the chad were detached. But this only produced 48 new Gore votes in the first 153 precincts (of 609 total). So late Friday, Circuit Court Judge John Miller suggested that the county canvassing board count "dimpled chads," that is, ballots that are merely indented.

Circuit Court Judge Jorge Labarga did something similar in Palm Beach County. As the Orlando Sentinal put it, "This has resulted in a large number of ballots being set aside for closer scrutiny by the county's three-member canvassing board. The ruling concerns

Republicans, because two of those board members are Democrats and the third is a nonpartisan judge." This should ramp up the Gore tallies.

It all gets curiouser and curiouser.

• The Miami Herald reports that "at least 39 felons—mostly Democrats—illegally cast absentee ballots" in Broward and Miami-Dade. Those same counties also reversed themselves and decided to hold manual counts, under severe Gore pressure.

• Democratic lawyer Bruce Rogow says that Gore lawyer Warren Christopher called him to lobby Mr. Rogow's client, elections supervisor Theresa LePore, to assure a manual recount in Palm Beach County. Mr. Rogow says this is inappropriate, but Palm Beach is now doing what Mr. Christopher asked.

• And, mysteriously, some 1,420 overseas ballots were rejected, perhaps as many as 1,100 of them from U.S. military personnel. That is, they dismissed the military ballots because they weren't cast through exacting procedures, but they've sent other ballots back to be counted a third, fourth and fifth time; dimpled chad now qualifies. Still, Mr. Bush won 63% of the overseas absentees that were counted. If Democratic vote canvassers can disqualify military ballots, why can't Katherine Harris do her job and enforce legal vote-counting deadlines?

All of this started, remember, not because of any fraud but because some voters in Palm Beach County believe they made mistakes on a ballot designed by a Democrat. From that blunder the Gore campaign has built what has become a classic railroad job. Look for the Supreme Court to issue its findings once the Gore counters have found enough dimpled chad to go ahead, and with the absentees in, they now know their target number.

Count and then recount, sue and then count again, change the rules and count again, and when that fails ask the Dexter Douglass Florida Supreme Court to let Al Gore count for as long as it takes to move ahead of George W. Bush. Then all hail "the will of the people."

Editorial Feature

How Democrats Wage Political War

By Cleta Mitchell

In case you're bewildered by the machinations of the Gore campaign-turned-law-firm, let there be no doubt that the goings on in Florida are perfectly in keeping with the way Democrats normally think and behave. Lawsuits are a key part of the Democrats' political strategy, so nothing about Florida should surprise anyone who has spent time in the Democratic Party.

Until 1995, I was a Democrat. I've been a Democratic elected official, a party official and an active party member, so I know how Democrats think.

Democrats know and internalize, understand and are motivated by, certain ideas, concepts and principles that seem to be foreign to Republicans. And Democrats are elated that Republicans don't know or function under the same ideas. These basic rules of Democratic thinking are at work in Florida. This primer should help explain what makes the Democrats tick.

Rule 1: If we don't win, we don't eat.

The fundamental motivation for Democrats is their understanding that winning control of government is tied to paychecks, jobs, government grants, public money for private groups and companies, government contracts, union bargaining advantages, rules by which trial lawyers bring lawsuits, and on and on. The use of government to feed friends and starve enemies is something Democrats know instinctively. Winning elections means getting or keeping a livelihood.

Say what you will about trial lawyers, but remember this: They only get paid if their clients win. Extending that principle to politics means that various Democratic constituencies are convinced that a Democratic victory means food on the table.

Rule 2: State courts are "home" to Democrats.

There is a reason why, of the more than two dozen lawsuits filed in Florida by various Democrats, virtually all have been filed in state courts. Democrats are at home in the state courts. It is where the judges are elected, often on partisan ballots. And the trial lawyers are the most ardent in overseeing who fills and keeps judicial positions.

William Bramhall

Trial lawyers normally hate federal court, where rules are stricter and standards much higher, and where attorneys can be, and often are, sanctioned for filing frivolous lawsuits.

Against the backdrop of the myriad state lawsuits filed by Democrats in Florida, and the call by the Gore campaign for even more trial lawyers to come and assist in the litigation battles there, the Bush campaign filed one legal action. It was filed in federal court as a challenge to the constitutional validity of the manual recount procedures in Florida and the absence in the statute of any objective standards for such recounts. The evidence to support the sole Republican lawsuit has unfolded on our television screens during the manual recounts conducted to date.

State courts are often a blank page to be filled in by the most clever manipulator in the courtroom. (No wonder the Democrats have brought in uber-litigator David Boies.) Only a state court judge would have entertained, much less ruled on, a lawsuit like the one filed by the Palm Beach Democratic Party, which argued that incomplete ("dimpled") ballots should nonetheless be counted. And that's just one example of the kinds of cases the Democrats have filed.

Republicans depart from their customary arguments in favor of federalism, decentralization of government power and devolution of authority to the states when the civil justice system and lawsuit reform are at issue. Then, the parties switch sides and it is Republicans who prefer federal courts and uniform national standards and Democrats who fight vigorously to protect their state court fiefdoms. This may seem inconsistent—but it isn't, when one understands the hometown advantage of the Democrats and trial lawyers in state courts. Remember Rule #1.

Rule 3, the "golden rule": He who makes the rules wins the gold.

The post-election fight in Florida is the best evidence in my lifetime of the absolute supremacy of the rules-as-gold principle. Democrats understand impressively well that the rules, the regulations, the procedures and the processes will almost always dictate the outcome. In a nutshell, rules provide victories—or defeats. Because the statutory process in Florida did not provide the result the Democrats wanted, they knew it was imperative to change the rules after the election.

When I was first elected to the Oklahoma legislature, a veteran Democrat member told me to learn the rules. He told me, "If you know the rules better than your opponent, you can beat him every time." He was right. I also learned that writing and rewriting the rules is as important as understanding them.

The legal wrangling this week in Florida is neither about "technicalities," nor about "fairness." It is about winning. See Rule #1. Changing the rules is why the Gore campaign dispatched lawyers and organizers to Florida in the early morning hours of election night—because the rules had to be rewritten under public pressure, either through executive or judicial decisions, in order for Al Gore to prevail.

Changing the rules required a massive public-relations effort by the Gore campaign to discredit the rules and procedures under which elections are normally conducted in the state of Florida. Changing the rules was the objective in the Gore campaign's vilification of Katherine Harris, the Republican secretary of state, for enforcing the existing laws and rules.

Any Republican who misses the lessons the Democrats are teaching us on national TV these past two weeks is terribly naive. If, as a result of all this, Republicans don't commit themselves to learning and practicing the art of political war, as well as its natural extension in the courtroom, there may not be much of a GOP to kick around anymore in the future.

Ms. Mitchell is a Washington attorney who has previously served as a Democratic member of the Oklahoma legislature.

November 24, 2000

REVIEW & OUTLOOK

President Dimples?

Al Gore can't win without the dimpled ballots. That is the single, irreducible, final truth of the 2000 campaign for the U.S. Presidency. No dimples, no White House for Al Gore.

Thus, like the Terminator robot, Al Gore grinds on across the state of Florida, programmed only to win. No sooner had his lawyers locked up the Florida Supreme Court Tuesday night, than the Miami-Dade canvassing board broke out of the compound Wednesday, declaring that the hand counting there was over and they were certifying their results from November 8. With Miami-Dade's dimples evaporating, the Gore lawyers went on a fruitless search for a Florida court to agree with them that "the law" should force Miami-Dade to do what Al Gore wants them to do: Count his dimpled ballots.

Al Gore

Now that every serious observer of Florida agrees that the outcome for Mr. Gore comes down to the dimpled ballots, we think it's reasonable to ask, why continue the nightmare? Does Mr. Gore truly want to become President on the basis of some cards that maybe, sort of, suggest what is delicately called "voter intent"?

Indeed, the Miami-Dade canvassing board's attempt to wind back the clock to the status quo ante of November 8 gives the rest of us an opportunity to look back and wonder just how much of this spectacle has been necessary. It now appears that the key moment in this election was 3:45 a.m., November 8. That was when Al Gore telephoned George Bush and withdrew the concession he had made at 2:15 a.m. when Governor Bush had a lead of 1,725 votes. In retrospect, the 2:15 concession qualified as the sort of statesmanship many have called missing in action during all this litigation.

Now, giving the Gore camp some benefit, one can concede that Florida law permits an automatic recount for such a small margin. But it is an automatic machine recount that the law allows. And after that machine recount, Governor Bush was still in the lead. Thus, the next key event here, pitching the nation into what it now endures, was Bill Daley, on successive days, asserting that Mr. Gore had won, based on the national popular vote, that they wouldn't accept the machine recount and would press for a manual recount until the "will of the people" was somehow discovered. This opening bell from Bill Daley is what brought into the ring the team of Gore lawyers and has transformed the presidential election into a WWF Smackdown.

Enough statistical commentary has been published on the vote to make it clear that Florida is a coin-flip result, and every ballot count produced since November 8 shows that the coin came up heads for George Bush. What we've been witnessing is Al Gore wanting the rules changed so that one of the coin-flips comes up tails for him. Instead of gracefully standing by his original concession or by the results of the legal machine recount, Mr. Gore was reportedly persuaded by his camp that "we can win this thing" with a manual recount. The whole world has now watched what Mr. Gore set in motion.

Despite it all, one theme in this effort stands out: Mr. Gore's attempts, often successful, to change the rules in the middle of the game, for no purpose other than a Gore victory. Never in politics have so many goal posts been moved so many times.

Looking back on what the country has been put through, there are a couple of points that can be made with finality: If Al Gore had been ahead by 1,725 votes that November 8 morning, George Bush would have conceded the election and gone home to Texas and the U.S. would be assembling a new government. Instead, Al Gore's "just win, baby" philosophy of government has diminished the election, diminished the candidates, and—no one disputes—diminished the next Presidency. Quite an accomplishment.

The time for worrying and weeping about the republic is long gone. If nothing else, the American people are getting an up-close look at a country run by trial lawyers and judges; it's a hellhole that average citizens and businesses disappear into every day of the week. As to the unseemly procedures in Florida, Al Gore made this bed, and the American people are going to have to lie in it for awhile.

Our view remains as it was expressed earlier this week, that the GOP has an obligation to fight and defeat this kind of politics at its own level. The activities of the past several days suggest that is exactly what the Republicans have decided to do. Indeed, it's beginning to look a lot like this is not your father's GOP. And if the apoplexy seizing the throats and pens of most liberal commentators is any indication, they aren't too comfy with a GOP ready to fight hard for something.

At the moment, it appears the GOP has a fair amount of ammunition for its legal counteroffensive. The decision by the Miami-Dade canvassing board to throw in the towel and certify its results back to November 8 was a watershed event, as was the Florida Supreme Court's Thanksgiving decision to let Miami-Dade's action stand.

There's been a lot of worrying that all of this has become so partisan. The only genuinely partisan activity in Florida took place on November 7, when the people of that state cast their votes either for the Democratic Presidential nominee or the Republican nominee. When those votes were counted, George Bush had won. When they were recounted, he had also won. We have arrived at the day after Thanksgiving, and having survived a hurricane of litigation up to the Florida Supreme Court, it is still clear that Mr. Bush has still won this election.

The time has arrived for Mr. Gore, or the Democratic party, to call off the dogs and revisit the statesmanship that existed in the early hours after the day that the United States voted for a new President.

November 24, 2000

Editorial Feature

Burgher Rebellion: GOP Turns Up Miami Heat

MIAMI—If it's possible to have a bourgeois riot, it happened here Wednesday. And it could end up saving the presidency for George W. Bush.

With both parties spinning, I thought I'd go south to see the Miami-Dade manual recount firsthand. Surely it couldn't be as arbitrary as it sounded from Washington? And it wasn't. It was worse. Little did I know it'd be bad enough to inspire 50-year-old white lawyers with cellphones and Hermes ties to behave, well, like Democrats.

Potomac Watch

By Paul A. Gigot

These normally placid burghers popped their corks after a week of watching a recount they felt was rigged for Al Gore. They kept mum but stewed for days as a three-member, Democratic-leaning canvassing board tried to divine the "intent" of the voter without any standards at all.

One of the canvassers, a career bureaucrat named David Leahy, had even declared the lack of any vote-counting standard a virtue. He needed "the flexibility," as his spokeswoman put it, to "look at the totality of the ballot to determine the intent of the voter."

Like other reporters, I had to watch from 10 feet away and strain to hear this subtle, epic search for "intent." Mr. Leahy would take a ballot and hunt not just for dimples but for any mark at all, even pregnant chads still in their first trimester. I saw him bend or twist several ballots, which can't be good for chads that have already been machine-counted three times.

Then he'd say, "that's a 6," meaning for Gore (who was sixth on the ballot) or a "no vote," or much more rarely, "a vote for 4" (Bush). He then handed the ballot to Lawrence King, a Democratic judge who looks like an older Charlie Sheen. Only once did I see him disagree with Mr. Leahy's declaration of a new Gore vote.

The challenge usually came, if it did at all, from the third board member, county judge and independent Myriam Lehr. She'd grimace and focus and turn the ballot over and over before saying she disagreed. But it didn't matter. A 2-to-1 vote—and I witnessed six in about 30 minutes—still counted for the veep.

Most of these ballots were clearly punched for a Senate candidate and other offices. Only the presidential mark was in doubt. So they weren't the ballots of seniors too confused or weak to punch through. They might have been those of voters who disliked both presidential candidates. But a partisan vote down the ballot was deemed to be one indication of intent.

Every Democrat described this guesswork recounting as "professional" or "fair." But every Republican was seething. "You should see what they're calling a dimple," said Neal Conolly, a mild-mannered New York lawyer who volunteered to spend his vacation here. "It's the most minor imperfection in the paper. I wouldn't even call it a crease."

In one instance, he says (and I witnessed his objection), a Gore chad was displaced but a smaller hole was also present in the Bush chad. They counted it for Mr. Gore. A reporter's reflex is to dismiss such complaints as "partisan." But having covered elections for 20 years, I hope I can distinguish real from synthetic protest. These folks were ready to blow.

The tipping point came Wednesday, after the Florida Supreme Court said manual counts must be included, but by a Sunday deadline. The three canvassers reacted first by dropping a complete recount, thus omitting pro-Bush Cuban precincts. They would only count the 10,750 ballots that machines had spit out for no presidential vote. These were mostly from Democratic precincts.

Then the Three Counting Sages repaired to semi-isolation, forcing TV cameras to watch through a window and keeping reporters 25 feet away. That did it. Street-smart New York Rep. John Sweeney, a visiting GOP monitor, told an aide to "Shut it down," and semi-spontaneous combustion took over.

The Republicans marched on the counting room en masse, chanting "Three Blind Mice" and "Fraud, Fraud, Fraud." True, it wasn't exactly Chicago 1968, but these are Republicans. Their normal idea of political protest is filling out the complaint card at a Marriott.

They also let it be known that 1,000 local Cuban Republicans were on the way—not a happy prospect for Anglo judges who must run for re-election. Inside the room, GOP lawyers also pointed out that the law—recall that quaint concept—required that any recount include all ballots.

The canvassers then stunned everybody and caved. They cancelled any recount and certified the original Nov. 7 election vote, claiming that the Sunday deadline didn't allow enough time to recount everywhere. Republicans rejoiced and hugged like they'd just won the lottery.

All of this leaves the Gore campaign as frustrated as Republicans were after watching Democrats trash Katherine Harris. Mr. Gore was counting on Miami-Dade dimples to give him at least 600 more votes. Now he'll have to get them from Palm Beach and Broward counties, but there may not be enough.

So, true to form, Mr. Gore's lawyers are suing the Miami-Dade canvassers to restart the hand count. But this contradicts the Florida Supreme Court decision that the vice president had heralded only the night before as a victory for "democracy." The court said that the decision to recount is up to the counties. A lower court rejected the Gore request late Wednesday, but his lawyers are now asking the Florida supremes to postpone their own deadline.

If Al Gore loses his brazen attempt to win on the dimples, one reason will be that he finally convinced enough Republicans to fight like Democrats.

November 27, 2000

REVIEW & OUTLOOK

Supremes to Al: Concede

The canvassers kept counting dimples yesterday and the nation got Florida Secretary of State Katherine Harris's dramatic announcement certifying George W. Bush as Florida's election winner.

Still, the weekend's most important event toward closing the circle for President-elect Bush was surely the decision by the Supreme Court of the United States to step into the middle of the 100-round Florida slugfest. It does not mean that the Supreme Court is going to declare Governor Bush the outright winner. What it does mean is that the American institution with the largest inventory of moral and political clout just now is about to lean hard on somebody. And in our view that somebody is Vice President Al Gore. We think that its acceptance of this case means that the Court is telling Mr. Gore it is time to stand down.

George W. Bush

The famous saying has it that the Supreme Court reads the election returns, like everyone else. Of course it does. And the returns it's been reading so far have had George W. Bush leading through several counts and recounts stretching back to November 7.

If you are a Democrat it is painful to lose by 537 out of 6 million cast. It would surely be better to win by 537 votes. But the only way that happens is if you are willing to affirm what various Florida canvassing boards, Mr. Gore's lawyers, and the Florida Supreme Court have done to the state's election laws as they existed on November 7, 2000. Or, as the Florida Supreme Court put it, letting "a hyper-technical reliance upon statutory provisions" get in the way. That is, they all changed the election law in the interest of what they believe to be a higher good, described as "the will of the people." Again, agreeing with the rightness and legality of all of this is the only way that dimpled ballots make Al Gore President. No one disputes this dynamic.

If the U.S. Supreme Court had agreed with all of this, specifically, with the state of Florida's authority to do whatever it wants while electing a President, it would have told Governor Bush's lawyers to get lost. Instead, it told the lawyers for both sides to show up Friday on Constitution Avenue.

The Court makes it pretty clear that it took the case because it is weighing whether to overrule the Florida high court and say that Secretary of State Harris should have been allowed to certify the original count. While the Justices probably have not conclusively made up their minds just yet, surely the likelihood of a pro-Bush decision from the Court would be greatly increased if there is a last-minute Gore surge in Broward and Palm Beach Counties, suggesting ever-changing counting standards. So with the Supreme Court standing by against that possibility, a Gore victory is harder than ever to envision.

We have felt from the beginning of this battle that the Gore team has been trying to fill an inside straight. They had to have hoped they could contain the case inside Florida's friendly judicial borders. And surely they knew from day one that the moment might arrive when Governor Bush's lawyers would ask the federal courts to rule that Florida was violating Title 3, Chapter I, Section 5 of the U.S. federal code, which states that "laws enacted prior" to the day of election "shall be conclusive and shall govern in the counting of the electoral votes as provided in the Constitution . . ." After all the Florida litigating, the predictable federal collision has arrived for Mr. Gore.

Even for people inclined to support the Florida high court's decision, the Gore team's audacious litigating must seem a travesty. Having won discretion for the canvassing boards, Mr. Gore's lawyers are now planning to sue these very same boards for not simply making Mr. Gore President.

They are going to sue Miami-Dade's Democratic board for shutting down its count in light of the supreme court's deadline. Most brazen yet, the Gore lawyers will sue Palm Beach County for failing to use the most liberal possible standard for identifying dimples favorable to Mr. Gore.

Then on Saturday the Broward canvassers surfaced a box of 500 absentee ballots to check for Gore dimples. But absentee voters punch out their ballots with a paper clip. There is no machine to confront. The notion of a dimpled chad on an absentee ballot is absurd. This is the abuse of a U.S. presidential election that has to be stopped, and Secretary of State's certification deadlines have been the appropriate mechanism for doing so.

The public-relations war never rests, of course, and so various liberal commentators have been frolicking with the assertion that conservatives have called in the highest federal court to stomp on Florida innocents merely for exercising their states rights. Dream on. The Florida Supreme Court's decision was the new century's greatest act of judicial activism, a reality the court itself didn't bother to deny ("a hyper-technical reliance"). The U.S. Court will of course limit its thoughts to protecting Title 3, but a decision against Florida would implicitly be the century's greatest blow against judicial activism.

If that happens, judicial liberals can dump their ire on Al Gore; he put this ball in play. Most likely, the pols on the Democratic side never expected that the Republicans could sustain two weeks of street-fighting. That was an odds-on bet. But the Democrats lost it. Al Gore has managed to transform an often pathetic Republican party into a unified fighting force. Not even Bill Clinton managed that feat.

As a footnote, Florida's horror show probably means that virtually every voting precinct in America is going to be subjected to a national effort to clean up voter fraud, inefficiency and abuse. Guess which party is least likely to benefit from that reform.

Purely at the level of political melodrama, it's hard not to sympathize with the Gore camp's excitement at the sight of the Bush vote total dropping as another 10 or 20 dimpled votes get squeezed out of Florida's overly ripe ballots. Al Gore thinks he can smell a win, and now intends to blow by the Harris certification and contest the election. Somewhere there must be Democrats who recognize that letting the Supreme Court hear this case on Friday is not in the long-term interests of their party.

REVIEW & OUTLOOK

Some Road to the Presidency

Al Gore is contesting the Presidential election not from clawing ambition, his spinners tell us, but because he has divined that he really won. Maybe so. A mind that can count a dimpled chad as a vote is capable of believing about anything.

Mr. Gore's professed high-mindedness would be easier to credit, though, if it were not washed in the casual attitude toward the truth that we have come to expect from the author of no controlling legal authority, the Buddhist Temple fund-raiser and the iced-tea defense.

The Vice President in his Monday speech to the nation repeated the professions of supermouthpiece David Boies, for example, that there were 10,000 votes in Miami-Dade uncounted. These are in fact votes that were machine-counted for other offices but did not register a vote for President. The common-sense view of such a ballot is that the voter wanted to be heard on other offices, but did not like either candidate for President. There were 175,000 such ballots across the state of Florida, and 1.25 million across the nation.

What Mr. Gore really wants is to pour over the 10,000 Miami-Dade ballots in search of the mysterious "dimpled chad" votes for him. Bear in mind that the county's board back on Nov. 14 shut down its first recount after a sampling of three precincts turned up only six more votes for Mr. Gore. That seemed in retrospect to be the sort of reasonable action so thought to be missing from this endless exercise. The Democrat sued, forcing Miami-Dade to resume.

The Gore team currently argues that Miami-Dade is an undiscovered mother lode of Gore votes because in the 135 of 614 precincts counted they produced a Gore gain of 157 votes. But the recount went through the precincts numerically, and the first tranche, heavily Democratic, are known to have voted overwhelmingly for Mr. Gore. While those 135 initially counted precincts gave Mr. Gore 73% of their vote, the Vice President's share of the whole county was 53%. Those potent projections of Gore numbers from a full recount that they're citing are undoubtedly an exaggeration.

The Gore lawsuit against Palm Beach is richer still. Here they are literally arguing that poor Judge Burton and his colleagues didn't use sufficiently low dimple standards, what the lawsuit calls "incorrect legal standards," to accept Gore votes. Here as well we have a Democratic county and board, upon whom the Gore folks were heaping praise less than two weeks ago, which they're now suing.

In Seminole County, "independent" Democrats have sued to kill absentee ballots certified for Governor Bush, who carried those votes by almost 2 to 1. Their case: The county's elections supervisor broke the law by letting GOP office workers enter voter indentification numbers left off of request forms sent in by absentee voters, who had otherwise complied by signing the form and listing the last four digits of their Social Security number. Want more detail? Normally the ID numbers are preprinted on the forms before they're sent out, which is what the Democrats did, but the GOP's software. . . . Oh well, the Democrats are suing.

So let's review the story so far. We had a Florida count Nov. 7, then a recount, and then we let Al Gore pick several famously Democratic counties to hand-count; we've let various amounts of ambiguous chads be counted, let his party officials eyeball the ballots, often going his way by a 2 to 1 vote, let a GOP counter in Broward resign, extended the pre-established deadline and, let's see, what else? Oh yes, Mr. Gore still lost.

The Gore/Boies strategy now is essentially to sue everyone in sight, hoping that some cache of votes reopens (Dade) or closes up (Seminole). His lawyers argued yesterday that he'd already be ahead if so many military ballots weren't counted. This is not "counting every vote"; it's asking lawyers to overturn an election, not once but several times. And it's becoming increasingly apparent to the

American people; two national polls put support for a Gore concession at 60%, a strikingly high number given the close election result.

As to the Democrats, a few have wavered publicly on joining the Gore long march, but mostly the party is circling the two exhausted candidates, on the one hand standing behind Mr. Gore's attempt to reverse the election, while simultaneously demanding to share power with the incoming Bush Administration.

All this said, we have in fact found one Gore gambit to really admire: Identifying that five-minute seam of network time for a speech at 8:55 p.m., five minutes before the start of Monday night football. Pretty clever. The dimpled-ballot standard may not stand up, but opening up that 8:55 prime-time window for political speech may last forever.

Editorial Feature

Gore Agonistes

By Peggy Noonan

The scene: Midnight, Tuesday, in a mansion in the city. Inside, on the second floor, a handsome man with dark hair and sharp but fleshy features thrashes about on a king-size bed. He can't sleep. It's the noise. They're chanting outside, across the street—"GET OUT OF DICK CHENEY'S HOUSE! GET OUT OF DICK CHENEY'S HOUSE!"

Close-up: The man in the bed puts a pillow over his head, around his ears. We hear his muffled internal dialogue:

"I'm gonna win this thing one way or the other, mark my words. Tie it up in the courts. Tie it up in controversy. I'll exhaust Bush into conceding for the good of the nation. Heck, time I'm done I'll exhaust the nation into conceding.

"Why not? What do I lose? If I win I win—everything. If I lose I still get to make a gracious-loser speech and say all I was looking for was justice. A really great 'Profiles in Courage' type speech. If we can get those yokel judges to string this thing along we can win back public opinion, and even if at the end I don't win by a dozen votes I'll still have clouded Bush's victory even more.

"If I walk now what do I get? Nothing. I'll be nothing. This is my life. What am I gonna do, run a government in exile? Who'd join? No one in the party likes me. What will I do with my resume? Go home and run? I couldn't even carry Tennessee. Make speeches at 50, 75 grand a pop? What does that get me? Tipper's no litigator. And Hillary could steal my thunder. A Clinton-Gore showdown in 2004— I'll lose that battle. In a primary she'll roast my chestnuts on an open fire, with Jack Frost nipping at my nose! Bill Clinton will help her— I'm Sore Loserman who blew the patrimony.

"I thought my speech Monday night was good. The flags, the emotion—'A vote is not just a piece of paper. A vote is a human voice . . .' I thought I got it across that this isn't about me. I'm protecting democracy.

"Learned that from Bill. The impeachment, Monica, the mess. He went around saying 'This isn't about me, this is about protecting the Constitution.' So that's what he was doing. Talk about multitasking! But it worked.

"Nobody caught the tense I used the other night when I talked about the outcome. 'If the American people choose me, so be it. If they choose Governor Bush, so be it . . .' Not chose—choose. Future tense for the future president. This election is not over. The campaign is not over. There is no outcome. It must be discovered. In the future.

"The polls are turning against me, so now I'm asking for a full state recount. It'll take days, weeks, months, to get this all sorted out in court. But I think it makes me look fair.

"I know they're making fun of me. They think I'm like Rhett in 'Gone with the Wind' after his daughter Bonnie Blue dies—he stays in the room with the coffin making believe she's not dead. They're all waiting for Miss Mellie to come in and tell me it's over.

"Well, there is no Miss Mellie. And it's not over. I get up every day and game-plan, just like I used to. I tell Billy Daley what to do, I tell the speechwriter what I want, I tell Tipper to get out there and wave. We're only buying ice cream, but so what?

"I saw Bush in his rinky-dink little speech. The way if the prompter doesn't move quick enough to the next line he stops and waits like a doofus. 'And so I will create a transition' pause, pause, pause, 'team.' He doesn't reassure with his strength. I reassure with my strength.

"And Reagan's. I did a full Reagan imitation Monday night and all Tuesday. I've studied the Gipper and do him better than anyone. Why doesn't anyone tag me on this? Get an old tape of Reagan standing at a lectern, the way he cocked his head, did a little shoulder roll, the good-natured chuckle. Can't they see I've totally ripped it all off and put it on like a suit? I've become him, his mannerisms are mine! I do this because he was good—and if I seem like him, people will think I'm good.

"But I'm no phony, I'm me: the man who understands media and who tries to seem like other men you like. I'm just looking for the most popular version of me. If the American people would settle down and pick the one they like best—Reagan Gore, Kennedy touch-football Gore—I'd stick with it. I have discipline. But can they decide? No. They lack discipline.

"Speaking of the president. He's loving all this. Me and Bush get to play the part of the warring children, he gets to play The Wise Judicious One. He gets to wear the Mideast Peace Face—'Surely we can reason together, Yasser.' That phony good-natured 'children will squabble' look he gets. He likes what's going

William Bramhall

on because it makes him feel like—well, not a child. Like a victor. Like the Man Who Didn't Need a Recount.

"Wait till I'm president and it's pardon time. I'll wear my good-natured Children Get Into Trouble face.

"I have friends telling me step back, who wants this dog's dinner of a presidency that's coming up? I'll be Asterisk Boy with an almost even Senate and a split House and no chance to do anything big, and the next guy gets the recession anyway. But maybe not. The economy's still so strong. And anyway, it looks like Big Bill is getting the dot-com recession. I'll walk in and turn it around. As for the split Congress, so what? It means I can't come through on my pledges— the big spending, the budget busting. I never would have gotten it anyway and if I had it would have hurt the economy. So I'll lay down on spending and get credit for wanting it and credit for bowing to reality and not pushing it. And as for a tax cut, we'll get one but it won't be Bush's big one, it will be my small one."

Again, chanting from outside. They seem to be saying a poem: "I'll count the ballots one by one/And hold each one up to the sun!"

Close-up again on the man in the bed:

"The Dr. Seuss poem again. It's all over the Internet. Everyone's sent it to me.

I hate it. I am not the Cat in the Hat."

The voices from outside continue: "I won't leave office! I'm staying here!/I've glued my desk chair to my rear!"

The man on the bed:

"When this is over I'm gonna find out the names of those guys and find out what they belong to and I'm gonna put together a RICO suit at Justice . . ."

Voices from outside: "How shall we count this ballot box?/Let's count it standing in our socks!/Shall we count that in a tree?/And who shall count it, you or me?"

The man on the bed: "Don't get mad, get even. Later for mad, now for planning. Gotta keep Democrats aboard, keep the media. Broder with that Thanksgiving column—if he were on my side he wouldn't be so sad. Gotta watch the Dean. Gotta keep Daschle and Gephardt. They looked embarrassed with the big phony phone call Monday. But so far they're with me.

"Sixty percent of the people in ABC's poll say I should leave. Zogby too. And Bush is getting some mileage out of leaking who'll be in the administration. Cheney, hand it to him, he's tough. But Powell won't jump aboard until it's very safe. Could be a problem if some-one like Sam Nunn jumps to Bush, but he plays it safe too. That's how they got where they are.

"The press picking up on that 'Bush is a uniter not a divider' stuff—that's taking. It's looking like maybe this is the first time since '94 the people have been with the Reps in a crisis. But here's the thing—this time I can win without the people. I can win it in court. My guy Boies said so the other day. He said 'This is something that's too important to be solved in a partisan environment. This is some-thing that ought to be decided by impartial judges.'

"Picking a president is too important to be decided by the people, take it to the judge! Uh oh, I thought. But he got away with it. And that's our plan. "You think I wouldn't fight this all the way to the point of getting information about that elector who's been through rehab twice and is drinking again, the elector with the little tax problem—you think my people won't lean on them?

You think we won't fight this through the floor of the House? You think we won't use any means, low and lower? You think I'm gonna wrap this up in a week? Only if Bush concedes in a week."

And now he was happy. And now he could sleep. But first he threw off the pillow, bounded from the bed, walked to the window and yanked it up. He leaned out and yelled. "Fasten your seatbelts. You ain't seen nothin' yet!"

But the crowd couldn't hear him above the chanting: "I will not say that I am done/Until the counting says I've won!" There was laughter then and he heard it, he listened for a moment. And then he slammed the window shut.

Ms. Noonan is a Journal contributing editor. Her column appears on Fridays in OpinionJournal.com.

December 1, 2000

REVIEW & OUTLOOK

Dimples Wild?

OK, belly up and ante up. The world's greatest democracy is going to play Miami-Dade. The game works like this: We will deal 625,000 punched cards, and salted among them will be 10,000 unpunched cards. When the pit boss sees an unpunched card, he can award it to either player at his discretion. Over in the poker pits they have deuces wild; here at the election table we have . . . dimples wild.

Watching the TV pictures of election counters poring over the dimpled chad, it's been hard to stand back and recognize that the

Al Gore

whole process is preposterous, not to mention wholly illegitimate. If a ballot is ambiguous, throw it out, stupid. In the case of punch card votes, this means the ballot has to be recognizable to a machine, as voters were instructed at the polls. How did we get to the point of allocating ambiguous ballots on the basis of 2-1 votes of the examiners?

Before November 7, dimples wild was not the rule in Palm Beach County. One fact to emerge from the Florida proceedings is that in 1990, Theresa LePore, then Palm Beach County's chief deputy elections supervisor, issued a counting guideline which said: "But a chad that is fully attached bearing only an indentation should not be counted as a vote."

-306-

Nor was it the rule in Broward County. Writing on this page Wednesday, Boyden Gray noted: "In a contest of a 1991 election in Broward County, a Florida court specifically recognized that it was proper 'to defer to the count of the tabulation equipment following proper calibration and testing,' rather than do a manual recount where undervotes resulted from the failure of voters to properly punch out chads."

Miami-Dade tried to hold on to the old way even after November 7; it did a 1% recount, decided the machines were working and voted to stop there. But Palm Beach voted to count the dimpled chad, refusing Judge Burton's request for a ruling by the Secretary of State, whose representative advised that recounts were not for the purpose of weighing whether voters had made errors. Broward also forged ahead, with the Republican examiner eventually resigning. Miami-Dade momentarily changed its mind and started to recount, but reverted to its earlier refusal when the Florida Supreme Court established a difficult if not impossible deadline.

The dimple-counting itself was even more ridiculous than it looked on TV. In Miami-Dade, the hunt wasn't just for dimples, but any mark at all. If counter No. 1 felt the "intent" was for Gore, the Democratic member simply confirmed it, producing a 2-1 vote for the Vice President. A Presidential dimple was counted as a full vote even if every other relevant chad on the card was punched clean through. In this world "intent" is a one-way street.

This is the kind of mystical divination that the Florida election laws were designed to avert. Dimples wild became the game the moment the Florida Supreme Court enjoined Secretary of State Katherine Harris from enforcing the deadlines established by state law to set an orderly procedure for contested elections. The deadline was the immediate issue, but the real issue was whether to delay certification to allow time for hand recounts that Mrs. Harris said were not justified under Florida law. The Florida Supreme Court overruled her, providing the time for a round of dimples wild.

In the event, Governor Bush came out ahead even under dimples-wild rules. The Democratic-dominated election boards simply could not bring themselves to exercise their discretion ruthlessly enough to suit the purpose of the Gore campaign. So the Gore campaign is suing them. It urges Judge N. Sanders Sauls to order more rounds with even more wild cards. Today, the Supreme Court of the United States will hear arguments on whether to overturn the Florida Supreme Court decision that set the currently, if recently, prevailing rules.

At first blush the High Court case seems moot because the changed rules did not change the outcome. But only to this point, as the persistence of the Gore litigation shows. It is still not beyond imagining that Al Gore will become President by virtue of his lawyers and his dimpled chad.

The High Court, however, can go far toward getting to sensible rules simply by saying that Mrs. Harris was right in the first place, that a close election and the existence of some unallocated ballots was no reason to delay the vote certification while election judges distributed wild cards by divided vote. This issue has significance far beyond the current mess in Florida. The Supreme Court should put a stake through the idea of dimples wild before it becomes a permanent blight on American democracy.

December 1, 2000

Editorial Feature

When the Going Gets Messy, There's Jesse

By Shelby Steele

When we see the Rev. Jesse Jackson once again descend on Florida, once again turn Democratic talking points into a bad poetry of protest ("it's the count not the clock"), and once again arrange black faces around himself in a crescent of indignation, it is clear that a very familiar lever in our political culture is being pressed.

Mr. Jackson is doing something that he is conditioned to do. When he and other civil-rights leaders press this lever, they are invariably rewarded with two things: an exceptionalism that excuses blacks (and in this case Democrats as well) from rules that others must live by, and the license to meet a less demanding standard than others must meet.

This is the lever that often licenses blacks to meet a lower standard in college admissions, or that wins them a $176 million discrimination settlement from Texaco when no discrimination has been proven, or that chalks up weak academic performance in black students to "subtle forms of racism." It is the same lever that Mr. Jackson now presses to turn black misvoting in Florida into "disenfranchisement."

Of course, everyone now thinks he has Jesse's number. We all see the race card coming and there is a widespread feeling that Mr. Jackson is an exhausted figure on the political landscape who long ago used up his moral capital. And yet on Nov. 21, the Florida

Supreme Court rendered what was essentially a "Jesse Jackson" decision. The court clearly saw itself as protecting the "disenfranchised" against a law that it must have felt was unjust. One of the justices worried openly in court that the Republican position of insisting on the law might "disenfranchise" certain voters.

This lever in our political culture works like the sideshow game in which a lever is hit and a clown is dropped into a tank of water. Here the lever is hit and an event is submerged in a paradigm of victimization and oppression.

Suddenly, people appear telling stories. There was something funny at a polling place, a hostility just beneath the surface, a registration that could not be located, a group of police lurking on a corner for no apparent reason, confusing ballots.

David Smith

Suddenly, it is as though Orville Faubus rather than Jeb Bush is governor, and there is the feeling that an old American evil has reared its ugly head. As the Rev. Martin Luther King Jr. once appealed to President Kennedy for federal intervention against a racist South, now Kweisi Mfume asks Janet Reno to intervene.

When reality is bent in this way, back to the great American shame of racism, we enter a surreal terrain in which history colors the present so that we see it as an opportunity to redeem the past. Now we will not stand by as we once did and let injustice hide behind the law. Now we will take the license to do the right thing and make the rule of law stand aside for the work of justice. (Where was the Florida Supreme Court back in 1960 when injustice was palpable all across that state?)

When Mr. Jackson rides into a situation like Florida, his purpose is always the same: to use racism to undermine the moral authority of laws or standards or rules so that excepting blacks from them can be seen as an act of justice. Yes, the law says the election must be certified seven days after the vote. But there is a whiff of racial oppression in the air. The word "disenfranchisement" has come into easy usage with its imagery of Jim Crow injustice. Now Florida's election law loses much of its moral authority. And now justice requires exceptionalism—that the terms of the law be set aside, that deadlines be extended, that recounts be allowed to the point of redundancy.

But this is Al Gore's election bid, not Mr. Jackson's. And one would think that Mr. Gore could fight his own battles. But in fact he cannot. Without Jesse and the great specter of black oppression, there is no depth or resonance to Mr. Gore's claim of unfairness. Jesse vets Mr. Gore—a privileged white guy—to ask for the same exceptionalism that normally only blacks have the moral authority to demand. Democrats are still in the Clinton era and one thing this means is that they may go to church as New Democrats but when they get into a street fight they go black.

Blacks are their muscle. When the law or the rules or the simplest standards of decency stand in their way, when it is time to scorch the earth, they whistle for blacks. At Bill Clinton's lowest moments during impeachment it was the Congressional Black Caucus that muscled for him. Maxine Waters, John Conyers, Charlie Rangel et al., crowding the talk shows, flacking for the moral relativism that gave Mr. Clinton cover, but a relativism that many white Democrats lacked the authority and nerve to flack for.

Now Mr. Gore is in a street fight and his deal with blacks, like Mr. Clinton's, is to offer exceptionalism (affirmative action) in return for moral muscle. The James Byrd commercial put out by the National Association for the Advancement of Colored People is but one example. Indeed, no rhyme intended, a Gore presidency would no doubt mean a Jackson lieutenancy.

There is great pathos, if not tragedy, in images of Mr. Jackson screaming "Keep hope alive" from the pulpits of black churches in Florida. After all, this is not the civil-rights movement. This is the political campaign of a privileged white baby boomer who has no more than pandered to black fears for his own gain.

To rally blacks into a monolith, as if Mr. Gore's candidacy were a liberation struggle, not only wastes moral capital but also makes blacks the easiest group in American politics to take for granted. They simply become a given, a constituency of "ultra" Democrats whose price is so cheap because their loyalty is so obvious.

What black America deserves is a leadership that ignites our energies with the idea that personal responsibility—despite past or even present suffering—is the only power that can truly deliver us to full parity with others. But today's black leadership only rallies blacks with a sense of their victimization into a voting campaign that promises nothing more than a little exceptionalism. And this as the sun begins to set on affirmative action.

Having lost faith in the capacities of its own people—having bought into the defamation that blacks are intractably weak without white intervention—this leadership uses hard-earned black moral capital to chase the likes of Mr. Gore, and flatters itself that it can provide him with muscle. This, after going to bat for O.J. Simpson and bodyguarding for a philandering president who thanked them by suggesting that his very philandering made him "the first black president."

At no time in American history have blacks suffered from a leadership so lost, and so absurd.

Mr. Steele is a research fellow at the Hoover Institution and author, most recently, of "A Dream Deferred: The Second Betrayal of Black Freedom in America" (HarperCollins, 1998).

REVIEW & OUTLOOK

Chad Buildup

At last. Someone on Al Gore's team has finally admitted that what he is doing has never been done before.

This pregnant chad, er, moment came in last Friday's Supreme Court oral argument. Justice Antonin Scalia asked a question of Paul Hancock, a lawyer for Florida Attorney General Bob Butterworth and ally of Mr. Gore:

"Do you know of any other elections in Florida in which recounts were conducted, manual recounts, because of an allegation that some voters did not punch the cards the way they should have, through their fault? No problem with the machinery, it's working fine, but, you know, there were, what, pregnant chads, hanging chads, so forth?"

Mr. Hancock: "No, justice."

Justice Scalia: "Did it ever happen before. . ."

Mr. Hancock: "I'm not aware of it ever happening before." There you have it. Even the lawyer for the Democratic attorney general admits that what they are doing is unprecedented.

There has never been a post-election challenge like Mr. Gore's in Florida. No candidate who lost on the first count, and then on the recount, has tried to use the courts to divine voter intention from first trimester pregnant chads.

This underreported exchange undercuts the entire Gore argument before the U.S. Supreme Court. That argument is that the Florida

Supreme Court was right to overturn Katherine Harris because the Florida secretary of state had abused her discretion. As Justice Ruth Bader Ginsburg helpfully put the Gore case, the oh-so-modest Florida judges were merely trying to "reconcile" the counting deadline with recount law.

This claim of judicial restraint by one of the High Court's activists is touching but fatuous. Everyone agrees that Ms. Harris had discretion to extend the deadline for good reason, immediately reconciling the conflict Justice Ginsburg imagines. The Secretary did not do this because recounting to correct voter error had never been considered an appropriate reason under Florida law.

Now even a Gore attorney agrees that was indeed the precedent before the Florida Supreme Court changed the rules. The habit in Florida had been to allow manual recounts only when there was machine failure. There was none of that here, as the Miami-Dade canvassing board found with its test of 1% of the precincts. Mr. Gore's endless legal obsession, not Ms. Harris's common-sense decision, is the real abuse of power.

We hope the Supreme Court puts the Florida court in its place and restores Ms. Harris's original deadline. But even if it punts the case back to the Florida court, we doubt the ongoing legal spectacle in that state will help Mr. Gore. The true absurdity of the Gore legal claim is now on display in Judge Sanders Sauls's court in Tallahassee.

The Gore team's star witness introduced the world on Saturday to the theory of "chad buildup." You see, chads can accumulate in voting machines and make it hard for voters to punch through ballots, resulting in those notorious dimples. And this is reason enough to overturn an election. Never mind that many ballots were punched clean through for Congress and Senate races but not for President. Chad "buildup" must be a special problem with presidential choices.

But even if Judge Sauls is impressed with the buildup theory, any future vote tally would still be entirely subjective. It's impossible to know whether someone "intended" a dimple to be a vote. Maybe the voter was stymied by chad buildup, but maybe he couldn't decide between Mr. Gore and George W. Bush. Mr. Gore can't abide this, so he's unleashed his lawyers to find any excuse to open up more dimples that can be subjectively declared as his votes.

A bit of media wisdom says the election was a "tie," and therefore

Mr. Gore is entitled to this legal jihad. And in a statistical sense, with six million votes cast in Florida and 100 million in America, the result was a tie. But there have been many such ties in American history, and no candidate for President has ever behaved like Mr. Gore. Nearly all narrow losers for much lesser offices bow out gracefully. They understand that for democracy to succeed losers must ratify the legitimacy of the winner.

It's time someone told Mr. Gore that he cannot become President. Even if he prevails in one of his lawsuits to add votes (Miami-Dade and Palm Beach), or in a proxy Democratic suit to subtract votes (Seminole), he will probably be trumped by the Florida legislature. The constitutionality of this was made clear by none other than Justice David Souter last Friday. He argued that the U.S. Supreme Court had no role in this case because the law already makes clear how Congress can settle such electoral disputes. This implies a role for the Florida legislature that is already preparing to vote the state's electors for Mr. Bush.

The only question left is how bloody-minded Mr. Gore wants to be. He can fight on and on, losing in the end but doing great damage to Mr. Bush, to his own reputation and to our democracy. Or he can salvage some honor and pack it in.

December 4, 2000

Editorial Feature

The Clinton Legacy: Rule or Ruin

With its unerring sense of drama, fate has provided the perfect capstone for the Clinton Presidency. We always should have known the Clinton legacy would be rule-or-ruin politics, as now waged in Florida by his putative successor.

The Florida words may be new, but the melody is hauntingly familiar. Doesn't "dimpled chad" sound a lot like "what the meaning of 'is' is"? An official trying to do her duty, Secretary of State Katherine Harris, is smeared as "partisan," just as Whitewater investigator Jean Lewis was. Meanwhile, of course, partisan votes allocate ambiguous ballots to Al Gore.

Thinking Things Over

By Robert L. Bartley

Mr. Gore's echelons of lawyers run from court to court trying to bend the law into victory, mouthing claims as brazen as the "protective privilege" Mr. Clinton had his legal eagles invent. All this is cloaked in pious high-mindedness—we only want to count all the votes (except the military ones and maybe Seminole County absentees). Victimization—the "vast right-wing conspiracy"—cannot be far behind.

On these pages we started eight years ago to write about "Arkansas mores." The citizens of that lovely state tended to take an offense we did not really intend, but they also took the point. In the post-Clinton era they've moved decisively to clean up their local politics. But the nation learned, and has even come to expect, a new style of politics, the "permanent campaign"—if the truth won't work, "we'll just have to win it then."

The corrosive effect of this was neatly captured by our new OpinionJournal columnist, former Delaware governor and presidential primary candidate Pete du Pont: "The result of all this dissembling, obfuscation and lying is that the law becomes what you can get away with. Smear the opposition; eradicate the evidence; turn on your own if you must; attack the opposition as biased and partisan, and argue every point to the bitter end regardless of the consequence to anyone but yourself. The end justifies the means."

The mores Bill Clinton brought from Arkansas distort the formal rules of the game, but utterly shred the informal ones that have long made politics work. You may disagree with your opponent, but you don't try to destroy him. You may fudge, but at some point the outright lie is restrained by a sense of shame. Especially with the presidency, there has been a residual sense that you hold the office in trust. That you have a duty not to damage the Republic or our institutions, not to debase the terms of our debate.

Thus you had Lyndon Johnson declining to stand for another term during Vietnam; he probably would have won, but at bitter cost. You had Richard Nixon agreeing to resign rather than force a Senate impeachment trial. And of course, you also have Mr. Nixon in 1960, holding reasons to contest a presidential defeat, but seeking to suppress them rather than pressing them to the hilt.

I have to wonder what Mr. Gore expects to win. Does he really want to prevail by imaginative counting of dimpled chad, as his lawyers now argue in court? He could also perhaps prevail through an over-the-top hypertechnical ruling by Judge Nikki Ann Clark, a protege of Florida Attorney General Robert Butterworth, who was instrumental in getting Al Gore to reverse his election-night concession to George W. Bush. Judge Clark is hearing a suit brought by a local plaintiffs lawyer asking that Seminole County absentee ballots be thrown out because the correct information on the applications was entered by the wrong people.

In either event, Mr. Gore would "win" by dint of clever lawyering to overturn three vote counts, certification by state authorities and a national feeling that Gov. Bush has won. Along the way, he would also have to overcome a certain vote by the Florida legislature asserting its right to name electors and a battle in Washington to decide between competing sets of electors. If Mr. Gore ran this gauntlet and became president, it might be a victory in the Johnnie Cochran sense. But would this be good for the Republic? Would it be good for Al Gore?

These questions have seldom if ever been asked in the Clinton era. For that matter, while Mr. Clinton brought war-room politics to new heights, the initial dam break was the campaign against Robert Bork's nomination to the Supreme Court. While "to Bork" became a verb, at least some Democrats tried to staunch the trend. But as the Clinton years progressed, Democratic dissent has been squelched. In the impeachment proceedings, the more brazen his defense, the more solidly his fellow Democrats united behind him.

So today Mr. Gore follows the "just win it" script in Florida. And other Democrats offer at most sotto voce reservations. Sen. Joe Lieberman, in particular, will have to spend a long time recovering his piety after serving as Florida point man. And Republicans, given their recent experience, suspect the Gore challenge is a kamikaze dive to denigrate the Bush presidency and set the stage for the next elections.

At the very least, the Florida imbroglio is an ill omen for Mr. Bush's proclaimed intention to seek bipartisanship and act as a unifier. Having tied the Republicans at 50 seats, Senate Democrats are talking of power sharing, but would they use their share of the power to seek common ground or to obstruct? The rule-or-ruin tactics in Florida are scarcely reassuring.

Conceivably, indeed, the presidential results will themselves be the first test of the new Senate balance. The new 50-50 Senate convenes on Jan. 3, and counts the electoral votes on Jan. 5, a Friday. As ultimate judge of the electoral vote, the Congress may yet have to decide between competing sets of Florida electors. Until Jan. 20, Al Gore will remain vice president, and have the deciding vote in the Senate. As it happens, Hubert Humphrey turned over the gavel under similar circumstances in 1968. And Florida Gov. Jeb Bush has recused himself from the current vote-counting there. But on current performance, can anyone doubt that Al Gore would take great relish in breaking a tie to make himself president?

Legally this would not be decisive, because the House would have to agree (and in case of disagreement the nod goes to electors certified by the executive of the state involved). Politically, though, a Gore tie-breaker would be poisonous. The decisive act in creating the 50-50 Senate split was Sen. John Ashcroft's decision not to offer a legal challenge to his loss to a dead man, Mel Carnahan. Rather than argue votes for an ineligible candidate are null and void, he stepped aside and let Missouri's Democratic governor appoint the widow. If Jean Carnahan's vote sets up mischief in the presidential selection, Mr. Ashcroft's kind of gallantry will be gone from American politics. Rule or ruin will be firmly established as the universal standard.

REVIEW & OUTLOOK

Controlling Legal Authority

Al Gore has been searching high and low for a judge politically pliable enough to order up the votes to make him President. Yesterday, in courts both high and low, several judges told the Vice President that they aren't playing along.

It's hard to lose a case as thoroughly as Mr. Gore lost in Judge Sanders Sauls's Leon County courtroom Monday evening. He and lawyer David Boies lost on the facts and they lost on the law. And they lost on all of his election-contest claims. Katherine Harris and the various county canvassing boards were all vindicated.

"There is no credible evidence and no other confident substantial evidence" to show that Mr. Gore won the election, Judge Sauls said. "The court further finds and concludes the evidence does not establish any illegality, dishonesty, gross negligence, improper influence, coercion or fraud in the balloting and counting processes."

In short, Mr. Gore's claims were frivolous. For reasons better left to a psychologist or historians, Mr. Gore has been taking the nation on a wild judge chase unattached to what Judge Sauls called any "reasonable probability" that the Vice President got the most votes. Mr. Gore's lawyers immediately said they'll appeal to the Florida Supreme Court, the home of his only legal victory so far. But there Mr. Gore must now contend with his other defeat yesterday, this one in the U.S. Supreme Court.

Chief Justice William Rehnquist turns out to be a better politician than his reputation. He somehow marshaled all of his colleagues behind an opinion that gently but firmly rebuked the Florida Supreme Court.

The unsigned per curiam—"for the court"—decision has all the earmarks of a grand intra-court compromise. We suspect the Chief Justice had a majority to overturn the Florida Supreme Court's rewriting of that state's election laws. But to get a unanimous opinion, and thus to protect the U.S. Supreme Court's institutional authority, the chief made concessions to the liberals.

Reading the tea leaves from last Friday's oral argument, we'd say Justice Stephen Breyer bargained for a simple remand to the Florida high court. Justice Ruth Bader Ginsburg won some kinder, gentler rhetoric toward the Florida panel. And Justice David Souter won a bow toward his belief that the High Court had a limited role because Congress has already legislated a path out of the Florida election impasse.

Justice Rehnquist

But Justices Rehnquist and Antonin Scalia got the muscle of the opinion. That was to vacate the Florida supremes with explicit instructions that any revised decision can't be rooted merely in their own political whim or the Florida Constitution. They must take into account both the U.S. Constitution and federal election law—specifically, the clauses and statutes raised by George W. Bush's lawyers in their appeal.

In short, if the Florida court decides to rewrite its opinion, it had better come up with a better argument. And that argument must come to terms with Article II, Section 1, Clause 2 of the U.S. Constitution, which gives "the Legislature" of each state the power to determine how Presidential electors are chosen. As the Supreme Court put it, "the legislature is not acting solely under the authority given it by the people of the State, but by virtue of a direct grant of authority made under" Article II.

Mr. Gore's spinners immediately cast the opinion as "neutral" and purely about procedure. But the Rehnquist court's opinion slam-dunked the notion, popular in Gore-land, that the Florida Supreme Court will be the final arbiter of the Florida results. Drafted out of retirement by Mr. Gore, Mario Cuomo has hit the airwaves saying the courts must decide who is President. And Joe Lieberman, his sincerity count falling by the hour, frets about a "constitutional crisis" if the Florida legislature somehow gets into the act.

Sorry, fellas, but yesterday's Supreme Court ruling gave both the Florida legislature and Congress a big green light. "Since [Section 5 of the U.S. code] contains a principle of federal law that would assure finality of the State's determination if made pursuant to a state law in effect before the election, a legislative wish to take advantage of the 'safe harbor' would counsel against any construction of the Election Code that Congress might deem to be a change in the law," the court said.

In plain English, the court is saying that the Florida legislature and Congress outrank judges in choosing a state's electors. Both can be skeptical toward, and may overrule, any slate of electors chosen because the Florida Supreme Court changed the election rules after Election Day.

This is bad news for Mr. Gore, whose last Presidential hope is that Florida judges award him Florida's electors and then that the GOP-controlled legislature lacks the nerve to respond. But the squeamish president of the Florida Senate, Republican John McKay, can now invoke the Supreme Court if he needs a backbone transplant.

All in all, yesterday was a good day for the American judiciary. It showed that at least some American courts recognize the limits of their power. And at least some judges understand that elected officials are better suited than they are to settle electoral disputes in a democracy. Now if only Vice President Gore would take these rather large hints, demonstrate a similar gracious modesty, and concede defeat.

December 11, 2000

Review & Outlook

What's the Law For?

With the course of an American presidential election changing by
the hour across four weeks in the state of Florida, it is hard not to
think that the U.S. political system has spun out of control. And for
all the time spent watching the affair live on television, it has been
hard to see much meaning beyond the battling teams of lawyers. But
with Saturday's stay of the counting by the U.S. Supreme Court, and
as the High Court gathers the Bush and Gore lawyers before it this
morning, it seems an appropriate moment to comment on the role of
the American legal system in this extraordinary event.

Democrats and liberal commentators are making much of an apparent role reversal in Florida, whereby conservatives cheer the
Supreme Court's "activist" overturning of a state supreme court. The
idea is that conservatives have railed for decades against activist
judiciaries but are cynically content to accept the benefits if it delivers a presidency.

Nebraska's Democratic Senator Bob Kerrey, who we expect is laying the ground here to run for his party's presidential nomination in
four years, put the matter clearly on the weekend: "It would be one
thing if this were the Warren court. This is the Rehnquist court. That
court that has established in case after case the principle of state sov-
ereignty."

We think that Mr. Kerrey and the rest are misstating the larger
significance of the role that the law and the courts have been forced

to play in the Florida events. Justice Scalia, as is his wont, clarified the underlying issue bluntly in his concurrence with the Saturday stay: "Count first, and rule upon legality afterwards, is not a recipe for producing election results that have the public acceptance democratic stability requires." That is, changing the rules in the middle of the game is judicial activism; opposing that is judicial restraint.

Indeed, there is a larger point to be made here about the law, and one can paraphrase Justice Scalia to make it: Leaning on the law until it produces outcomes you desire is not a recipe for producing a legal system that has the public acceptance democratic stability requires.

By noting what they think is a role reversal in legal philosophy here, Democrats and liberals are of course implicitly acknowledging that it is they who have most ardently supported expansive judicial decisions, most often in pursuit of what they have felt to be some public good, which, right now, should trump any prior legal precedent. Thus in Florida, "every vote counts," no matter what the standard, should trump whatever Florida law or standard existed on November 7. It was this indisputable act of legal activism in Florida that the Supreme Court vacated on December 4.

There is a broader, historical battle revealing itself in Florida. As we and others have written for well over 20 years, the Democrats, unable to get what they want by winning votes in legislatures, in Congress or in the states, have legislated through activist courts. The golden age of legislature-based activism essentially ended with the Great Society, and most of what liberals have achieved since has come through activist courtrooms, activist enforcement bureaucracies and Clinton-like executive orders.

This is a long, long way from the legislative arduousness the Founding Fathers thought they were creating. When in time the public appetite waned for grandiose legislative enactments, Democratic liberals became impatient with the difficult system we had for almost 200 years and found a way to create an alternative system—court-based legislation.

Now, if you are a liberal Democrat, you see nothing to apologize for here. But conservatives warned repeatedly that using the legal system for large social purposes meant to be debated and concluded in the elected branches of government in time would breed public cynicism about the courts and the law. All this was before the emergence of plaintiffs' lawyers using the legal system to extract grandiose settlements for "damages" against huge classes of victims, as in the tobacco suits made famous in Florida and elsewhere.

The plaintiffs bar knows no self-restraint. The trial lawyer ethos is to contort the rules to your benefit. They are all about finding, or inventing, new causes of action. Today everyone from corporate executives enduring plaintiffs suits against their stock price on down to inner-city residents believe that the legal system is essentially a game rigged by lawyers. And now, allied explicitly and financially with the Democratic Party, trial lawyers have now found a cause of action to overturn an election.

It is not enough for Democrats to scream that Florida is about simple fairness. That is rhetoric, and perhaps powerful rhetoric. But it is not the law. This is the crucially important distinction that Florida Chief Justice Charles Wells, a Democrat joined by other Democrats, drove home in his dissent.

So it has come to pass that an impossibly close presidential election teeters on the fulcrum of this long-running argument over the proper role of the law in American society. And it is perhaps ironic that this great issue now rests on the meaning of Article II, Section 1, Clause 2 of the U.S. Constitution, which established the role and the authority of state legislatures, that is, the state lawmaking bodies, in creating the nation's highest elected official.

Either that piece of the U.S. Constitution means what it expressly says, as the Supreme Court suggested last week, or it means nothing, or whatever you think it should mean this year. If the Supreme Court somehow concludes it is now the latter, and that the next President may be discovered among the Florida dimples, then public sentiment toward the uses of our laws and courts won't be what it was last week. It will be even worse.

December 13, 2000

REVIEW & OUTLOOK

7 to 2

To restate what should now be obvious: When the voting in an American presidential election is this close, the loser should graciously concede for the good of the political system created by our Founders. Whatever the arguments of Mr. Gore's lawyers on behalf of fairness the past month, his purpose clearly was to force a recount in one or another Florida county that would make his number larger than Governor Bush's.

Mr. Bush no doubt surprised Democratic expectations by fighting back hard, and out of this morass of litigation the election twice arrived at the U.S. Supreme Court, which at 10 p.m. last night decided 7 to 2 that the Florida Supreme Court's intervention violated the Constitution of the United States. The High Court ruled that the varying standards of assigning ballot wins, on view to the entire nation for a month, could not pass Constitutional muster.

Justices Souter and Breyer thought another recount possible, but the majority concluded that federal law made Mr. Bush's electors legal at last night's midnight deadline. The electors' deadline is no mere artifact; it dates back to the close Hayes-Tilden election of 1876, and was intended to ensure that electors would survive congressional challenge by January 6. That is, it exists in the interest of finality. And it means there will be no recount.

Mr. Gore took what opportunities the law allowed, and now the law has exhausted his opportunities. There will be time in the days ahead to sort out the nuances, but what we know irrefutably is that

Mr. Gore's bid foundered on the supreme law of the land. It is over. We suspect the nation concurs.

The nation has been exhausted by this remarkable election. There is little appetite for retribution. Most voters do not depend for their life's blood on the profession of politics. The nation votes for leadership, and the moment has arrived to provide it to them.

December 14, 2000

REVIEW & OUTLOOK

Supreme Irony

So Al Gore is a statesman for finally conceding defeat after 36 days of legal street-fighting. But Chief Justice William Rehnquist has "scarred" our institutions by doing his duty and deciding a case he preferred not to hear.

This is the conventional wisdom in the wake of Tuesday's Supreme Court verdict against the Vice President. Too bad it turns history on its head.

Mr. Gore's concession last night was gracious and much needed. It repairs some of the damage his unprecedented legal challenge has wrought. He can take pride in winning the popular vote, and we think history will be kinder to his pre-election campaign than today's media have been. Bill Clinton's ethical legacy cost Mr. Gore the electoral votes of Tennessee and the heartland more than anything the Vice President did.

But Mr. Gore's ferocious post-election campaign is another story, which shouldn't now vanish as if it were routine. He and four members of the Florida Supreme Court are responsible for the political wreckage since November 7. They are the exceptions who violated the informal rule required for democratic consensus that a loser admits defeat in a timely fashion.

This rule is all the more important the higher the office and closer the election. But Mr. Gore tried to steal the election by changing the rules after November 7. His lawyers never asked for the statewide manual recount with a uniform standard that Justice Stephen

Breyer proposed in his Supreme Court dissent. Asked directly in Florida court if his client wanted such a recount, David Boies declined. Mr. Gore asked instead for a recount of only some ballots, in largely Democratic precincts, to be conducted by mainly Democratic vote counters under standards of their own choosing.

At several stages, moreover, Mr. Gore could have conceded and salvaged more respect. He might have stopped after the machine recount; after Democratic Judge Terry Lewis said Katherine Harris behaved correctly; after some of the Democratic canvassing boards decided not to count dimpled chads; after Mrs. Harris's certification, which met the Florida Supreme Court's first deadline extension, or especially after Democratic Judge Sanders Sauls ruled against his election "contest."

But Mr. Gore charged on, abetted by the brazen Florida Supremes. They enjoined Mrs. Harris without even being asked, overturned Judge Lewis to mandate one recount scheme, and then overturned Judge Sauls and local canvassing boards to mandate another, even in the face of a gentle but firm rebuke by the U.S. Supreme Court to heed federal law.

Amid this bloody-mindedness, how could Chief Justice Rehnquist and his colleagues decline to take the case? Were they supposed to ignore this nose-thumbing by a lower court? A nose-thumbing deplored by that lower court's own chief justice in dissent?

Mr. Rehnquist clearly did not want the High Court to be seen as deciding an election. But he had no choice once the Florida Supreme Court decided it could rewrite election rules in a way that favored Mr. Gore. As the majority states, "When contending parties invoke the process of the courts, however, it becomes our unsought responsibility to resolve the federal and constitutional issues the judicial system has been forced to confront."

The irony is that Mr. Gore was finally defeated by the very legal process he sought to exploit. Much is now being made of a "fractured" High Court. But seven of the nine justices found that the Florida Supreme Court's recount scheme was unconstitutional. Somehow all of this reality—from the recounting in selective Democratic counties to the constitutional problems identified by even Justices Breyer and Souter—is swept aside by Democrats now wailing about fairness.

Justice David Souter's half-dissent called the multiple recount standards "wholly arbitrary" and a violation of one-man, one-vote jurisprudence. Justice Stephen Breyer's dissent acknowledges that "the use of different standards could favor one or the other of the candidates." This seven-vote majority more than justifies the High Court's decision to stop the recount in its tracks on Saturday.

No doubt Mr. Rehnquist wanted Justices Souter and Breyer to join his remedy of halting the recount, as well. But at least he assembled five votes that drew a line in the sand against Florida's judicial activism. As the Chief's concurring opinion puts it, "This inquiry does not imply a disrespect for state courts but rather a respect for the constitutionally prescribed role of state legislatures."

Legislatures are at least elected. Voters delegate power to them to write laws that set the terms of elections in advance. They do not delegate to courts the right to rewrite those rules after the fact to benefit one candidate or another. For defending these principles, this week's decision was William Rehnquist's finest hour.

End of an Era

With economic storm clouds gathering on the horizon, Bill Clinton spent the waning days of his Presidency taking an extended victory lap. He issued executive orders, created national monuments, and toured sites of earlier victories, including New Hampshire and Arkansas. A Clinton spokesman attacked President-elect Bush, saying his team was "talking down the economy" and injecting "fear and anxiety."

Mr. Clinton's penchant for style and spin over substance remained to the very end. He "has spent the eight years of his presidency going from photo-op to photo-op," Journal editor Robert L. Bartley wrote, ending his tenure with "some 450 photo op orders and proclamations, nearly every one of them an economic drag."

As Inauguration Day approached, Mr. Clinton remained in legal peril. Independent Counsel Robert Ray would soon decide whether to indict him for perjury and obstruction of justice in the Lewinsky affair. "Whether or not the President is above the law is ultimately the issue Mr. Ray faces," the Journal noted. His job "is to serve justice today, and uphold its principles for the future. Yes, Mr. Clinton should be indicted, upholding the principle that even Presidents and ex-Presidents are not above the law."

A day before leaving office, in a deal with the independent counsel, President Clinton admitted he made false statements in the Lewinsky case and surrendered his law license for five years. Mr. Ray declined prosecution of Mr. Clinton for perjury and obstruction.

The agreement effectively ended the long Whitewater investigation, which began with questions about the Clintons' land dealings in Arkansas but expanded into Oval Office conduct.

On January 20th, George W. Bush was sworn in as 43rd President of the United States. The Clinton Era was over.

REVIEW & OUTLOOK

Yes, Indict Clinton

They never apologized to the country for impeachment, they never apologized for all the things they've done. . . . And they've spent, what, $52 million on Whitewater and what have they admitted—that there was nothing to Whitewater, nothing to the file controversy, nothing to the Travel Office controversy. . . . So after all this time, and they've spent over $100 million on all those special prosecutors and congressional investigations, trying to make the whole story of the administration, and they have yet to come up with one example of official misconduct in office—not one.

—Bill Clinton's December interview with Esquire magazine

Bill Clinton

Here's one: lying to a federal grand jury. Perjury by a sitting President, not only the chief law enforcement officer of the nation, but sworn to preserve and protect the Constitution. Mr. Clinton will leave office in a few weeks, but his campaign for exoneration is in full swing—in the face of history and in the face of an ongoing inquiry by Independent Counsel Robert Ray. Mr. Ray says he will move swiftly in deciding whether to seek an indictment for perjury in the Lewinsky matter after the President leaves office.

Mr. Clinton will soon be a former President and as such his fate somehow involves us all. It's hard not to have some sympathy with the sentiments the elder George Bush expressed when asked on ABC's "This Week" about the possibility of a Clinton indictment: "I don't want something bad to happen. He's been through a lot. The country's been through a lot. Let's heal and forget."

But as demonstrated in his Esquire remarks above, and elsewhere, Mr. Clinton is making magnanimity anything but easy. He is manifestly guilty of perjury in his Paula Jones testimony, but even today clings to the "what the meaning of 'is' is" defense. So consider Mr. Ray's dilemma: If he should decide to give the President a pass in terms of a larger public interest, the President will surely then claim his preposterous defense was vindicated, that he was the victim. This continuing corruption of our national discourse certainly serves no larger public interest.

Consider Mr. Ray's own experience. He gave the First Lady every benefit of doubt in his inquiry into whether she improperly exerted influence in the White House Travel Office firings, and then lied to federal investigators in denying any role. His report concluded that, "as a matter of historical fact, Mrs. Clinton's input into the process was a significant—if not the significant—factor influencing the pace of events in the Travel Office firings and the ultimate decision to fire the employees." Mr. Ray decided not to seek an indictment because there was "insufficient evidence to prove beyond a reasonable doubt that Mrs. Clinton's statements to this Office or to Congress were knowingly false." In President Clinton's rhetoric, this finding translates into "nothing to the Travel Office controversy."

Similarly, Mr. Clinton says "they"—presumably the Office of Independent Counsel—have "admitted that there was nothing to Whitewater." Mr. Ray found that in the Whitewater matter "the evidence was insufficient to prove to a jury beyond a reasonable doubt that either President Clinton or Mrs. Clinton knowingly participated in any criminal conduct." That is not to say no evidence, and indeed there remain possibly telling open details, such as whether the Clinton tax returns properly reported Jim McDougal's gift in assuming all Whitewater losses. The Whitewater probe also saw the convictions of 14 figures associated with the Clintons, including former Associate Attorney General Webster Hubbell, the then-sitting Governor of Arkansas, Jim Guy Tucker, and the Clintons' former Whitewater Development Co. partners, Mr. McDougal and his wife Susan.

For sheer brazenness, no one in contemporary political life can beat Mr. Clinton. His Administration of course was filled with examples of misconduct. The installation of a crooked Arkansas crony, Mr. Hubbell, as the number three man in the Justice Department. The vicious smear job on a hapless yet determined former Arkansas state employee named Paula Jones. The shredding of campaign finance laws. A permanent campaign of witness intimidation and rhetorical assaults by an attack machine operating out of the White House counsel's office.

All of this in a sense worked. Mrs. Clinton escaped indictment and became a Senator. President Clinton, impeached by the House of Representatives, now bids history to find that he had a little trouble in his personal life but did nothing wrong with or in the office of President. With tainted campaign finance figure Terry McAuliffe, a close Clinton associate, installed as Democratic National Committee chairman and scandal-plagued Washington insider Harold Ickes masterminding Hillary Clinton's New York demarche, the Arkansas couple remain a force to be reckoned with. And a game plan for future Presidential corruption has been established: Marshal a high-powered legal team; make sure key documents disappear or delay producing them for years; smear the opposition with relentless assaults; intimidate witnesses; see that the central players are either kept quiet or discredited. Declare victory.

This is the legacy that Mr. Ray must weigh in reaching his decision. The facts and the law, of course, must be the major factors, but prosecutors, especially in important cases, also bear a general responsibility for the public good. History's burden on Mr. Ray is that a decision not to indict serves the Clinton revisionism—that it was all about "nothing." Not indicting also sends a somewhat more subtle and sinister message from the Clinton camp to future generations: "Here's how we got away with it."

To review the facts, Mr. Clinton's conduct in the Lewinsky matter constitutes a strong case for a perjury indictment. Both Independent Counsel Kenneth Starr and David Schippers, the chief counsel for the House Judiciary Committee during the impeachment proceedings, reported that Mr. Clinton committed multiple acts of perjury in his August 17, 1998, testimony before a federal grand jury in the Lewinsky matter. In their minds, the issue was whether the law applied to Mr. Clinton, or whether a President is above the law.

Mr. Clinton was cited for contempt by U.S. District Judge Susan Webber Wright for lying in the Jones case. Judge Wright fined the President $90,000 for providing "false, misleading and evasive answers" in a sworn deposition. Judge Wright wrote of the need "to deter others who might themselves consider emulating the President of the United States by engaging in misconduct that undermines the integrity of the judicial system." Those words should resonate in any debate over indictment.

Article One of the House impeachment resolution charged the President with "perjurious" testimony to the grand jury about his relationship with Ms. Lewinsky, his attempts to influence witnesses, and statements he made under oath in a civil deposition in the Paula Jones sexual harassment lawsuit. During the impeachment debate, many senior members of the President's own party opposed his removal from office, but agreed that the courts were the proper forum for deciding whether Mr. Clinton had committed perjury and possibly obstruction of justice.

Mr. Clinton is not "above the law," said Senator Herb Kohl of Wisconsin. "His conduct should not be excused, nor will it. The President can be criminally prosecuted, especially once he leaves office." Senator Barbara Boxer of California said that the Democrats' rejection of the articles of impeachment "does not place this President above the law. As the Constitution clearly says, he remains subject to the laws of the land just like any other citizen of the United States." Recent Vice Presidential candidate Joseph Lieberman said at the time, "Whether any of his conduct constitutes a criminal offense such as perjury and obstruction of justice is not for me to decide. That, appropriately, should and must be left to the criminal justice system, which will uphold the rule of law in President Clinton's case as it would for any other American."

Whether or not the President is above the law is ultimately the issue Mr. Ray faces. Yes, Mr. Clinton was embarrassed, but will his flouting of the law escape even symbolic legal sanctions? Even the Arkansas disbarment proceedings threaten to dissolve into farce, with a parade of judges disqualifying themselves over various conflicts of interest.

Mr. Ray's job is to serve justice today, and uphold its principles for the future. Yes, Mr. Clinton should be indicted, upholding the principle that even Presidents and ex-Presidents are not above the law. The sympathies expressed by the elder George Bush need not be entirely dismissed, but they can be weighed in other forums. If Mr. Clinton would stop denying his wrongdoings, for example, he could be considered for a Presidential pardon.

Editorial Feature

Make Way for Hillary

BY PEGGY NOONAN

I return from 10 days away to find on the front page of every newspaper in America the official swearing-in of Hillary Clinton, Sen. Clinton, dressed in a pantsuit of robin's-egg blue, her right hand raised, a radiant smile upon her face. Moments later, Strom Thur-

Hillary Clinton

mond rose and asked if he could hug her, which made everyone in the chamber chuckle.

And so it begins. And appropriately enough with what appears to be another of Mrs. Clinton's transformations. She appears to be in the middle of another metamorphosis. The last was of her outward appearance—there is almost no recognizing the Hillary of 1997 in the Hillary of the campaign trail three years later. But the latest transformation seems to be connected to personality, or even character—from full of pre-

sumption to lit by humility, from imperious to collegial, enraged to endearing. She no longer seems like the kind of person who, in Dick Morris's words, sets off the alarms when she walks past a bank. Since her victory in November, gone has been the Hillary of the Angry Visage. As she breezes into parties and past the press, as she greets her new colleagues and makes sure other, lesser known freshmen get in the picture, she seems not at all like the strange and cunning lady who railed bitterly at the White House staff, got Billy Dale canned, attacked conservatives, maneuvered and misled.

This is a sudden change, and there are probably two kinds of people who can change so suddenly. The first is a person with a lot inside, a person of true depth who is capable of true growth, and who might be transformed by desire and commitment, by a hunger to be a better human being, and who might get the strength for this mighty work from religious conversion, or a serious and successful therapy.

The second kind of person might appear to change, and easily and quickly, not because he is so full but because he is so empty. If your inner self is essentially absent, or is only a bundle of desires and habitual responses to them, it's no great deal to change, or seem to. It's like turning a ship with an empty hull: It takes less strength. A change of course can be made quickly, with little strain, and more changes can follow.

Mrs. Clinton, of course, has a great deal to be happy about—a new kind of political power, an independent base, a bright future in her party, new wealth. Good fortune makes most of us smile, and perhaps it's only that.

One of the things that is most amazing and impressive is how Mrs. Clinton continues to get politically like-minded individuals and groups to underwrite her career. The great institution of American publishing, for instance, which is, in general, politically and culturally liberal, is giving her $8 million for a book—which she reportedly demanded in a lump-sum advance. This shows that she truly is not a normal writer, and I say this meaning that she is different not only in that she cannot write.

The agreement looks for all the world as if she were being given money not as an advance, but to advance an agenda—her own. Or perhaps it is simply a shrewd investment. Mrs. Clinton will soon be in a position to smile or frown on the interests of the publisher's parent company, Viacom, a communications empire with much, always, at stake in Congress and before numerous government agencies.

With the $8 million, the publisher pays for her new Washington mansion, where the senator can function as a powerhouse fund-raiser for other candidates for national office, who will, when they win, pledge their loyalty to her, and to Clintonism. When Hollywood shows the home of a senator in a movie, it's a McLean mansion, but most senators share apartments or have houses out of town. Mrs. Clinton's living arrangements will be truly extraordinary.

But what is important to note is that this is the left underwriting the left, not with the usual fellowships and grants and MacArthur "genius" awards, but underwriting Mrs. Clinton's daily concrete ability to proselytize for, and build, and institutionalize, her particular kind of leftism in America.

The publisher has suggested that the $8 million advance is in lieu of the stratospheric sales that will be spurred by Mrs. Clinton's stunning revelations. This, they seem to be saying, will move millions of books. But they must know this is not true. Mrs. Clinton has been many things the past eight years, but forthcoming is surely not one of them; she has shown no tropism toward the truth, and in any case would be foolish to start telling it now. She is more like what was said of Nixon, that he doesn't think honesty is the best policy but he does think it's a policy. If she now tells the full truth about the scandals, from Travelgate to the Puerto Rican FALN terrorists, she will undermine her own past statements and insistences.

All she can do now is repeat with new words. Nor is she likely to tell the truth about her politics, which, again, she has not done in the past. She will continue to cloak, with words like "concern" and "compassion"—for those who bowl alone, for those who suffer from various diseases—her apparent desire for a maximum accrual of wealth and power to a government run by those whose higher understanding entitles them to run it. That would be her, and her friends.

In the broadest sense, Mrs. Clinton, like Tony Blair, like every sophisticate in Europe and bureaucrat in Brussels, seems to be in pursuit of one world—of the end of nations, and the beginning of a world federation. This would make a bleaker world—more regimented, more uniform, more controlled by the values and desires of an elite, less free, less spacious.

But I don't imagine Mrs. Clinton will start talking about that, whatever the promptings of the person who ultimately writes the book, or those who publish it, whose motives are no doubt more immediate. Mrs. Clinton knows what the $8 million is about, and what it can be used for, and will no doubt use it well.

Ms. Noonan is a contributing editor of the Journal. Her column appears on OpinionJournal.com on Fridays.

Editorial Feature

The Clinton Years

A decade ago it would have been hard to imagine a program like the five-part "Nightline" series beginning tonight (11:35 p.m. EST, on ABC), but then, the Clinton years have made much imaginable that was inconceivable before. By the time it ends viewers will have heard unvarnished opinion, and data such as no former staffers have ever before publicly uttered about any outgoing president and first lady—

Critic at Large

By Dorothy Rabinowitz

a first lady fearfully volatile and punishing when challenged, as Bill Clinton's former press secretary, Dee Dee Myers, is not alone in noting. Mr. Clinton had a temper of his own—a legendary one—but it is clear, both from the "Nightline" series and from its companion report airing on "Frontline" next week (Tuesday, Jan. 16, at 9 p.m. EST on PBS) that it is Hillary Clinton's accusatory rages that remain unforgiven and unforgotten.

After "Troopergate" (the charges that when he was governor of Arkansas Mr. Clinton used state troopers to arrange amorous liaisons) and the Paula Jones charges, and the stonewalling on Whitewater, then senior White House adviser George Stephanopoulos recalls concluding that it was necessary for the president to appoint an independent counsel, and advising that there was no longer any choice but to do so. Mrs. Clinton responded with accusations of disloyalty, telling him "You never stood for us."

Anyone who stood up and tried to tell her that her policy was a bad idea was, says Dee Myers, "smashed down" and belittled "very personally." Ms. Myers, who suffered severe dressings down of her own at Mr. Clinton's hands, one of which she describes in detail, nevertheless announces that, in the end, she still feels a certain affection for him, for reasons she doesn't quite comprehend. Neither she nor any other of the commentators here seem inclined to any similar expression of affection for Mrs. Clinton—not altogether surprising, given the portrait of the first lady that emerges in these anecdote-rich productions. They feared her in a way they never feared the president, their huggy scamp in the White House whose misadventures caused them nightmares and tears and regular bouts of fury.

Mr. Stephanopoulos couldn't believe his ears when he heard Mr. Clinton's voice on the telephone tapes that Gennifer Flowers recorded—how stupid can you be, to make such a call in the middle of a campaign, he wants to know, now. He would have roughly the same response just after the state trooper stories emerged and the president began calling the troopers. It infuriated him, it was just like the calls to Gennifer. All the trouble came from "this maneuvering," he tells "Frontline." And this time it was worse—calling these people from the Oval Office. "Just nuts."

The "Nightline" series (which offers roughly the same material as the somewhat more detailed "Frontline" documentary) takes us through the Clinton presidency chronologically, beginning with the 1992 campaign. A lot of years have passed since Bill and Hillary Clinton confronted their first nationally publicized crisis. Who knew—as they testified to their mutual devotion on "60 Minutes" and Mrs. Clinton declared, in accents that have since lost a certain heartland twang, that she wasn't Tammy Wynette standing by her man—what was yet to come? The troopers, maybe, and a few others, but surely not the core staffers who had come, as "Nightline" reports, trembling over the prospect that this scandal might destroy the campaign. James Carville cried a river. And all for nothing. The team had not yet learned what the comeback kid could do—though not, to be sure, without the help of his wife.

"Nightline" delivers a vast amount of material in shapely fashion, capturing, in one vivid scene after another, almost every key drama of the Clinton years. There is the first great issue, summed up in Brit

Hume's semi-question, hurled during a raucous press conference, in which he pointed out that instead of an instant laser focus on the economy, as the president had promised, he was busy leading gays-in-the-military week. It wasn't that they wanted this entanglement just then, Ms. Myers observes, they simply didn't know how to get out of it.

In due time, the problem of Whitewater came knocking and the Washington Post wanted documents. Republican David Gergen, who had come on to help out in what had begun to be perceived as a failing presidency, had some advice for Mr. Clinton which was, in brief, that the documents should be handed over. As far as he was concerned that was fine, the president said—now all that was necessary was to convince Mrs. Clinton. An impossible task since, as Mr. Gergen relates, the first lady simply refused to return any of his phone calls. She had already made up her mind; no one was turning any papers over.

If Mr. Gergen's arrival disturbed the core Clinton team, Dick Morris's entry was cause for hair-tearing. The group's detestation of him is visceral. He isn't one of them, politically. Robert Reich complains that he was a cabinet member after all, and he had to tolerate submitting ideas to Mr. Morris, who would then take a poll to see if they flew. Mr. Morris himself relates, with relish, how he wrote the State of the Union address in secret. Such was his power, for a time, that every important plan and strategy the other staffers developed could all be upended by a single phone call between the president and Dick Morris. No doubt they all felt im-

Paula Jones

mensely superior to him, for all the reasons Messrs. Stephaopoulos and Reich and the rest describe—but it's hard to avoid the feeling that he was also the handiest vessel for frustration in the hotbed of paranoia that was the Clinton White House.

Still, they had periods of pride and triumph. With Mr. Clinton's victory in the face-off over the government shutdown, Leon Panetta, for one, felt powerfully reassured in all the reasons he'd come to work for this president. In the midst of calamity, they found causes for pride, none of them enough, in the end, to make any one of these witnesses to the Clinton presidency look other than grim, or confused, or both, as they try to assess Mr. Clinton's works and his place in history. There is, on the other hand, nothing confused or grim about these extraordinary documentaries.

Ms. Rabinowitz is a member of the Journal's editorial board.

Editorial Feature

A Photo-Op Presidency: The Finale

In a better world this column would be strictly about the economy, much in the news with the manufacturing sector in outright decline and the Fed reaching for the emergency cord. But as with everything else in the administration, the economy is inextricable from presidential character, never more in evidence than in the final days of Bill Clinton's tenure.

Item A is not in fact the economy, but the compulsive grandstanding in the Middle East. The Clinton plan to have Israel give up the Temple Mount for the Palestinians' abandoning the "right of return" is a nonstarter on two counts. One, Israel happens to be a democracy and Prime Minister Barak does not control the Knesset, which is not about to give up the Temple Mount. Two, the Palestinian mini-state and most Arab nations happen to be dictatorships, depending on their grievance against Israel to bolster internal legitimacy; they are not about to deed legitimacy to the Jewish state.

Thinking Things Over

By Robert L. Bartley

Given these realities, what is all this fuss about? Well, it's about one big final photo-op for Bill Clinton. President-elect Bush says he appreciates this effort "so very much," and indeed it may demonstrate that the land-for-peace formula is unworkable and help refocus policy on the military balance of power. But Mr. Clinton's clear intent is to wrap up a deal with Mr. Barak and Mr. Arafat that neither can or will deliver, letting the incoming president pick up the pieces after his own peace-in-our-times photo-op.

We've already had the Esquire-interview photo-op (see photo), showing the same taste as the Mussolini walk at the Democratic National Convention. We've had the first-black-President photo-op, with Mr. Clinton shredding promises to the Senate about recess appointments so he can name one more black judge, at least for a year. We've had the war-crimes photo-op, adding the International Criminal Court to the long list of treaties Mr. Clinton has signed despite no chance of Senate ratification.

But then, we've had rescission of the 1993 ethics photo-op, with Mr. Clinton repealing the rules he issued in the first hour of his presidency about a five-year moratorium on lobbying by former executive branch employees.

On the economy, we've rehearsed the old Clinton ploy of sending a minion out to turn the tables on your critics and pose as the victim. Of course, chief economic adviser Gene Sperling did not exactly talk of hundred-dollar bills and trailer parks. Instead, he complained that "what you're seeing is President-elect Bush and his team actually talking down our economy" and injecting "fear and anxiety." They'd observed that a recession risk has suddenly appeared, and that their proposed tax cut looks like a better idea than ever.

By now it should be evident even within the White House that recession risk is not something dreamed up in Austin. After all, the economy is so perilous that the Federal Reserve felt it had to cut its target interest rates by a full 50 basis points only two weeks after it left them unchanged. It's preposterous to assert, let alone believe, that this was caused by a few remarks by the incoming administration much milder than some already heard along Wall Street.

Only a minority of economists, to be sure, has concluded that we are experiencing a recession, two quarters of contraction. We can still hope, as I certainly do, that the consensus prediction of a "soft landing" proves correct. But it's under severe test from the abruptness of the downturn and its seeming acceleration. Nor is it clear that the Fed's sudden change of heart will make a quick difference; monetary policy affects real economic variables like production and employment only with a lag—some say as long as two years.

The "talking down the economy" line is a rather pathetic effort to deflect blame for any serious problems forward into the Bush administration. Any sensible person will see that any recession starting with the current sourness would not be the Bush recession but the Clinton recession.

Some of course are already seeing a Greenspan recession; the hunt for policy errors starts with monetary policy. But back in the summer and fall I agreed that Mr. Greenspan had one big inflationary sign to worry about, namely the price of oil, which I do not dismiss as casually as some of my friends do. Yes, the dollar was strong and the gold price low; perhaps Mr. Greenspan could have eased sooner. But with oil soaring to $35 a barrel, this was far from clear at the time.

Even in the Greenspan era, you cannot expect monetary policy to be perpetually errorless, so you also have to look at the rest of the policy mix. On the fiscal side, the federal government is taking more of economic output in taxes than it ever has since World War II; should we be surprised that a touch on the monetary brakes might have an untoward effect? Nor is running a surplus to pay down debt a stimulative policy; where are the Keynesians when we could use them?

Add to this the Clinton regulatory morass. A big lawsuit against Microsoft is another good photo-op, but not exactly the way to keep the productivity surge rolling. The broadband and wireless revolutions have been stopped in their tracks by the antitrust division and the FCC. The Clinton veto of tort reform opened the field for his plaintiff lawyer friends/contributors to suck blood from American business.

While the price of oil has now declined, natural gas prices have quadrupled and electricity has become scarce. Why? Because environmental photo-ops have stopped energy investment. California has not sited a power plant for 15 years, and suddenly the long run is here.

Mr. Clinton, similarly, has spent the eight years of his presidency going from photo-op to photo-op. Beyond discovering the virtue of paying down the debt after the election of a GOP Congress in 1994, his administration has seldom thought beyond the next news cycle. We will be better off if his luck holds into a soft landing. But it now seems possible that the long run is arriving before he gets out of town.

So how is he spending his final days in office? With some 450 photo-op orders and proclamations, nearly every one an economic drag. The safety photo-op burdens business with new ergonomic standards. The public lands photo-op locks up 58 million acres in 39 states from logging or energy development. The Clinton EPA is pouring out new regulations, and the Landmark Legal Foundation has filed suit for an injunction against destroying relevant documents.

REVIEW & OUTLOOK

Pending Justice: Labor v. Ashcroft

With Linda Chavez brought down, Democrats are loudly proclaiming that Attorney General-designate John Ashcroft will be next. Issuing a war declaration against Senator Ashcroft and Interior nominee Gale Norton, AFL-CIO President John Sweeney said, "We pledge to do everything in our power, working with our allies in the civil rights, women's rights and environmental communities to persuade the Senate to reject these nominations."

PENDING JUSTICE

When the Ashcroft hearings commence next week, the Capitol will virtually levitate on the winds of moral dudgeon over Bob Jones University, Missouri Judge Ronnie White and someone's freedom to abort. But these are no more the fundamental issue than an illegal immigrant was in the Linda Chavez episode. The Clinton coterie has been filled with individuals skimming along the edges of federal criminal investigations stifled in the current Justice Department, and have much reason to undermine any incoming Attorney General. John Sweeney, in particular, has to worry about the legal exposure of AFL-CIO Secretary Richard Trumka. Also of Terry McAuliffe, the newly named Democratic National Committee chairman.

Both of these figures have been mentioned in one of the most important prosecutions of recent years. In November 1999, former

International Brotherhood of Teamsters political director William Hamilton was convicted of fraud and conspiracy in a complex series of schemes to embezzle the union's funds to aid the 1996 re-election effort of then-Teamster President Ron Carey. As presented by prosecutors under Mary Jo White, U.S. attorney for Southern District of New York in Manhattan, the case suggests a criminal conspiracy reaching into the top levels of the Clinton-Gore-Labor network.

Since the 1999 Hamilton conviction for fraud and conspiracy, however, the case has gone nowhere. A senior aide to U.S. Attorney White tells us "the investigation is continuing." The Democrats' problem with John Ashcroft is that he looks just like a fellow who might bring such cases back to life.

The AFL-CIO's No. 2, Richard Trumka, has in some ways been the union's most visible Democratic powerbroker. He appeared in Iowa as an early and important backer of Al Gore, bestowing crucial public support on the Veep against Bill Bradley. At the Hamilton trial, the prosecution noted that Mr. Trumka was a player in two schemes that went before the jury.

In one, according to testimony by a Hamilton co-conspirator, Mr. Trumka and top labor leaders Gerald McEntee of the American Federation of State, County & Municipal Employees and Andy Stern of the Service Employees International Union conspired to make $50,000 donations each to Teamster President Carey's re-election effort, illegal under federal law. None of the men has been charged.

In the second scheme, Mr. Trumka allegedly helped launder $150,000 of his union's funds to Mr. Carey through a Democrat-aligned activist group. Mr. Trumka has denied wrongdoing, but when questioned by government investigators asserted his Fifth Amendment privilege against self-incrimination. The AFL-CIO's code of conduct says no officer who takes the Fifth can hold office; John Sweeney waived the rule for Mr. Trumka.

Following Al Gore's defeat, Bill Clinton immediately named Terry McAuliffe DNC chairman. Head of the Clinton-Gore re-election effort in 1996 and one-time prospective financier of the Clintons' Westchester home, Mr. McAuliffe worked with one of the key, named co-conspirators in the Hamilton trial, Martin Davis.

At the trial, former DNC finance director Richard Sullivan testified that Mr. Davis and Mr. McAuliffe attempted to carry out an illegal scheme in which the DNC would find a donor for the Carey re-election campaign, and in turn the Teamsters would donate money to Democratic groups. Mr. McAuliffe's lawyer has said his client was not involved in any wrongdoing and cooperated with the investigation.

Mr. Davis pleaded guilty to conspiring to funnel union funds and agreed to cooperate with the prosecution. But on the eve of the trial, news came that Mr. Davis would not testify. Prosecutors told the presiding judge that his plea bargain was "under review." Mr. Davis still awaits sentencing, as do several other figures in the case.

The final call on this and other unsolved mysteries of the Reno-Clinton years will fall to the new Attorney General. There is as well the stalled campaign finance task force at Main Justice, the China spy tangles and Independent Counsel David Barrett's probe into possible obstruction of justice by Justice Department officials in the Henry Cisneros investigation. The pending Southern District investigation threatening Messrs. McAuliffe and Trumka is merely item one in the stakes Democrats have to defend by cutting up Mr. Ashcroft.

Yes, some of Mr. Ashcroft's critics want to use his nomination to hyperventilate about abortion and the like. But there are also plenty of reasons Democrats do not want a vigorous Attorney General dedicated to the impartial pursuit of justice. The real threat to his nomination comes from those who seek to impede and obstruct justice.

REVIEW & OUTLOOK

Damaged Justice

There is a good reason why Democrats tomorrow will try to focus the nation's attention on John Ashcroft: Down the street the Justice Department is moving fast to shut down the probe of the Clinton-Gore campaign finance operation before a new Attorney General takes over. Last week, Justice concluded a wrist-slap plea deal with James Riady, the Indonesian billionaire and Clinton patron at the epicenter of the 1996 campaign-finance scandal. Mr. Riady agreed to plead guilty to one count of conspiracy to defraud through obstructing the work of the Federal Election Commission. He'll pay an $8.6 million fine for illegal contributions, most of it funneled to the Democratic National Committee from his Lippo Group conglomerate from, note the dates, 1988 to 1994.

The Justice Department deal appears to stop short of any conspiracy in the crucial 1995 to 1996 period. If that's off the table, it is good news for Mr. Clinton. It is now well established that money from Mr. Riady and his friends in 1995 and 1996 helped fuel a huge barrage of TV ads damaging GOP candidate Bob Dole, giving Mr. Clinton a decisive early edge in the election.

Recall that Mr. Riady attended an Oval Office meeting on September 13, 1995, with the President, an unknown Commerce Department official named John Huang, close Clinton aide Bruce Lindsey, and Arkansas businessman Joseph Giroir. It was at that meeting that Mr. Huang, a former senior Riady employee at Lippo, was dispatched to the Democratic National Committee and a conspiracy began to subsidize the 1996 presidential election with huge infusions of illegal money.

That is not simply our opinion but the investigative theory of senior law enforcement officials, including FBI Director Louis Freeh and one-time Justice Department task force head Charles La Bella. In four years of detailed memos to Attorney General Reno, painstakingly unearthed last year by Representative Dan Burton, Mr. Freeh argued for an independent counsel to probe a "core group," including President Clinton, aided by a floating cast of "opportunists." Mr. La Bella called the scheme a "loose enterprise" conspiracy. Janet Reno repeatedly rejected the independent counsel requests, often over the objections of senior staff.

The status of this investigation as well as others, such as the Cisneros/IRS probe, are all live matters inside Main Justice. Thus we were startled to be told last week on good authority that the incoming Bush team might be thinking of appointing Ms. Reno's primary deputy and close Clinton ally, Eric Holder, as interim Attorney General until Sen. Ashcroft is confirmed. This would be the single worst choice for interim AG, giving Judiciary Democrats an incentive to delay the Ashcroft vote as long as possible. Surely a better choice can be found.

Mr. Riady lives in Indonesia but has agreed to come to the United States and cooperate with investigators. His influence was sweeping and much of it remains mysterious. In an August 1992 limousine ride with candidate Clinton, Mr. Riady pledged $1 million to him; Mr. Clinton told federal investigators in April, implausibly to say the least, that he had no "specific recollection" of the huge pledge. Government documents in the plea filing show over 80 illegal contributions to various political entities by Mr. Riady's Lippo Bank of California.

A Riady venture in Indonesia now employs Jim Guy Tucker, Mr. Clinton's successor as Governor of Arkansas, convicted in a Whitewater-related fraud case by Independent Counsel Starr. In 1994, Mr. Riady provided a $100,000 consulting payment to Arkansas insider Webster Hubbell, the former Associate Attorney General at Reno Justice, then under pressure to cooperate with Mr. Starr. Mr. Hubbell did not cooperate and went to prison on fraud charges. What Mr. Tucker, Mr. Riady and Mr. Hubbell share, of course, is potentially damaging information about Bill and Hillary Clinton.

Mr. Freeh and Mr. La Bella were on the right track with the "loose enterprise" theory of a conspiracy directed out of the White House. That avenue was shut down by Ms. Reno. Also, questions of Chinese influence on the political process and related national security matters need thorough exploration. There is Buddhist Temple fund-raiser Maria Hsia, who was convicted in the scheme last year but awaits sentencing. And there is the disposition of the host of figures in U.S. Attorney Mary Jo White's Teamster election-fraud case in New York.

It's hard not to have some sympathy for the Bush view to let the Clinton scandals fade into the past. But the problems at Justice are not about the past. Mr. Ashcroft, should he be confirmed, will inherit a damaged Justice Department. The Burton memos and a stream of news reports leave no doubt that Main Justice morale has been devastated by pressure from the Clinton coterie, internal battles over Ms. Reno's refusal to appoint an independent counsel in the campaign finance affair, wars with independent counsels Ken Starr, Donald Smaltz and David Barrett, China espionage cases and other matters. Many good people have left Justice and others have fallen silent as prosecutions and reforms languish.

A new Attorney General would go a long way to restoring confidence in Justice with a thorough audit and accounting of these matters. Sweeping it into the dustbin serves neither history nor the rule of law.

Editorial Feature

The Clinton Legacy: President Paradox

By Francis Fukuyama

Now that the New York Times has weighed in with another of its interminable series on the "Clinton Legacy," what more is there to be said about the eight years that are now coming to a close? Perhaps it is best to drop down below the level of the North American Free Trade Agreement, of welfare reform or the peace process, and look at how the social and cultural texture of America has changed under the presidency now ending.

The **CLINTON LEGACY**

Social statistics tell us that things have gotten better. The relentless cultural decline that at the beginning of the 1990s seemed like a fact of nature ground to a halt and, miraculously, reversed direction while Bill Clinton was president. As most Americans are well aware, crime rates have gone down by about 20% nationally and much more steeply in individual cities like New York.

Lower crime rates had a variety of positive spillover effects in terms of great social trust: Urban spaces could be reclaimed for urbane uses by the middle class, rather than being dominated by the extremely rich and extremely poor. The proportion of unwed mothers stopped increasing by 1994 and even declined slightly thereafter. Teenage pregnancy rates dropped more dramatically, and the rate of divorce drifted downward.

So far so good. But the social reality of what Tom Wolfe calls our "wild, bizarre, unpredictable, Hog-stomping Baroque country" during the Clinton years can be unbelievably contradictory and complex. Ballroom dancing, home schooling, and sexual abstinence can all be major trends next to body piercing and downing ecstasy pills. This contradictory reality is probably better described by a novelist (as Mr. Wolfe himself has done effectively) than by a social scientist armed with statistics.

Take the question of class. It is true that income inequality slowed its rate of increase in the 1990s. But it didn't decline, either, and the meaning of working class, middle class, and rich all changed.

Back in the 1950s, America's sizable working class—people who work in factories, build houses, or police the streets—could think of itself as middle class because class was defined in terms of ownership of assets like a home, a car, and a washing machine.

One consequence of the 1990s "knowledge economy" was the emergence of a new economic gulf, as the working class, now a much smaller part of the labor force, moved downward in status and income, and the middle and professional classes moved up. The latter reconciled themselves to Reaganite economics as half of all households came to own equities by the late 1990s. Liberals in this group were taken aback by the anger of working Americans over Nafta, China and globalization. But culturally, there was a convergence as the working class drifted to the left while prosperous baby boomers now raising families became more traditional.

The situation of better-educated people who still thought of themselves as middle class changed in other ways. With so many women moving into the work force, it once again became a common experience for people who didn't think of themselves as rich to have servants. There is in Colorado a new school for servants that teaches its female students not to be too pretty, lest they threaten the lady of the house. Its graduates work for people who, by and large, have not grown up with servants themselves, and who try to be on a first-name basis with their butlers. This sort of egalitarianism, it turns out, doesn't work any better in the 1990s than in the 1890s.

In the Clinton years, the rich got unbelievably rich. In the 1980s, having a net worth in multiples of $100 million seemed like a lot of money. Today, that's a technology baron's chump change. The areas surrounding New York, Boston, San Francisco and Washington are now filled in with new subdivisions of trophy homes where a husband, wife (perhaps herself a trophy), and a child or two occupy a minimum of 10,000 square feet.

It is amazing what happens when a society of well-educated people has money to burn. The high end of everything exploded during the 1990s. Cigars, microbrew beers, camping gear, gas barbecues, home theaters, and mountain bikes now all have legions of devotees. There are firms that specialize in refurbishing antique license plates, or that manufacture vacuum tubes out of production since the 1930s. In today's America, you can easily pay $10,000 for a pair of wires to connect your high-end CD player to your high-end amplifier, and read reviews of how they "sound" compared to other five-figure cables.

The self-perception of the newly rich changed in significant ways. The media managed to label the Reagan years the "decade of greed," symbolized by corporate takeovers, a booming stock market and Nancy Reagan's dresses. The Clinton years, which have seen even larger corporate takeovers, a headier stock market, and Monica Lewinsky's stained dress, thought much better of itself and its own "remarkable," even "exuberant," prosperity. This contrast is due in part to the fact that the baby-boom generation, which includes much of the media and the opinion leaders of the chattering classes, themselves got rich only in the 1990s and could no longer point a resentful finger at other people who were making off like bandits.

But there is something more at work here. The newly well-to-do could feel good about themselves because they had morphed into what David Brooks calls a "bobo," or the bohemian-bourgeoisie. The basic idea is that it's OK to be crassly materialistic and ill-behaved as long as you have good intentions, which by the 1990s meant having the right opinions about the environment, race, gender and poverty. The Clintons are perfect exemplars of this trend, since they quite honestly seemed to think that the goodness of their intentions justified their commodity deals, lying under oath, and astronomical book deals. Those who got rich off the tech boom could think of themselves as pioneers on the new "electronic frontier."

Another area of contradictory social trends is race. In their book "America in Black and White," Stephan and Abigail Thernstrom presented an overwhelming statistical case that while inequality still remained a stubborn fact, African-Americans over the past generation had improved their material and social situation relative to whites in virtually every respect. But as the objective differences narrow, the perceived injustice of those inequalities still remaining seem to become all the more unbearable.

To hear many black leaders talk in the wake of the Florida recount, the current situation is not all that different from Selma, 1963. For all of Mr. Clinton's gestures toward racial healing, the distinctiveness of black perceptions of events has grown. This became painfully evident during the O.J. Simpson trial, when liberal white women expected their black sisters to denounce male violence, only to find one well-educated black talking head after another taking O.J.'s side. While whites were sharply divided over the Clinton impeachment, blacks were monolithically on his side; Al Gore got an even higher proportion of the black vote than did our first "black" president. The gulf that separates blacks and whites is increasingly a cultural rather than socioeconomic one.

All of these trends indicate that the most important changes of the Clinton years were in the end cultural rather than economic. This explains the central political paradox of this period: Why it is that one of the most conservative presidents from the Democratic Party could have ended up being so intensely hated by the right, and polarized American politics like no other?

The reason was that the Clintons were quintessential "bobos": crudely materialistic, self-absorbed, and power-hungry, but at the same time unable to admit any of this to themselves because they believed their intelligence, education and sophistication entitled them to a higher level of respect. Like others in his generation, the man presiding over America's most recent decade of greed could look himself in the mirror and pronounce himself satisfied with what he saw.

Mr. Fukuyama is a professor of public policy at George Mason University.

Editorial Feature

Two Presidencies in One

BY DICK MORRIS

What will be Bill Clinton's legacy? Which legacy? Which Clinton? When Sunday Morning Clinton was balancing the budget, Saturday Night Bill was prowling the halls of the West Wing looking for prey. As the good Clinton reformed welfare, the bad one paid detectives to dig up dirt on the women in his past. While the one made education a key national focus, the other borrowed heavily from Joseph McCarthy and Richard Nixon in smearing political opponents.

The CLINTON
LEGACY

The two versions of the same man ruled together in Washington for eight years, locked in a constant struggle for supremacy and power. By the second term, it was clear that Saturday Night Bill had won.

Fenced in by his villainous co-personality, Sunday Morning Clinton had no choice but to focus on defeating impeachment even though that meant paying such obeisance to the Democratic Party's congressional caucus that nothing would pass and no progress would be made for four years. Surrounded by the females whom Saturday Night Bill had seduced, abandoned, harassed, abused and probably raped, the collective Clinton personality had to hire secret police to silence women, troopers and witnesses by blackmail, intimidation and coercion.

But before Saturday Night Bill took over, Sunday Morning Clinton had amassed a record that would have been the envy of any other administration. It began with a crucial insight—that Fed Chairman Alan Greenspan must be appeased. By raising taxes, particularly the gas tax, Mr. Clinton convinced the Fed that he was sufficiently serious about closing the deficit that interest rates could be cut without fear of igniting inflation. This fundamental deal between the leader of the nation and the boss of the economy set the stage for eight years of prosperity, elimination of the deficit, and, eventually, even the repayment of the national debt.

The Sunday morning president did not squander this prosperity but set about a deliberate, well-planned and systematic effort to use it to raise the living standards of the poor and crack the seemingly intractable problem of the underclass in our society.

First, he sharply raised the Earned Income Tax Credit so that wage supplements made it financially rewarding for welfare families to work, even at low-wage jobs. Then he raised the minimum wage so that bottom-rung jobs paid more. Next, he signed an executive order requiring that this higher minimum wage be paid to welfare recipients forced to work under the new welfare-reform bill that he had signed into law. Finally, he used tax credits and jawboning to create one million jobs specifically tailored for those formerly on welfare.

The result? The percentage of those in poverty dropped for the first time since the 1960s and the gap between the rich and the poor closed as it had not for 20 years.

But Sunday Morning Clinton realized that reducing poverty was only the first step—that crime must also come down if the causes of the racism that gnawed at our social fabric were to be alleviated. In his 1994 crime bill, he provided, for the first time, adequate federal funds for prison construction and then required state judges and parole boards to make criminals serve at least 85% of their sentences as a condition of getting the money.

With a federally funded increase of almost 20% in the number of police officers, and tough new gun controls, Sunday Morning Clinton was able to increase the number of inmates in state and federal prisons by more than 50%. With more than 500,000 fewer men on the street to rape, rob and kill us, crime dropped and dropped and dropped.

With the cut in unemployment, welfare and crime, racism also receded. The elections of 2000 were the first in our nation's history in which racial bigotry against blacks or Hispanics, in any of its issue disguises, played no role.

Meanwhile, Saturday Night Bill was feeling enabled and empowered by skating free from the Gennifer Flowers scandal and frustrating prosecutors seeking the truth of the Whitewater and FBI file scandals. Roaming the surreal corridors of the West Wing during the days of the government shutdown, he pounced on Monica Lewinsky, thong and all.

Re-elected, the Sunday morning president proceeded to make good on his campaign promise and signed a budget deal with the GOP setting the nation on a course of prosperity and balanced budgets as far as one can see. But no sooner was his signature dry than the ominous signs that the Paula Jones litigation was drawing nearer fenced him in. When Monica Lewinsky's name came to the fore, Saturday Night Bill and his sidekick Hillary stepped in and took over.

Detectives were dispatched to dig up dirt on his latest sexual conquest. Cover stories were sold to the gullible White House staff. Disinformation leaked to the media. Saturday Night Bill had taken charge. When his semen stain was found on Ms. Lewinsky's dress, lying became untenable and he hunkered down to survive impeachment.

Cutting a deal with House and Senate Democrats, Saturday Night Bill promised to lock his alter ego up in the offices of the National Security Council and keep him out of domestic policy. No longer, Saturday Night Bill pledged, would his good doppelganger try to cut deals with the GOP to protect Social Security or Medicare or to cut taxes. Instead, he promised, would come vetoes designed to keep issues alive for the congressional elections of 2000.

Consigned to foreign policy, Sunday Morning Clinton did his best. He brought North Korea in from the cold and laid the basis for reconciliation in the world's most dangerous hot spot. He labored long and hard to bring peace to Ireland and the Middle East with varying degrees of success. He bombed Kosovo and kept troops in Bosnia so that the Balkans would not again shatter the peace.

At home, Saturday Night Bill celebrated yet another escape as impeachment failed and Juanita Broaddrick's accusations were largely ignored. Then Saturday Night Bill paid his debt to co-conspirator Hillary and orchestrated the final fraud—her election as senator in a state in which she had been barely a tourist.

At the end it was Saturday Night Bill in the Oval Office, cursing his fate, damning the media, and howling his outrage for all to hear. Sunday Morning Clinton had long since left through the Rose Garden, taking his legacy of solved problems and constructive achievement with him into the night.

Mr. Morris served as a political adviser to President Clinton. He is author of "The New Prince" (Renaissance Books, 2000)

REVIEW & OUTLOOK

Who Is Bill Clinton?

Back on March 12, 1992, with that year's Presidential election still nine months away, we published an editorial entitled "Who Is Bill Clinton?" destined to become the first of a long series of "Who Is . . ." titles exploring the vagaries of his Presidency. Even then there was reason to believe that Bill Clinton was going to be a little different than most of the men who've sought the Presidency.

"So it now appears," the editorial said, "we will get to know, or try to get to know Bill and Hillary Clinton. The Gennifer Flowers tank has already rumbled by. But where's the rest of them?"

Bill Clinton

Nearly nine years later, the question remains as relevant as ever. To put the matter concisely, "a Clinton Presidency" turned out to be an oxymoron, a notion inherently at odds with itself. Instead of a Presidency, we've had two terms of Clinton agonistes.

All the retrospectives out now on the Clinton Presidency feel obliged to regret that his innate political skills never produced an expected level of political accomplishment. This is seen as some tragic flaw. We have come to the view by now that Mr. Clinton's failures didn't have much of anything to do with politics. Bill Clinton's flaw is that he sees everything in the whole wide world as his personal property. Mr. Clinton seems to have believed that he could use everything as he wished, not because he is an officer of the state of Arkansas or of the United States, but because he is Bill Clinton.

And so the things he saw as belonging mainly to him included the Presidency of the United States, the Oval Office, Monica Lewinsky, Paula Jones, the Secret Service of the United States, the lawyers of the White House counsel's office, Ron Brown's Commerce Department, the Democratic National Committee, the Department of Justice, the landing patterns at Los Angeles Airport, Madison Guaranty, the Lincoln Bedroom and, not least, the rest of the world. Nearly every account one reads describes his frantic two-minute drill on the Middle East as aimed at the "Clinton legacy." Thankfully, FDR didn't look into the flames of Pearl Harbor and see the Nobel Peace Prize.

These columns have argued that this behavior is sociopathic. Psychiatrists who don't trust their profession's categories objected, but whatever the medical precision, a neurotic recklessness was clear enough. Yes, other personally reckless men have risen into the Presidency, but none were so oblivious to the need for personal or political temperance while serving as the nation's first public officer. He asked an army of federal officials and federal institutions to protect him from the consequences. His legacy is that they did so.

What even Democrats and liberals regard as the mysterious "failure" or unfilled promise of his Presidency is in fact a function of his inability to put public purpose firmly ahead of personal need. Ultimately this impossible tangle, requiring endless lies and stratagems to keep from undermining his public office, led to the second term's impeachment proceedings.

Any other serious President one can think of had some obvious sense of public purpose beyond himself. With Bill Clinton, all was reversed: For eight years he was larger than life, and kept the American Presidency smaller.

Politically, it was not necessary. The North American trade agreement of 1993 and the 1996 passage of welfare reform proved bipartisan achievement could occur and on the centrist terms Mr. Clinton promised in his first campaign. We are perfectly willing to dismiss HillaryCare as the price of private White House peace, but there simply was no reason for this Presidency's legislative achievement to stop there. Reform of Medicare and Social Security, certainly not about sex, were within reach of his skills. But after the party's liberals stood with him through impeachment, centrist reforms were dead.

The great paradox of the Clinton Presidency is that even as it achieved so little, the economy flourished beginning in 1994, a break-point in the Clinton Presidency. In fact, bonds, as an index of economic well-being, languished midway through the first Clinton term, then rose smartly in November 1994 precisely when the GOP won control of the House.

Prior to the GOP Congress, indeed, the Clinton Presidency in 1994 had been headed downward. On January 20, Janet Reno appointed an independent counsel to investigate, not fund raising or Monica, but Whitewater. Two months later, Webster Hubbell, the Arkansas crony planted to watch the Justice Department, resigned. Paula Jones filed her lawsuit on May 6. In November, the GOP won its historic victory. Amid this mess, the White House, of all things, forces the trumped-up indictment of former Travel Office director Billy Dale. At this point, anyone seeking some larger public purpose in this Presidency would have been distracted by walls of attorneys and public-relations specialists trying to defend one man from personal disgrace or impeachment.

The spin game continued until this one man stood before the American people and lied to them, and sat silently while his attorney made statements to a federal judge that Mr. Clinton knew were false. Months later, the judge held the President of the United States in contempt.

At points along the way the past eight years, Bill Clinton's defenders have suggested that the criticism of him has been personal and that his vices were private. Any student of history understands that politics, especially democratic politics, is the product of mortals and that no office, no matter how high, is immune from the complexities of private life or politics. The history of the Clinton Presidency, however, indeed the history of Bill Clinton's life, is the tale of a man for whom much has been allowed and much forgiven—many, many times.

It has been great theater, but ruinous to the nation's political civility. A man who in return for all this forbearance learn nothing may remain a charming rogue to his friends. But it is another thing for an American President to assume with bottomless insouciance that a whole nation must condone his profligacy, both personal and political. The Clinton "legacy" is a cheapening of our national life, and the question is how long it will take to repair the damage.

January 22, 2001

REVIEW & OUTLOOK

Bill Cops a Plea

The reaction to Independent Counsel Robert Ray's plea bargain with Bill Clinton seems to be a collective sigh of relief that we can now put the Clinton era behind us. The only problem is that the now former President has no such intention.

We certainly sympathize with the dilemma faced by Mr. Ray. These columns have argued that the evidence warranted an indictment that allowed the legal system to play itself out as it would for any normal defendant. But the country does want a fresh political start, and prosecuting a former President would not have been painless or easy. In return for no indictment, moreover, Mr. Ray managed to wrestle from Mr. Clinton what history will understand to be a clear admission of guilt. The former President essentially copped a perjury plea.

Bill Clinton

His "agreed order of discipline" with the Arkansas Supreme Court Committee on Professional Conduct states that "Mr. Clinton admits and acknowledges, and the Court, therefore, finds" that "he knowingly gave evasive and misleading answers" in an attempt to cover up his relationship with Monica Lewinsky.

And that in so doing, Mr. Clinton "engaged in conduct that is prejudicial to the administration of justice." His intentional deception "interfered with the conduct of the Jones case by causing the court and counsel for the parties to expend unnecessary time, effort, and resources, setting a poor example for other litigants, and causing the court to issue a 32-page Order civilly sanctioning Mr. Clinton."

With this admission he avoided the humiliation of disbarment, though he did have to agree to the considerable embarrassment of a five-year suspension of his law license. He joins Richard Nixon as the only Presidents to be so sanctioned.

In his own White House statement, Mr. Clinton also finally admitted that his testimony was "false." Yes, this was couched in the usual Clintonian parsing that "I tried to walk a fine line between acting lawfully and testifying falsely." This means he tried to lie without getting caught. But he was nonetheless forced to concede that "I now recognize that I did not fully accomplish this goal and that certain of my responses to questions about Ms. Lewinsky were false."

Any normal defendant would leave bad enough alone. But Mr. Clinton quickly sent out his spinners to deny what he had just admitted on paper. Lawyer David Kendall insisted that "he did not lie." Court jester James Carville drew the hilarious conclusion that the plea repudiated impeachment and could have been concluded in 1998. Everyone else knows that Mr. Clinton would still be denying everything if it were not for his DNA on Monica's blue dress.

We suspect Mr. Clinton's self-justifying will only get worse as time passes. Having violated all the normal rules as President, he will no doubt violate all of the rules for ex-Presidents. This includes the convention not to criticize his successor.

It's obvious that, far from ending their era, both Bill and Hillary Clinton view George W. Bush's Inaugural as the start of their own restoration. Mr. Clinton has already twice cast doubt on Mr. Bush's legitimacy. They have done their best to eclipse Al Gore as leader of the Democratic Party, installing their own chief fund-raiser to run the Democratic National Committee. Mr. Clinton's "farewell" speech in Arkansas last week was less a valedictory than a State of the Union address. In one of his final talks on Jan. 20, he told a friendly crowd that "you've got a senator over here who will be a voice for you"—Hillary.

Mr. Clinton also tried to clear the ethical decks with an astonishing 176 last-minute pardons. The beneficiaries include several of Hillary's New York constituents as well as Whitewater partner Susan

McDougal. Thus was Ms. McDougal rewarded for refusing to cooperate with Independent Counsel Ken Starr. Webb Hubbell was somehow overlooked for a pardon, perhaps because he was convicted for defrauding Hillary's former law firm.

Like Mr. Ray and most Americans, these columns have had their fill of the Clintons and long to "move on" to a less cynical era. If only Bill Clinton would let us.

A Whitewater Chronology

Editor's note: *This comprehensive chronology has been updated through the end of the Clinton Presidency. It covers the events shaping Bill Clinton's journey from Little Rock to the Oval Office and during the eight years of his Presidency. It supersedes the chronologies in earlier volumes of* **A Journal Briefing: Whitewater.**

1976

Bill Clinton is elected Arkansas Attorney General.

Little Rock investment banker Jackson Stephens forms Stephens Finance with Indonesian banker Mochtar Riady to do business in Asia.

1977

Hillary Rodham Clinton joins the Rose Law Firm.

Jackson Stephens joins with former Carter administration budget director Bert Lance and a group of Mideast investors—later identified as key figures in the corrupt Bank of Credit & Commerce International—in an unsuccessful attempt to acquire Financial General Bankshares in Washington, D.C. Amid the legal maneuvers surrounding the takeover attempt, a brief is submitted by the Stephens-controlled bank data processing firm Systematics; two of the lawyers signing the brief are Hillary Rodham and Webster Hubbell.

1978

August: The Clintons purchase a 230-acre land tract along Arkansas's White River, in partnership with Jim and Susan McDougal.

October: Mrs. Clinton, now a partner at the Rose Firm, begins a series of commodities trades under the guidance of Tyson Foods executive Jim Blair, earning nearly $100,000. The trades are not revealed until March 1994.

November: Bill Clinton is elected Governor of Arkansas. He makes Jim McDougal a top economic adviser.

1979

Feb. 16: The Federal Reserve rejects the bid by BCCI frontmen to take over Financial General Bankshares.

June: The Clintons and McDougals form Whitewater Development Co. to engage in real estate transactions.

1980

November: Gov. Clinton is defeated by Republican Frank White. He joins his trusted friend Bruce Lindsey at the Little Rock law firm of Wright, Lindsey and Jennings.

1981

Jim McDougal purchases Madison Bank and Trust.

Aug. 25: The Federal Reserve approves a new bid—by largely the same group of BCCI frontmen—to acquire Financial General Bankshares.

1982

Financial General changes its name to First American and Democratic Party icon Clark Clifford is appointed chairman. BCCI fronts begin acquiring controlling interest in banks and other American financial institutions.

In Arkansas, Jim McDougal purchases Madison Guaranty Savings & Loan. It begins a period of rapid expansion.

November: Bill Clinton defeats Frank White, winning back the governor's seat.

1983
Capital Management Services, a federally insured small business investment company owned by Judge David Hale, begins making loans to the Arkansas political elite.

Jackson Stephens forms United Pacific Trading with Mochtar Riady to do business in the U.S. and Asia.

1984
Stephens and Riady join forces to buy First Arkansas Bankstock Corp., changing its name to Worthen Bank and installing 28-year-old James Riady as president.

Jan. 20: The Federal Home Loan Bank Board issues a report on Madison Guaranty questioning its lending practices and financial stability. The Arkansas Securities Department begins to take steps to close it down.

August: According to Jim McDougal, Gov. Clinton drops by his office during a morning jog and asks that Madison steer some business to Mrs. Clinton at the Rose Law Firm.

November: Gov. Clinton wins re-election with 64% of the vote.

1985
January: Roger Clinton pleads guilty to cocaine distribution charges and is given immunity from further prosecution in exchange for cooperation. He testifies before a federal grand jury and serves a brief prison sentence.

Jan. 16: Gov. Clinton appoints Beverly Bassett Schaffer, a longtime associate, to serve as Arkansas State Securities Commissioner.

March: Mrs. Clinton receives from Madison Guaranty the first payment of a $2,000-per-month retainer. Madison's accounting firm, Frost & Co., issues a report declaring the savings and loan solvent.

April 4:   Jim McDougal hosts a fund-raiser to help Gov. Clinton repay campaign debts. Contributions at the fund-raiser later draw the scrutiny of Whitewater investigators.

April 7:   The New Jersey securities firm Bevill, Bresler & Schulman files for bankruptcy amid fraud charges and an estimated $240 million in losses; one of the biggest apparent losers is Stephens-dominated Worthen Bank, which holds with Bevill $52 million of Arkansas state funds in uncollateralized repurchase agreements.

April 30:   Hillary Clinton sends a recapitalization offer for the foundering Madison Guaranty to the Arkansas Securities Commission. Two weeks later, Ms. Schaffer informs Mrs. Clinton the plan is approved, but it is never implemented.

October: Governor and Mrs. Clinton lead a trade delegation to Taiwan and Japan.

              Jim McDougal launches the Castle Grande land deal.

1986

Jan. 17:   The U. S. Attorney for the Western District of Arkansas drops a money laundering and narcotics-conspiracy case against Arkansas associates of international drug smuggler Barry Seal. Arkansas State Police Investigator Russell Welch and Internal Revenue Service Investigator Bill Duncan, the lead agents on the case, protest; later, both are driven from their jobs.

Feb. 19:   Barry Seal is gunned down by Colombian hitmen in Baton Rouge, La. He becomes the touchstone in murky allegations of covert operations, cocaine trafficking and gun running swirling around his base at Mena airfield in western Arkansas.

March 4: The Federal Home Loan Bank Board issues a second, sharply critical report of Madison, accusing Jim McDougal of diverting funds to insiders.

April: Roger Clinton is paroled from prison.

James Riady steps down as president of Worthen Bank.

April 3: David Hale's Capital Management Services makes a $300,000 loan to Susan McDougal in the name of a front, Master Marketing. Some of the funds wind up in a Whitewater Development Co. account. Indicted for fraud on an unrelated transaction in 1993, Mr. Hale claims that then-Gov. Clinton and Jim McDougal pressured him into making the loan.

August: Federal regulators remove Mr. McDougal from Madison's board of directors.

Oct. 5: Deceased Mena drug smuggler Barry Seal's C-123K is shot down over Nicaragua with an Arkansas pilot at the controls and a load of weapons and Contra-supporter Eugene Hasenfus in the cargo bay.

Oct. 24: Clinton friend and "bond daddy" Dan Lasater and nine others, most from the Little Rock bond trading community, are indicted on cocaine charges. Roger Clinton, who has cooperated with the prosecution, is named an unindicted co-conspirator.

November: Gov. Clinton wins re-election. Gubernatorial terms are extended from two years to four.

1987
According to Susan McDougal, Whitewater records are taken to the Governor's Mansion and turned over to Mrs. Clinton sometime during the year.

Officials at investment giant Stephens Inc., including longtime Clinton friend David Edwards, take steps to rescue Harken Energy, a struggling Texas oil company with George W. Bush on its board. Over the next three years, Mr. Edwards brings BCCI-linked investors and advisers into Harken deals. One of them, Abdullah Bakhsh, purchases $10 million in shares of Stephens-dominated Worthen Bank.

Jan. 15: Dan Lasater begins serving a 30-month sentence for cocaine distribution. In July, he is paroled to a Little Rock halfway house.

Aug. 23: In a mysterious case later ruled a murder and linked to drug corruption, teenagers Kevin Ives and Don Henry are run over by a train in a remote locale a few miles southwest of Little Rock.

1988

October: A Florida grand jury indicts BCCI figures on charges of laundering drug money. It is the first sign of serious trouble at the international bank.

1989

Manhattan District Attorney Robert Morgenthau begins a wide-ranging probe of BCCI.

March: Federal regulators shut down Madison Guaranty Savings & Loan, at a taxpayer loss of about $60 million. Jim McDougal is indicted for bank fraud.

June 16: Mena investigator Bill Duncan resigns from the Internal Revenue Service following clashes with Washington supervisors over the probe.

1990

May: Jim McDougal goes to trial on bank fraud and is acquitted.

November: Gov. Clinton is elected to a second four-year term, promising to serve it out and not seek the presidency in 1992.

Dec. 3: The Federal Deposit Insurance Corp. cites the Riady family's Lippo Bank in Los Angeles for poor loans and inadequate capital.

1991

Yah Lin "Charlie" Trie, Clinton friend and Little Rock restaurateur, opens Daihatsu International Trading Co., with offices in Arkansas, Washington and Beijing. He later emerges as a central figure in the Clinton-Gore campaign scandal.

January: The Federal Reserve orders an investigation of BCCI's alleged control of First American Bank.

July 5: Regulators world-wide shut down BCCI amid wide-spread charges of bank fraud and allegations of links to laundered drug money, terrorists and intelligence agencies.

Aug. 13: Chairman Clark Clifford and top aide Robert Altman resign from First American.

Oct. 3: Bill Clinton announces his candidacy for president, denouncing "S&L crooks and self-serving CEOs."

1992

March 8: New York Times reporter Jeff Gerth discloses the Clintons' dealings with Madison and Whitewater.

March 20: Washington Times reporter Jerry Seper discloses Hillary Clinton's $2,000-per-month retainer from Madison.

March 23: In a hasty report arranged by the Clinton campaign, Denver lawyer James Lyons states the Clintons lost $68,000 on the Whitewater investment and clears them of improprieties. The issue fades from the campaign.

July 16:   Bill Clinton accepts the Democratic Party's presidential nomination in New York.

July 22:   A Manhattan grand jury hands up sealed indictments against BCCI principals, including Clark Clifford and Robert Altman. A week later, a grand jury in Washington and the Federal Reserve issue separate actions against Clifford and Altman.

August: Clinton friend David Edwards arranges a $3.5 million lead gift from Saudi Arabian benefactors to the University of Arkansas for a Middle East studies center.

Aug. 31:   Resolution Trust Corporation field officers complete criminal referral #C0004 on Madison Guaranty and forward it to Charles Banks, U.S. Attorney for the Eastern District of Arkansas. The referral alleges an elaborate check-kiting scheme by Madison owners Jim and Susan McDougal and names the Clintons and Jim Guy Tucker as possible beneficiaries. Later, Mr. Banks forwards the referral to Washington. In the heat of the campaign, the issue is sidelined.

Nov. 3:   Bill Clinton is elected President of the United States.

December: Vincent Foster, representing the Clintons, meets with James McDougal and arranges for him to buy the Clintons' remaining shares in Whitewater Development Co. for $1,000. Mr. McDougal is loaned the money for the purchase by Tyson Foods counsel Jim Blair, a longtime Clinton friend and commodities adviser. The loan is never repaid.

1993

Jan. 20:   Bill Clinton is sworn in as 42nd President of the United States.

February: Arkansas Gov. Jim Guy Tucker announces a $20 million Saudi gift to the University of Arkansas for a Middle East studies center.

Feb. 11: President Clinton nominates Miami prosecutor Janet Reno for the post of Attorney General

March 23: At her first news conference as Attorney General, Janet Reno announces the firing of all U.S. Attorneys, the 93 top federal prosecutors in the nation, saying the administration wants to put in its own people.

March 24: Year-old press clips about Whitewater are faxed from Deputy Treasury Secretary Roger Altman to White House Counsel Bernard Nussbaum. Mr. Altman also is serving as acting head of the Resolution Trust Corporation, an independent federal agency.

April 3: After serving as White House liaison to the Justice Department, Arkansas insider Webster Hubbell is named Associate Attorney General.

April 20: Arkansas businessman Joseph Giroir, former chairman of the Rose Law Firm, incorporates the Arkansas International Development Corp. to bring Indonesia's Lippo Group together with American companies seeking to do business in Indonesia and China; Mr. Giroir later emerges as a player in the campaign-finance scandal.

May 19: The White House fires seven employees of its Travel Office, following a review by Associate Counsel William Kennedy III, a former member of the Rose Law Firm. Mr. Kennedy's actions, which included attempts to involve the FBI and the Internal Revenue Service in a criminal investigation of the Travel Office, are sharply criticized. Deputy White House Counsel Vincent Foster also is rebuked.

June 21: Whitewater corporate tax returns for 1989 through 1991, prepared by Mr. Foster, are delivered to Jim McDougal's attorney.

July 17: According to a White House chronology, Mr. Foster completes work on a blind trust for the Clintons. In Little Rock for a weekend visit, President Clinton has a four-hour dinner alone with old friend David Edwards, an investment adviser and currency trader.

July 20: The Little Rock FBI obtains a warrant to search the office of David Hale as part of its investigation into Capital Management Services. In Washington, Deputy White House Counsel Vincent Foster drives to Ft. Marcy Park and commits suicide. That evening, White House Counsel Bernard Nussbaum, Clinton aide Patsy Thomasson, and Mrs. Clinton's chief of staff Maggie Williams visit Mr. Foster's office. According to testimony by a uniformed Secret Service officer, Ms. Williams exits the counsel's suite with an armful of folders.

July 21: Early-morning calls are exchanged between Mrs. Clinton in Little Rock and White House operatives, including Maggie Williams and Susan Thomases. According to later Congressional testimony, Mrs. Clinton's concerns about investigators having "unfettered access" to the Foster office are conveyed to Mr. Nussbaum. A figure of later controversy, White House personnel security chief Craig Livingstone, is spotted in the Foster office area.

July 22: Mr. Nussbaum again searches Mr. Foster's office, but denies access to Park Police and Justice Department investigators. In an angry phone call, Deputy Attorney General Philip Heymann asks, "Bernie, are you hiding something?" Documents, including Whitewater files, are removed. Details on the removal of Whitewater files do not emerge for months.

July 26:   A torn-up note is found in Mr. Foster's briefcase.

Aug. 14:   In New York, Robert Altman is acquitted of bank fraud in the BCCI case; Clark Clifford's trial is indefinitely postponed due to ill health.

Aug. 16:   Paula Casey, a longtime associate of the Clintons, takes office in Little Rock as U.S. attorney.

September: Ms. Casey turns down plea bargain attempts from David Hale's lawyer, who had offered to share information on the "banking and borrowing practices of some individuals in the elite political circles of the State of Arkansas."

Sept. 23:   Mr. Hale is indicted for fraud.

Sept. 29:   Treasury Department General Counsel Jean Hanson warns Mr. Nussbaum that the RTC plans to issue criminal referrals asking the Justice Department to investigate Madison. The referrals are said to name the Clintons as witnesses to, and possible beneficiaries of, illegal actions. The current Governor of Arkansas, Jim Guy Tucker, also is said to be a target of the investigation. Mr. Nussbaum passes the information to Bruce Lindsey, a top Clinton aide.

Oct. 4 or 5: Mr. Lindsey informs President Clinton about the confidential referrals. Mr. Lindsey later tells Congress he did not mention any specific target of the referrals.

Oct. 6:   President Clinton meets with Arkansas Gov. Jim Guy Tucker at the White House.

Oct. 8:   Nine new criminal referrals on Madison Guaranty are forwarded to U.S. Attorney Paula Casey in Little Rock.

Oct. 14:   A meeting is held in Mr. Nussbaum's office with senior White House and Treasury personnel to discuss the RTC and Madison. Participants at the meeting later tell Congress that they discussed only how to handle press inquiries.

Oct. 27:   The RTC's first criminal referral is rejected in Little Rock by U.S. Attorney Casey.

Nov. 3:   Associate Attorney General Webster Hubbell recuses himself from the Whitewater case.

Nov. 9:   In Little Rock, U.S. Attorney Casey recuses herself from the Madison case; in Kansas City, RTC investigator Jean Lewis is taken off the probe.

Nov. 18:   President Clinton meets with Gov. Tucker in Seattle.

Dec. 19:   Allegations by Arkansas state troopers of the president's sexual infidelities while governor surface in The American Spectator magazine and the Los Angeles Times.

Dec. 20:   Washington Times correspondent Jerry Seper reports that Whitewater files were removed from Mr. Foster's office.

Dec. 30:   At a New Year's retreat, President Clinton asks Comptroller of the Currency Eugene Ludwig, an old friend, for "advice" about how to handle the growing Whitewater storm.

1994

Jan. 20:   Amid mounting political pressure, Attorney General Janet Reno appoints Robert Fiske as special counsel to investigate Whitewater.

Jan. 27:   Deputy Attorney General Philip Heymann resigns.

Feb. 2:   Roger Altman meets with Mr. Nussbaum and other senior White House staff to give them a "heads-up" about the Madison probe. Washington RTC attorney April Breslaw flies to Kansas City and meets with investigator Jean Lewis; in a secretly taped conversation, Ms. Breslaw states that top RTC officials "would like to be able to say that Whitewater did not cause a loss to Madison."

Feb. 24: Mr. Altman gives incomplete testimony to the Senate Banking Committee about discussions between the White House and Treasury on the Madison referrals.

Feb. 25: Mr. Altman recuses himself from the Madison investigation and announces he will step down as acting head of the RTC.

March: Top Clinton aides Thomas McLarty, Erskine Bowles, Mickey Kantor and others begin a series of meetings and calls to arrange financial aid for Webster Hubbell, then facing charges of bilking his former Rose Law Firm partners and under growing pressure to cooperate with the Whitewater probe; the meetings are not revealed until April 1997.

March 5: White House Counsel Bernard Nussbaum resigns.

March 8: Lloyd Cutler is named White House Counsel.

March 14: Associate Attorney General Webster Hubbell resigns.

March 18: The New York Times reports Mrs. Clinton's spectacular 1978 $100,000 commodity trades.

March 23: The Association of American Physicians and Surgeons files suit against Mrs. Clinton's health reform task force for violating the Federal Advisory Committee Act by holding secret meetings.

May 3: President Clinton meets with top advisers, including deputy chief of staff Harold Ickes, to discuss raising millions of dollars for the 1996 campaign.

May 6: Former Little Rock resident Paula Corbin Jones files

suit against President Clinton, charging he sexually harassed her while Governor.

June: Indonesia's Lippo Group pays Webster Hubbell about $100,000 for undisclosed services as pressure grows for Mr. Hubbell to cooperate with the Whitewater probe; also in June, Lippo scion James Riady and associates meet at least five times with President Clinton and aides; reports of the payments and meetings emerge in 1996 and 1997.

June 30: Special Counsel Robert Fiske concludes that Mr. Foster's death was a suicide and clears the White House and Treasury Department of obstruction of justice on the RTC contacts, opening the way for Congressional hearings limited to the two subjects.

July: John Huang, president of U.S. operations for Indonesia's Lippo Group, joins the Commerce Department as a senior official with a top-secret clearance to oversee international trade.

July 26: Whitewater hearings open in Congress.

Aug. 1: The White House reveals that the Whitewater files removed from Mr. Foster's office were kept for five days in the Clintons' residence before being turned over to their personal lawyer.

Aug. 5: A three-judge panel removes Mr. Fiske and appoints Kenneth Starr as independent counsel. Mr. Starr continues to investigate all aspects of Whitewater, including Mr. Foster's death.

Aug. 12: The RTC informs Madison investigator Jean Lewis and two colleagues that they will be placed on "administrative leave" for two weeks.

Aug. 17: Deputy Treasury Secretary Roger Altman resigns.

Aug. 18:	Treasury Department General Counsel Jean Hanson resigns.
Sept. 12:	Donald Smaltz is named independent counsel to investigate Agriculture Secretary Mike Espy.
Oct. 1:	Abner Mikva replaces Lloyd Cutler as White House Counsel.
Oct. 3:	Agriculture Secretary Mike Espy resigns.
Nov. 8:	In a political earthquake, Republicans gain control of the House and the Senate.
Dec. 5:	In Little Rock, Madison Guaranty real-estate appraiser Robert Palmer pleads guilty to one felony count of conspiracy and agrees to cooperate with the Starr probe.
Dec. 6:	Former Associate Attorney General Webster Hubbell pleads guilty to two felonies in a scheme to defraud his former Rose Law Firm partners and says he will cooperate with the independent counsel.
Dec. 7:	Former Travel Office director Billy Dale is indicted on charges of embezzling office funds.
Dec. 19:	The FDIC sanctions the Riady family's Lippo Bank in Los Angeles for failing to adhere to money-laundering regulations governing large cash transactions.

1995

Jan. 3:	Republicans on the Senate Banking Committee, poised to move into the majority and renew the Whitewater hearings, issue a sharply critical report based on the summer hearings. It accuses Clinton administration officials of "serious misconduct and malfeasance" in the matters of the RTC criminal referrals and later congressional testimony.
Feb. 28:	Arkansas banker Neal Ainley is indicted on five felony

counts relating to Bill Clinton's 1990 gubernatorial campaign. He later pleads guilty to reduced charges and agrees to cooperate with the independent counsel.

March 21: Whitewater real-estate broker Chris Wade pleads guilty to two felonies.

March 27: Legal Times reports that Independent Counsel Donald Smaltz's probe has been "significantly curtailed by the Justice Department." In recent months, Mr. Smaltz had been exploring Arkansas poultry giant Tyson Foods.

May 5: Mena investigator Russell Welch fights off an attempt by the Arkansas State Police to discredit him, but is forced into early retirement.

May 24: David Barrett is appointed independent counsel to probe charges that Housing Secretary Henry Cisneros made false statements to the FBI.

June: Monica Lewinsky begins work at the White House as an unpaid intern in the office of Chief of Staff Leon Panetta.

June 7: An Arkansas grand jury hands up indictments against Gov. Jim Guy Tucker and two business associates in a complex scheme to buy and sell cable television systems.

June 23: A report for the RTC by the law firm Pillsbury, Madison & Sutro says that funds flowed to the Whitewater account from other Madison accounts, but adds that the Clintons "had little direct involvement" in the investment before 1988.

July 6: Daniel Pearson is named independent counsel to probe business dealings of Commerce Secretary Ron Brown.

July 18: The special Senate Whitewater Committee opens a new round of hearings in Washington; they quickly become mired in partisan disputes.

Aug. 8: In testimony before the House Banking Committee, RTC investigator Jean Lewis says there was a "concerted effort to obstruct, hamper and manipulate" the Madison investigation.

Aug. 17: Independent Counsel Kenneth Starr indicts Arkansas Gov. Jim Guy Tucker and former Madison Guaranty owners Jim and Susan McDougal for bank fraud and conspiracy.

Sept. 5: Federal District Judge Henry Woods dismisses the cable TV fraud case against Gov. Tucker and two associates, saying Mr. Starr has exceeded his jurisdiction; the independent counsel appeals the decision to the Eighth Circuit court in St. Louis; the separate indictment against Gov. Tucker and the McDougals stands.

Sept. 13: At a White House meeting including President Clinton, Commerce official John Huang, Lippo Group scion James Riady, senior Clinton aide Bruce Lindsey and Arkansas businessman Joseph Giroir, a decision is reached to dispatch Mr. Huang to the Democratic National Comittee as a senior fund-raiser.

Sept. 20: White House Counsel Abner Mikva announces his resignation. The President names Jack Quinn, Vice President Al Gore's chief of staff, as his fourth White House counsel.

November: House Banking Committee Chairman Jim Leach informs colleagues that he will investigate allegations of drug smuggling and money laundering at Mena airport.

Nov. 16: After deliberating less than two hours, a Washington jury acquits former White House Travel Office head Billy Dale of embezzlement charges.

Dec. 13: Drug suspect Jorge Cabrera attends a White House Christmas party after donating $20,000 to Democrats; three weeks later, he is arrested in Florida with 6,000 pounds of cocaine.

Dec. 29: A memo from former White House aide David Watkins, placing responsibility for the Travel Office firings on Mrs. Clinton, is discovered at the White House.

1996

January: John Huang leaves the Commerce Department to join the Democratic National Committee as a senior fund-raiser.

Jan. 5: The White House announces that Mrs. Clinton's Rose Law Firm billing records, sought by the Independent Counsel and Congress for two years, have been discovered on a table in the "book room" of the personal residence.

Jan. 11: At a news conference, President Clinton says he is nearly broke and owes about $1.6 million in legal fees stemming from Whitewater and the Paula Jones sexual harassment suit.

Jan. 22: The White House announces that Mrs. Clinton has been subpoenaed to testify before a Whitewater grand jury about the missing billing records.

Feb. 5: Federal District Judge George Howard Jr. rules that President Clinton must appear as a defense witness in the bank fraud case against Jim Guy Tucker and the McDougals.

Feb. 6: Charlie Trie escorts Chinese arms merchant Wang Jun to a White House reception for donors.

Feb. 8: The Wall Street Journal discloses that two of President Clinton's insurance policies have paid $900,000 into his legal defense fund.

Feb. 20:	Arkansas bankers Herby Branscum Jr. and Robert Hill are indicted on bank fraud and conspiracy charges relating to Bill Clinton's 1990 gubernatorial campaign.
Feb. 29:	The Whitewater Committee's mandate expires and Senate Democrats launch a filibuster to block an extension of the probe.
March 4:	Gov. Tucker and the McDougals go on trial for bank fraud and conspiracy in Little Rock.
March 15:	A three-judge panel of the Eighth Circuit Court of Appeals reinstates Independent Counsel Starr's indictment of Gov. Tucker and two associates in the cable television fraud scheme, and directs that Federal District Judge Henry Woods be removed from the case "to preserve the appearance of impartiality."
March 22:	Independent Counsel Starr's jurisdiction is expanded to cover the Travel Office affair.
March 25:	Arkansas insider David Hale is sentenced to 28 months in prison for defrauding the federal government.
April:	Monica Lewinsky is transferred from the White House to the Pentagon for "immature behavior." She meets former White House aide Linda Tripp, who later tapes their telephone conversations.
April 3:	Commerce Secretary Ron Brown and 32 others are killed in a plane crash in Croatia.
April 28:	President Clinton gives four hours of videotaped testimony in the White House as a defense witness in the Arkansas trial of Gov. Tucker and the McDougals.
April 29:	Vice President Al Gore attends a fund-raiser at the Hsi Lai Buddhist Temple in California, raising $100,000 later found to be illegal.

May 28:   An Arkansas jury convicts Gov. Tucker and the McDougals on 24 counts of bank fraud and conspiracy.

June 5:   Documents obtained after a long struggle by the House Government Reform and Oversight Committee reveal that the White House has improperly obtained confidential FBI background files. "Filegate" mushrooms into another scandal.

June 17:   The trial of Arkansas bankers Branscum and Hill on charges of bank fraud relating to the 1990 Clinton gubernatorial campaign begins in Little Rock.

June 18:   The Senate Whitewater Committee releases a 650-page final report detailing a "pattern of obstruction" by Clinton Administration officials.

June 21:   Independent Counsel Starr's jurisdiction is broadened to cover "Filegate."

June 25:   The Supreme Court agrees to hear President Clinton's procedural appeal in the Paula Jones harassment suit, effectively delaying trial until after the November election.

June 26:   In an appearance before a House oversight committee investigating the Filegate affair, White House personnel security chief Craig Livingstone announces his resignation.

July 7:   President Clinton gives videotaped testimony in the White House as a defense witness in the trial of Arkansas bankers Branscum and Hill.

July 15:   After a tumultuous day of political drama, Jim Guy Tucker steps down and Republican Mike Huckabee takes over as Governor of Arkansas.

Aug. 1:   A federal jury in Little Rock acquits Arkansas bankers Branscum and Hill on four bank fraud charges relating to the 1990 Clinton gubernatorial campaign; a mistrial is declared on seven other counts on which the jury deadlocks.

Aug. 15: After months of stonewalling, the White House releases 2,000 pages of documents to the House Government Reform and Oversight Committee; included is a long "task list" for dealing with the sprawling Whitewater probe.

Aug. 19: Awaiting a liver transplant, former Arkansas Gov. Jim Guy Tucker is given a four-year suspended sentence in the Madison Guaranty bank fraud case.

Aug. 21: Susan McDougal is sentenced to two years in prison for her part in the Master Marketing fraud scheme.

Sept. 4: Susan McDougal refuses to answer questions about Bill Clinton before a Whitewater grand jury and is ordered jailed for contempt.

Sept. 23: In a PBS interview, President Clinton says he has not ruled out pardons for Whitewater figures, touching off a campaign controversy.

Sept. 24: In the probe by Independent Counsel Smaltz, a federal jury convicts agribusiness giant Sun-Diamond of giving illegal gifts to Agriculture Secretary Mike Espy.

Oct. 8: Following disclosures by The Wall Street Journal of large illegal foreign donations, the campaign-finance story emerges as a major national issue one month before the presidential election.

Oct. 18: Democratic National Committee finance vice chairman John Huang is suspended after growing reports of improper campaign solicitations.

Nov. 5: Bill Clinton is re-elected President of the United States.

| Nov. 8: | In a declassified summary of a report to Rep. Jim Leach, the CIA for the first time admits it was present at remote Mena, Ark., but denies any association with drug trafficking or other illegal activities. |

Nov. 8:   In a declassified summary of a report to Rep. Jim Leach, the CIA for the first time admits it was present at remote Mena, Ark., but denies any association with drug trafficking or other illegal activities.

Nov. 29:   Attorney General Janet Reno declines to name an independent counsel in the campaign-finance affair, retaining the matter as a Justice Department probe.

Dec. 13:   Jack Quinn, President Clinton's fourth White House counsel, announces his resignation.

Dec. 14:   Susan McDougal is transferred to California to stand trial on charges of embezzling $150,000 from conductor Zubin Mehta and his wife; she remains jailed on civil contempt charges stemming from her refusal to testify before a Whitewater grand jury.

Dec. 16:   President Clinton's legal defense fund announces it has returned $640,000 in suspect donations from Clinton friend Charlie Trie.

1997

Jan 7:   Charles Ruff is named President Clinton's fifth White House counsel.

Jan. 13:   The Supreme Court hears oral arguments as to whether the Paula Jones sexual harassment case should be delayed until after Bill Clinton leaves office.

Jan. 20:   Bill Clinton is sworn in for a second term as President of the United States.

Feb. 13:   Webster Hubbell is released from federal custody after serving 15 months for mail fraud and tax evasion.

Feb. 17:   Kenneth Starr unexpectedly announces he will step down as independent counsel to become dean of Pepperdine University Law School in California.

Feb. 21:	After a storm of criticism, Mr. Starr reverses his decision to leave the Whitewater probe, saying he will stay on until investigations and prosecutions are "substantially completed."
March 3:	Drawn deep into the campaign-finance scandal, Vice President Al Gore defends himself at a press conference, declaring that "no controlling legal authority" indicates his actions were illegal.
March 31:	For the third time in seven years, the FDIC sanctions Lippo Bank, imposing a stiff cease-and-desist order due to bad loans and financial losses.
April 1:	Facing imminent news reports, the White House discloses that in early 1994 top Clinton aides set out to funnel money to Arkansas insider Webster Hubbell, then under pressure to cooperate with the Whitewater probe.
April 14:	Following a sentencing recommendation by Independent Counsel Starr about significant cooperation, Jim McDougal is given a sharply reduced three-year prison term for his role in the Madison Guaranty bank fraud case.
April 15:	In a new public-corruption drive in Arkansas, former county prosecutor Dan Harmon is indicted on multiple drug and racketeering counts.
April 30:	For a second time, Attorney General Reno turns down requests for an independent counsel in the campaign finance affair.
May 2:	The White House announces it will appeal to the Supreme Court a previously sealed Eighth Circuit ruling that government lawyers must turn over to Independent Counsel Starr notes taken during conversations with Hillary Clinton.

May 27: The Supreme Court issues a unanimous decision ruling that Paula Jones's sexual harassment suit may proceed against President Clinton while he is in office.

June 11: An Arkansas jury convicts former county prosecutor Dan Harmon of running a drug-related criminal enterprise.

June 23: The Supreme Court declines to grant certiorari on Mrs. Clinton's notes, effectively compelling the White House to turn them over to Mr. Starr.

July 8: Hearings into the campaign finance affair open before Senator Fred Thompson's Governmental Affairs Committee.

Aug. 27: A federal grand jury hands up a 39-count indictment accusing former Agriculture Secretary Mike Espy of illegally soliciting more than $35,000 in gifts from companies regulated by his department and attempting to conceal his actions.

Sept. 16: Under fire and with the Justice Department probe in disarray, Attorney Reno names a new prosecutor, Washington outsider Charles La Bella, to head her campaign finance investigation.

Sept. 19: News reports disclose that three associates of Teamsters union president Ron Carey have recently pleaded guilty to fraud charges in a fund-raising conspiracy involving labor movement figures and Democratic Party activists.

Oct. 10: Confirming the findings of earlier investigations, Independent Counsel Starr issues an exhaustive report concluding that deputy White House counsel Vincent Foster committed suicide in Ft. Marcy Park, Va.

Oct. 31: Senator Fred Thompson suspends hearings into the campaign finance affair after nearly four months of bitter partisan warfare.

Dec. 1: Former Agriculture Secretary Mike Espy's chief of staff, Ronald Blackley, is convicted of lying to investigators about receiving $22,000 from associates who had dealings with the agency.

Dec. 2: Attorney General Reno rejects appointment of an independent counsel to investigate campaign fund-raising calls made by President Clinton and Vice President Al Gore, saying she acted on "the facts and the law—not pressure, politics or any other factor." It is her third rejection of a special prosecutor for the campaign finance affair.

Dec. 17: Monica Lewinsky and Linda Tripp are subpoenaed by the Paula Jones legal team seeking evidence of sexual misconduct by the President.

Dec. 28: Monica Lewinsky reportedly visits Bill Clinton at the White House for the last time. News reports cite 36 previous visits.

Dec. 29: Tyson Foods Inc. pleads guilty to providing former Agriculture Secretary Espy with $12,000 in illegal gratuities and agrees to pay $6 million in fines.

1998

Jan. 7: In an affidavit filed in the Jones sexual harassment case, Monica Lewinsky denies a sexual relationship with Bill Clinton. According to later news reports, Ms. Lewinsky tells Ms. Tripp that she too must make false statements in the Jones case.

Jan. 12: Linda Tripp reportedly turns over to Starr prosecutors 20 hours of surreptitiously taped telephone conversations with Ms. Lewinsky, including descriptions of efforts by the President to direct false testimony and obstruct justice, and graphic accounts of Oval Office sex.

Jan. 16:   Attorney General Reno secretly petitions the Special Division of the U.S. Court of Appeals for an expansion of Mr. Starr's jurisdiction into the Lewinsky affair, citing possible witness tampering and obstruction of justice.

Jan. 17:   In a six-hour deposition for the Jones case, President Clinton denies that he had an affair with Monica Lewinsky.

Jan. 21:   In a bombshell story, the Washington Post discloses the Lewinsky affair and the Starr investigation, touching off a media frenzy and the biggest crisis of the Clinton Presidency.

Jan. 26:   In a forceful televised denial following a White House event, President Clinton says that he "never had sexual relations with that woman, Ms. Lewinsky," and that he "never told anyone to lie."

Jan. 27:   Hillary Clinton appears on the "Today" show and blames her husband's problems on a "vast right-wing conspiracy."

Jan. 29:   U.S. District Judge Susan Webber Wright, ruling in the Paula Jones sexual harassment case, excludes all evidence relating to Monica Lewinsky, saying it is not "essential to the core issues" in the lawsuit.

Feb. 3:   Wanted Democratic fund-raiser Charlie Trie returns to the U.S. from China and Macau and surrenders to the FBI.

Feb. 11:   Attorney General Reno asks for an independent counsel to probe Interior Secretary Bruce Babbitt's role in his department's decision to reject a casino application opposed by major Democratic Party contributors.

Feb. 18:   Democratic Party fund-raiser Maria Hsia is indicted by a federal grand jury on charges of arranging to disguise illegal campaign contributions growing out of a fund-raising trip by Vice President Gore to the Hsi Lai Buddhist Temple in California.

March 5: Senator Thompson's Governmental Affairs Committee votes out a 1,100-page report chronicling massive campaign finance abuses during the 1996 presidential race. At a Washington grand jury, in a plea bargain with federal prosecutors, Democratic fund-raiser Johnny Chung is charged with funneling illegal contributions to the Clinton-Gore campaign.

March 8: Jim McDougal, 57, dies after a heart attack in a Texas prison, where he was serving a three-year Whitewater fraud sentence.

March 15: Former White House volunteer Kathleen Willey appears on "60 Minutes" and says that President Clinton made a crude sexual advance and groped her at the White House, and that his associates later sought to assure her silence.

March 20: President Clinton's lawyers invoke executive privilege for senior aides before the Starr grand jury in the Lewinsky obstruction probe.

April 1: Federal Judge Susan Webber Wright of Arkansas dismisses the Paula Jones sexual harassment suit against Bill Clinton, ruling that Mrs. Jones had failed to demonstrate emotional or career harm. The President's spokesman declares "vindication."

April 13: Jeff Gerth of the New York Times reports that the Clinton White House approved the transfer of missile technology to China at the behest of a major Democratic party donor, sparking a new campaign-finance controversy.

April 21: The Clinton Administration invokes a new "protective function" privilege to prevent Secret Service officers from testifying before the Starr grand jury in the Lewinsky matter.

April 24: Attorney General Reno confirms that Charles La Bella, installed only seven months earlier to inject credibility into the Justice Department's listless campaign-finance investigation, is departing to become interim U.S. Attorney in San Diego.

May 5: U.S. District Judge Norma Holloway Johnson rejects President Clinton's effort to use executive privilege and attorney-client privilege to block testimony by senior aides in the Monica Lewinsky investigation.

May 22: Judge Johnson rejects the administration's claim of a protective function privilege for the Secret Service. The Justice Department readies an appeal.

June 2: Monica Lewinsky fires loquacious California malpractice lawyer William Ginsburg and hires veteran Washington attorneys Jacob Stein and Plato Cacheris. Negotiations on immunity for Ms. Lewinsky, stalled for five months, resume.

June 4: The Supreme Court rejects Independent Counsel Starr's request for fast-track hearings on attorney-client and protective function privilege, remanding the matters to the U.S. Court of Appeals.

June 25: Four months into a two-year Whitewater fraud sentence, and after serving 18 months in prison for refusing to talk to an Arkansas grand jury about Bill Clinton, Susan McDougal is released from jail by a federal judge due to medical problems. She faces embezzlement charges in California unrelated to Whitewater, and an obstruction prosecution by Mr. Starr in Arkansas.

July 1: U.S. District Court Judge James Robertson throws out Mr. Starr's tax evasion case against Webster Hubbell, saying the Independent Counsel strayed too far from his mandate. Mr. Starr says he will appeal.

July 7:   A three-judge panel of the U.S. Court of Appeals for the D.C. Circuit rejects a Justice Department appeal on protective function privilege.

July 16:   In a day of high legal drama, the full U.S. Court of Appeals for the D.C. Circuit refuses to reconsider the decision by its three-judge panel ordering the Secret Service to testify in the Lewinsky matter. The White House rushes an emergency petition to Chief Justice William Rehnquist, asking him to issue a stay and block testimony.

July 17:   Chief Justice Rehnquist declines to intervene in the protective function matter. Within hours, Secret Service officers are testifying before the Starr grand jury.

July 23:   The New York Times discloses that departing Justice Department task force head, Charles La Bella, has delivered a report to Attorney General Reno strongly advising her to seek an independent counsel in the campaign-finance affair.

July 25:   The White House reveals that Independent Counsel Starr, in a dramatic and unprecedented maneuver, has subpoenaed President Clinton to testify before the grand jury in the Lewinsky matter. Mr. Clinton had rebuffed earlier requests for voluntary testimony. The historic subpoena is later withdrawn after the President agrees to testify.

July 27:   The U.S. Court of Appeals for the D.C. Circuit rejects administration arguments that President Clinton's conversations with White House lawyers are shielded by attorney-client privilege, clearing the way for Mr. Starr to question deputy counsel Bruce Lindsey, a key Clinton confidant.

July 28:	Monica Lewinsky is granted blanket immunity in exchange for full and truthful testimony before the Starr grand jury.
July 31:	Paula Jones asks a U.S. appeals panel in St. Louis to reinstate her sexual harassment case against Mr. Clinton.
Aug. 6:	Monica Lewinsky testifies before the Starr grand jury. According to news accounts, she details numerous sexual liaisons with the President, recants her sworn testimony in the Paula Jones lawsuit denying an affair, and contradicts sworn and televised statements by Mr. Clinton. On Capitol Hill, the House Government Reform and Oversight Committee votes to hold Attorney General Reno in contempt of Congress for failing to turn over memos by FBI Director Louis Freeh and Justice task force head Charles La Bella concerning the campaign-finance probe. The sanction awaits a vote by the full House.
Aug. 17:	President Clinton testifies, via closed-circuit television from the White House, for four hours before the Starr grand jury. In an angry speech to the nation that night, he admits to an "inappropriate relationship" with Ms. Lewinsky, denies criminal wrongdoing, and attacks Independent Counsel Starr. Political support begins to erode.
Aug. 20:	Interrupting his vacation in Martha's Vineyard, Mass., President Clinton announces missile strikes against "terrorist-related facilities" in Afghanistan and Sudan.
Sept. 9:	Independent Counsel Starr sends Congress a report containing, in the words of his mandate, "substantial and credible information" that "may constitute grounds for impeachment" of President Clinton.
Sept. 10:	Mr. Clinton apologizes to Senate Democrats and his Cabinet for his misconduct in the Lewinsky affair.

Sept. 11:   Mr. Clinton apologizes to religious leaders at a national prayer breakfast, telling them, "I have sinned." The House of Representatives votes to release the 445-page Starr report, posting it on the Internet. With its explicit sexual details, the report draws a storm of controversy and criticism.

Sept. 21:   The House releases the videotape of President Clinton's Aug. 17 grand jury testimony.

Oct. 2:   The House releases 4,600 pages of supporting evidence from the Starr referral, including transcripts of taped conversations between Monica Lewinsky and Linda Tripp.

Oct. 4:   Pornographer Larry Flynt, publisher of Hustler magazine, places an ad in the Washington Post, offering up to $1 million for "evidence of illicit sexual relations" with top federal lawmakers.

Oct. 8:   The House votes 258-176 to open an impeachment inquiry into the President, only the third such proceeding in U.S. history. Thirty-one Democrats join Republicans in voting for the inquiry.

Oct. 30:   A federal judge supervising Mr. Starr's Washington grand jury discloses she has named a "special master" to determine whether the Office of Independent Counsel has illegally leaked secret grand jury information to the media.

Nov. 3:   In an electoral upset, Democrats mount a strong showing in midterm elections. The GOP loses ground in the House, emerging with a slim 12-seat majority; it retains a ten-seat margin in the Senate and a nearly two-to-one edge in governorships.

Nov. 6:   As unrest over GOP electoral losses mounts, House Speaker Newt Gingrich, leader of the Republican resurgence in the House, announces his resignation.

Nov. 9:	Constitutional scholars debate impeachment and censure before the House Judiciary Committee's Subcommittee on the Constitution.
Nov. 13:	President Clinton agrees to pay Paula Jones $850,000 to settle her sexual harassment lawsuit; the President does not admit guilt or offer an apology. In a separate development, Independent Counsel Starr indicts Clinton associate Webster Hubbell a third time, for fraud and obstruction related to investigations into the Castle Grande land scheme in Arkansas; Hillary Clinton figures in the indictment as the Rose Law Firm "billing partner."
Nov. 16:	News reports say that former White House intern Monica Lewinsky has negotiated a seven-figure media deal for book and television rights to her story.
Nov. 17:	The House Judiciary Committee releases 22 hours of secretly recorded conversations between Linda Tripp and Monica Lewinsky.
Nov. 19:	The House Judiciary Committee opens impeachment hearings and calls Independent Counsel Starr as the first witness. Mr. Starr testifies for 12 hours.
Nov. 23:	Whitewater figure Susan McDougal is acquitted in a California court in a fraud and embezzlement case unrelated to Mr. Starr's inquiry.
Nov. 24:	Following a preliminary review, Attorney General Reno declines to name an independent counsel to investigate whether Vice President Gore lied to federal investigators about his knowledge of 1996 fund-raising activities.
Nov. 30:	President Clinton responds to 81 questions from the Judiciary Committee about the Lewinsky matter. Republicans denounce the President's answers as "evasive and legalistic."

Dec. 2:	In a sweeping corruption prosecution brought by Independent Counsel Donald Smaltz, former Agriculture Secretary Mike Espy is acquitted on all 30 counts of illegally accepting $33,000 in gifts and travel from companies regulated by the Agriculture Department.
Dec. 7:	Following a preliminary review, Attorney General Reno declines to name an independent counsel to investigate whether President Clinton or Vice President Gore illegally used 1996 campaign funds for television advertising.
Dec. 8:	The White House opens its impeachment defense with an apologetic statement from Special Counsel Greg Craig saying the President's conduct was "sinful" but not impeachable.
Dec. 9:	Despite an appeal from White House Counsel Charles Ruff to spare the nation the "horror" of a Senate trial, the Republican majority of the House Judiciary Committee proposes four articles of impeachment, charging President Clinton with obstruction of justice, abuse of power, and two counts of perjury.
Dec. 10:	Following closing arguments from Democratic and Republican chief counsels, the Judiciary Committee begins final debate on the articles of impeachment.
Dec. 11:	In a party-line vote, the Judiciary Committee approves three articles of impeachment alleging perjury and obstruction of justice and sends them to the full House for consideration.
Dec. 12:	The Judiciary Committee approves a fourth article of impeachment alleging abuse of power. Democratic efforts to censure, rather than impeach, are defeated.
Dec. 16:	As the full House prepares to debate the articles of impeachment, President Clinton orders airstrikes

against Iraq for violating United Nations sanctions. Impeachment debate is delayed. Some Republicans accuse the President of using the airstrikes to divert attention from impeachment proceedings.

Dec. 18:   Impeachment debate begins in the House, reflecting harsh partisan divisions.

Dec. 19:   In a day of turmoil and high political drama, the House of Representatives approves two articles of impeachment, for perjury before a grand jury and obstruction of justice, against President Clinton. It rejects two other articles alleging perjury in the Paula Jones civil deposition and abuse of power. In a dramatic announcement before the House vote, spurred by reports of an impending story by Hustler magazine publisher Larry Flynt, Speaker-elect Bob Livingston says he will resign because of marital infidelity.

1999

Jan. 7:   The trial of William Jefferson Clinton on two articles of impeachment officially opens with Supreme Court Chief Justice William Rehnquist sworn in as presiding officer. All 100 Senators are sworn in. House Judiciary Committee Chairman Henry Hyde, leader of the thirteen House "managers" prosecuting the case, reads the impeachment charges.

Jan. 8:   Senators approve a bipartisan plan for the trial of President Clinton, deferring the contentious issue of witnesses until after opening arguments.

Jan. 12:   President Clinton pays Paula Jones $850,000 to settle her sexual harassment lawsuit.

Jan. 14:   The House managers open their case, charging that President Clinton betrayed his oath of office and broke the law in attempting to cover up his affair with Ms. Lewinsky.

Jan. 19:   The White House opens its defense of President Clinton, saying his behavior, while deplorable, does not rise to the level of impeachment. Later, the President delivers the State of the Union address.

Jan. 21:   Following a scathing attack on the evidence presented by the House managers, the White House closes its defense, saying the charges are false and do not warrant impeachment.

Jan. 22:   Under questioning by the Senators, the House managers and White House defense team clash over interpretations of the evidence. Democrat Robert Byrd of West Virginia announces he will offer a motion to dismiss the case.

Jan. 27:   Following debate behind closed doors to bring the trial to an end, the Senate votes to take videotaped depositions from three witnesses—Ms. Lewinsky, White House aide Sidney Blumenthal, and Clinton friend Vernon Jordan. The Senate rejects a Democratic motion to dismiss the perjury and obstruction charges.

Jan. 29:   Attorney General Reno declines to name an independent counsel to investigate perjury allegations against White House aide Harold Ickes related to the 1996 campaign.

Feb. 3:   Former Justice Department campaign finance task force head Charles La Bella resigns as acting U.S. Attorney in San Diego, saying he no longer has the confidence of Attorney General Reno and top Justice Department officials.

Feb. 4:   The Senate rejects calling live witnesses but allows videotaped testimony to be shown.

Feb. 6:   Clips from the videotaped depositions of Ms. Lewinsky, Mr. Blumenthal and Mr. Jordan are presented by both sides in the case.

Feb. 8:	House managers and White House lawyers present closing arguments.
Feb. 12:	Following deliberations behind closed doors, the Senate acquits President Clinton on both articles of impeachment. The vote on the first article, perjury, is 45 guilty, 55 not guilty; the vote on the second article, obstruction, is 50 guilty, 50 not guilty. A two-thirds majority of 67 votes is necessary for conviction.
Feb. 16:	In Little Rock, Judge Susan Webber Wright says she is considering holding President Clinton in contempt for providing misleading testimony in his deposition in the Paula Jones lawsuit.
Feb. 19:	The Wall Street Journal reports allegations by Arkansas businesswoman Juanita Broaddrick that she was raped by then-Arkansas Attorney General Bill Clinton in 1978. Lawyers for Mr. Clinton deny the charge.
Feb. 24:	Hearings into the controversial Independent Counsel Statute open before the Senate Governmental Affairs Committee. With the statute set to expire in June, a wide array of politicians and pundits pronounce it dead. In a separate development, after holding the story for more than a month and under mounting pressure from competitors, NBC airs a report on Clinton accuser Juanita Broaddrick.
March 8:	Whitewater figure Susan McDougal goes on trial in Little Rock, charged with contempt and obstruction for failing to answer questions from a federal grand jury about Bill Clinton's knowledge of illegal Whitewater financial transactions.
March 11:	Starr spokesman Charles Bakaly resigns amid charges that he leaked information to the New York Times and then lied about it when questioned under oath.
March 18:	Testifying at the Susan McDougal trial, Deputy Inde-

pendent Counsel Hickman Ewing discloses that a draft indictment of Mrs. Clinton in Whitewater matters was prepared but never presented to a grand jury.

March 31: President Clinton tells CBS's Dan Rather that he does not regard impeachment as "some great badge of shame" but is "honored" to have had "the opportunity to defend the Constitution."

April 11: Ms. McDougal's trial ends with acquittal on an obstruction charge and a hung jury on criminal contempt for refusing to answer questions from a federal grand jury.

April 12: U.S. District Judge Susan Webber Wright finds President Clinton in contempt for "intentionally false" statements under oath and "willful failure" to testify truthfully in the Paula Jones sexual harrasment case. Judge Wright's verdict is the first ever to hold a U.S. president in contempt of court.

May 25: Rep. Chris Cox's Select Committee on U.S. National Security publishes a detailed report on Chinese espionage coups. The Cox inquiry grew out of reports that a top Democratic Party contributor's donations may have influenced White House decisions on China.

June 16: Vice President Al Gore announces his candidacy for the Democratic presidential nomination.

June 30: The Independent Counsel law expires. Congress does not renew it. Independent Counsel Starr's investigation continues, but there will be no new counsels.

July 6: News reports disclose that in a highly unusual proceeding, former Starr spokesman Charles Bakaly has been charged with criminal contempt in a sealed court filing. Mr. Bakaly had been the target of a Justice Department probe into whether he lied under oath about leaks to the media in the Lewinsky affair.

| July 7: | On a farm outside Oneonta, New York, Hillary Rodham Clinton announces her bid for a seat in the U.S. Senate. |

July 7:   On a farm outside Oneonta, New York, Hillary Rodham Clinton announces her bid for a seat in the U.S. Senate.

July 29:   Judge Wright of Arkansas orders President Clinton to pay $90,686 in sanctions to Paula Jones and her attorneys for lying under oath in the Jones case.

July 30:   Linda Tripp, whose secretly recorded tapes of telephone conversations with Monica Lewinsky played a key role in the impeachment affair, is indicted by a Maryland grand jury on charges she violated state wiretapping laws.

Sept. 27:   Ms. Tripp files a civil lawsuit accusing White House and Defense Department officials of unlawfully disclosing confidential records in a campaign to discredit her.

Oct. 18:   Kenneth Starr steps down as independent counsel. Robert Ray, an experienced federal prosecutor, is sworn in as his successor.

Nov. 19:   In a case that saw testimony involving senior Democratic National Committee and labor figures, a federal jury convicts former Teamsters' political director William Hamilton on multiple counts of fraud and embezzlement.

2000

March 2:   A federal jury convicts Gore associate Maria Hsia on five felony counts related to illegal contributions in the Buddhist Temple fund-raiser.

March 16:   In the Filegate affair, Independent Counsel Ray files a report stating there is "no substantial and credible evidence" that President or Mrs. Clinton sought information on Republican figures contained in confidential FBI background checks of former White House personnel.

April 13:   Speaking to a meeting of the American Society of Newspaper Editors, President Clinton declares that he is "not ashamed of the fact that they impeached me. That was their decision, not mine, and it was wrong."

May 24:   Maryland prosecutors drop their wiretapping case against Linda Tripp.

June 21:   The head of the Justice Department's campaign task force recommends that a special prosecutor be appointed to investigate whether Vice President Al Gore lied about his knowledge of the Buddhist Temple affair and other matters. Attorney General Reno later rejects the recommendation.

June 22:   Reporting on the White House Travel Office affair, Independent Counsel Ray declines prosecution of Mrs. Clinton. Mr. Ray notes that while there was "substantial evidence" that Mrs. Clinton had played a role in the firings of Travel Office personnel, he could not prove beyond a reasonable doubt that she had made false statements under oath.

June 30:   A panel of the Arkansas Supreme Court moves to strip Bill Clinton of his license to practice law. The suit accuses the President of "dishonesty, deceit, fraud and misrepresentation" in the Jones case. Mr. Clinton is given the opportunity to defend himself in court.

Sept. 11:   In a case growing out of allegations of improper Chinese influence on the U.S. electoral process, the prosecution of former Los Alamos physicist Wen Ho Lee collapses. Mr. Lee pleads guilty to a minor charge and leaves jail.

Sept. 20:   Reporting on the Whitewater land deal, Independent Counsel Ray releases a statement saying there is "insufficient evidence" to bring criminal charges against the Clintons. "The coverup worked," the Journal declares in an editorial.

Oct. 6:	Former Starr spokesman Charles Bakaly is acquitted of contempt of court charges in a case stemming from allegations that he lied under oath about news leaks to the media.
Nov. 7:	In one of the closest elections in U.S. history, George W. Bush wins Florida's twenty-five electoral votes, and thus the presidency, by a tiny margin. Al Gore launches a lengthy recount battle. In New York, Hillary Clinton wins a seat in the U.S. Senate.
Nov. 17:	Following a fierce legal battle in the lower courts, the Florida Supreme Court blocks Florida's secretary of state from certifying Mr. Bush the victor by 930 votes, following the counting of overseas ballots.
Nov. 19:	Charles Ruff, former White House counsel and chief counsel for the president during impeachment, dies in his sleep.
Dec. 4:	With battles waging in the Florida lower courts and the Florida legislature moving to take action, the U.S. Supreme Court instructs the Florida Supreme Court to reconsider its ruling.
Dec. 12:	With an electoral college deadline looming and Vice President Gore pressing appeals and recounts activity, the U.S. Supreme Court moves decisively, ruling that the Florida high court's rulings favoring Mr. Gore are unconstitutional.
Dec. 13:	Mr. Gore concedes. George W. Bush is president-elect.
Dec. 19:	Facing possible indictment for perjury and obstruction by Independent Counsel Ray after leaving office, President Clinton tells CBS News he would "stand and fight" the charges.
Dec. 22	President Clinton pardons Archie Schaffer, a Tyson Foods executive caught up in Independent Counsel

Donald Smaltz's probe of Agriculture Secretary Mike Espy.

2001

Jan. 19   In a deal with Independent Counsel Ray, President Clinton admits that he made false statements in the Monica Lewinsky case and surrenders his law license for five years. Mr. Ray declines prosecution of Mr. Clinton for perjury and obstruction of justice. The agreement effectively ends the Whitewater investigation, which began with questions about the Clintons' land dealings in Arkansas but expanded into Oval Office conduct.

Jan. 20   Hours before ending his term in office, President Clinton issues 140 pardons. Included on the list is the Clintons' former Whitewater Development Co. partner, Susan McDougal.

George W. Bush is sworn in as 43rd President of the United States.

Acknowledgments

"A Journal Briefing — Whitewater" — six volumes and a CD-ROM — represents the efforts of many people at The Wall Street Journal. This project was mostly done in-house, which is to say, it was written, edited, proofread, designed and laid out by energetic newspaper men and women who developed and executed it at the same time as they were putting out a daily newspaper. Thanks to all of them.

Following is a list of the writers, editors, production staff and office assistants who research, write, edit and produce The Journal's U.S. editorial pages every day. Many of their bios are available on the editorial page's Web site, OpinionJournal.com.

Robert L. Bartley, Editor
Daniel Henninger, Deputy Editor, Editorial Page

April Anderson
Max Boot
Patricia Broderick
Ginny Bubek
Ned Crabb
Ken De Witt
Jacqueline Dowdell
Erich Eichman
Kate Flatley

Paul A. Gigot
Marian Hieda
Holman W. Jenkins Jr.
Joann Joseph
Michael Judge
Melanie Kirkpatrick
Susan Lee
Collin Levey
William McGurn

George Melloan
Brendan Miniter
Micah Morrison
Carol Muller
Mary O'Grady
Maria Perignon
Rob Pollock

Dorothy Rabinowitz
Jason Riley
Judy Rodriguez
Claudia Rosett
Nancy deWolf Smith
Kimberley Strassel

Thanks also to colleagues from other parts of Dow Jones & Company, including: Rod Copeland, Frank Gallucci, Pamela Gaudette, Susan Lillo, Paul Martin Jr., Marie Sticco, and Hector Santiago and the Mail Center staff.

Index

A

Abraham, Spencer (Senator), 60

Abrams, Elliott, 51

AcrossAsia, 197–198

AFL-CIO, campaign finance investigation concerning, 96, 114, 120–122, 167–169

Altman, Roger, 51

American Bar Association, 76–77

American Spectator magazine, 74, 190

Amodeo, Anthony ("Chickie"), 235

Anderson, Kate, 163

Ashcroft, John, 250, 275, 319

      nomination as Attorney General, 349–354

B

Babbitt, Bruce, 223

Babcock, Charles, 88

Bakaly, Charles III, 189-192

Baker, James, 280

Bartley, Robert, 132-134, 157, 178-181, 189-192, 203, 214-217, 239-242, 246-249, 316-319, 331, 345-348

Battalino, Barbara (Dr.), 83-84

Beckel, Bob, 274

Begala, Paul, 279

Bennett, Robert, 1-3

Bennett, William, 209

Ben Veniste, Richard, 119, 169

Berger, Sandy, 45, 227

Berman, Ronald (Representative), 83

Blair, Jim, 13

Blumenthal, Sidney, 151, 164

Bohener, John (Representative), 75

Boies, David, 268-269, 274, 280, 298-300, 320, 329

Bork, Robert, 76, 248, 318

Bowles, Erskine, 223

Boxer, Barbara (Senator), 85, 103, 336

Bradley, Bill, 257

Brazile, Donna, 248

Breaux, John (Senator), 83-84, 86, 104, 257

Breaux Medicare Commission, 15, 216

Breslin, Jimmy, 63-64

Breyer, Stephen (Justice), 321, 326, 330

Brooks, David, 357

Brown, Ron, 41, 45

Bruce, Carol Elder, 223

Bryan, Richard (Senator), 85, 103

Buddhist Temple investigation, 41, 43, 53, 91-92, 123, 137-139, 141, 178-181, 204, 212, 222-224

Burton, Charles (Judge), 259, 265, 269, 299

Burton, Dan (Representative), 107, 139, 162, 180, 196-199, 353

Bush, George W., 133-134, 143

    Clinton's commentary on, 206-207

    debate performances of, 241

    drunk driving charges against, 232, 243, 246-249

    Florida election controversy, 255-257, 262-269, 295-297

    nomination of, 203

Bush, Jeb, 264
Butterworth, Robert, 271-272, 313-315, 317
Buyer, Steve (Representative), 125-126
Byrd, Robert (Senator), 7, 35

C

Cameron, Carl, 46
Campaign finance investigations
    Buddhist Temple investigation, 41, 43, 53, 91-92, 123, 137-139, 141, 178-181
    Chinese contributions investigated, 2, 18-20, 33, 44-47
    Congressional investigation of, 106
    Freeh memo concerning, 172-177
    Ickes' role in, 237-238
    Justice Department's role in, 96-101, 107, 165-166
    La Bella's role in, 72, 79-80
    review of, 165-166
    Teamsters union ties to Democrats and, 53, 96, 113-115, 120-122, 167-169
Capital Management Service, 11
Carey, Ron, 96, 113-115, 120-122, 167-169
Carnahan, Jean, 250, 275, 319
Carville, James, 368
Castellano, Paul, 235
Castle Grande scandal, 14, 27, 51
CATO Institute, 191
Central Intelligence Agency, security lapses in, 159-161
Chavez, Linda, 349
Chernomyrdin, Victor, 240-241
Cheney, Dick, 203
    Clinton's commentary on, 206-207
Childs, William (Judge), 247
China
    espionage activities of, 44-47, 78-81, 159-161, 225-228
    U.S. relations with, 18-23, 40-43
    Chinese campaign contributions, investigation of, 2, 18-23, 33
Christopher, Warren, 274, 284
Chung, Johnny, 18-20, 41-43, 46, 80, 225

Citizens Against Government Waste, 117
Citizenship USA program, 218-221
Clark, Nikki Ann (Judge), 317-318
Clinton, Hillary Rodham
        campaign finance investigations and, 142-143
        elected as New York senator, 250
        Ickes as consultant to, 234-238
        indictment drafted against, 8-9, 125-128
        senatorial campaign of, 55-56, 62-71, 107, 154, 206, 232
        sworn in as New York senator, 338-340
        Travelgate scandal and, 190-191
        videotaped depositions of, 12
        Whitewater investigation into, 106
Clinton, William Jefferson
        ABA keynote address, 76-77
        Bartley assessment of, 214-217
        campaign finance investigation and, 100-101
        China policy of, 18-23, 40-43
        commentary on Republicans by, 205-207
        contempt charges against, 31-32, 36-39
        disbarment action against, 170-172
        Esquire Magazine interview, 333-337, 346-347
        final policy initiatives of, 345-348
        foreign policy assessed, 15-20
        impeachment of, 1-2, 333-336
        indictment considered against, 331-337
        legacy of, 355-366
        Madison bank scandal and, 9-14
        "Nightline" program on, 341-344
        perjury charges against, 11-12, 56, 82-86, 102-107, 143-144, 153, 331-332
        post-presidential legal challenges to, 331-332
        Ray plea bargain with, 367-369
        revisionism concerning, 152-158
        role in 2000 presidential campaign, 123-124
Coble, Howard (representative), 135-136
Coelho, Tony, 93-94, 121-122
Cohen, Richard, 151
Coia, Arthur, 236-237

Conason, Joe, 153–158
Connolly, Tom, 247
Conrad, Kent (Senator), 86, 104
Conrad, Robert J., 165, 178, 195–199, 200–202, 204
Cox, Chris (Representative), 31–32, 44–47, 226–227
Cudahy, Richard, 82
Cunningham, William, 235
Cuomo, Mario, 322

D

Dale, Billy, 52, 74, 151, 190
Daley, William, 259, 275, 279–280
D'Amato, Al, 71
Davis, Martin, 114–115, 168–169, 350–351
Dean, John, 28
DeGrinney, John, 247
Democratic National Committee, campaign finance investigation
    into, 53, 96, 113–115, 120–122, 167–169, 350–351
Dershowitz, Alan, 269, 274
Deutch, John, 159
Deutsch, Peter, 270
Dodd, Chris (Senator), 58
Doerr, John, 58
Dole, Robert, 134
Donovan, Ray, 33
Douglass, Dexter, 269, 283
Drusman, Marzuki, 197
Du Pont, Pete, 316

E

Edelman, Marion Wright, 70
Eggleston, Neil, 190–191
Ekberg, Gregory, 195
E-mail investigation, 162–164, 192–195, 223–224
Epstein, Edward Jay, 89–94
Epstein, Julian, 189
Esposito, William, 171–172

Ewing, Hickman Jr., 9

F

Fabiani, Mark, 265
Farbrother, Douglas, 219-221
Fay, Peter (Judge), 82
Federal Internal Security Act (FISA), 79
Filegate investigation, 125-126, 150-151
Florida election controversy, 250-254
    ballot recount efforts, 255-257, 262-281, 289-294, 298-308
    state court intervention in, 282-288, 307-308
    Supreme Court intervention in, 258-261, 295-297, 308, 313-315, 320-330
Flowers, Gennifer, 342
Foster, Vincent, 12-13, 52, 127-128
Freeh, Louis, 5, 34, 46, 52-53, 72
    campaign finance investigation memo, 97-101, 141, 165, 171-178, 191-192, 196, 201-202, 222-224, 353
    Lee investigation and, 228
Friedman, Paul (Judge), 135-136, 146
Fuerth, Leon, 92
Fukuyama, Francis, 355-358
Fund, John, 247, 283

G

Gage, Robert, 115
Gallagher, Neal, 172
Geragos, Mark, 7-9, 12, 14
Gergen, David, 343
Gigot, Paul, on Hillary Clinton Senate campaign, 59-61, 69-71, 292-294
Gilligan, James, 193
Gingrich, Newt, 45, 134, 248
Ginsburg, Ruth Bader (Justice), 314, 321
Giroir, Joseph, 41-42, 46, 80, 197, 202, 352-354
Giuliani, Rudy (Mayor), 61, 71, 154
Glaeser, Edward, 256, 259, 262-263

Glenn, John, 19

Glicken, Howard, 136, 146

Goaes, Ed, 53

Good, Terry, 150

Gorbachev, Mikhail, 22

Gore, Al

    campaign finance investigations and, 2, 46, 87-94, 123-124, 136-144, 164, 178-181, 196-199, 222-224

    campaign issues of, 243-245

    character assessment of, 218-221, 239-242

    Clinton's links to, 133-134

    concession speech by, 328-330

    Florida election controversy and, 255-257, 262-269, 273-284, 289-291, 295-300, 311-322

    fund-raising investigations of, 53

    Lieberman picked as running mate, 208-213

    mining properties of, 182-188

    nomination of, 203

    presidential campaign launched by, 55-58

    senatorial campaign of Hillary Clinton and, 60-61

    Teamsters' links to, 168-169

Gore, Albert Senior (Senator), 87-94

Gorton, Slade (Senator), 60

Graham, Lindsey (Representative), 151

Green, Ernest, 139

Greenspan, Alan, 347, 360

Griesa, Thomas (Judge), 115, 122

Grove, Andrew, 58

H

Hale, David, 11, 25, 230

Hall, Sheryl, 194-195

Hamilton, William, 96, 113-115, 120-122, 168-169

Hammer, Armand, 87-94, 182-188, 212

Hancock, Paul, 313-315

Harlan, Dwight, 197-198

Harris, Katherine

    Florida ballot controversy, 253-254, 265, 267-269, 273-276,

306-308

state court intervention in certification process, 282-284

Supreme Court intervention and, 295, 314, 316, 320, 329

Hartigan, John, 12-13

Hartigan, Laura, 115

Hatch, Orrin (Senator), 123-124, 129-134

Heissner, Karl, 163

Heritage Foundation, 117

Hill, Anita, 248

Hoffa, James, 114, 121-122, 167-169

Holder, Eric, 353

Holtzman, Liz, 119

Hoover, J. Edgar, 90

Howard, George Jr., 7

Hsia, Maria

    Buddist Temple scandal and, 41, 43, 53, 91-92, 123

    trial of, 136-139, 146, 165-166

Huang, John

    Buddhist Temple incident and, 53, 92, 137-138

    campaign finance investigations and, 46, 143, 197-198, 202, 352-354

    Justice Department investigation of, 80

    U.S.-Chinese relations and, 41-43

Hubbell, Webster

    address to ABA, 76-77

    Castle Grande scandal and, 27

    Clinton testimony concerning, 200-202

    guilty plea of, 51

    at Justice Department, 34-35, 153

    Starr indictment of, 13-14, 48, 128, 152

    trial of, 74, 135-136, 146-147, 353

    Whitewater investigation and, 230

Huber, Carolyn, 125-127

Hughes, Karen, 248

Hughes Electronics, 45

I

Ickes, Harold, 63, 126, 142, 234-238

Immigration and Naturalization Service, Congressional investigation of, 218-221
Impeachment
    aftermath of, 1-2
    public opinion polls on, 53-54
Independent Counsel Act
    Congressional hearings on, 3-5, 31, 33-35, 49-54
    opposition to, 179
Ingersoll, Laura, 98-99
Internal Revenue Service (IRS), Clinton "enemies" list and audits by, 28-30, 117-119
Intriago scandal, 53
Iorio, Pam, 269

J

Jackson, Jesse, 309-312
Jansing, Chris, 66
Jimenez, Mark, 136, 146
Ji Shengde, 18-20, 42
Jobs, Steve, 58
John Paul II (Pope), 22
Johnson, Norma Holloway (Judge), 74, 135-136, 145-148, 163-164, 190
Jones, Paula, 11, 24-25, 32
Jordan, Vernon, 136
Judicial Watch, 150-151
Justice Department
    Ashcroft nomination and, 352-354
    campaign finance investigations and role of, 96-101, 107, 165-166, 178-181
    Clinton presidency and, 34-35

K

Kaiser, Robert, 209
Kamarck, Elaine, 219-221
Kamiya, Gary, 248
Kanchanalak, Pauline, 136

Kantor, Mickey, 90-91

Kelly, Michael, 278

Kendall, David, 13, 170-172, 368

Kennedy, Henry H. Jr. (Judge), 29, 136, 146

Kerrey, Bob (Senator), 323-324

Kettle, Martin, 66

Khalil, Abdul Raouf, 53

Knight, Peter, 92-94

Kohl, Herbert (Senator), 83, 85-86, 103, 336

Kornblum, Allan, 79

Kosovo bombings, assessment of, 15-17

L

Labarga, Jorge (Judge), 271, 283-284

La Bella, Charles, 34-35, 46, 52-53, 72, 80

    campaign finance investigation and, 98-101, 200-202, 237-238, 353

    independent counsel memo of, 123-124, 140-143, 163-164, 178, 191-192, 196

Laborers International Union of North America (LIUNA), 236-237

Lake, Celinda, 53

Lamberth, Royce (Judge), 142, 149-151, 163-164, 193-195, 223-224

Lambuth, Betty, 151, 194-195

Landmark Legal Foundation, 28-29, 117-119

Landow, Nathan, 91-93

Lautenberg, Frank (Senator), 86, 104

Lazio, Rick, 61, 71

Leach, Jim, 12

Lee, Robert W. (Judge), 268, 270-272

Lee, Wen Ho, 45, 78-81, 204, 225-228

Lehane, Chris, 247-248

LePore, Theresa, 259, 264-265, 284, 306

Lerach, Bill, 58

Levin, Carl, 19

Levin, Mark, 29-30

Lewinsky, Monica, 11, 25

    Clinton testimony concerning, 31-32, 82-84, 128, 335-336

    Ray plea bargain with Clinton over, 367-369

Tripp and, 73-75

Lewis, Anthony, 154

Lewis, Jean, 9-10, 51, 230, 316

Lewis, Terry (Judge), 269, 282-284, 329

Lieberman, Joseph (Senator)

    criticism of Clinton by, 79-81, 85, 98-99, 103, 336

    Florida election controversy and, 318, 322

    nomination as vice presidential candidate, 202, 208-213, 240-241

Lindsay, Mark, 224

Lindsey, Bruce, 41, 46, 80, 202, 353

Lippo Group, 41-42, 92, 196-199, 201, 352-354

Liu Chaoying, 45-46

Livingstone, Craig, 91

Lockhart, Joe, 106

Lofgren, Zoe (Representative), 86, 104

Loral Space & Communications, 33, 42, 45

Lowey, Nita, 63

Lunde, Brian, 63

Luu, Robert, 46-47

Lyndon, Neil, 89

Lyons, Gene, 153-158

M

Madison Bank, 10

Madison Guaranty Savings & Loan

    McDougal testimony on, 6-7, 9-10, 14, 25-26

    Whitewater investigation and, 229-231

Mapili, Maria, 99

Mazo, Earl, 251

McAuliffe, Terry, 63, 114-115, 121-122, 168-169, 349-351

McCain, John, 139, 143

    Babbit investigation and, 223

    Clinton's commentary on, 206

McDermott, Jim (Representative), 74

McDermott, Michael (Jdget), 271-272

McDougal, James, 7, 9-11, 25, 64, 152, 156-157, 229-231

McDougal, Susan

acquittal on criminal contempt charges, 1-2, 24-27
Clinton pardon of, 368-369
trial on criminal contempt charges, 6-14, 152, 156-157
Whitewater investigation and, 229-230
McDowell, Gary, 1-3, 56, 82-84
McEntee, Gerald, 350
McGurn, William, 28-30
McLarty, Mack, 41-42
McLendon, Marna, 75
Meehan, Marty, 119
Meese, Ed, 33, 51
Mehta, Nancy, 7-9
Meissner, Doris, 219-221
Messinger, Ruth, 63
Meyer Suozzi law firm, 236, 238
Middlebrooks, Donald M. (Judge), 259-260
Middleton, Mark, 41-42, 139
Milken, Michael, 93
Miller, Alan, 141
Miller, John (Judge), 283
Mills, Cheryl, 150-151, 162
Milosevic, Slobodan, 16-17
Mitchell, Cleta, 285-288
Mitchell, John, 51
Molten Metals Technology, 93
Morgenthau, Robert, 53
Morris, Dick, 63, 343. 359-362
Morrison, Alexia, 33
Morrison, Micah, 8-14, 19, 24-27, 87-94, 105-107, 113-115, 152-158,
182-188, 216-217, 234-238
Moynihan, Daniel Patrick (Senator), 55, 62, 65-66, 70-71
Murray, Patty (Senator), 58
Myers, Dee Dee, 341-342

N

Nader, Ralph, 241
National Association for the Advancement of Colored People
(NAACP), 256

National Performance Review, 219

New Republic, The, 60

Ng Lap Seng, 19-20, 22, 41-42, 46, 98

Nixon, Richard, 22, 28, 51, 119, 251-252, 258, 275

Noonan, Peggy, 55, 65-68, 154, 246-247, 277-281, 301-305, 338-340

Norton, Gale, 349-351

Novak, Robert, 270

O

Occidental Petroleum Corporation, 87-94, 182-188, 212

O'Leary, Hazel, 226

Olson, Barbara K., 125-128

Olson, Ted, 33

Oreskes, Michael, 153-154

P

Panetta, Leon, 142, 343-344

Parker, Roberta, 99

Parkinson, Larry, 172

Pataki, George (Governor), 71

Patkus, Michael, 11

Philbro-Salomon, 12

Posner, Richard, 155-158

Potts, Stephen, 121

Provenzano, Anthony, 236

R

Rabinowitz, Dorothy, 341-344

Radek, Lee, 98, 141, 171-172, 179-181

Ray, Robert

    e-mail scandal investigation, 224

    indictment considered against Clinton, 331-337

    investigations by, 139, 144, 181, 191

    named Independent Counsel, 95-96, 102-107, 125-127

    plea bargain with Clinton, 367-369

    Whitewater investigation ended by, 229-231

Reagan, Ronald, 22

Real, Manuel L. (Judge), 20

Rehnquist, William (Chief Justice), 320-322, 328-330

Reich, Robert, 343

Reid, Chip, 66

Rempel, Bill, 141

Reno, Janet
    campaign fundraising investigations and, 43, 46, 142, 165-166, 173-181, 191, 196, 204, 222-224
    Chinese espionage investigation and, 79-81, 226
    Clinton's China policy and, 41, 43
    special prosecutor appointments by, 52
    tenure at Justice Department of, 34-35, 51

Resolution Trust Corporation, 2, 9, 26, 230

Revell, Oliver "Buck," 159-161

Riady, James, 42, 46, 80, 92, 139, 196-202, 216-217, 352-354

Riady, Mochtar, 139, 196-199

Rice, Condoleezza, Clinton's commentary on, 206

Rice, Robert, 113-115, 121-122

Richardson, Bill, 44

Rivera, Geraldo, 7

Roberts, Carol, 259, 264, 271

Robertson, James (Judge), 135-136, 146-148

Rogow, Bruce, 284

Rohapaugh, Robin, 270

Rotunda, Ronald D., 145-148

Rudman, Warren (Senator), 80

Runkel, David, 13

S

Saddam Hussein, 16

Sauls, N. Sanders (Judge), 307-308, 314-315, 320, 329

Scaife, Richard, 74, 248

Scalia, Antonin (Justice), 313-314, 321, 324

Schaffer, Archie, 106

Schippers, David, 83, 105, 140-141, 218-221, 224, 335-336

Schumer, Charles, 64, 83

Schwartz, Bernard, 33, 42, 45

Seikaly, Daniel, 79

Sentelle, David, 82

Severin, Jay, 68

Shaheen, Michael, 74, 190

Shays, Chris, 162–164

Sheinkopf, Hank, 63

Shrum, Bob, 248

Skaggs, David (Representative), 117

Slater, Wayne, 248

Smaltz, Donald, 106

Smith, I. C., 97–101

Souter, David (Justice), 315, 321, 326, 330

Specter, Arlen (Senator), 100, 107, 179

Sperry, Paul, 100

Stans, Maurice, 90

Starr, Ken
> assesses his investigation of Clinton, 108–111
> assessment of, 6–7, 152–158, 230, 239–240
> final report on Clinton issued, 48–49
> Freeh letter to, 116
> grand jury testimony leaks alleged against, 116
> immunity to Tripp granted by, 75
> McDougal trial and, 8–9, 12
> misconduct charges against, 171
> opposition to Independent Counsel Act, 33
> perjury charges against Clinton, 82–84, 335–336
> resignation of, 95–96, 102, 105
> Whitewater investigations of, 24–27

State Department, security lapses in, 159–161

Steele, Shelby, 309–312

Stephanopoulos, George, 341–342

Stephens, Jackson, 157

Stern, Andy, 350

Stern, Gertrude, 91

Sullivan, Richard, 350

Supreme Court (U.S.), role in Florida election dispute, 258–261,
> 295–297, 308, 313–315, 320–330

Sweeney, John, 168, 349

T

Taylor, W. H., 99

Teamsters Union, campaign finance investigation of, 53, 96, 113-115, 120-122, 167-169

Thatcher, Margaret, 22

Thernstrom, Stephan and Abigail, 357-358

Thomas, Clarence (Justice), 248

Thomases, Susan, 63

Thompson, Fred (Senator), 3, 19, 43, 79-81, 97-98, 100-101, 139, 191, 197-198

Toobin, Jeffrey, 153-158

Torricelli, Robert (Senator), 19, 126, 128, 257

Travel Office firings, 102, 126-127, 153, 190

Tribe, Lawrence, 119

Trie, Charlie, 19, 41-43, 46, 74, 80, 98-101, 225
    sentencing of, 112
    testimony of, 143
    trial of, 135-136, 138-139

Tripp, Linda, 73-75, 190

Trumka, Richard, 96, 114, 120-122, 167-169, 349-350

Tucker, Jim Guy, 7, 9, 25, 152, 197, 353-354

Turley, Jonathan, 36-39

Tyson, Don, 99

V

Vallone, Peter, 63

Vrooman, Robert, 78-81

W

Walpin, Gerald, 77

Walsh, Lawrence, 33, 51, 248

Wang Jun, 42

Weddington, Sarah, 115

Wehr, Daniel, 99

Weinberger, Caspar, 51

Wells, Charles (Chief Justice), 324

White, Mary Jo, 96, 113-115, 120-122, 167-169, 350

White, Ronnie (Judge), 349

Whitewater Development Company, 6-7, 10-11, 13, 127-128
    end of investigation into, 229-231, 333-336

Will, George, 278

Willey, Kathleen, 91-92, 102, 106, 149-151

Williams, Jack, 106

Wolf, Frank (Representative), 225

Wolfe, Tom, 356

Woodward, Bob, 103

World Trade Organization (WTO), Chinese membership in, 20-23,
    40-43

Wright, Susan Webber (Judge), 6-7, 31-32, 36-39, 82-83, 105-106,
    143-144, 170-171

Wyke, Rebecca, 247

Y

Y2K legislation, 57-58

Yost, Pete, 135

Z

Zelnick, Bob, 92

Zhu Rongji, 18-23, 40